P9-BYW-523

THE MYSTICAL, MAGICAL, MARVELOUS WORLD OF DREAMS

Other books by the same author:

Follow Your Dreamzzz: A How-to Book on Dream Interpretation

The
Mystical, Magical, Marvelous
World of Dreams

Wilda B. Tanner

Sparrow Hawk Press

Tahlequah, Oklahoma

Sparrow Hawk Press
11 Summit Ridge Drive
Tahlequah, OK 74464

©1988 by Wilda B. Tanner
All rights reserved. Published 1988
Printed in the United States of America

Book design and cover: Dianna K. Christenson

Library of Congress Catalog Card Number 88-60774
ISBN 0-945027-02-8

First printing	May	1988	Eighth printing	April	1994
Second printing	April	1989	Ninth printing	July	1995
Third printing	Feb.	1990	Tenth printing	July	1996
Fourth printing	Nov.	1990	Eleventh printing	Aug.	1997
Fifth printing	April	1991	Twelfth printing	June	1998
Sixth printing	June	1992	Thirteenth printing	Feb.	2000
Seventh printing	May	1993	Fourteenth printing	Aug.	2001

"You, O king, as you lay in bed, were thinking of the future, speculating as to what should come to pass hereafter, and He who Reveals Secrets disclosed to you what is going to happen...that you, O king, may understand the thoughts of your own heart."

Daniel 2:29-30

CONTENTS

FOREWORD

Our dreams give us a key to one-third of our lives, perhaps unrevealed. At the edge of the mind is a hidden creator of high drama and each of us has the potential to access information this dream-maker seems to possess.

With sparkling clarity these pages call us to excitement and enthusiasm for a kind of work we relish exploring from time to time. If dream-study becomes too weighty, we give up its possibilities. If the instructions promise too much too easily, we don't buy into the real effort required; we struggle to find encouragement for a task that stimulates hope but sometimes seems too laborious.

To travel this inward passageway we need to have had an experience that assures us there is something the inner knows that we want, or we have to be intrigued by a promise that simply hooks us into the idea. This manuscript certainly can excite and promise. If we already have had proof through experience, here we find helpful hints to enhance our excitement.

Inward travel is best accomplished under the embrace of an experienced guide and Ms. Tanner has been this route time and time again. Not only am I familiar with her earlier book, *Follow Your Dreams*, I have seen her helpful manner tested through the medium of writing and find her techniques highly effective. Her years of experience, earned excellence and play with dream reality already have taught numerous persons to enjoy dreaming, recording and pondering—and then reaping the rewards. She has scouted the path—the high places and the low—and can be a beacon for us. I would choose Wilda Tanner as a guide for myself, so I can recommend her as a guide for you.

If we want to penetrate the promised land under the direction of the Knower, we must be willing to make the effort. All technique is just that until we do the work and bear the fruit. It takes time and effort and an investment of ourselves to find what waits just out of sight.

Techniques intrigue, but can they work? They need testing and this demands time. Our author has spent years developing, integrating and determining her preferences for how to work; herein we find a way to go ahead on our journey under expert tutelage.

It behooves us to remember that what we learn as we work with subtle threads of consciousness at one level of our being is transferred easily to other methods of gaining insight.

I compliment Wilda on the clarity of instructions, analyses and wonderful, helpful hints. Record-keeping, triggering and pondering the results can be fruitful work.

Thank goodness we have here the help that makes it fun. I rejoice as we learn to share our hard-earned information in light, happy ways as the voice of a friend.

Why would we want to open up another third of our life when what we have is so full already if there were not hope for positive assistance? We are reaching for high consciousness from the reflected Source. Can it be that as we process we grow more quickly and more easily into our own wholeness—or holiness? I trust it is so.

I believe in an interlocking relationship between our meditations, our intuitive awareness and our dream level. The same wonderful, gossamer-like impressions that linger behind the dream can be found in the quiet of meditation or in the slight prompting of that inner-knowing we experience from time to time. I have found, both personally and as a teacher, that each aspect of self we enhance brings new capabilities to the other.

The thread we weave in our dream studies helps us pull to ourselves the wispy impression that is called heavenly aid. The meditation thought seems whispered from the silence but may trigger that inner knower to give us the drama needed to explain pain or joy, to tempt us in adventure or to warn of mishap. This secret third of our lives seems to me to be related intricately to the other two-thirds and, with its rich creativity to share, I believe it can enhance the whole.

Dream work is a kind of high play that can intertwine the basic nature of the conscious mind and the Wise One who dwells just at the edge of reach. The unique character of this book is summed up in the techniques that allow us freedom to develop perspective and find tools that enhance the quest we are already pondering. To delve one more step inward is exciting—especially when the tool is magical.

I salute our author for her excellent work. Enter in and gain powerful insight.

CAROL W. PARRISH

ACKNOWLEDGEMENTS

Loving acknowledgements to Linda McCachran, Noreen Wessling, and Carl E. Meier who gave needed help and encouragement; and to Carol Parrish and Richard Reavill who took the time, effort and patience to help bring this book together.

My thanks and blessings!

PART I

CHAPTER 1

The Magical Things
Your Dreams Can Do for You

*Dreams show us how to find a meaning in our lives, how to fulfill our own
destiny, how to realize the greater potential of life within us.*
— *Marie-Louise von Franz*

Why do we dream? Is there a purpose in dreams, or are they mere nonsensical
meanderings of the mind as some claim? Perhaps the Bible says it best when Daniel
explains the king's dream, "You, O king, as you lay in bed, were thinking of the future,
speculating as to what should come to pass hereafter, and He who reveals secrets disclosed to you what is going to happen...that you, O king, may understand the
thoughts of your own heart." (Daniel 2:29-30, EV.)

American Indians believe that the Great Spirit gives dreams to guide and inspire the
soul. Edgar Cayce, the great American psychic, once declared that "Visions and
dreams are given for the benefit of the individual, would they but interpret them correctly" (Reading 294-15). He further stated that guidance only comes to "those who
are doing something with their lives." (McGarey).

Problem Solving: The Major Purpose of Dreams

The most important single thing dreams do for us is that of helping us to solve our
problems. We are all constantly beset with problems of one kind or another and are always looking either for answers or for better ways to perform. Nobel prize winner Albert Gyorgi stated it so well when he said, "My work is not finished when I leave my
workbench in the afternoon. I go on thinking about my problems all the time and my
brain must continue to think about them when I sleep because I wake up...with
answers to questions that have been puzzling me."

Robert Louis Stevenson in his autobiography *Across the Plains* tells how he asked his "dream helpers," as he called them, to give him a marketable story, and they gave him what he termed, "Better tales than he could fashion himself!" The whole plot for *Dr. Jekyll and Mr. Hyde* came from a dream, as did many of his stories.

Elias Howe was having great difficulty creating a needle that would catch the bobbin thread on the sewing machine he was trying to create. Nothing seemed to work. Puzzled and frustrated, he went to sleep with the problem on his mind and dreamed of being attacked by African natives with spears which had a hole in the point...as if to say, "Here is your answer, coming right at you! Hope you get the point!" Elias did, and as we all know, the new needle design worked perfectly. As a result, all of us now wear clothing made on sewing machines.

Much of our greatest music came from dream levels: Handel's *Messiah*, "Silent Night," and much of Richard Wagner's works, to name just a few. We could go on and on, but the point is that this knowledge is available to all of us when, and if, we learn how to "tune in" and remember our dreams.

Thomas Edison, who once said, "Ideas come from space!" kept a cot in his work area. Whenever he faced a problem, needed a new idea or a better way to design one of his many, many inventions, he would lie down and doze off lightly with his **mind concentrated on the solution**. This was his secret. He was keenly aware that by just relaxing his body and mind he would then be able to receive new ideas from "space."

Straining for answers tends to block all intuitive flow, while relaxing seems to open the flood gates to Universal Mind. It is not a matter of making things happen, more of letting ideas flow in; but you must guide the direction your mind is to take. Mastering the art of meditation is extremely helpful to anyone learning to consciously dip into the deeper levels of mind for either relaxation or problem solving.

Your Magic Lamp

We can't all have a cot in our office space, but we can take time out to close our eyes and relax our minds and bodies at our place of work when we need answers. In our lack of understanding about how things really work, we often fail to be all that we could be simply because we are not aware that this vast store of knowledge is readily available to all of us, and that it can be so easily reached.

If you are new at this, the easiest way to get your answers is by writing out a specific question, problem, or concept you wish to know more about before going to bed. Memorize the question, then repeat it over and over as you drift off to sleep. Enter into sleep **expecting** an answer, making sure you have pen and paper handy to write it out when it comes.

In the practice of asking questions and working with the answers on a regular basis, you establish a mental path or corridor in your mind so that with each usage it becomes easier and easier to contact your superconscious or intuitive levels of mind and bring back good, usable, even brilliant ideas and information. This process, in turn, brings further rewards of broadening your mind, improving your mental range, and increasing your awareness and intuitive abilities. It also helps you get in touch with subconscious memories and information not usually available to you.

Ideas, Solutions, and Insights

Our dreams can be literal gold mines of information, especially when we ask for specific help or answers. There is nothing we can't ask about; there are no limits to the amount of knowledge we can request. We are told in the Bible to "Ask, and ye shall receive..." Many of us forget to ask. We can tap into what is called "universal knowledge" in dreams—it is ours to use. If you don't get an answer the first time, ask again. Sometimes it takes three days of asking, but the insights and information *will* be given.

Occasionally our questions are not specifically answered in a dream but are answered by means of a book, a TV program, a conversation we just "happened" to hear, a "chance" meeting, a magazine article, and so forth. The possibilities are endless, so let's not limit our answers to one source. They can come to us in a wide variety of ways, and dreams are only one of the many. But working with dreams seems to be the gateway that leads to greater opportunities for expansion of knowledge. We were never meant to stay in ignorance or poverty, nor need we be slaves to expensive teachers. All wisdom is available to us on dream levels—it is up to us to "tap in."

When problems seem overwhelming, we often concentrate so intently on one particular subject that our dreams will be totally involved with its solution. At such times, all other requests for information will be temporarily set aside until the main project is finished or the problem solved. Then, and only then, will the less important matters or questions be dealt with, so keep this in mind when answers seem not to be forthcoming.

Problems and Programs

In the book *Edgar Cayce on Dreams* (Bro 1968), Mr. Cayce is quoted as saying, "Dreams work to solve the problems of the dreamer's conscious, waking life, and they work to quicken in the dreamer new potentials which are his to claim." Such is the potential of our dreams.

Whenever you purchase a complicated gadget at your favorite store, there is always an instruction manual to help you to put it all together and to keep it running smoothly. Since the human being is undoubtedly the most complicated structure on earth, we too come with an instruction manual: a built-in computer-like device we call the subconscious mind, which is constantly monitored, re-programmed, up-dated, and corrected by way of our dreams.

Learning Our Lessons

Tertullian, the first important Christian writer, declared, "Almost the greater part of mankind get their knowledge...from dreams." In fact, each night we view approximately five to seven dreams which comment on problems, attitudes, actions, and reactions of the previous day. We are given lessons, guidance, information, insights, understanding, knowledge, and encouragement. When we get "off course" or "off track," our dreams may show picture stories, such as a derailed train, to alert us of our error.

Some of these messages are directly from our subconscious levels, particularly information about the physical body and its needs. Others come from conscious levels: miscellaneous facts, figures, and bits of information to deal with our present day problems. But most of our lessons come from the superconscious level, our God-self or High Self. These come as spiritual lessons and insights to help with problem-solving on all levels to give us greater understanding of our goals, our mental and spiritual growth processes, and even reminders of our soul purpose for this lifetime, *provided* we pay attention to our dreams. Without this we may wander further and further off course until we wonder, "What is life all about?" "What am I here for?"

How It Works

The human mind is similar to a giant computer which acts and reacts according to its programming. All too often the programs are faulty, erroneous, and misleading. This gets us into all kinds of trouble and may even halt our progress completely.

While our active programming starts the day we are born, there are influences imprinting our conscious minds long before birth. We are conditioned as to what is "good" and what is "bad." We are continuously told what we can and cannot do, should or shouldn't do. We may be told that we are bad, good, smart, or dumb; too old to do this and too young to do that. Or we may hear the comment that we are "just like Uncle Joe" (who is feeble minded or eighty pounds overweight), insinuating that we, too, have these faults. Unknown to most of us, our subconscious mind *accepts all these things as truths!* Later on in life we may wonder why we have a weight problem.

Then, to compound matters, we go to school and possibly to church where more ideas and concepts, often highly biased, prejudiced, narrow-minded, or just plain inaccurate are added. On top of all this, psychologists tell us we are "a part of everything we see, hear and feel!" (Think of all the TV programs and commercials filed away in our subconscious minds..."I can't believe I ate the whole thing...") All of this information, good and bad, true or false, is *permanently filed* in the subconscious mind unless and *until we consciously do something to remove it.*

These seemingly harmless misconceptions then become an integral part our store of knowledge and our **basic belief system** from which we continually draw when decisions are to be made, just like the computer: "Garbage in, garbage out!"

Such things as "Obesity runs in the family," "You can't get there from here," "Sex is dirty," "You gotta work hard for a living," "You just can't win," "God's gonna getcha for that," or "Money is the root of all evil"— all these things and many others become entrenched in our minds while we are too young to realize how false they are, with the result that these "beliefs" influence our lives and our decisions without our even being aware of them.

By the time we are grown we may have collected more untruths than truths, and sooner or later in our lives we begin to run into conflict between these false impressions and our own deep desires and inner instincts. An excellent example is the problem young women run into with the "Sex is dirty" idea and the marriage concept. Some women never get that one resolved! They may be labeled frigid, incompatible, or worse. Many of our present-day problems are due to these subconscious misconceptions and erroneous beliefs.

In this regard, our dreams act as our inner guidance system, helping us to locate, isolate, correct, and delete the errors and ignorant beliefs which not only hinder our progress but cause most of our conflicts. Our dreams will guide, correct, encourage, retrieve forgotten facts, show us new ideas and ways of doing things, and generally help us to solve whatever problem is uppermost in our minds when we go to sleep.

How Dreams Help You to Live a Better Life

Not only do dreams relate to the problems and concerns that were on your mind prior to sleep, but they give you insights and understanding on:

RELATIONSHIPS: How you get along with others, the problems and some possible solutions. You may be shown the basic cause of your present difficulty or some aspect of the problem of which you were totally unaware. Dreams help you see things from a different point of view to aid in your understanding.

ATTITUDES: Your attitudes, beliefs, and prejudices toward your work, people, and the circumstances which strongly affect your life and affairs. Dreams often point out the misunderstandings or misconceptions which stand in the way of your progress, making way for the correcting of difficult situations in a peaceful manner.

THE WAY YOU SEE YOURSELF: A dream is the mirror of the soul, bringing us a clear view of ourselves and the learning situations in which we are involved. These dreams are often quite revealing in content, showing us aspects of ourselves we hadn't noticed, letting us see the roles we are playing, and revealing how we think we appear as opposed to how we **really** are. (These are portrayed by the people in our dreams.)

We may, in dreams, act out the part of a king or a servant, a work horse, a loner, a victim or victor. We may lead one time and be led, pushed, ignored, or manipulated another time. All of these incidents give us important insights about our lifestyles which help us to understand ourselves better and to make our lives more complete and satisfying.

UNSEEN FACTS: When someone is trying to "pull the wool over our eyes," we may dream just that scene, or we may see a person wearing a mask, costume, or some other symbolic apparel which says to us, "There is something wrong here, something false, or hidden." Finding ourselves "in the dark" in dreams is an important clue which suggests that we do not have enough information, that we need more "light" on the subject before going on. It can even warn of unseen danger lurking in a current situation.

WARNINGS: Dreams can alert us to acts of subterfuge or bring to our minds conflicting statements, inconsistencies, falsehoods, and little deceptions we may have missed during the busy day. These are candidly pointed out at night, which is part of the protection and edification which comes to us in our dreams.

PROBLEMS: During the day there is a strong tendency to handle physical problems in a purely physical way, especially when things go wrong. We may use physical force to make a point, slamming doors and throwing things. We may use our emotions to cry, pout, yell, "fuss and cuss," or use mental force to try to out-talk an opponent. We may react in fear, swallowing our pride and ending our day with stress. These tactics may temporarily get things "out of the system," but they do not solve our problems. Later, as we drift off to sleep, our mind will review the day's events and begin to analyze what was done. This is almost always followed by a dream which will comment on the way we dealt or refused to deal with the situation. Insights and information may be given. We may be shown pictures which delineate our mistaken attitudes or our false pride. Alternative measures may be suggested and new ideas given. A nightmare may point out our fears, implying that we cannot run from them. Dreams can even indicate where we need to stand up and fight for our rights!

All of our unsolved problems show up first in our dreams. When these are ignored we will have recurring dreams, which in time turn into nightmares as we continue to neglect to face our fears. Meanwhile, on the physical level our unsolved problems may begin to surface in the form of headaches. If the cause is not looked into and corrected as our dreams suggest, it will begin to manifest itself in the electromagnetic energy field as a dark spot in the aura. Still later, it becomes a physical problem or disease which may appear to have no cause, or we may have an accident or injury in the appropriate area. Most modern, orthodox doctors, unlike the old-fashioned family doctor, see no correlation between our mental or emotional problems and our body illnesses, but holistic doctors now understand that body, mind, and spirit act as a whole unit. What goes on in one part of us definitely affects the rest, like a pebble thrown into a still pond. The ancient wisdom speaks of correspondences between emotions and resulting diseases, as well as definite areas of the body relating to particular types of activity. Example: Head represents thinking; feet relate to understanding.

MANIPULATIONS: Many people, most especially our parents and often our bosses, have a way of manipulating us in such a subtle way that often we are not even aware of it, yet we are affected strongly. This often makes us irritable without realizing the source of our exasperations; and worse yet, we become frustrated with ourselves for not understanding why we are upset!

Parents aren't the only ones, however; almost all authority figures do it to some extent, and often our families or our very best friends put us in positions where we feel obligated to do something we really don't want to do. Bear in mind there is a **big** difference between **being useful and being used.** In the first case, **we choose** what, where, when, and how we want to give. In the second, we find ourselves doing something we really didn't want to do and wonder, "How did I get myself into this?" Dreams invariably point out these manipulations, helping us to see the situation for what it really is, so that we can deal with it in an intelligent and unemotional manner.

The symbolism for manipulation may be someone driving your car, pushing you in some way, or leading you around by a string, the nose, or whatever symbol will get the point across. Watch your dreams for these subtle symbols. They are important. God never meant for you to be subservient to other people. You were meant to be free, whole, and happy. Your dreams will unerringly point you in that direction.

The Real Magic of Dreams

Your dreams help you get in touch with your High Self, your True Self, the God-part of you in such a way as to instill confidence in all the beauty, love, wisdom, power, and wonder that comprises the **real** you! Through dreams you can make that all-important God-connection. This is the real magic of dreams!

The Mystical, Magical, Marvelous World of Dreams

CHAPTER 2

The Temple of Dreams, Ancient and Modern

Is it not known to all people that the dream is the most usual way that God reveals himself to man?

— Tertullian

Although we spend approximately one third of our lives in sleep, few of us really understand the processes of sleep and dreaming, nor do we realize the tremendous importance of dreams in our spiritual growth and daily affairs.

The Antiquity of Dreams

In ancient times such was not the case, for then dreams were highly esteemed. Beautiful temples were built and maintained as havens to entice and encourage dreams. People would travel many miles for the great privilege of entering the Temple of Dreams, for it was well-known that dreams were a source of deep truth which could be used for healing, solving problems, or attaining guidance in matters of health, wealth, happiness, and understanding.

In those days, a person with an illness or a weighty problem would patiently travel many miles, often on foot, to visit one of these dream temples, the most famous of which was at Epidaurus near Corinth. These temples, begun as centers of worship for Aesculapius, the revered Greek god of healing, were soon fitted with beds and became the first hospitals, so great were the healing energies working through dreams. Even his staff with the winding snake was adapted into the caduceus, symbol of healing both then and now.

Those unable to travel to the temples would often send a trusted friend or relative to procure a healing or an answer to an important problem.

Once there, the weary traveler would be met by friendly temple aides and after a bath, food, and drink would talk to a priest about his problems. The kindly temple priests were well trained in the art of dream interpretation and in the ability to discover the cause and cure of an illness through dream information. They could even foretell future events based on knowledge gleaned from dreams.

After consultation and a night's rest, the next day or so would be spent in prayer, fasting, and preparations for the hoped-for healing, guidance, or dream-answer. This would be followed by a long purification bath with pleasantly scented oils. The pilgrim, then ready, would don a clean, white robe and enter the temple. There would be a small sacrifice, followed by music, chanting, and an impressive ceremony led by the priests imploring Aesculapius to come to the aid of the supplicant. Last, there would be an elaborate dream incubation ritual succeeded by a well-deserved night's sleep in a specially prepared room in the Temple of Dreams.

On this long-awaited night it was not at all unusual for the seeker to have a vision of the great god offering a needed solution, wise counsel, or perhaps the suggestion of certain herbs, potions, or other remedies which would effect a cure.

On occasion, Aesculapius would render a healing touch to the body, and the pilgrim would wake fully healed. According to legend, wayfarers frequently came in on crutches or by cart and left the temple dancing, skipping, and laughing.

Our modern-day dream incubation techniques and practices are based on this ancient truth and are surprisingly effective.

Dreams and the Bible

One of the oldest books known to man is the Bible, which mentions over seven hundred dreams and visions, all showing an important connection to the lives, problems, and well-being of the people involved. One of best known is recorded in Matthew 2:13-14, when Joseph was cautioned by an angel to flee into Egypt with Mary and Jesus to avoid the coming wrath of Herod. In the preceding verses, the Wise Men were also warned in a dream, "Not to return to Herod, but to go home another way." The first two chapters of Matthew contain no less than five recorded dreams which gave valuable warnings or advice. The Old Testament stories of Daniel and Joseph revolved around dreams.

"Every major writer in the first four centuries of Christianity regarded dreams as one way that God offered healing and guidance to mankind," says Reverend John Sanford, author of *Dreams: God's Forgotten Language*. In his book he tells us, "I started to remember and record my dreams and began…a lifelong adventure with my dream life. I soon found that my dreams were leading me out of confusion into a relationship with myself, and acting for all the world like the voice of the Holy Spirit." Of such is the power of dreams for all who care to listen.

Modern Research

In spite of all this, only a few centuries later psychologists were blatantly proclaiming that dreams were "useless meanderings of the mind," with the result that many people, even now, actually believe that dreams are nonsense.

Today, however, our modern psychologists lead the way in researching the processes of sleep and the usefulness of dreams.

Sigmund Freud brought the world's attention back to an avid interest in dreams with his famous book *The Interpretation of Dreams*, published in 1900. This work was first joined, then enhanced, by Carl Jung. More recently, Dr. Calvin Hall researched over ten thousand dreams for his book *The Meaning of Dreams*. At the present time there are a dozen or more sleep/dream research laboratories actively exploring this intriguing phenomenon.

In the search for more information on sleep and the dreaming processes, researchers have recruited volunteers willing to sleep under laboratory conditions with a series of tiny wires attached to their heads. Using elaborate brain-wave measuring devices called electroencephalographs, better known as EEG machines, it has been found that there are several distinct levels of consciousness shown in our brain-wave patterns. The fastest waves, called Beta, occur during our wide-awake, thinking, and acting states and can range from as low as 12 to 14 cycles per second (cps). This may vary slightly from person to person, going much higher if we are extra tense or excited.

It has been found through testing that whenever we become bored or drowsy, our brain waves move more and more slowly, our eyes begin to droop, and we start to drift into the Alpha wave pattern of 8 to 13 cps. It is at this state that we can move in and out of what we term "reality." Altered states of consciousness begin here. During this stage, we may find ourselves drifting back and forth, bobbing like a cork, in and out of Beta and Alpha several times before finally slipping into the deeper levels of sleep.

As this happens the brain waves continue their slowing process, and we drift rather rapidly through Alpha, into Theta, and on into Delta in a matter of moments.

Rapid Eye Movements

About ninety minutes later, the brain waves begin to speed up again and we drift back through Theta and on into the Alpha stage. At this point, our bodies become quite still as though very intent upon watching something (which is indeed true), and it is in this stillness that dreams take place.

Our eyes begin to move quickly beneath closed lids, a sure signal for the start of the dream state. This "rapid eye movement" has been dubbed *REM* by researchers and is used as a criterion to recognize both the beginning and the end of the dreaming state.

After approximately three to five minutes of REM, our consciousness moves back again into the slow roll brainwave pattern typical of the Delta phase, to remain there another ninety minutes before returning once more to Alpha for a second dream cycle. This whole process repeats itself at ninety minute intervals all through the night, giving a total of four or five dreams per night depending on the number of hours spent in sleep.

As the usual waking time approaches, roughly eight hours later, the consciousness begins moving slowly from the deeper stages of sleep, through the Alpha levels and on to the Beta, with the dream process going on from the lower borders of Alpha until the moment of awakening. This dream may last as long as an hour and is the one most likely to be remembered, whether it is recalled consciously or not.

Our Many Levels of Consciousness

Alpha

The Alpha stage is actually made up of several mini-levels which are unnamed. The first stage, Alpha One or Al-Beta, is neither Alpha nor Beta but a combination of both. Here the brain waves hover at about 12-14 cps. The body is relaxed; the mind is quiet, yet alert and keenly aware of the input from the five physical senses, while also in touch with the Alpha levels of the intuitive mind—a balanced combination of both right and left brain input, the **rhythm of genius!**

This is the same level we use when brainstorming, day-dreaming, and in tuning-in to the *universal mind* or *cosmic consciousness*. New and ingenious ideas, inventions, and solutions enter here.

In Alpha II, in the general range of 10 to 12 cps, the mind is in a delicate balance between awake and asleep. The outer sensory input seems to be cut off or at least greatly muted, while the mind is highly alert, aware, sensitive, and in an extremely receptive condition. Daydreaming, light meditation, intuitive knowing, cosmic consciousness, extra sensory perception (ESP), flashes of insight, and even visions may occur at this stage.

However, because there is such a delicate balance between these two levels, we often cannot hold this state for very long; we either move rapidly on toward sleep or "pop" awake.

When this phase can be held, it appears to be the gateway to what is known as *lucid dreaming*, a point where we realize that we are dreaming or in an altered state. Here our clarity and perceptions can reach new heights. At this stage we can experience full control of our dreams and can consciously change the action and content of our dream. We may choose to astral travel to any desired place, have an out-of-the-body experience (OOB or OOBE), or move on to a high spiritual experience—the ultimate goal in dreaming.

Alpha III is often associated with deep meditation, trance, and hypnotic levels as well as with light sleep. This cycles at about 8 to 10 cps, with spurts dipping lower or higher at intervals. Often in Alpha III we think we are awake, since we can hear sounds like planes, birds, or voices all around us. However, if anything startles us, we "pop" back to Beta with a jerk, often quite surprised because we didn't realize that we had been "gone!" States of consciousness are elusive to pin down and describe.

At only a slightly lower cycling we reach Alpha IV, a stage where dreams occur and where they seem to be stored in our subconscious mind. (This explains how we can suddenly recall a seemingly forgotten dream while in meditation or even in the daydreaming state.) Actually, all these layers are extremely close together and seem to interweave. Those of you who meditate may be well aware of these stages.

Theta

The next level is Theta, ranging from 4-7 cps. This is a stage of deep sleep where there is a vague type of dreaming or thought process which scientists call *Non-REM* or *NREM*. We note that the mind, even in deep sleep, seems never to be entirely stilled.

Delta

Delta cycles from .5 to 3.5 cps and is our deepest level of consciousness. Here, most believe, dreams do not occur. This is the point of sleep where our bodies receive extensive repair and renewal, which may explain why deep sleep is said to be so therapeutic. Delta is the only stage in which this restoration process is carried on. This fact may be significant in understanding the aging processes in the elderly for, according to recent scientific findings, there is **no actual reason for losing our youthful appearance**—our bodies completely renew themselves every night. Since older people are known to be light sleepers, perhaps it is the lack of Delta level sleep which results in the appearance of aging.

Sleep Walking

Both sleep walking and bed wetting are said by researchers to occur only during Delta sleep. Doctors now believe that sleep-walking is an expression of emotional conflicts which have been repressed during the day and are therefore released during deep sleep. (A dieter sleep walking to a well-stocked refrigerator would be a good example of this.)

A. E. Powell, in his book *The Astral Body*, states, "The physical body may be working automatically, and by force of habit, uncontrolled by the man himself. Instances of this occur where servants rise in the middle of the night and...attend to household duties to which they are accustomed, or...the sleeping body carries out...the idea dominant in the mind before falling to sleep." Some doctors now feel that these traits may be psychological abnormalities which can run in a family.

Bed Wetting

The bed wetting problem has only recently been connected to family tensions and stresses, particularly in the case of a high-strung or emotionally volatile parent. The fear of a parent or other authority figure in the family situation seems to be the main culprit, although there are a few cases where other fears such as darkness, ghosts, "scary" movies before bedtime, or other emotionally upsetting situations were found to be heavy contributing factors. In one case, a frightening and (to the child) threatening picture which hung on the wall and had to be passed before reaching the bathroom was discovered to be the source of the problem. Once removed, there was no more bedwetting!

Snoring

Researchers now agree that the problem of snoring is not limited to the sleeping position—usually on one's back—but is confined to the NREM states and ceases during the dream state. Allergies and sinus problems which tend to block the nasal passages are the greatest causative factors, while greasy foods, heavy meats, and alcohol and/or drugs are strong contributing factors.

Sleep Learning

Much research has been done in this area, and test findings show that sleep learning occurs only when the EEG shows Alpha waves; even this learning is apt to be sketchy, since the mind is intent on the dream content during the night. This leaves only the early evening drifting-off-to-sleep stages open to learning, because in NREM states the input from our five physical senses is greatly censored, acting like a closed circuit TV. Our attention seems to be riveted on the inner senses exclusively.

Non-REM (NREM)

Non-REM (no dream) states occur during Theta and Delta stages. Here the brain waves are very slow, breathing is deep, and heart and pulse rates are noticeably lowered. Those awakened from these levels describe their experiences as having "drifting thoughts," a feeling of observing things, or watching and learning with none of the action and participation found in the REM states. Elsie Sechrist, author of *Dreams, Your Magic Mirror,* says, "The highest revelation usually comes without sound, picture, or emotional disturbance. It is an intuitive experience akin to the still, small voice."

The Importance of Your Dreams

In investigating the value of REM, students being tested were allowed to have their full eight hours of sleep but were **denied their usual dream periods**, being awakened at the beginning of each dream. After only three days of REM deprivation, some of the students developed strong excitability, irritability, disorientation, hallucinations, abnormal behavior patterns, and in some cases signs of psychosis. Symptoms in all students were similar, with some less pronounced. However, **all** showed signs of mental and behavioral abnormalities; one young man flatly refused to do any further testing after only one dreamless night! Apparently the loss of dreams disturbed him profoundly.

When the REM deprivation test was over, these same students were allowed a normal, uninterrupted night's sleep, after which they not only returned to normal behavior but as a group spent a ***greatly increased amount of time*** in the REM states during the next few nights. It was as though they were making up for the loss of dream time as quickly as possible! Obviously, our dreams are highly important in relation to our mental processes and our overall sense of balance and well-being.

Dr. Wm. Dement, a man well-known in the area of sleep and dream research, has written many articles on the subject of dreams and has been quoted in many more. In one of these (Dement 1976), he announced that "REM-deprived subjects showed anxiety, irritability and difficulty in concentrating." He further stated his belief that the condition known as *delirium tremens* (D.T.'s) is "an accumulation of deprived REM."

Dream Deterrents

Dream studies have also disclosed that the consumption of drugs, alcohol, sleeping pills, and certain medicines including anti-histamines tend to keep the consciousness in the very deepest levels of Delta, thus depriving us of the REM periods so necessary for balance and sanity. Dr. Dement says, "The pills people take to regulate their sleep cause ***profoundly disturbed sleep*** [emphasis added]." This is a common cause of inability to remember dreams.

Dream Recall

Researchers have also reported that people awakened during or immediately after dreaming had vivid and seemingly complete dream recall; but when these same people were awakened as little as five minutes after the dream ended, part of the dream was already forgotten. If as much as ten minutes were allowed to elapse before being awakened, only a small fragment could be remembered. It is evident that we need to train ourselves to awaken immediately after a dream in order to obtain complete recall.

While there are those who recommend that we train ourselves to awaken after *every* dream and record it immediately, I personally do not feel this is necessary. For one thing, it tends to interfere with a good night's sleep, which is reason enough for most of us. Secondly, the earlier dreams tend to be more or less a series of problem-solving exercises, eliminating the lesser alternatives and working purposefully toward the best solution. This last dream seems to combine and coordinate the best possible options, answers, advice, fact-recall, or whatever is needed into one final theme which is given just before waking. It is *this* dream you want to remember, record, and understand, for much wisdom is given in dreams.

GENERAL SLEEP PATTERNS
(Based on Electroencephalogram brain wave measurements)

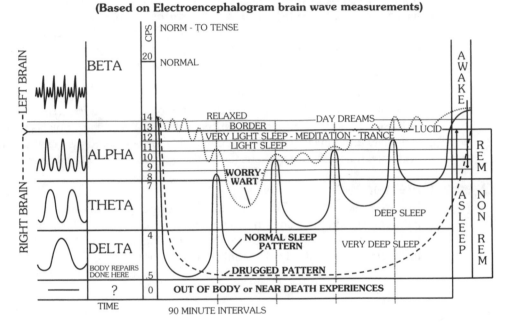

The Mystical, Magical, Marvelous World of Dreams

CHAPTER **3**

The Realm of Dreams

It is in our idleness, in our dreams, that the submerged truth sometimes comes to the top.

— Virginia Woolf

Most of us have been taught that we are "only human," that we are nothing but the physical body. This is like telling the carpenter that he is nothing but the hammer he uses!

One of the first principles to grasp in the study of dreams is that just as the human mind has several unseen levels of function, Beta through Delta, the human body also has its hidden layers. We are infinitely more than the physical being that we perceive in the mirror, for immediately surrounding our bodies is what scientists refer to as the *electromagnetic field*. This "field" is an extension of ourselves and our finer sensitivities which, while not often seen with normal vision, can be seen, heard, and felt by those with extra sensitivity. It is also seen, known, and painted as the human *aura* or the familiar *halo* found around the heads and bodies of various saints.

There is now a special kind of photography called *Kirlian* which can actually capture on film the auras found around us "ordinary" people!

Busy Bodies

This electromagnetic energy field surrounds and interpenetrates the human body in an egg-shaped oval extending out some three feet or more, depending on the development and condition of the individual. It can be seen as distinct layers around the body by those with what is called *extended vision* or *clairvoyance*.

The body's closest stratum is called the *etheric layer*, or *vital body*. This extends from one quarter to one and one-half inches from the physical body and is considered an integral part of the physical. Next is the *emotional body*, also called the *astral body*.

Energy Fields Comprising the Human Aura

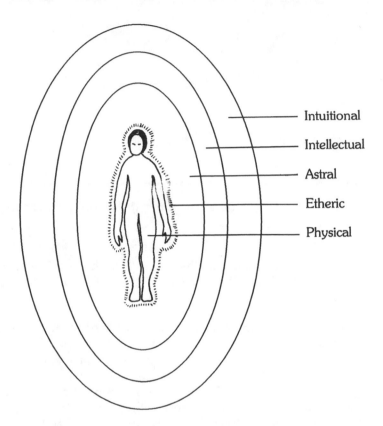

Intuitional

Intellectual

Astral

Etheric

Physical

Then, the *intellectual body* (lower mental or mental body). Beyond that is the *intuitional body* (also known as *buddhic, causal* or *higher mental body*).

All of these bodies are incorporated into what we call the *real self*. Our real self includes all of these as a whole, not just the physical body alone. The physical body is actually just a vehicle which Spirit uses to work in and through. It is when we think and act from the **whole** of ourselves that we are *one*, whole, or *holy*.

Because a dream experience may occur in any or all of these subtle bodies, we will use the term *dream body* throughout this book to refer generically to the non-physical bodies. Your dream body can move in and out of the physical one whenever you drift off to sleep, faint, or "pass out" (of the body) from drugs, shock, injury, or

The Mystical, Magical, Marvelous World of Dreams

anesthetic. Other literature may refer to the same thing by a variety of names: it may be called the phantom, astral, etheric, soul, or even ghostly body, since it has the general shape of the physical body it has just left and can be seen and recognized by others.

When the dream body leaves the physical, it can function and experience on many different levels, or *planes* of existence. To distinguish these levels from the physical, and because the Bible tells us that the Kingdom of Heaven lies within, we will use the term *inner planes* to refer to the worlds of our dream experience.

Entering the Dream World

"Falling" Asleep

If you have ever held a drowsy child, you are well aware of the sudden shift in weight and feeling so evident the moment the youth falls asleep. You may even have made the comment, "He's gone," or, "He's out of it!" without stopping to think seriously about your choice of words. Yet, how true this is!

No matter how many exciting and wonderful things were going on around that little one, he was totally oblivious of it all. He was definitely **not there.** A certain part of his consciousness was out of the body and off into another plane of existence where the sights and sounds of the physical world did not seem to enter. But you were not concerned, for you knew he would *return* shortly. And so it is with all of us when we *go* to sleep.

Starting the Dream Journey

As we begin to relax, our non-physical bodies, moving as a unit, begin to slip gently out of the physical casing as we cross the border between Beta and Alpha. We may linger awhile at the border, bobbing in and out as our brainwaves continue to slow down. Then we let go completely and we are gone. Our conscious awareness then goes back home to the inner planes for lessons and problem-solving experiences.

This process is often referred to as *astral travel*, and the chances are you have experienced at least some of the related phenomena associated with this procedure without knowing what it was. For example, whenever you are extremely tired you may notice that you have trouble getting to sleep. You may start to drift off, only to have the slightest noise or muscle twitch bring you back to full consciousness with a jolt. Furthermore, this action may repeat itself several times before you can finally relax enough to let go of the physical body and *go* to sleep. This jerking sensation is caused by your dream body rushing back into the physical vehicle again after it was partially out. Once the dream body is fully released to flow to other planes of existence, you may have the sensation of flying. Many flying and floating dreams are simply memories of this fascinating experience.

In case of any emergency, such as the doorbell ringing, your dream body has the ability to return to the sleeping physical body with extreme rapidity. Many so-called "falling dreams" are simply the half-remembered sensation of rushing back into the body at the sound of a barking dog, a ringing telephone, an alarm clock, or any unfamiliar noise or sense of trouble. There is absolutely no danger involved, because the dream body is at all times firmly connected to the physical one by what appears to be a silver-like rope which the Bible refers to as the *silver cord* (Ecc. 12:6).

Many people who are able to clearly recall their nightly travels have reported seeing this cord attached to and trailing along behind them. Whenever there is even the slightest threat to the sleeping body, the subconscious mind sends a signal along this cord to our wandering spirit which instantly responds, returning swiftly to handle the matter. All of this works smoothly and perfectly **unless** we ourselves disrupt the process with drugs, chemicals, or alcohol.

Perhaps you can recall a time when you were sound asleep and heard someone calling you from far, far away, but when you awakened (returned to your body) you found they were quite close; *you* were the one who was far away! Or, possibly you have experienced the feeling of being down in a deep, deep place. When someone called you it seemed to take a long, long time to get back to the surface. Both of these are examples of being out of the body during sleep. This is neither strange nor mystical—it is a common occurrence. We all leave our physical bodies every time we "fall" asleep—we just don't always recall the experience of coming or going.

In fact, when teaching dream workshops the most frequently asked question is about the falling dream. People wonder if it is true that when they fall in dreams, they will die if they don't wake up before they hit the ground. Of course, the answer is *no*. The experience of falling is simply the memory of returning swiftly to your sleeping body, but we may at times return with a jolt, experiencing a jarring sensation as we wake!

When We "Go" to Sleep, Where Do We Go?

According to ancient wisdom teachings, we may in our astral travels not only go to other countries, but to other planes and planets as well. You might note that the word *astral* means *star*. Astral travel truly means travel among the stars!

I can recall many, many times thinking as I awakened, "Oh...I'm back," accompanied by a feeling of reluctance or disappointment. Obviously the place where I had been was far more pleasant and interesting than the place of my return! This reminds me of a personal incident I'd like to share with you.

I was going through an extremely difficult and unhappy time in my life, painfully working through my current lesson. Sleep seemed to be my only pleasure. As I was dreaming in a beautiful, peaceful place, the time came for me to return to earth...and my problems. I vividly remember clinging desperately to marble pillars, stubbornly refusing to leave the celestial planes, never wanting to return to the earth again; when suddenly I seemed to be the recipient of an angelic push from behind, and *pop!* I awoke in my bed, abashed and astonished that "they" could do such a thing (how **could** they?)—and not a little ashamed of myself! (The apostle Paul wrote of these "heavens" in his letter to the Corinthians 12:2.)

Out of the Body Experiences

As more and more people have become aware of their dream states, many have reported returning to their bedroom and viewing their sleeping body from a vantage point high above, sometimes as much as thirty or forty feet, which indicates they were looking right through both roof and ceiling with no problems at all!

The first time something like this occurs, it can be rather frightening or at least puzzling to see oneself (or someone else, for that matter) in what seems to be two places at once. Actually, this is a fairly common phenomenon. The same kind of thing happens when one faints or when one is rendered unconscious ("knocked out" of the body), whether by accident, drugs, shock, drink, pain, anesthesia, or by whatever means. Our language implies an obvious understanding of the process when we say, "He passed out."

Another saying is, "She was beside herself," meaning the shock was so great that the dream body was knocked out of alignment, appearing *beside* the body rather than *in* it. We sometimes remark, "I'm not all here today!"

We may declare, "I haven't got it all together," or, "I've got to get myself together!" All of this implies a lost ability to perceive these things clairvoyantly or to realize when the spiritual body is outside of or not correctly aligned within the physical one. While these are not unusual events, they are frequently misunderstood. Undoubtedly you have heard or read at least one story about someone who "died and came back," who had an "out of the body experience" (OOBE), or had astral traveled somewhere and remembered it. There are now so many books and articles available concerning such events that people feel safer about revealing these encounters. Today both physicians and religious leaders are beginning to take a serious look at the many accounts and experiences of those who were pronounced "dead" and returned to talk about it.

The interesting thing is that all of these reports, coming from a wide variety of people, cultures, and places, and over a period of many years, seem to tell of essentially the same experiences—only the details differ. Most individuals speak of floating upward, after either an accident or anesthetic, and looking down upon their "lifeless" bodies. All are acutely aware of being out of their bodies and of dispassionately watching others working frantically to "bring them back." After this, they proceed to visit some heavenly realm and see a Being of great love and light who often asks them, "What have you done for others?" then gently tells them that they have *work to finish*. Finally, they **reluctantly** return to tell of their adventures. Some of these accounts have been carefully checked, recorded, and reported by prominent physicians.

Does this sound incredible? There is really nothing sensational about this except our general lack of information on the matter. We all leave our bodies every time we go to sleep. Some leave when they meditate. (The floating sensation many experience is the gentle exit of the dream body from the physical one.) Should this prove frightening in any way, you need only to open your eyes and your bodies will immediately merge.

During the day we work through a physical body. At night we slip out of the body and go back to the inner planes from whence we came. It is interesting to note that the much-feared and dreaded act of dying is just as simple, painless, and effortless as going to sleep. The only difference is that we don't return to the physical body again in the morning.

Delta Travel

Under normal circumstances, as we drift off to sleep, our brain continues to process the problems of the day, sorting through its computer files for relevant information, facts, and ideas for coping with whatever problem is uppermost in our minds.

Our guardian angel (or High Self) meanwhile adds to this with knowledge and instruction from higher realms, so to speak, helping our minds put together various plausible solutions to our current difficulties.

Night School

As our sleep deepens, our brain waves slow down to the Delta pattern. Here, while the physical body is being repaired, the dream body is deep in lessons. These instructions or experiences are often so deep and profound that they cannot be translated into words. This is the so-called dreamless sleep or Non-REM. We learn much at these deeper levels.

We may begin our studies with lessons in the solving of a particular problem about which we are concerned. We will also have lessons for our overall spiritual growth and development. Often the two are interwoven, the physical problem pushing us to learn some needed spiritual lessons. Perhaps you can recall glimpses of being in a school, college, seminary, or some favorite place of learning. You may even remember some of your schoolmates or one of your teachers when you wake.

At times we may burst awake with the joyous knowledge of a problem solved, an answer found, or a forgotten needed fact recalled. Most of the time we arise totally unaware of the learning that has taken place at deeper levels, yet we may have just worked out a very satisfactory solution to a situation we were unable to handle only the day before.

During the night, several possibilities or alternatives to a puzzling situation may be viewed. Eventually the best one is chosen, and by morning we wake with a needed answer or at least a workable theory to try.

Often we are unaware of the dream processes involved—we may not even remember dreaming, much less the solution; but when we again face the problem, we suddenly "get an idea," or a flash of inspiration, and we **know** what to do. Seldom do we stop to question where the answer came from or connect the "new" knowledge with our dream life.

When we travel to the inner planes, we find that all knowledge is available to us. Many of the so-called *geniuses* were simply people who were aware enough to be able to bring this information back from the dream states.

Albert Einstein, for instance, freely admitted that the *Einstein Theory* was not his, but came to him in a daydream. Thomas Edison, knowing that knowledge was available through dreams, kept a cot at his office and deliberately took "cat naps," focusing on the desired solution whenever he needed new ideas! It is said that at least fifty percent of all creative ideas, art, music, and inventions come from our dreams.

Recording Our Lessons

After approximately ninety minutes of lessons we drift back into Alpha, where the concepts we have been learning are condensed and encapsulated into a symbolic dream form and literally stored at the Alpha level as a dream. Remember, the Alpha level can be reached in the meditative state; in other words, it is "filed" where we can reach it. After this, we slip back into Delta again; only this time we don't go quite as deep, gradually working our way back to the waking level in gentle cycles, with learning going on all through the night.

Homework

When our lessons are over, we may get some practice in exercising the knowledge just learned while still visiting the inner planes. We often give help to others we know and care about, especially those people for whom we are concerned or those on our prayer list. We may work with healing or counseling concepts for our friends, family, or even strangers. We may visit with friends and relatives who are no longer living on the earth plane while we are "in the neighborhood," so to speak.

Visiting With the So-Called Dead

Contacts with loved ones who have "departed" are as easy and frequent as we want them to be. In the case of someone very dear to you who has recently "gone on," you may not recall the dream encounter for awhile, simply because the memories are still too painful to recall; this tends to prolong the ache on the physical plane. Your visits will be remembered later when the experience is less traumatic and emotionally upsetting to you.

Charting Our Course in Life

The well-known philosopher and author, James Allen, states that, "Man is where he is that he may learn, that he may grow. And as he learns the spiritual lessons which individual circumstances hold for him, they pass away and give way to others." Our most important concern at night is to plan and design our lives. Edgar Cayce, America's most famous clairvoyant, said that nothing important ever happens to us without *first being previewed in our dreams* (Bro 1970). We not only *pre-view* it, we *pre-plan* it as well!

At night, we talk with our guardian angel or teacher about our lives, planning, deciding, and *agreeing to every major event* we will experience. We *know* what will happen (ESP), because *we choose the events!* Our soul knows the lessons we need to learn; we select the circumstances and the situations in which to learn them. When it is all over, we ourselves judge how well we did and whether or not we have learned the needed lesson. Then, we set a new course accordingly.

Nothing ever happens to us by accident! Everything is planned—not predestined, but preplanned by us for our greatest spiritual growth. Now, from a purely intellectual point of view we may very well say, "I would *never* have planned that," or, "I wouldn't have done that to myself!" This may be true, but from the inner planes we see things much differently and far more clearly. There, we see from a spiritual-progress-needed point of view; our judgment is unbiased, unprejudiced, totally fair, and far-reaching in scope.

This may seem like a strange concept until you begin to work seriously with your dreams. Then you may experience for yourself the schools, the teachings, and planning. You may suddenly recall having agreed to certain circumstances, or you may catch yourself thinking, "I know I have to do this..." but may not remember *why*. You could find yourself aware of what will happen next or what someone is going to say next. Almost everyone has had this experience.

Decision Making

Often in dreams we find ourselves at a fork or crossroad in our lives where important decisions must be made. We may then, in a series of dreams, explore a number of alternatives or possible courses. This can last several days, or even a week or two, while we select what we feel is best suited to our needs. These decisions are chosen with our spiritual growth and well-being in mind, not for our physical ease and pleasure; although we are allowed little vacations in between problems, especially if we have had a series of difficulties to overcome.

Our main lesson? Basically, it is to learn to **love one another**. Although we know this intellectually, few of us have learned to live by this principle. Ultimately, we must come to the place where we reach complete harmlessness in our physical and mental outlook and sincerely wish no one less than that which is best for him. We must develop an overall attitude of good will to all with **no** exceptions, for as long as we harbor ill-will, hate, or vengeance in our hearts, we have lessons to learn.

Almost all of our lessons are based on our attitudes and relationships with people and circumstances. When we have truly learned to do all things in love, to have peaceful, harmonious relationships with everyone and everything, then we are graduated from the earth plane and no longer need to return. We move on to better things, higher learning, and to the "many mansions" prepared for us.

Re-Entry

As daylight comes and it is time for us to return to our sleeping bodies, we come up out of Delta and Theta levels into Alpha, dreaming all the way.

If we are physically well-rested, our awareness may linger in the various Alpha levels, bringing us to a point where we can become aware that we are dreaming—the lucid state. Here we may stay only a moment before moving on to Beta awakeness, or we may move into the lucid state where we can take control of our dreams and decide where we want to go and what we want to do.

Waking from these upper layers of Alpha is smooth, easy, and pleasant, for the dream body is poised and hovering over the physical one, ready to move gently in, provided our bodies are in good condition and that we have had a sufficient amount of sleep.

Crash Landings

When we are over-tired, over-stressed, ill, or under the influence of toxins of any kind, we may experience a real rude awakening when the alarm sounds. Being under-rested, our consciousness stays in the deeper Delta layers longer for needed body repairs and may still be down in these depths when the clock explodes into action. If so, we come rushing back to the physical level without sufficient time for our bodies to "line up" before re-entry, and we literally have a crash landing!

We may wake with a jolt—the jarring return can cause a slight headache, vague discomfort, and even a rapid heart palpitation which could last for several minutes. Some people experience a slight disorientation upon waking in this manner; others may go to such extremes that they actually do not know where they are. They may still be energetically involved in the action of their dream as they wake and may require much time to reorient themselves to here and now.

If this should happen to you, try turning over and going back to sleep, or at least relax into Alpha for a few moments to allow your body to get lined up and synchronized once more. Without this, you may groan and grope your way out of bed feeling tired, groggy, uncoordinated, and completely "out of it," which is quite literally true.

When your body isn't well-rested, it may take anywhere from a few minutes to several hours after waking before you feel like your usual self. This is at least partially due to the disruptive jolt of the crash landing and the resulting misalignment of the physical and dream bodies. The "out of it" feeling tends to disappear when your bodies eventually realign and become correctly positioned. Then you can truly say "I've got it all together!"

Sleeping Problems

Some people experience disorientation every morning. You may even know someone who is clumsy, unsynchronized, and scarcely able to cope for up to an hour or more after waking—people who "can't do a thing until after their morning coffee." Be aware that the problem is not the lack of coffee, but the misalignment of bodies. This condition can usually be alleviated by simply going to bed earlier and getting a longer night's sleep. The body may need an extra hour or so to catch up, or the person may habitually short-change himself of needed sleep.

Stress and Worry-Warts

One definition for worry is "going around and around a problem without ever coming to a conclusion." This kind of thinking can rob you of valuable sleep. Try making a bargain with yourself to either come to a conclusion of some sort or to put the problem away in a locked trunk for the night so you can get some sleep. Better yet, ask for insights and answers as to how best to deal with the situation, and then *sleep on it!*

Stress is more difficult to deal with, but you might need to know that one of the best ways of handling stress is vigorous exercise. This releases the tightness naturally. Otherwise, your tensions are literally stored in your muscle tissues until you finally work out the difficulties. Often stress is due to a build-up of unresolved problems.

Program yourself to face up to a problem situation **as soon as** it develops rather than to ignore it in the vague hope that it will go away. Again, here is a circumstance where the practice of working with your dreams can be extremely helpful. Try asking yourself, "Just exactly what is bothering me? How can I fix it? What is the best way to handle this?" If you have no immediate answer, then write out the question in your dream book and expect to get an answer or an insight by morning.

Naps as Stress-Breakers

If and when it is possible, a nap during the day keeps you from being excessively tired at night so that your sleep is not quite so deep in the morning, allowing you to slip in and out more easily. Remember, drugged sleep makes the condition worse.

Immobilization

Once in awhile someone has the problem of waking to find they cannot move at all! Needless to say, this can be an extremely frightening experience. If this should happen to you, don't panic. Just realize your two bodies are not yet together. Relax, breathe deeply, and give your bodies time to get settled back in place before trying to move. This shouldn't last more than a moment or two. While this is not a common occurrence, it does happen.

Drugs and Dreams

Many things can affect the quality and depth of our sleep and dreams: antihistamines, sleeping pills, hallucinogens, alcohol, "pot," plus various chemicals and medications. These act as toxins, lowering the vibrations of the body as a whole and the brain waves in particular. When one goes to sleep under the influence of any of these, the dream body may slip out of the physical body as usual, but it will be unable to go to the spiritual planes as it should. Its vibrations, lowered by drugs or drink, are simply not high enough to enter the higher planes. Therefore, it hovers over its sleeping counterpart until the effects of the toxins have worn off. Only then can it go to the Delta levels for lessons. Body repairs, recuperation, and general revitalizing do not occur until the dream body is released. It is fairly easy to see how a habit of taking drugs or having a few drinks every night can seriously interfere with our dreams, our spiritual lessons, body repair, and rejuvenation as well as our psychological balance as shown in REM denial experiments cited earlier.

In the case of heavier doses of chemicals or toxins, the dream body, once separated, may be unable to re-enter the physical body under any circumstances until some degree of mental and physical balance is restored.

In either case there are no dreams, no lessons, no REM, no communications. Should a problem occur such as a fire, the subconscious may duly signal, but the dream body may not be able to re-enter the drugged body to activate it and remove it from danger until at least some of the toxic effects have dissipated. This can be dangerous to your health!

CHAPTER 4

The Many Kinds of Dreams

Edgar Cayce, the great American psychic (1877-1945), tells us there are three main types of dreams: physical, subconscious, and superconscious ("Your Dreams").

THE PHYSICAL DREAM

These dreams are caused strictly by physical noises, such as police sirens, honking horns, singing cats, and banging shutters or such discomforts as too much pizza, pickles, and ice cream, an elbow in your back, cold wind or rain blowing over you, or perhaps a pet pouncing on your bed. Dreams of this type are often strictly physical in nature and can usually be forgotten. However, we may at times have a combination of both, when the subconscious mind incorporates physical feelings and sounds into a very meaningful dream. Think twice before discarding any dream.

DREAMS FROM THE SUBCONSCIOUS

Dreams from the subconscious levels of the mind are mostly couched in symbolic or picture language which needs to be interpreted. They mostly concern the conditions of the body, symbolized by vehicles; the mind, represented by hair and clothing; and emotions, often indicated by water. These dreams are to help us become aware of our problems, and to bring aid in solving them. Most of our dreams fall into this category.

DREAMS FROM THE SUPERCONSCIOUS

Dreams from the superconscious are usually classified as visions, spiritual experiences, or revelations and are not to be interpreted in the same way as symbolic dreams. ESP dreams may also fall in this class.

Symbolic Dreams

Dreams coming from the subconscious levels are consistently symbolic in nature, being loaded with symbols of all kinds. Some are quite obvious, such as seeing yourself driving a zebra-striped automobile or finding yourself wearing a type of clothing you don't own and maybe would never wear. You may dream of living in a house you haven't seen in years or possibly one which was torn down long ago. All these things which do not fit your present reality are symbolic and need to be thoughtfully interpreted to get the full meaning.

Under the general heading of symbolic dreams we have many varieties, some of which are covered more fully in other chapters.

Action and Inaction

If most of your dreams show you animatedly participating in the dream action, you are in pretty good shape. This shows that you are actively involved in the learning, doing processes. On the other hand, if you are always sitting down, lying down, watching TV, or watching other people doing things, this would point out either a lack of interest or insufficient involvement on your part, which is a hint to get busy.

When this is occasional, your dream may be saying that you are not doing anything about a particular condition or that you are simply observing the situation. Dreams may indicate some hidden factors or suggest that you do not have any particular goal at this time, especially if you have a series of inactive, do-nothing dreams. You may be reminded that you are not really trying, not working, or not taking part in your life's events when perhaps you need to be applying yourself more diligently.

Daydreams

We all have daydreams from time to time, which generally fall in two categories. One we deliberately make up as we wish for something special in our lives; the other is the dream that just happens. We may catch ourselves out "wool-gathering," as we sometimes call it, and suddenly pop back into waking consciousness, sheepishly realizing that we have been gone.

It is this latter daydream that is so meaningful. Often these show us our innermost hopes, yearnings, and wishes of the heart that we tend to repress. The very fact that we dreamed it points to the fact that there is some need that is longing to be expressed in our lives.

These dreams deserve some thoughtful consideration. They are trying to tell us something we need to hear, so it may be wise to record them in our dream book lest we forget.

Disjointed Dreams

Occasionally, we have dreams which suddenly switch from one scene or theme to another so quickly we wonder if the dream could possibly have a meaning for us. Whenever the dream seems clear enough in each segment, it can symbolize the way in which one thing can lead to another. For example, if you do **this** then **that**

The Mystical, Magical, Marvelous World of Dreams

will happen, which in turn may cause still another situation. In such cases you will need to analyze each segment separately as a *dreamlette* first, and then try to string them together in sequence to see what point or relationship of events the dream is trying to depict. (See *Multiple Dream Themes* under *Further Exploration of Dreams*.)

If the dream itself is vague and the symbols are fuzzy, the chances are you are only recalling bits and pieces. Always try to work with what you have in the realization that this may be something you really don't want to look at, and therefore may be much more important than you supposed. Make an effort to understand the main symbols and their relationships with each other. If this doesn't solve the problem, then ask for another dream to give you more clarity. Sometimes, when we are working with a really **BIG** hangup within ourselves, it becomes necessary to take the message in small segments so that we can acclimate ourselves to the needed changes and slowly turn our thinking around.

Dream-Within-a-Dream

At times you may dream you are asleep and wake within the dream. Generally speaking, to dream you are dreaming is to say that you are not awake, unaware, or not paying attention to this situation. The action which follows when you "wake up" in the dream is doubly emphasized and therefore of extra significance. Your subconscious mind is trying to stress its importance, so even though the dream-within-a-dream is only a dreamlette, be sure to give it your full attention. This is your cue to **wake up and look** at what is going on around you.

On the other hand, waking within a dream can be a signal that you are becoming aware you are dreaming and can, at this point, move into the lucid state.

Dreamlettes or Fragmentary Bits of Dreams

There are times, especially when we first begin to work with dreams, when we can recall only a piece of what we know to be a much longer dream. **Be not dismayed!** See that fragment as the most important part of the dream, the main message, the bottom line, the **point**. Learn to work with what you have, and apply the lesson of the dreamlette to your life. It is a well-known fact that when we use what we have, our dreams become correspondingly longer, have greater clarity, and can be remembered with far greater ease.

A good example of this is one I call *The Giving Bowl*, a simple but powerful dreamlette (overleaf).

Falling

From time to time we experience the sensation of falling, or we may have a dream of falling, which can be frightening. Usually in these we never touch the ground, which is a sure sign this is another part of the out-of-the-body experience. We are just remembering a part of our return trip to the sleeping body.

DREAMLETTE: THE GIVING BOWL

A bowl of fruit on a table. I reach out to take one,
then withdraw empty-handed two or three times.

Filled Bowl: An offering, gift, invitation to accept some thing good, free for the taking.

Reaching Out: Desire to have, hope to attain, receive.

Withdrawing Empty-handed: Refusing or unable to accept the good that is offered. Self denial.

Meaning: I am refusing to accept the good things offered me.

Short, simple, straight to the point, and POWERFUL in scope.

On the other hand, we may dream of tripping, falling, or being pushed and actually hitting the ground or surface. This type of fall is likely to be a warning that there is danger in some decision or plan you have made. You may be "headed for a fall," or the dream may say, "Beware of pushy people!" If you are dealing in the stock market, it could imply a fall in your stock, especially if you had this matter in mind as you went to sleep.

Such dreams could indicate a physical fall, a social fall, a business failure, being fired or demoted, or even a fall from grace! Take a good look at the background setting, the overall actions, your feelings, and your present life situation to determine the correct implication.

Flying Dreams

Your dreams of flying are often simply the remembering of all or part of your astral flight to and from your sleeping body and are not connected to your dreams, but occasionally these may occur within the dream itself. Often this is your indication that you are moving into a lucid state; that is, you are about to become aware that you are dreaming.

Should you find yourself flying in a symbolic dream (one with a plot), it may indicate a need for you to rise above the present problem or situation. It could be suggesting that you try to see things from a higher and more spiritual point of view.

When this is part of a meandering dream which seems to have no particular plot, it is more likely to be an astral travel remembrance. Again, it could be a signal that you are near that Al-Beta level between sleep and waking, where you begin to realize that you must be dreaming and can begin to move into the lucid state. This is something you want to watch for. See the chapter on *Lucid Dreaming*.

Meandering Dreams

These dreams wander around without making any point and do not seem to have any plot or direction. You may seem to be first here, then there, without much action of any kind. If you have more than one of these in a row, your dreams are indicating a lack of progress in your life or are possibly depicting your habit of drifting through life without any clear purpose or direction, which may be a strong suggestion that you start setting some realistic goals for yourself.

Outrageous Dreams

Dreams we label as *outrageous* may simply be a pun pointing out our own outrageous behavior—a playful spoof on what we have been doing; or, when the symbols are carefully analyzed, they may make a very valid point.

Recurring Dreams

Dreams repeat themselves because we have not as yet gotten the point; we haven't understood the situation or taken any action on the problem. Sometimes they are simply stating, "This is how you perceive this," or "This is your problem," or "This is how you really feel about your life." These dreams tend to continue showing up from time to time until we eventually work through the situation. Ignored long enough, recurring dreams may return as nightmares!

Some recurring dreams or dream-themes may have their roots in a past life or trauma. Dreams of falling, drowning, bombing, warfare, or being shot or killed are often relived at least in part within the context of other dreams. Watch for other symbols of former lifetimes in the clothing, buildings, and background area. Often these are sources of great pain, shock, dread, fear, or unforgiven acts which need to be recognized and confronted.

The Silly Dreams

These are dreams which seem to make no sense at all upon waking. The more symbolism they contain, the more ridiculous they appear to the conscious mind. Since there is a great tendency in each of us to reject anything that does not instantly make good sense, we need to be especially careful about rejecting these seemingly nonsensical fantasies.

One of the first lessons to learn in working with dreams is to discipline ourselves to accept and write down all of our dreams without question because, invariably, when properly understood, those outrageous, funny, or silly dreams are giving us an important, coded message about ourselves.

Dreams From the Superconscious

One of the surest ways to recognize a spiritual dream is by the background setting. These are almost always outdoors, on a mountain top, or by a beautiful, flowing river.

Colors are unusually clear, bright, and beautiful. The scene is filled with sunshine or brilliant light, there may be lovely trees, flowers, birds, and scenes of great splendor. Often there is a special feeling of love, peace, serenity, inspiration, and joy accompanying the spiritual dream.

You may see yourself climbing up a mountain, and since mountains almost always suggest higher states of consciousness, this would be your symbol of moving closer to God. Your progress, or lack of it, may be indicated by your feelings and the way in which you are climbing, as well as by the heights you have reached. Notice any obstacles in your path.

Swimming often denotes spiritual activity, especially when you are swimming in a clear and beautiful lake or river. Perhaps you will be sailing a boat over peaceful waters. If the ship is large and beautiful, well and good; if it has a hole in the bottom, it may suggest a "hole" or flaw in your thinking, acting, or perception of things. You may be all alone or in a crowd, struggling and paddling against the current, or sailing smoothly, making good progress or none at all.

Dreams of boating, of the captain of the ship, its crew, cargo, and destination are frequent symbols of your spiritual journey, with the captain portraying your Godself or High Self, you representing yourself or your conscious mind, and the crew depicting other aspects of yourself. Note the overall cooperation and harmony or lack of it.

The act of fishing can be a spiritual activity, as fish often symbolize Christ, Christianity, or spiritual food. Our fishing lines can denote a desire for spiritual things or a reaching out for spiritual knowledge. Observe carefully how you go about fishing and what, if anything, you catch.

A rainbow is always a sign of God's promises, blessings, or His protection, while a ray of sunlight could mean wisdom, knowledge, blessings, or enlightenment coming to you. The feeling in this kind of dream is also highly significant in understanding the overall meaning.

Healing

Although healing dreams may occur in symbolic form, they are mostly Superconscious in origin. Healing may occur in your bed, out in "nature," or in a beautiful temple. This can be quite direct, such as a touch from an angelic being, or may be symbolized as a visit from a doctor, priest, or some unknown but loving being. You may be given an herb, pill, a "shot" of medicine, an operation, or a simple beam of light. Sometimes this is accompanied by directions for a change in diet, habits, your thinking, or some other suggestions to aid in your recovery. The results may be dramatic and immediate or may take awhile to complete. At the very least this would mark a turning point in your illness. These healings are usually the result of prayers: yours, other people's, or both.

Visions

A vision may come while fully awake, half-way between sleep and waking, or during sleep. Most often these seem to occur at the half-way point. The most outstanding qualities are the combination of brilliant colors (sometimes colors we have never seen before) and the clarity and tremendous depth of feelings which coincide. A vision usually leaves us with a deep sense of awe and an accompanying sensation of devotion and gratitude. We are definitely *impressed*.

Visions usually indicate something of vital importance. It may be instruction or the revealing of your soul purpose, especially if you have been seeking this experience. (Many races have *Vision Quests* as part of the rite of passage into maturity.) Often these visions reveal the future in some way. Most visions, unlike ESP dreams, can **not** be changed (although these are sometimes altered or canceled when enough people get together and make positive changes in their thoughts and actions).

The vision itself will stand pretty much as is, with the possible exception that some of the main symbols, such as a snow-capped mountain, can signify a higher state of consciousness, high spiritual planes, being closer to God, meditation, high spirituality, and so on. The basic meanings do not change, but can often be stated in several ways, according to one's understanding. Most importantly, visions seem to grow on you so that with time you may become aware of deeper and greater meanings within the original message.

Spiritual Progress Reports

Frequently, when one first begins to pay attention to dreams, the very first one to be remembered is what I term the *Spiritual Progress Report*. These dreams seem to be revealing to the dreamer his spiritual condition and are usually rather long and detailed. Once started, they may recur at fairly regular intervals so that we may view our progress or lack of it and act accordingly. Our biggest clue here is the ending, which indicates how we are doing. If we arise happy and eager to go on, all is well and good; but if we wake sad, depressed, or gloomy, it is a clear warning that we are neglecting the spiritual side of our lives or that we are in the process of doing something that will be detrimental to our spiritual growth.

Such dreams may go back to our childhood and involve many people and events which have affected our lives. Some of our misconceptions and incorrect programming may be viewed at this time, as well as other influences from our past.

Overall, the Superconscious dreams may be said to come from the High Self and are important guideposts, warnings, or messages to comfort and aid us in our spiritual journey through life. We do not walk alone.

CHAPTER 5

Goals

Dreams guide and help us after we set goals and ideals for our lives.
                                                    — *Edgar Cayce**

Dreams show us the pattern of our lives but focus mainly around the problems and events of the previous day **in the light of the goals we have set for ourselves**. Therefore, the process of writing out our goals becomes an important measuring device to judge our progress. Understanding this point can be extremely enlightening in the interpretation of our dreams.

We may think that what we wanted most at the age of ten has nothing at all to do with what is happening to us in the present moment; but the truth is that our goals, remembered or not, exert a continuing influence on us. Our subconscious mind retains all our ancient beliefs and ideals, and our lives are run by the old programming **until something newer replaces it**. We could still be caught up in trying to please our parents or work for pennies!

Without definite goals, we tend to drift through life. We find other people are the **do**ers and we are the ones **done unto!** We become the victim and never the victor. The Bible states, "Without a vision the people perish." What is your vision for yourself? Is it something like, "You can't get there from here," or do you have a good, positive, success-oriented picture in mind? If you are not sure what you want, if you can't see yourself **being there**, your whole life becomes subject to the goals and manipulations of others and is bound to be disappointing.

Why not give some thought to setting up some definite, new goals for yourself today? This simple act will not only motivate your whole life into more successful directions but will aid you in dream interpretation as well.

---

* A.R.E. Journal, No. 6, 1972, p. 279.

PERSONAL OVERVIEW

1. How do you feel about your LIFE to date? Do you need to forgive anyone, including yourself? List.

2. What has been your OVERALL GOAL?

3. What have you done about your goals?

4. How do you feel about your JOB?

5. How do you feel about your BODY?

6. How do you feel about your HOME?

7. How do you feel about your SPIRITUAL LIFE?

8. What new goals or changes do you need to make in each category?

Let us start with a brief review of what has happened from early childhood until now to serve as a reference point.

When finished, write a brief summary in your dream journal as a point of reference for dream questions. Also list your new goals, possibly in red ink, as handy reminders.

MY NEW GOALS

Physical:

> Body:
> Home:
> Career:
> General:

Mental And Emotional Goals:

Spiritual Goals:

> Prayer/Meditation
> Study
> Disciplines

Once you have made a commitment to a purpose or a goal, it seems to immediately begin to draw to you a flow of ideas, opportunities, and the general wherewithal needed to accomplish that which you have envisioned. Doors open, help is offered, needed strength, tools, or money appear as if from out of nowhere; and you are on your way to success. But without that first commitment, nothing moves. For, as James Allen puts it, "Until thought is linked with purpose, there is no intelligent accomplishment...They who have no central purpose in their life fall easy prey to petty worries, fears and self-pity, all of which are indications of weakness."

A Word of Caution

There are three main causes of stress and frustration in our lives. Simply stated, they are: our expectations of others, other people's expectations of us, and our expectations of ourselves.

Our expectations of others. We tend to hold definite ideas as to how other people should act, perform their duties, and keep their promises. We expect certain amenities and considerations from those with whom we live and work. When they do not measure up to these ideals, we are disappointed, hurt, angry, and upset. Once we realize it is *our expectations* which cause us pain, we can reevaluate the situation, let go of our misplaced aspirations for others, and concentrate on the only persons we have any right to change—ourselves.

Other people's expectations of us. We find both friends and family, especially parents, projecting *their* expectations, standards, hopes, and goals upon us in such a way as to make us feel guilty when we don't conform to *their* patterns. True, those ideals were needed when we were children; but as adults these are no longer valid. It is important to grasp this situation in its entirety, then *deliberately break free of their goals* and create your own—it is your rite of passage into maturity and independence. Without it you remain owned, dependent, and manipulated.

Our expectations of ourselves. Alas, we often make goals for ourselves which are impossible to reach, thus dooming ourselves to failure and disappointment. It is far better for us to make reasonable, *reachable* ideals will which allow us to enjoy the success, prosperity, and happiness that goes along with our attainment. Then, *feeling successful and good about ourselves*, we can set new, higher, and attainable goals. Since success breeds success, this is the way to insure victory in your chosen area.

Your Spiritual Path

Once you have made a commitment to following the *Path* and are determined to work on your spiritual development, your dreams serve as a sounding board and guidance system for your growth. You can ask such things as "What is my biggest blockage to self-mastery?" or "What do I need to work on most?" and get answers which help you move speedily along your chosen route; and, because you are interested, your dreams give you more and more insights on where you need to make changes and how best to bring these about. There are times when great wisdom pours through your dreams, but not before you are ready for it.

Meditation proves invaluable here, for its regular practice intensifies the quality and clarity of your dreams, particularly when you are applying the lessons learned from them. Meditation also deepens your awareness and enhances your ability to move in and out of the Alpha states freely, which in turn greatly facilitates your psychic abilities. The combination of dreams, goals, and meditation gives you deeper insights and greater acceptance of your fellow man and of the Universe.

Affirmations

The New Age trend of living is leaning more and more to affirmations, positive thinking, re-training the mind, and reprogramming the subconscious belief system. As you work with these concepts, you will find your dreams reflecting this. They will actually give you progress reports on your attainments. For example, suppose your dreams are pinpointing your poor self-esteem which is impeding your advancement. You may decide to reprogram yourself by repeating something like, "I am a good, loving person and I am now drawing success and prosperity into my life." As you repeat this phrase, vocally or in writing, you may be aware of bringing about significant changes in yourself; but more likely you will be wondering whether your efforts are accomplishing anything at all. At such times you may have a dream indicating that your affirmation is about half-formed. By this, you *know* it is working and that you have more work to do in order to finish.

Or, suppose you are in dire need of money and that you have decided to program some prosperity into your life. Your next dream may point out your difficulty with wealth, revealing that you have a "money is the root of all evil" belief, a feeling that wealth is a heavy responsibility, or depicting some other kind of thinking which blocks your road to riches. Actually, all of us who are not in the flow of wealth have some kind of basic, subconscious blockage to opulence.

The same can be said about health. Those who are ill have accepted this condition for a reason, and dreams can help them to grasp the truth about their need to be sick. People tend to punish themselves in strange ways for even stranger reasons, but what has been done can be undone by the same process—creative thinking.

Dreams may also show you when your goals need changing or may indicate when your religious beliefs are getting in the way of real, spiritual Truth.

Questions and Answers

Asking a question of the Universe is much like a child asking a question in school—the questioning hand is raised and the teacher gives the desired instruction. Ask and ye shall receive. Let us not forget to ask or seek for something higher than we now have; for to truly live life we must continually grow, and dreams are an excellent way of getting needed answers.

To take this just a step further I would like to mention the now well-documented cases of what is known as *Near Death Experiences* (NDE). These stories first surfaced, to the best of my knowledge, in the late 1960's. Since then there has been an avalanche of recorded episodes where people were pronounced dead by qualified doctors or were feared dead for some moments before "returning" to life. In every case, the accounts were surprisingly similar (Ring 1984). Each one had a feeling of peace and well-being after leaving the body; each saw a brilliant white light. Most were aware of the valiant rescue efforts of others to keep them alive, even as they moved blissfully toward the Light. All reported a feeling of love and acceptance from the *Light Being,* and many had their whole life experience pass swiftly before their eyes. Some were told they had to return, as they had not yet finished what they had set out to do. Others were given a choice of staying or returning. Many were asked, **"What have you done for others?"**— a good question. One which, it seems, all of us will have to answer sooner or later.

Consider this well as you determine your goals and write in your journal. Ponder on the best questions to ask your High Self in order to make the most of your life and find the greatest joys of living.

CHAPTER **6**

Your Journal:
A Useful Dream Tool

---

*Truth is within ourselves; it takes no rise from outward things, whatever you may
believe. There is an inmost center in all of us where truth abides in fullness...To
know consists in opening a way out whence the imprisoned splendor may
escape. Not in effecting entry for a light supposed to be without.*

— Buddha

Your dream journal can be a marvelous tool both for dream interpretation and as a
record of your spiritual growth, if you will take time each evening to review the day's
events, your actions, reactions, and honest feelings about these things. It is wise to
write down successes as well as any failures or disappointments. Include your hopes,
fears, plans, expectations, and especially your goals, since your dreams are constantly
commenting on your thoughts and actions of the previous day **as measured by the
yardstick of your goals**.

In counseling others, we find that most people can tell exactly what is wrong with their
lives and how to make the necessary corrections as well; all they really need is a
chance to put their thoughts into words, and as they do so their problems become
clear, the answers apparent. Journaling produces the same effect without the high cost
of counseling!

As you set up definite goals and ideals for your life, your journal writing serves as a
focus for all you are currently experiencing and how you really feel about your life
situation. Most of all, this practice helps you to look deeply into your life, seeing what
you are doing and why—where you are going, the lessons you are learning, and what
changes are needed in order to create a more fulfilling lifestyle. Significantly, this also
helps you to exert more control over your life. By making a habit of looking at your
lifestyle on a regular basis, you tend to be much more aware of the stream of events

flowing about you and of the many manipulations, games, and situations which are coming into play. You are therefore far better equipped to both understand your challenges and to quickly face them head-on, rather than being swept away by the subtle undertow of circumstances.

Journaling

Your journal can be your special place to talk to your best friend and counselor (you), writing out your current events and feelings so the crux of your problem becomes apparent and your mind is cleared to ask the appropriate questions as a framework for your dreams.

To begin seriously working with your dreams, your first and best step is to faithfully keep a spiritual diary, writing out all the important things you are thinking, feeling, and experiencing at the end of each day. It is said that one should, as a daily spiritual practice, make a self-examination and evaluation; in so doing, valuable dream-learning time is not wasted in performing this spiritually-necessary task after going to sleep. This gets you off to a head start, so to speak. To facilitate this you may find it more convenient to keep your dreams, meditation notes, and your journal all in the same notebook under the day's date, rather than having separate books for each. Experiment to find what works best for you!

The main idea is to look at the events of your day, in a ***detached*** manner, evaluating the ways in which you worked, acted, or reacted, and how you handled the events. Weigh your actions in the ***light of the goals you have set for yourself***, being sure to include your feelings about these. ***Lovingly evaluate*** what you did, noting where and how you could improve your performance. This is not meant to be a put-down exercise, belittling yourself for every little mistake, but an impartial appraisal of what was done and how it might be improved upon in the future. Don't forget to add all incoming information such as classes, books, tapes, and even movies, as all these things exert subtle influences on the way you think, therefore the way you live.

Be careful not to judge yourself harshly. Remember that every so-called mistake is actually another step in your learning processes and, as such, is to be understood and treasured, not condemned. Try to love yourself just as you are, realizing that the problem people and situations in your life are teaching you something ***you have chosen to learn***. Accept these challenges for what they are: your *lessons in life*. Then, journaling can be a nightly practice in loving self-evaluation and improvement, done with your most cherished hopes and goals in mind.

This continued self-search of your goals, motives, actions, and overall lifestyle greatly aids in accurately assessing your progress in life and in understanding the why and how of the problems facing you. It facilitates the learning of your lessons or the overcoming of difficulties and obstacles far more speedily than ever before. It also

SUGGESTED POINTS TO REVIEW
FOR JOURNALING

1. PRESENT GOAL(S) (repeated briefly to remind yourself what you want to do).

2. OVERALL PATTERN of events this week (or month).

3. HAPPENINGS of the day? RECURRING PATTERNS?

4. ACTION/REACTION to events? To people?

5. Were actions IN LINE with goals?

6. How do I FEEL about this?

7. What seems to be my MAIN CHALLENGE or lesson to learn? (Anything that repeats itself is pointing out an area that needs to be confronted and worked through.)

8. What are my DREAMS TELLING ME about this?

9. What have I done about my GOALS today? (Be sure to compliment yourself for every success or improvement!)

10. What CHANGES, improvements do I need to make?

prepares the way for guidance from your High Self to come through dreams with greater clarity, paving the way to lucid dreaming—a much-to-be-desired achievement.

Writing Your Dream Request

When your review is done, form your request for new ideas, advice, or help from your dreams. Write this out carefully, for regardless of how clear the question may be tonight, you may find it completely forgotten by morning! I can still recall waking one morning with a beautiful dream, a wonderful answer, but...*I couldn't remember the question!*

Once written, the next step is to reduce any lengthy requests to the simplest, briefest possible statement. For instance, if you are starting the journaling process, you may want to write out several lines asking in detail for an overview of your life to date and some sense of direction as to what you need most to do or change in your life right now. Having done this, you can restate it briefly as, "A past overview and future direction," or if you prefer a rhyme you could write, "Past and future let me see, for a better me to be."

You want to state your query in words easily remembered so that you can repeat the phrase over and over as you drift off to sleep, since your last waking thought before slumber strongly influences the dream content. You might further implant the idea by placing your request under your pillow, so you can literally *sleep on it!*

When this is done, you are ready to begin your enlightening adventures in dreaming!

CHAPTER 7

Recalling Your Dreams

Sleep [is] that period when the soul takes stock of that [which] it has acted upon from one rest period to another.

—Edgar Cayce*

We often hear the comment, "I never dream"; yet science has proven that we all dream, not once, but several times every night. The truth is that most of us simply do not remember.

Why Do We Forget?

The most common cause of forgotten dreams is that we ***do not really want to remember***. There are a variety of reasons for this. Often, it is because we have closed our minds to spiritual things; other contributing factors are an over-tired body, sleeping pills, various drugs and medications, or heavy drinking. The most commonly found reason is our childhood programming. Most of us have been told repeatedly in our youth to "forget it, it's only a dream..." and being obedient children, we "forget"; and our minds, being similar to a computer, having once been programmed to forget, will continue to ignore dreams until reprogrammed to remember. The only exception to this is an occasional nightmare or extremely vivid dream which seems to crash through all our defenses.

For some people, a frightening dream experience will cause a shut off of all dream recall. People with vivid ESP dreams—especially those which warn of some unfortunate experience such as a death—are prone to feel frightened and somewhat guilty when the dream comes true, as if they should have somehow prevented it. They then determine, often quite unconsciously, never to dream again, which can cut off dream recall most effectively.

---

* Reading 5754-2.

This is a legitimate problem, but it can be dealt with by simply affirming to yourself, "I *want* to remember my dreams, but I do *not want* any ESP dreams." Or, you may say, "No more death dreams." Just remember you are in control, and you can make the rules any way you wish to satisfy your own needs. Your subconscious mind is your willing servant and will do for you as you command.

Another deterrent to recall is waking to a noisy radio, alarm, or talkative roommate. Even your own waking thoughts, when allowed to wander, can be distracting and may erase all dream memory before it can be brought to the surface of your conscious mind.

A lack of interest in your dreams is another contributing factor to poor dream recall, as is sleeping too long after the dream has ended. Remember, five minutes after the dream is finished half the content is forgotten; in ten minutes ninety percent is lost.

Several things can help you get back in touch with your dreams:

- *Eliminate* all the dream deterrents.
- *Tell* your subconscious mind that you really *want to remember* your dreams. (Do this at least three times.)
- *Buy a special notebook* for recording your dreams.
- *Program your subconscious* mind to remember that you want to re-enter gently when you return to your body.
- *Read* books and magazine articles on dreams.
- *Talk about dreams* with friends, preferably those who are interested in them, of course!
- *Pay attention* to your dreams! Recall to mind the last dream you can remember and *ponder* it's meaning.
- *Treat dreams with respect* and appreciation. Act as though they contain valuable and important messages just for you.
- If possible, *join* a dream group.
- *Beware of rejecting any dream!*

How To Recall Your Dreams

Your first step, naturally, would be to eliminate all the deterrents mentioned earlier. Since you can't very well throw away your noisy alarm clock or your roommate, you may want to program yourself to wake up five minutes before the alarm (or roommate) goes off. This is amazingly easy to do. The subconscious mind is easily impressed with instructions from the conscious mind. Simply tell yourself what you want done, and repeat it several times to impress the message firmly. (Reaffirm this again as you drift off to sleep, just to reinforce it.)

Secondly, you need to convince yourself that you **really want to remember your dreams**. Repeat this to yourself off and on during the day and especially just before falling asleep.

Respect Your Dream Source

Avoid writing your valuable dreams on just any old scrap of paper which happens to be handy. Buy a new notebook **especially for your dreams**. (This further impresses your subconscious mind that you are in earnest about remembering.) Keep both book and pen within easy reach. If a tape recorder suits you better, then by all means use what works best for you!

Since your dreams almost always refer to the events and problems of the day before, you can make things much easier for yourself by making a habit of journaling the night before, paying special attention to your feelings about the parade of events in your life. Follow this self-analysis by either asking for insights on a problem or for an answer to a specific question. You will find that choosing your topic ahead of time makes dream interpretation much, much easier! Follow this by repeating your request as you drift off to sleep, because your last waking thoughts and memories strongly influence the dream content.

Obtaining Answers to Your Questions:

- Program mentally what you want to know all through the day, e.g. "Tonight I want some insights on my health problem."
- Write out your request in your dream book.
- Have dream book and pen handy, **expecting** an answer.
- Tell yourself, "I will remember my dreams."
- Determine to wake up immediately after your dream and remember it.
- Hold your dream request firmly in mind as you drift off to sleep.

If you are having an especially difficult challenge, you may have to work on the same question for three consecutive days; but your answer **will** come.

Be aware that the answer you seek may not always come in the form of a dream but can come in the form of a person, book, magazine, T.V. program, an overheard conversation, or in some other totally unexpected manner. Apparently this keeps us alert and open to guidance from all directions! Your answer, when it comes, is valid from whatever source and lets you know Somebody-Up-There **cares about you!**

As You Wake

Discipline yourself to waken gently, lying still rather than turning or stirring, and promptly begin to recall all that you have dreamed before permitting your mind to go to other matters. (To digress to workaday matters at this point can effectively erase the whole dream!)

Capturing the Elusive Dream

Be aware that since you dream at Alpha levels, it is necessary for you to deliberately *pull* your dream *up* from the subconscious levels and firmly impress it on your intellect. As you waken, gently recall whatever tidbit of your dream you can capture and run this through your conscious mind; then ask, "What else?" Repeat this process until you have as much of the dream as you can regain, then go back again, trying to recall as much detail and feeling as possible, remembering colors, background, and anything else that may be relevant. When you have finished, turn to another sleeping position to see if you can dredge up any more memories. You may be surprised at the added information!

Only when you have brought back as much information as possible to your conscious mind do you dare to reach for your notebook. Record immediately before details become lost or hazy.

If you cannot recall the dream, don't be discouraged. Discipline yourself to write **something**—a single symbol, an emotion you felt on awakening, and **any** fragment of your dream **regardless** of how small or insignificant it may seem. This is a starting point. The faithful recording in a dream notebook will impress the subconscious mind of your serious intention to remember your dreams. Next time you will do much better.

Recording Your Dream

Try to keep both people and outside influences out of your space during this time, even if you have to retreat to the privacy of the bathroom to do so. (If possible, get your roommate to work on his/her dreams, or at least respect your desire to remember yours.) Make every effort to keep this moment inviolate, treating your dream material as a precious message from God to you, which in essence it is.

It is best to write out your dream fully as soon as possible. Be sure to include colors, names, numbers, song or book titles—any and every detail you can recall. When you are finished, embellish your dream with an appropriate title. It would be wise to remember the news reporter's old rule of: Who, What, Where, When, How, and Why.

Picture Symbols are Invaluable

If there is something you can't put in words, draw a picture so you don't lose the symbol. In fact, make as many sketches as possible, for they are invaluable as memory prompters; often these symbols have hidden meanings which may surface later. If you like to doodle, try doodling some of the symbols and impressions that come with the dream, pondering these during the day.

Capture That Feeling!

Be sure to record the feeling that went along with the dream. It may seem insignificant as you waken; but when it comes to interpreting, the sentiments you had in the dream can play a most important role, so be sure to include the sensations you had as you woke and any emotions within the dream.

Dreamlettes

If you have only a fragment of a dream, don't despair; it is at least a start in the right direction, especially if you haven't remembered a dream in a long time. Applaud yourself mentally for having the dreamlette. Write it down carefully and gratefully. Work with what you have, treating it as important and thinking of it as often as possible during the day; ponder its meaning. Take the time to interpret it just as you would a longer one. All of this serves to stimulate your mind to more vivid dream recall and encourages your subconscious to produce longer dreams.

Meanwhile, consider the dreamlette as the most important point of a longer dream, the best part, the most significant. *Do not treat it lightly!*

If time won't permit a full writing in the morning, make it a habit to jot down your *feeling*, the *main action*, and the most *important symbols* before trotting off to work. Promise yourself to fill in the details at the first available opportunity, possibly while having breakfast or riding to work. If a tape recorder is handy, you might dictate your dream as you bathe, dine, or dress. If you have access to a computer, you may enjoy using it for your dream work. Use whatever works best for you.

Weekend Dreamer

Not everyone has the time or the inclination to work with dreams every morning, even when we would like to, but don't let that discourage you—become a *weekend dreamer!*

Tell yourself you really are interested in dreams, but your busy schedule won't let you write long dreams in the morning; so if there is an important message it will have to be in a very brief form or wait for a weekend. (This leaves you a little space for emergencies.)

Next, make up your mind firmly that Saturday and Sunday mornings will be your **prime time** for dream viewing. Set aside this time **exclusively** for your dream work, then honor your commitment.

Carry through by having your dream notebook close by your bed, and on Friday night faithfully do your journaling, writing out your dream request **with the expectation** of having your week's dream information poured out into the time span you have set aside.

Many busy people do this and find it works well.

Silly Dreams

Override the tendency to reject a dream because it seems silly. This is an easy thing to do, but bear in mind that to reject a dream for any reason leads to non-remembering. In actual practice, the silly dreams have some of the greatest and most memorable symbols of all; often, when interpreted, they are of utmost importance to you. Try to honor all of your dreams, disciplining yourself to record each one. You can always analyze later.

You may also have a tendency to reject dreams because they closely resemble a movie or TV program you have just seen. This is not valid reasoning. Your dreams use symbolism from any and all sources, and one is just as legitimate as the other! The movie symbols are simply fresher in your mind, so decode these dreams in the usual manner.

Beware of the temptation to reject any dream! There are three main reasons for this.

1. You think it is silly (Most dreams seem silly on waking.)

2. It's "only a fragment" or dreamlette.

3. You don't want to look at it!

The dreams you tend most to forget, throw out, or ignore are consistently the **most important ones** for you to write and interpret! So, discipline yourself to write down every dream, not just those that appeal to you. The one you reject is probably the one you most need.

Remember, your dreams are important coded messages to yourself, from yourself, for yourself.

CHAPTER **8**

Interpreting Your Dreams

A dream that is not understood is like a letter not opened.

— The Talmud

Dreams are fascinating—you never quite know what to expect, but you can be sure to learn something of interest about yourself in each one. If dream interpretation is a new adventure, you will find it best to begin with an open mind and a good, workable routine to develop your skills in dream work. The expanded outline given below is adapted from the *Five Step Approach* developed by Montague Ullman, M.D. using principles in the Edgar Cayce readings on dream interpretation. I suggest you follow this for a month or so, then adjust things to suit yourself.

Procedure

Awakening

Beware of rejecting your dream because it seems silly or is only a fragment. Lie quietly a moment and recall the details of your dream. Sometimes, as you wake and ponder the dream in that Al-beta state, you will if you ask receive either an interpretation or a strong impression as to the dream meaning. Encourage this.

Writing

Respectfully record all you can remember *in your dream notebook*, not on a scrap of paper! Form the habit of treating your dream as a valuable document. If time does not permit a full writing, re-read the sections on *Recording Your Dream* and *Weekend Dreamer.*

Feelings

Once you have finished writing down your dream, make it a habit to record your feelings: happy, sad, angry, elated, uneasy, frustrated, determined, frightened, or whatever your mood or emotion was as you awakened. Take enough time to clarify the feeling(s), such as extremely disappointed, mildly frustrated, or supremely happy.

You might also note what kind of dream you felt this was: ESP, lucid, vision, nightmare, symbolic, superconscious, or whatever.

Most Outstanding Symbol

This is especially important for those who cannot take time to work out dream meanings before starting their busy day. Pick out one outstanding symbol and ponder its meaning.

Action or Dream Theme

Go through your dream, preferably with a colored pen or see-through marker, and underline the verbs—this gives you a look at the dream action. Make this into a brief sentence such as, "someone is buying new clothes," "someone is climbing a ladder," or "someone is playing a game." This gives you the dream theme.

Frequently you will find several small themes within the overall dream, so that you may have someone running, someone hiding something, someone playing a game, **and** someone watching. Keep this brief; you just want a quick overview of the action before you become caught up in the dream symbols. This helps you keep your perspective. (Detailed information on multiple dream themes can be found in *Further Exploration of Dreams.*)

Background

Where does your dream take place? Is it indoors or outdoors? Is the area reminiscent of home and family? Work? Health? Is it light or dark? What kind of buildings? Are they old and familiar? New? What feeling does the setting evoke? Are you confident, pleased, worried?

These questions will give you some idea as to the particular part of your life the dream is emphasizing. Your feelings should confirm this. If not, you may need to recheck the background scenery. Once you have determined the theme and the area of your life it concerns, you have made a major step in finding the dream's purpose and are ready for the details.

Sketch Those Special Symbols

Whether you think you are artistic or not, try to sketch, draw, doodle, or caricature as many symbols as possible. This is the very best way to capture a dream symbol. If you feel this takes more time or effort than you care to give, then at least draw the more unusual symbols, especially those which are difficult to describe. This serves as a permanent reminder, for it is not unusual to find new insights and innuendoes days or even months later, and you'll be glad you had the sketch to use in making comparisons or confirming your findings.

Key Words

Going back through the dream again, underline all the important words, phrases, puns, and spoken sentences. Below your written dream list the key words as shown in the sample, giving yourself plenty of space to write all the feelings and meanings you associate with them, starting with the easiest and most obvious. Remember, your dreams are painting pictures of your attitudes and emotions, often pointing out unconscious responses and habits or throwing a spotlight on areas of your life which need changing.

Watch for slang expressions, puns, and various word-plays; and be alert for words or symbols which repeat themselves within the dream as well as those which continually crop up in a series of dreams. You may also find several different symbols, all with the same meaning, in one dream. These repetitions are accenting an important theme, making sure you *get the point!* If you have a computer, by all means use it; it makes your interpretation easier, and you'll have a neatly printed document when you finish.

Go as far as you can in writing down what each word or phrase means to you before using any book as reference, for it is **your** feelings, **your** emotions, memories, and responses which are triggered by the symbols; and these are **the most important** meanings as well as the only correct ones.

Example: Dog.
To most people, dogs are symbols of loyalty, friendliness, devotion, and protection. Many are considered to be part of the family! But, someone who has been bitten or badly frightened by a dog feels differently. His associations would be fear, pain, and mistrust. Others may consider dogs as pests which bark all night and overturn garbage cans or kill chickens and make messes. Each interpretation is correct for that person.

Since all symbols have this potential of duality, the most important thing to consider is that of being **totally honest** with yourself as to **what it means to you**.

When you find the right meaning for you, there is often a certain *gut feeling* about it: a tingle, a chill, or an *Aha!* which you come to recognize as your signal of correct interpretation.

If after careful study you are still unsure of a meaning, take an intuitive guess. Doing the best you can, write out in full whatever you think it means to you. Often your suppositions are incredibly accurate. You might want to ask yourself, "What old feelings, memories, or associations were stirred by that dream symbol? What was my honest reaction to it?" Bear in mind that the dream shows your immediate situation, your feelings, and the particular way in which you are viewing things at this time.

Spoken Words: In dreams, most of the communications are telepathic. Few, if any, words are actually spoken; therefore, whenever you or anyone else makes a statement, it is of vital importance and often is the main point of your dream. Generally, anything you say outloud is something of significance that you are telling yourself, so you will want to pay special attention to this.

At times, an aspect of yourself may make the first comment and your reply can show you how you *really* feel about this.

Ringing Bells: The telephone, doorbell, alarm clock, buzzer, or any kind of bell-like sound in your dream serves to draw your attention to whatever is said or done next. It is a way of bringing strong emphasis to that part of the dream; therefore, you will want to pay special attention to whatever follows.

People in Your Dreams: Generally speaking every person, animal, or thing in your dream graphically symbolizes some aspect of you, such as the moody part of you, the comedian, the parent figure, or your animal nature, while the dream action depicts how you act and interact with these fragments. (Our usual response is to deny or disown the less-than-lovely parts of ourselves.) Note any points of conflict, realizing that *everything in your dream is telling you something important about yourself.*

Meaning

When you have finished with your symbols and keywords, you are ready to decide what the dream seems to be telling you. First consider the three basic components of the dream:

- *Feelings* (On waking)
- *Overall action* (Who is doing what to whom)
- *Background setting* (Home, health, study, career, etc.)

Examine these. See where and how they fit with your dream question, your present problem, or your lifestyle. Look at your question or your journal writing to help you understand what the dream is about. You might also recheck the background setting for any further clues or implications.

There will be days when you find that the dream symbols fall right into place and the meaning is quite clear; other times there will be a word or phrase that eludes you. Don't be in a hurry with this. Ponder its meaning—take all day if necessary—just so you come to some sort of conclusion about your dream on the same day. Look up the possible meanings in this book, and *if* one feels right to you, use it. If not, continue to search for the meaning that is **just right for you**. You are the only one who can interpret your dreams correctly, so, **trust yourself!**

Once you have worked through the action, background, people, keywords, and probable purpose of your dream, you need to write out what you think it is saying to you. If you are not sure, take a good intuitive guess. The main idea is to write out a general statement to yourself about the most likely meaning of the dream.

Summary

After writing the dream meaning in full, which helps clarify your thinking, you may want to conclude with a brief summary—possibly a one-sentence statement—to be used for quick reference in your monthly dream reviews as well as for food for thought in your meditations.

Title

Once you have the meaning of your dream it is wise to give it an appropriate title, just like a movie. This serves as an aid in remembering the whole dream and gives you a handle to work with or to meditate upon for even further insights.

Decision

It does little good to discover your dream message if you do nothing about it. Dreams are an important self-help system designed to inspire, enlighten, and enrich your life; but they are powerless unless you apply the lessons learned, so don't allow yourself to skip this highly important step in dream work. Determine just how you are going to use the insights you have just received. Think it over carefully (don't allow yourself to put it off), then write out your decision.

Application

Your next step is in how to apply what you have learned. You may need to make some new goals or affirmations as to how you will handle things from now on or perhaps list your new plans on a calendar or your "Things To Do" list.

Follow Through

Make a firm commitment to yourself to follow through on these, listing any steps needed to implement this.

FINISHING TOUCHES:

- **Record new symbols**: Use the space provided in this book to record new symbols.

- **Weekly follow up**: Look over your dreams once a week, picking a **definite day**. Review titles and summaries. Watch for recurring symbols, recurring dreams, repeated themes, or a series of dreams on a particular subject. (These may change as you accept a talent of an aspect of yourself and begin to integrate this quality into your being.)

- **Monthly review**: Examine the month's dreams to get an overview of patterns, series, themes, and recurrences. List dream titles and summaries for the month. Write a brief digest of the month's messages.

- **Yearly**: Survey titles and summaries for the year, again noting recurring dreams, themes, and patterns, making a brief digest of what you feel are the most important messages and trends. Use this as a basis for your New Year's resolutions.

This may sound like an arduous process at first, but it can be tremendously helpful, informative, and totally transforming in its scope; tell yourself that you are worth the time and effort. Be kind to yourself. Most of all, love yourself; for if you don't love yourself, you can't truly love others, and **love is all there is!**

This routine is a well-worn, time-proven method which is the easiest and most efficient manner of dream work I've found, so give it a good try before making any changes. Once the pattern becomes habit, it will keep you from overlooking any important steps in interpreting your valuable dreams.

Once you have worked through a few dreams the routine will become familiar to you, and all you will need is a brief reminder of the steps to follow. At the end of this chapter you will find a sample dream interpreted according to this method and an abbreviated outline for your convenience.

Please bear in mind that to obtain the greatest possible benefit from your dreams, you need to **faithfully** do the following:

- Write your dreams
- Work out your symbols in detail
- Decide on the meaning
- Write your summary
- Keep each month's titles and summaries on a separate sheet
- Look over your dreams on a regular basis

This gives you not only an excellent overview of your dream content but brings you in close touch with the loving care and guidance of your High Self, and it gives you glimpses of both your life direction and your soul's purpose.

SAMPLE DREAM INTERPRETATION

Date: April 3, 1988

Journal Entry: I have been struggling to get my book written, but for the past week there have been so many interruptions that I am frustrated and not accomplishing much.

Dream: I am driving my car downtown and I run into a passing parade of people and things. I have to pull over to one side. I feel I am parked where I should not be, but cannot do anything about it. I am blocked in by a pile of boxes. I tell myself, "I need to get myself out of this."

Feeling: Frustration!!!

Theme(s): I am driving. I am blocked. I want out.

Background: Downtown, business area, material concerns, hustle, bustle, hurry. Center of activity.

Most Important Symbol: Passing parade.

List of Key Words:

Driving My Car: I am in control, I have chosen this lifestyle and this situation, so it is up to me to change it.

Downtown: Busy area of my life. Practical, material matters.

Run Into: Something in my path blocks, stops my progress.

Passing Parade: Long line of people, events, attitudes, aspects of me parading, making themselves highly visible. Something I can't ignore, must work through. Need to stop and look at this. Also feel this represents the "parade" of many people passing through my life now; personal visits, phone calls and interruptions keep me from my chosen work.

Pull to Side: Off course, sidetracked from goals, purpose.

Parked: Completely stopped, not going anywhere, no progress.

Where I Shouldn't Be: Warning, I should not allow this stoppage, should not be in this situation. Need to do something about this.

Can Not Do Anything: Can't or won't take action. Feeling helpless.

Being Blocked: How I feel: life, progress blocked, can't see my way out.

Pile of Boxes: Many blocks, limits, boxed in by many things, yet the boxes are empty, not heavy, they can be moved. I am allowing myself to be boxed in by my limited ideas about how to handle things. Need a new outlook, must find a way out.

Statement: Need to Get Myself Out: I must find a way out now and not put this off any longer.

Meaning: I am allowing myself to be sidetracked from my goals and am letting myself be blocked, boxed in, limited, sidetracked from my true purpose by either my wrong thinking or by allowing other people's ideas, goals, and visits (parade) to stop me from my goals. I have been wanting to get on with teaching metaphysics and writing my dream book, but problems with my family and an over-abundance of calls and visits from friends keep interfering. I realize I am still trying to "people-please" which comes from my lack of self worth. I need to work on this attitude in order to find a satisfactory and harmonious way out of my predicament.

Summary: I have allowed myself to be sidetracked by "people-pleasing." Need to get myself back on course.

Title: Passing Parade

Decision: I need to set aside a certain block of time for me to do my work uninterrupted, and another block of time to deal with my friends so that these aspects of my life are in better balance and I won't feel so frustrated. I must value myself and my time for creative writing. It is my gift to the world. Purchasing a phone answering device will facilitate this. No calls or callers from 9AM to 5PM. I WILL carry this out. I WILL honor myself and my needs.

Application:

1. I will buy a phone answering device this week.

2. I will enforce the 9AM to 5PM schecule with NO exceptions!

Follow Through:

1. Put an answering machine on my shopping list.

2. Call a friend or two about the best kind to buy.

3. Let my friends know of my new schedule.

4. Write my schedule on a calendar so I can see it every day.

5. Affirm, "To thine own self be true!"

```
┌─────────────────────────────────────────────────────┐
│                                                       │
│               ABBREVIATED OUTLINE                     │
│             FOR DREAM INTERPRETATION                  │
│                                                       │
│   EVENING: (MUST)                                     │
│                                                       │
│           1. Journaling                               │
│                                                       │
│           2. Dream Question                           │
│                                                       │
│   MORNING: (MUST)                                     │
│                                                       │
│           1. Recall                                   │
│                                                       │
│           2. Write                                    │
│                                                       │
│           3. Feelings                                 │
│                                                       │
│           4. Outstanding Symbol                       │
│                                                       │
│   WHEN THERE IS SUFFICIENT TIME, follow through with: │
│                                                       │
│           1. Dream Theme                              │
│                                                       │
│           2. Background                               │
│                                                       │
│           3. Keywords                                 │
│                                                       │
│           4. Meaning                                  │
│                                                       │
│           5. Summary                                  │
│                                                       │
│           6. Title                                    │
│                                                       │
│           7. Decision                                 │
│                                                       │
│           8. Application                              │
│                                                       │
│           9. Follow Through                           │
│                                                       │
└─────────────────────────────────────────────────────┘
```

The Mystical, Magical, Marvelous World of Dreams

CHAPTER **9**

Working With
Your Dream Symbols

You have probably wondered why we dream in symbols. The answer lies in the phrase, "One picture is worth a thousand words." A dream symbol is a word picture showing you, in the simplest possible form, a situation or emotion that might take hundreds of words to fully describe. You might think of your dreams as being similar to the game of charades, where an idea or phrase is portrayed through action.

Actually, we all think in symbols whether we realize it or not. We do not truly understand a concept until we have a mental picture of it, then we say, "I *see* what you mean!" or, "I get the picture." Do you "see" what I mean?

Basically, symbols make us think. Perhaps you have noticed that many of Jesus's most important teachings were given in parables, which were full of symbolic forms so that people from all walks of life, educated or not, could think out the meaning for themselves. One truly picturesque symbol can remain in your mind for years, while a long-winded lecture is forgotten in minutes! See the example at the top of the next page.

Universal Symbols

We all see symbols every day. We associate the sign of the cross with religion, a fish with Christianity, a lion with courage, an elephant with good memory, and a light of any kind from candle to sunbeam represents wisdom, learning, knowledge, or understanding. Advertising is full of symbols and logos familiar to all of us, as are some of the new international, no-word signs designed to be understood by everyone.

National Symbols

Some symbols are peculiar to a particular race, religion, or nation such as a national flag, the Eiffel Tower, the Statue of Liberty, Big Ben, pyramids, totem poles, Indian

EXAMPLE SYMBOL: GLASS WAGON

I had been working very hard trying to do many things, despite a broken foot, when I had a dream...of just one scene...a glass wagon. An old-fashioned, work-type farm wagon. (Vehicles represent one's body or life-style.) The symbol haunted me.

I grumbled to my High Self, "A GLASS wagon?" But that's silly!

High Self: Oh?

Me: But, why glass? Why not wood?

HS: THINK about it.

ME: Well, a farm wagon is for hard work, but glass would break!

HS: Right!

GLASS WAGON: Fragile vehicle, must be handled with care!

That symbol is now a constant reminder to take care of my body and avoid overloading!

---

tribal signs, and so on. Symbols are a quick way to get the message across, whether we "speak the language" or not.

Personal Symbols

Personal symbols are those which have one meaning for you and quite a different one for someone else. Take an airplane, for example. When you mention flying to me I think travel, vacation, freedom, and happiness. To a commercial pilot, it may be just a routine job. To some people, it brings dread because they are afraid of flying. To others, it can be the thrill and excitement of sky-diving or piloting their own plane, crop-dusting, cloud seeding...and so it goes.

Personal symbols may also be full of puns, often using your favorite phrases and cliches such as, "He drives me up a wall!" Yet, if you dreamed of driving your car straight up a wall, you would undoubtedly say, "That sure was a *silly* dream!"

Puns in dreams are common as well as elusive. Coins, for instance, can mean change, small change, or many changes in your life, and not allude to money at all. Generally, dreams tend to use the same puns and slang words that you use. Watch for catchy phrases and expressions, titles of songs, books, or movies, as well as for any play on words such as "gilt" to represent guilt or "sole" to depict soul.

There may be suggestive names like "Mr. Moody" to depict the moody aspect of you as well as names like Doolittle, Cheatham, Fairfax, Taylor, Baker, and other subtle and not so subtle titles for the various aspects of yourself.

Some symbols can mean more than one thing. A fire can indicate that you are all "burned up" about something; it could represent warmth, comfort, something cooking, cleansing, transformation, purification, anger, or a raging fever. In order to make the right decision among all these choices, you need to remember your feeling about that fire, possibly closing your eyes for a moment and mentally going back into the dream to see how it felt then. This often solves the dilemma. Learn to use your own good judgment, rather than depending on any book or person. Again we say *trust yourself!*

Changing Symbols

From time to time you may have a symbol which changes from one thing or person into another. This kind of transition often signifies how one person, quality, or characteristic can lead to another, which may or may not be welcomed; or it may designate the connection between one kind of attitude or action and its ultimate effect. It can show relationships or causes between one action and another, demonstrating how one thing, quality, or attitude, if continued, can lead to or bring about a situation or problem you neither wanted nor expected. Sometimes transitions indicate what is likely to happen, while at other times they may show you how to make a needed change from an unpleasant situation into something much more to your liking.

For example: you may dream of talking to someone you consider kind and friendly, but after a drink or two s/he turns into a snarling wolf or a grouchy old bear. This could very well indicate what happens to *you* when you drink! So take a good, careful look at these changing symbols to see what direction things are taking.

Objects in dreams may also be describing and accenting—acting as adjectives to further delineate the main symbol, action, or feeling. Pay special attention to changing feelings and emotions in sequence.

Enlarged Symbols

Anything enlarged is usually being accented or exaggerated in order to make a point. For example, an extra-large coffee cup may be suggesting that you are drinking too much coffee! In the same vein, anything disproportionate in size or shape would be an emphasis on the item or situation to draw your attention to the fact that it is out of balance and needs correction, adjustment, or whatever.

Most Outstanding Symbols

There is usually one of these in every dream. It is a good practice to draw or write these in the margins or some special place for easy access later, as they are important and often become recurring symbols.

Arbitrary Meanings

Be wary of dream books with arbitrary meanings such as, "Spider means bad luck" or, "Bear means hibernation." These could apply, but so might a dozen other meanings. A bear may symbolize something you have to "bear," being overbearing, forbearance, bare facts, bad temper, bad breath, and so on, depending on the rest of the dream. The main point always is *what does it mean to you?* In working with the symbols in your dream, you need to think about what you associate with that word: what memories, feelings, ideas, guilts, or experiences are linked with them. Ask yourself, "How does this relate to what I have been thinking, feeling, planning, or doing lately?"

Bear in mind that dreams generally tend to deal with the events and problems of the preceding day, unless you have written a specific question. They often suggest new and creative ways to handle situations or point out the basic cause or contributing factor to a current difficulty.

You rarely dream of things you have mastered but rather of the areas in your life which are in the greatest need of correction. Most dreams are telling you about your problems, goals, physical health, and physical concerns for the express purpose of leading you to higher levels of wholeness and perfection. The regular practice of meditation aids greatly in all these processes, especially in your spiritual growth and overall dream recall.

New Ways to Work with Your Symbols

Every symbol in your dream, whether a person, object or situation, *stands for a part of you*, understood or not. The dream makes a statement about you, your attitudes, habits, and your relationships to the rest of the world. The only exceptions would be the people you have *programed* to play themselves, their friends, and possessions. See chapter on *People*.

Occasionally, a symbol will seem to defy all attempts at interpretation. Whenever you are unsure what a word or phrase means, try the renaming process: substitute different words that mean the same thing, re-state the phrase in a different way, or rewrite the whole sentence in several ways. For instance, a "bottom step" can also be the first step, a last step, a beginning step, a small step, a step up, or even a step in the right direction. Try playing around with words and phrases, have fun with them, and remember to keep a light touch and a sense of humor about you at all times.

When a symbol proves to be particularly elusive, try using a separate piece of paper to write out all the possible meanings, associations, feelings, and connections you can think of to see if one or more of those definitions will feel right to you. Remember, your feelings give the symbols life and clarity, so use your sensing abilities to the utmost.

A Few Tricks to Try

When a symbol's meaning completely escapes you, try closing your eyes and picturing the elusive object as it was in the dream. Turn it around, look at it from all four sides, from the top, then underneath. You may even open it up and look inside! This can bring you some surprising new insights.

You might also try making a sketch of your symbol, as this often helps you to get in touch with the inner meaning.

Amplification Process

If all else fails, try mentally talking to the symbol with your eyes closed. Ask, "What are you doing in my dream? What are you trying to tell me, or what do you represent?"

Experiment in uniting with the symbol, for example a violin. Mentally **become the instrument**, then ask yourself, "How do I feel as a violin?" Beautiful? Creative? Holy? Joyous? Or angry, used, unappreciated, and worn out? Getting in touch with your **real** feelings, represented by the symbol, is the name of the game! Another method is to ask yourself:

- What does it mean to me?
- What meanings do I associate with it?
- How do I feel about it?

After each question, relax. Allow your subconscious mind to speak to you. Refrain from questioning what comes to mind and just flow with what you see or feel for a moment, then write out your impression. Think about it. See if it brings a positive response from deep within. If not, you can always discard the idea. The point is to be receptive to new ideas, possibilities, and impressions, being careful not to block the input during the questioning process.

If you are still unsure, try a dictionary or a thesaurus for additional meanings. If this fails, look through the dream categories and suggestions in this book to try to find something that **feels right** to you.

There will be times when nothing seems to fit and you have to set aside the part you don't understand, continuing to ponder its meaning off and on during the day. Often, when you least expect it, the answer suddenly comes!

Sharing Dreams With Others

When nothing seems to work, even after using all the associations you can think of, try talking about your dream to a trusted, understanding friend. Often another person can see what you could not or can make a connection you didn't consider. Sharing dreams with others, alone or in groups, is one of the best ways to learn dream interpretation.

Thoughts Are Things

Your thoughts are far more important than you have been taught to believe. They are totally creative in nature. If you persist in saying or thinking something like, "He gives me a pain in the neck!" life guarantees that within a few days you will have a pain in the neck, a stiff neck, a sore throat, or some other similar circumstance which relates directly to the thought you held in mind and have, therefore, built.

James Allen observes, "You are today where your thoughts have brought you. You cannot escape the results of your thoughts." The great Edgar Cayce often remarked, "Mind is the builder" (Reading 1436), then added, "Thoughts are things" (Reading 1562-1).

The thoughts you hold in your mind actually build a form which can be seen clairvoyantly. Even those of us who can't see these can often sense them. These thought-forms produce the circumstances in your world. If you don't like the way your world is, you need to change your thinking! Many of the New Age religions now stress this point, but Jesus said it first: "As a man thinketh in his heart, so is he." What kind of thoughts have you been thinking all day? What kind of world are you creating? Your dreams may show you!

Not all of our thoughts are beautiful. When we indulge in thoughts of hate, anger, greed, and negativity, we create ugly forms which linger in our auras. (Whatever we send out eventually comes back to us and is often seen in our dreams.) Some of the nasty things which appear in dreams are our own hate-thoughts built over a period of time. The more we dwell mentally on a thought or fear, the bigger, stronger, and more hardened it becomes. If these thoughts are not stopped, corrected, cleansed, forgiven, or otherwise erased, they will eventually take on a physical form and manifest themselves in our lives as some bitter experience. The mind is a powerful tool!

Our dreams try to show us exactly what we are creating by constantly out-picturing the results of our thinking, fears, prejudices, attitudes, pet phrases, and the ways in which we act or react. Because of this, your journal should reflect at least some of what you have been thinking and feeling during the day. These ideas, when written down, give you a better grasp as to what kind of thoughts, goals, emotions, and ideals your dreams are bringing to your attention. Understanding this process greatly facilitates your dream interpretation.

The ultimate goal is to have your spiritual beingness in control over your physical, emotional, and mental bodies so that only loving thoughts can prevail. Your dreams help you to reach that goal ever so slowly by pointing out your erroneous attitudes, giving you a higher perspective, or urging you to clean up your angers and vent your emotions in healthy ways. Your thoughts, your journal, your meditations, and your dreams are tightly interwoven.

If you are really interested in your spiritual journey, your dreams and your journal, along with clearly defined goals, will greatly speed you on your way. Spiritual growth does not just happen; it develops directly from your daily thoughts, goals, ideals, desires, and efforts. No goals, no progress.

Recurring Symbols

Occasionally recurring dreams and themes have their roots in former lifetimes; but most often recurring dreams and repeating symbols are an attempt to emphasize a problem we have not solved, a pattern we have not overcome, a situation we have been avoiding, or something we have not yet learned. It is important that we dig deep within ourselves to learn what, how, or why.

In my own dreams, boxes have been recurring symbols surfacing many, many times. From their very frequency I have learned that for me they represent obstructions, blocks, and limitations which *I have allowed* to obstruct my path. The question I have to ask myself is, "Why?" The answer is usually some kind of fear of the unknown...of what might happen if I were to actually accomplish that which I long to do...or of other uncertainties I have allowed to creep into my thinking. Boxes represent old, insecure, or uncertain habit patterns which halt my progress.

We learn in time that one dream does not, cannot, give all the answers; but a series of dreams can. Therefore, it becomes necessary to review and rethink these dreams from time to time, especially when the same symbols keep showing up consistently. This is a sure signal of a trouble spot which needs our attention.

Some symbols are used repeatedly in order to depict your progress, growth, or maturity in relation to it. For example, in the area of your health you may dream of an automobile, representing your body, in very poor condition—fenders dented, paint peeling, and perhaps a few rusted parts. Often the vehicle is one issued in the year of your birth to further emphasize this as your body—not your lifestyle, which may be quite modern. Then, as you begin to do your exercises, take your vitamins, watch your diet, and generally start taking better care of yourself, you may see that same model looking progressively better and better in each dream until finally it may look as good as new or may even have turned into a Mercedes or Rolls Royce!

For the state of your consciousness, usually represented by a building of some sort, you may find yourself starting out in a log cabin, gradually adding rooms and improvements until you have a truly beautiful building. This may take place over a number of years, however, so it won't be noticeable unless you do your dream reviews and summaries from time to time so that you have the necessary overview.

Recording Your Symbols

When you have worked out your symbols it is a good idea to write them down in the pages provided in this book or elsewhere, starting your own personal dictionary of what those symbols mean to you. Once the interpretation has been established, it usually signifies the same thing each and every time. However, you may find exceptions to this, seeing totally new dimensions added to an old symbol; or it can take on a whole new meaning for you over a period of time. The same thing can happen with the people in your dreams.

It's a good idea to keep your recorded dreams in a private but handy place where you can easily review them on a regular basis. Dreams which seem vague and obscure today have a way of becoming brazenly clear after a week or more, so make it a habit to review them often. This has the added advantage of keeping your current messages fresh in your mind.

CHAPTER **10**

Lucid Dreaming

Our truest life is when we are in dreams awake.

— Thoreau

In the early morning hours when our physical bodies are fully rested, our consciousness begins to drift from the deeper layers of sleep into the upper alpha layers and we spend more time in the dreaming state. Then, as we drift nearer to the waking state, close to the Alpha-Beta border, we may become aware of incongruities in our dreams and suddenly realize that we *must be dreaming!*

It is at this point of recognition that we can become *lucid*—awakening fully within the framework of the dream. Instantly everything becomes brighter, clearer, and far better comprehended than only a moment before. We find ourselves reasoning with great clarity, able to act swiftly and take full control of the drama unfolding about us. We are mysteriously able to change the script or rewrite the play, making things happen in accordance with our slightest desires. We seem to be in a whole new world with no limits to our abilities.

Sometimes this lasts for only a moment or two before we are once more swept back into the dream; then again, we may remain lucid right up to the time we awaken in the morning. Apparently it takes an alert sense of balance and awareness to maintain the lucid state. There are many who have never experienced a lucid dream, some have done so only on rare occasions, while others have long and frequent lucid dreams as well as excursions into other planes of existence.

Dr. Stephen LaBerge of the Sleep Research Center at Stanford University in California defines lucid dreaming as our "untapped human ability with astounding potential for self-exploration." He points out that learning to dream lucidly is like "having a personal laboratory or playground for trying out new behaviors and ways of being." He describes lucidity as an "expanded mental state" (Rubin).

Tibetan masters, as well as mystics from many other cultures, have always maintained that *dreaming true,* as it is sometimes called, is a level of high spiritual consciousness—a place where wisdom and knowledge can be greatly expanded and therefore a much-to-be-desired state. Fortunately, lucidity is a teachable, learnable skill for those of us who desire to know more; and there are many ways to improve our chances of having lucid dreams as well as for prolonging the experience.

Laying the Groundwork for Lucid Dreaming

The most important prerequisite for lucid dreaming appears to be a well-disciplined mind and an ability to hold a focus. People who have never learned to concentrate have less chance of recognizing and maintaining lucidity. They also tend to have *fuzzy* dreams. Those with moderate self-discipline may have lucid moments but can seldom retain them. It is the well-disciplined mind which seems to have the greatest frequency of clear, lucid dreams; and it is these people who can freely walk through God's door into other dimensions.

Charles Leadbeater, in his book *Dreams,* declares, "If a man wishes to reap in his waking consciousness the benefit of what his ego may learn during sleep, it is absolutely necessary for him to acquire control over his thoughts, to subdue all lower passions, and to attune his mind to higher things." The regular practice of meditation, yoga, body workouts, or other skills which require mental discipline are highly recommended as a basic, general rule for any kind of spiritual progress. Working with dreams and applying their messages is another type of mental training.

Your Plan of Action

When you reach the point where you realize you are dreaming and begin to move into the much desired lucid state...then what? If you don't have some kind of predetermined response, you are more likely to slip back into just plain dreaming. Experienced lucid dreamers plan to have a healing, get an answer to a special question, pray, meditate, have a spiritual experience, or achieve some special desire. They are prepared and expectant of making the most of their lucid opportunities, knowing they offer possibilities for great mental and spiritual advancement. As one lucid dreamer put it, "I become aware of the presence of God and feel spontaneous great joy."

Your personal plan of action may include:

- A purpose for becoming lucid, such as spiritual enlightenment, union with God, healing, transformation, learning, overcoming a problem or fear.

- A predetermined task, action, question, learning, or desired experience related to your purpose. To put these into the form of an affirmation or poem you can remember easily and to repeat this as you drift off to sleep is extremely helpful. You may want to write this out and repeat it often during the day in order to thoroughly impress it on your mind.

- Respect for the lucid process as a learning, uplifting growth experience. Be willing to confront and cooperate with the dream symbols while retaining your individuality.

On becoming lucid, determine to concentrate on a fixed symbol to stabilize lucidity, then concentrate on your purpose. Use your affirmation.

Determination

A strong desire to have a lucid dream often helps to precipitate one, especially if this request is repeated as you drift into sleep. Often it is necessary to prepare yourself mentally, emotionally, and spiritually for the experience, especially if you have never before experienced dreaming true. You might begin by resolving that you are serious about seeking a truly meaningful, inspirational encounter, then write your request or tell your subconscious mind that you fully intend to have this adventure. Make your goals clear and your intentions strong.

Affirmation

Next, you may tell yourself often during the day, "I am going to have a lucid dream tonight," or, "I really want to become aware that I am dreaming tonight," or to be very brief, say, "Tonight I will sleep and become aware." Find a phrase that suits you and repeat this over and over during the day, especially just before going to sleep. If your goal is one of enlightenment more than just a desire for adventure, it is more likely to be fulfilled.

An outline of suggested daily practices to promote lucid dreaming appears on the next page. This procedure will be ample for most beginners; however, for those who are seeking even greater spiritual enlightenment and understanding, here are a few words taken from *The Astral Body* by A. E. Powell:

"Every one should determine each night to do something useful on the astral plane: to comfort someone in trouble: to use the will to pour strength into a friend who is weak or ill: to calm someone who is excited or hysterical: or to perform some similar service...(you) will often receive indications in the physical world of definite results achieved."

Mr. Powell states that this service practically assures us of awakening from the dream state into the astral plane or lucid state. He adds that one might also make a "steady and persistent effort to clear away the mist from within...resolve to try when one leaves the body, to awaken himself and see...or do some useful work." He strongly emphasizes the importance of "fixing the last thought before falling to sleep, on high and noble things...it [lucidity] should be practiced regularly by those who wish to bring their dream under control."

Suggested Daily Practices for Lucid Dreaming

MEDITATION: Discipline yourself to meditate deeply, with love and devotion, on a daily basis with the purpose of seeking greater light.

APPLICATION: Determine to apply to your lifestyle that which you are given in dreams and meditation.

PRACTICE DETACHMENT and SELF-OBSERVATION as much as possible during the day.

SERVICE: Practice loving kindness and thoughtful service to others on a daily basis.

AFFIRM your desire to have a lucid dream regularly during the day.

ASK yourself frequently, "Am I dreaming?" Then do something to assure that you are indeed awake.

EXERCISE: Work out vigorously each day to assure sound sleep.

AVOID strong drink and all kinds of drugs, even over-the-counter varieties.

Final Preparations Before Sleep

1. Faithfully work with your dream journal in self-reflection, evaluation, goal setting and updating.

2. Establish a CLEAR PURPOSE for having a lucid dream and determine in advance what you wish to do on becoming lucid. This is IMPORTANT.

3. Read inspiring or uplifting literature before retiring.

4. Place yourself in as high a spiritual state as you can reach before sleep by means of prayer, meditation, or both.

5. Remind yourself to watch for the incongruities in dreams.

6. DETERMINE TO FLY in your dreams tonight.

7. Repeat your affirmation about becoming lucid as you drift off to sleep.

Recognizing the Pre-lucid State

A key criterion for recognizing the pre-lucid state, which practically insures lucidity, is a predetermined attitude of analytical, critical watchfulness. Be determined to recognize any strange, incongruent, or absurd happening which can trigger the realization that you must be dreaming!

We often have definite signs which warn us of approaching lucidity. The most common of these is the experience of flying or floating. This is *your signal* to say, "*I must be dreaming*," and to move into greater clarity and awareness.

Another frequently found indication is that of dreaming you are asleep (recognizing your sleep state), then waking within the dream. Again, this is your cue to becoming consciously aware that you are dreaming.

Occasionally, the occurrence of a brilliant white or golden light will announce the arrival of possible lucidity. A shift to more brightly colored objects may be another indication, or the sudden changing from one dream scene into another which makes no sense to you can be your clue.

Actually, any strange phenomena or occurance which is inconsistent with known facts can alert your awareness that you must be dreaming. Prepare your subconscious mind to watch for these signs; then, if you continue to dream on in spite of these signals, you will have to rigorously program your subconscious until it gets the message and you finally begin to become aware of the discrepancies and absurdities in your dreams.

A personal symbol may be the sight of a huge truck flying! Other triggering devices may be speaking with a "deceased" person, floating, flying, falling, driving a car you do not own, or the sight of any strange, unusual happening. Whenever you find yourself in a brilliantly lit place, you should suspect lucidity.

Anything that stirs your awareness can be you own particular symbol of pre-lucidity. Making a mental note of *your special symbol* will increase the probability of its working well for you. If there are several, write them all down as future reference points. Meanwhile, you may find your "vocabulary" of signals increasing in number as time goes by.

Semi-Lucid

There are many shades of lucidity, with more and more being discovered and researched daily. In the semi-lucid state one may experience greater light, the emotional high, and greater clarity of mind, yet not be fully awake or aware of dreaming. A good way to test the amount of awareness or lucidity is to try to fly. Let the act of flying be both your test and affirmation of awareness within the dream.

Waking Within the Dream

This may occur within or outside the semi-lucid state and often precedes the fully lucid stage.

Moving Into the Lucid State

The lucid world is as clear, rational, and vivid as your usual waking state to the point that it is often difficult to know which is which. However, once you have discovered that you are dreaming, you seem to move into a heightened awareness. Everything becomes exceptionally clear, and there is often a sense of excitement and deeper emotion along with a perception of greater light, brighter colors, and vastness of space. Sight, sound, and ideas are keenly experienced.

When this occurs, you *know* you are lucid and need to determine to hold the delicate balance between the dream content and your conscious awareness without allowing yourself to be drawn back into the dream, or to awaken. This calls for your instant concentration on some stable object, usually your hands or some other part of your body, which will allow you to establish and maintain lucidity. Often it is necessary to follow this with a determined concentration to carry out whatever you had planned to do when lucid.

Once concentration is established, it is then possible to change both the direction and the content of the dream. You may find a solution to a problem, ask questions, overcome obstacles, discover new ways of doing things, invent something, or obtain ideas, alternatives, or inspiration. You can seek aid, healing, or a spiritual experience. You may visit Jupiter, Neptune, or the pyramids of Egypt. The Universe is at your command, providing you can hold on to your lucidity. You may need to remind yourself to remain centered, to be at peace, and reaffirm your purpose in becoming lucid.

Prolonging Lucidity

In Carlos Castaneda's book, *A Journey to Ixtlan*, his teacher carefully instructs him in the fine art of dreaming, first reminding him that, "Every time you look at anything in your dreams it changes shape. The trick is...not just to look at things but to sustain the sight of them." (Concentration again.) Later he suggests that to do this, one needs to focus his attention on his hands as a starting point, then shift to other items. "If you only glance briefly the images do not shift," he maintains.

There is a constant tendency in dreams to either merge with the dream symbols, which pulls one back into the dream plot, or to move toward becoming awake; therefore, it becomes vitally important for you keep that fine balance between wakefulness and sleeping. It is also necessary at the same time to be able to distinguish clearly between yourself and the dream images, keeping yourself *set apart* from them. This is why we need to look at our hands or at one spot until our lucid identity is firmly established and we *know* ourselves to be separate and in control.

Lucid Learning

Ken Kelzer, a psychotherapist and avid lucid dreamer, says, "The lucid dream is a perfect metaphor for the awakening of the human soul into a higher state of consciousness" (Kelzer 1978).

An important part of the lucid dream is to be able to confront and to accept parts or traits of ourselves which we have rejected, disowned, or cannot accept. All too often when dark, threatening people are seen in our dreams (or nightmares), we tend to try escape by waking, rather than by facing up to the unknown and confronting or making peace with this mysterious part of ourselves. Frequently our dream state fights and conflicts symbolize wrestling with our own conscience or with our unwanted traits—coming to grips, so to speak, with ourselves.

Carl Jung declares (Jung 1961), "A man cannot always think and feel the good, the true and the beautiful, and in trying to keep up an ideal attitude, everything that ***does not fit in*** with it is automatically repressed [emphasis added]." It is these repressed, unknown, and disowned parts of ourselves we need most to face and work with. For example, if you are single you may try to repress all sexual urges as being unfit or unacceptable. Recognizing these feelings in your dream as an essential part of you does not necessarily mean that you will rush into promiscuity but allows you to admit these feelings openly so that you can deal with them honestly and decide on appropriate measures, such as vigorous exercise or other acceptable means to alleviate the pressures.

It is important to remember that you are in control and that it is desirable to bring your dream activities to a positive, happy conclusion, rather than to run away or choose to awaken. Remember, dreams are opportunities to increase our potentials and discover new alternatives to our problems. Dr. LaBerge believes the actions and emotions experienced during our lucid dreams have very real effects upon our mental and physical conditions. He views a lucid dream as a kind of working model through which we can try out a variety of ideas and alternatives. We can face and overcome our fears, solve our most difficult problems, and even initiate healing processes within our bodies. Lucidity seems to open up whole new worlds for us to discover, and the possibilities seem to be endless. From the platform of lucidity we may have visions, religious and spiritual experiences, healing, and/or various out-of-body journeys, to name a few. The research has only just begun in this new field.

Out-of-Body Experiences

It is not at all unusual for one to move from the lucid state into an out-of-the-body experience. Sometimes these seem to happen with no conscious control—we just suddenly find ourselves in a different city, state, country, or even on another planet. As long as colors are brilliant and your perception is clear, you know you are in a lucid state and can control the action from there ***if you want to***.

Sometimes it is nice to just go along for the ride just to see what will happen. It is possible to meet people in foreign countries, view strange customs, and taste exotic foods. Again, our innermost wishes and desires tend to pre-set the stage, whether we know it or not.

Let's suppose you are perplexed about something and genuinely want to understand how it works or the principles surrounding it. You may be shown, in marvelous detail, exactly what you wished to know! All things are possible in dreams. On the other hand, if you have always wanted to go to Egypt, for instance, you may suddenly find yourself there without any conscious commanding of your own—and you may find yourself whisked back home just as unexpectedly. Try to remember that you have a choice—that you are in control. At the slightest desire to return to your body...zap! You are there!

Removing Blocks to Lucidity

If you have tried to experience a lucid dream without success, you may need to program some leading questions into your dream journal to find out what the problem is. Ask how or why you are blocking these highly spiritual dreams or what can be done to induce them.

Helping Yourself to Lucidity

One of the most difficult things to do in dreams is to be alert and self-conscious enough to recognize the obvious inconsistencies which help you to realize that you are dreaming. Programing persistently for this awareness will help, of course, and on waking you can usually count at least a dozen incongruities you *could* have noticed as lucid warnings, but didn't. Keep these symbols in mind—they will come in handy later.

Consistent lucid dreamers confide that nearly all of their lucidity occurs in the early morning hours, somewhere between 5:00 A.M. and their regular waking time. Obviously, this is the best time for beginners to try to practice this art.

Choose a morning when you can sleep a bit longer, reminding yourself that you definitely want this enlightening, lucid experience as you go to sleep. Then, in the morning as you awaken, still in that drowsy, half-awake state, stop and review the dream you just had. Determine that you will not come to full wakefulness but will prolong your semi-dream state. If your dream has slipped through your mental fingers, be still and recall anything you can remember well; re-run it in your mind, reliving all the feelings it involved. Recollect any inconsistencies that could have been pre-lucid warnings. Then, with the dream content firmly in mind, replay the dream in your consciousness, stopping at the first incongruence, and announce, "I know I am dreaming."

From this point, begin to reconstruct the dream in a positive, rewarding way. In this manner you are practicing the art of becoming lucid, and you may suddenly find yourself actually dreaming true before the exercise is completed. If not, there will be other opportunities. Actually, anytime you wake during the night is a good time to try this; eventually, persistence will bring its own reward.

One way to enter lucidity is to deliberately daydream your way back to sleep immediately after waking. Since you are already relaxed, slipping back into the dream state is relatively easy. All you have to do is to direct your thoughts to the subject matter of your choice, then *flow with it* back into a lucid state, remembering that you are making it up and in control. Again, there is a very fine line of balance, and you can easily drift off into sleep or become wide awake. Try to hold on to your conscious control with a very gentle touch.

Some Tricks to Try

Many lucid dreaming "experts" believe that the practice of meditation for ten or fifteen minutes after awakening in the early morning hours is highly conducive to having a lucid dream when you once again fall asleep, especially when you set your mind to that purpose.

A simple way to stimulate lucid dreaming would be to use the general dream incubation techniques described in the next chapter as a springboard to help you get started. You may need to pursue this for at least three days, possibly longer, for best results.

A further suggestion is to try, while incubating, to program yourself to fly or float in your dreams, using this as a lucidity triggering device. Again, a three-day minimum is suggested. In this case the longer you persevere, the better chance of good results.

Another idea you may wish to try is to drink several glasses of water before retiring, which will assure you of waking in the middle of the night. Later, after returning to bed, try one of the suggested exercises. If you drift back to sleep there is no harm done, but meanwhile you are enjoying some needed practice in working out your problems in the dream or semi-dream state.

You may want to experiment with several different approaches to find what works best for you, but whatever you do, be sure to record all of your personal, pre-lucid symbols!

Final Check Points

Lucidity seems to occur most frequently when you:

- Strongly desire and **expect** the lucid experience (preferably for spiritual reasons).
- Work with, respect, value, and use your dream material.
- Go into deep meditation regularly.

- Observe yourself and your reactions to life's events on a regular basis, using detachment.
- Develop deep love, rapport, and caring for others.
- Practice seeking the light.
- Are willing to confront dream figures and situations.
- Try to carry your waking consciousness into the dream as you drift off to sleep.

Again, experiment to find which suggestions work best for you, possibly working at least a week with each one and recording the results in your journal.

May your dreams bring you much wisdom!

My Personal Pre-lucid Symbols:

CHAPTER 11

Further Exploration of Dreams

Your circumstances may be uncongenial, but they shall not long remain so if you but perceive an ideal and strive to reach it. One cannot travel within and stand still without.

— James Allen

Once you have mastered the basic concepts of working with dreams for information and guidance, you may wish to widen your horizons with additional techniques for gaining specific information and sharpening your abilities to interpret your dreams.

To encourage dreams that are clear and meaningful is an art. Dr. Richard Goldwater, a psychiatrist, declares, "Dreams are like fairies...they won't come around unless you create a hospitable place for them" (Barasch). Dream research studies held at the Association for Research and Enlightenment have concluded that dreams occur with greater frequency and tend to be clearer and more constructive in content when meditation has been practiced the day before. Results are even better when meditation is done on a regular basis; and, if one has applied what he has learned, dreams seem to become even more frequent, clear, specific, and helpful.

Dream Incubation: Gathering Specific Information

There are some special things we can do to help attune our minds to receiving specific information whenever it is needed. One of these processes is called incubation. The method of dream incubation which follows is a variation on the method first described by Gayle Delaney, Ph.D. in her book *Living Your Dreams* (Delaney 1979). Dr. Delaney has made major contributions to the field of dream study, and her work is highly recommended to those wishing to do additional reading on the subject.

Dream Incubation Technique

1. Place your request under your pillow, so that you literally "sleep on it."

2. Make some special sleeping arrangements (in lieu of having a Grecian Temple to visit) such as:

   - Sleep in a different place like a guestroom or porch, or change the position of your bed.

   - Use special bedding—your best sheets, a sleeping bag, a satin pillowcase, or special pillow.

   - Wear unique nightwear—fancy gown, pajamas, favorite T-shirt, whatever, as long as it differs from your usual habits. If you sleep nude, wear something!

   - Light a scented candle, burn incense, sprinkle herbs, or have fragrant flowers by your bed prior to sleep.

3. Plan to have plenty of time to write your dream in full, along with your feelings about it, before dashing out the door in the morning.

4. Make up your mind you will NOT REJECT your dream no matter how irrelevant, short, or silly it may seem. (They always seem silly in the early light of dawn!)

5. Have your dream journal ready and waiting in easy reach in EXPECTATION of that answer.

6. Repeat your dream request over and over as you drift off to sleep.

Begin by first going over the details of your present predicament, preferably writing out the main ingredients. For example:

- When did the problem begin?

- What do you think caused it?

- How have you handled it so far?

- How do you feel about it?
- How do you think it should be corrected?
- What would you like to see happen?
- How does this situation fit with your life goals?

In going over your difficulties in your journal, you pave the way for new ideas and insights. Then, when you have settled on the general theme of the problem, compose your dream question in detail. Once this is done, you may choose to rewrite it in the briefest possible form to make it easier to remember. The fewer words the better. If you like you may make it into a rhyme or mantra. Use what is most comfortable for you.

Next, find a way to impress your mind with the importance of your quest. Choose one or all of the suggestions on the facing page.

For best results use steps one through six, making your own variations to suit yourself. You may find it wise to use dream incubation techniques only for special requests and occasions, for this can lose its effectiveness if it is used too often.

Working Out Dream Themes

Most dreams seem to have one main theme running throughout, with all the action being more or less variations on a theme, such as you found in *The Passing Parade*. The whole plot centered around the parade. Other dreams may have more complex themes, with the first of the dream having one kind of action and the second half a different one; or you may have a series of scenes and actions all totally different and seemingly unrelated to one another to the point where you aren't quite sure whether this was all one dream or several mini-dreams—these are multiple themes.

The Multiple Theme Dream

When you begin to work with the multi-theme dream, the first step after writing your feelings is to extract each separate theme, making a brief statement to describe each segment. For example:

Theme 1: I am driving my car hard and fast.

Theme 2: I watch a man drive his car into a rock wall.

Theme 3: Someone is waving a gun and shooting everybody.

Theme 4: Someone is sick and wants to die.

Having extracted the themes, proceed to string them back together again, for this type of dream is showing you how one thing, situation, or action leads to another.

In theme one, the dreamer sees himself driving his car (himself) hard and fast.

In theme two, he sees someone running into a barrier. This someone is an aspect of himself who is:

- driving himself "up a wall" by pushing himself too hard.
- running into self-made barriers, limitations, and blocks to his progress by not giving himself time to think things through.
- causing his own problems.
- possibly all of the above.

In theme three, someone is shooting everyone in sight. Shooting could mean "shooting off" his mouth, firing angry words, an explosion of temper, or loss of control. The dreamer does not own or recognize this someone as himself.

In theme four, someone is sick. This can mean:

- an aspect of himself is "sick" of this behavior.
- behavior pattern can lead to physical illness.
- person is physically ill.
- all of the above.

Final meaning, assuming all the symbols seem to concur, would be that the dreamer:

- pushes himself much too "hard and fast."
- causes his own problems and blocks by so doing, but perceives the cause as someone else—not himself.
- having pushed himself to his physical, mental, and emotional limits, loses control of his temper and hurts others, again perceiving this as other than himself.
- is making himself sick in the process.

The final decision would be made according to whether or not the dreamer recognizes the behavior as his own or continues to pretend this is someone else.

When you are lacking a clue as to the meaning of a dream, refer to the next page for some thought-provoking questions you can ask to help yourself along.

Once you have tried all of these ways to understand your dream and still can't come to a conclusion as to what it is saying to you, try writing out what you think it means and go with that interpretation for the time being. Make your decision and follow through just as though you were certain. Chances are that you are absolutely right. Meanwhile, toy with the symbols in your mind during the day, considering additional meanings and possibilities. As you ponder your dream, deeper layers may

Questions to Ask to Clarify Dreams

1. What is the major action or dream theme? (Who is doing what to whom?) Are you involved? How much?

2. Does the dream make a point?

3. Who is in control?

4. What kind of a dream was it? Symbolic? ESP? Physical?

5. Did you express your feelings? How well?

6. Did you touch someone? Did someone try to get "in touch" with you? Do you move toward or away from contacts?

7. What is the major concern in your life right now?

8. Does the dream tie in with this concern in any way?

---

be revealed. Correctly interpreted, dreams should make sense to you in terms of your present life situation and help you to make constructive changes. They may make a simple statement of how things are or how you perceive events, but they **never**, ever put you down. Remember they are spiritual in origin and are there to help—not hinder or criticize—so never allow yourself to become discouraged by your dreams.

Dreams tend to occur in a series, stating the situation over and over in different ways until you get the point, but you don't want to remain undecided over your dreams while waiting for more to come. Always take time to write down what you think they mean, even when you are unsure; then, decide how you would apply that knowledge. If you guess wrong, you will get a correction or re-direction. The thing you want to avoid is the habit of not coming to any conclusion at all, for this is your conscious mind's sneaky way of saying, "I don't want to deal with this!"

Be watchful concerning the many ways in which we all try to evade the issue or try to fool ourselves by pretending we don't understand. It is an old trick of the mind. Don't fall for it!

More Information from Dreams

I have found that when one is studying a particular subject or reading something that is difficult to understand, it is within the realm of possibility to ask for added insight, knowledge, or understanding from the author or from the Universe, and through dreams get the help or information needed. Sometimes the author may answer in person!

Our dream adventures are something like the magic mirror in *Alice in Wonderland* in that they can take us to all sorts of wonderful places for interesting adventures.

Sample Questions You Might Try:

- May I have some inspiration for my latest _____ ? (painting, poem, story, invention, etc.)
- What is the source of the problem between me and _____ ?
- What is the lesson I need most to learn now?
- Give me an overview of my spiritual progress to date.
- What career course should I set for myself?
- What is the cause of my illness/injury/disease?
- What is the cause of my weight problem?
- Why am I afraid of _____ ?
- Why do I dislike _____ ?
- Show me a better way to handle _____ .
- What is blocking _____ ?

Undoubtedly you can think of more of these as you go along, but this will give you a start in exploring the wonderful world of dreams with the problem-solving genie at your fingertips.

Another approach you might like is to address a question or proposition to your Dream Self such as:

Dream Self: Please show me some new ideas and pleasant ways for becoming prosperous. Thank you very much.

Or, Dream Self: Please show me what I need to do for better health. Thank you.

On such subjects as these, it would be best to repeat the question for at least a week, taking up to a month for this procedure if you like—it can produce a multitude of ideas and useful information on any given subject.

Encouraging ESP Dreams

From time to time you may want to program or incubate an ESP dream. This too is possible; in fact, almost anything you need to know, provided it is not outside the realm of what is called "your business," can be asked for and answered by way of your dreams.

Dream Sharing

In the area of dream interpretation we find that discussing dreams with friends, family, or with a group which meets for that specific purpose is not only conducive to better dreaming but also promotes a greater development of one's interpretive skills as well. Often we find that another person can perceive a connection or correlation that we ourselves have missed or can point out a pun or parallel in our lives we might never have seen alone.

If your family is interested in dreams, you might try to instigate a dream discussion at your breakfast table, sharing ideas and insights which may have to do with family concerns as well as personal and community ones. My own family is somewhat scattered now, but we still keep in touch by letter or phone, especially when our dreams concern the needs, problems, or health of other family members. In this way we all become aware of another's needs, even when they are too busy or too proud to ask for help or support. It is a good family tie, keeping us together while apart.

If dream sharing is not possible with your family or does not fit into your personal scheme of things, you might want to share your dreams with a friend or two on a fairly regular basis or get a group of interested persons to meet on a weekly basis to discuss dreams. You may be pleasantly surprised at how much you can learn about yourself from the simple act of group dream sharing. Dr. Montague Ullman, a psychoanalyst who wrote the book *Working With Dreams*, declares, "There exists a need for people to share intimate parts of themselves in a safe, social context. In dream groups, people learn that sharing and self-disclosure are the fist steps toward communion."

Suggested rules for group dream sharing can be found on the next page.

Your Spiritual Growth

Dreams are part of God's plan, our roadmap to realizing our greatest potential. They promote harmony between ourselves and our surroundings. Those who are sincerely interested in their spiritual progress can gain much through dreams, for they are tools that bridge the gap between the physical life and the spiritual one. They are your hot line to love, wisdom, and understanding. Questions on spiritual matters are gladly answered, and loving assistance is given to all who sincerely seek it.

There is also a gift which you may give to the spiritual planes as we mentioned earlier, by offering yourself to be of help to others during your sleeping hours. This practice helps you gain in knowledge, spurs your inner growth and understanding, hastens your overall evolution, and hastens the development of lucidity. There is nothing to lose and everything to gain with this practice.

It is my sincerest hope that your mind will be greatly expanded and your life immensely enriched by your regular participation in dream work.

Blessings!

Rules for Group Dream-sharing

1. Keep it simple. Food and drink often distract and take up valuable sharing time.

2. Let each person bring a RECENT written dream to share.

3. Share the complete dream first, looking at the purpose or intent of the whole, then let the group share ideas and insights.

4. If this fails to unravel the dream, work on one paragraph at a time with suggestions from the group.

5. If necessary, take the dream apart one symbol at a time.

6. Let the dreamer alone decide if the interpretation feels right, then move on. No one is to IMPOSE an opinion.

7. When there is difficulty, try having the dreamer act out part of each symbol, getting both conversation and action going on between the symbols until the meaning or relationship becomes clear.

8. If the group is large you might want to work on only one section of each person's dream so as to give everyone a chance to learn and share. (Often we understand most of the dream anyway, and there is only a small part which eludes us.)

PART II

CHAPTER 12

Animals

Many societies respect and revere birds and animals for their fine qualities such as strength, courage, cunning, keenness of vision, speed, and accuracy; yet the so-called "civilized" societies tend to look down on the animal kingdom as something to be exploited for food, fur, tusks, or whatever. Therefore, much of the interpretation as to what the animal may symbolize will depend upon your honesty within yourself as to what characteristics you associate with that particular member of the animal kingdom.

The animals we find in our dreams often represent the animal instincts, urges, habits, and aspects we attribute to them which are also found in ourselves. This would include both the good and the so-called "bad." Animals may symbolize our strong emotional qualities, survival instincts, basic animal drive, attitudes and behavior, sub-conscious urges, untamed desires, or our wildest of hopes and tendencies. On the other hand, they can represent our playful, uninhibited feelings and expressions, natural urges, and intuition.

Since each animal has some special trait or peculiarity for which it is well-known, the dream animal usually represents this particular attribute in ourselves or this phase in our development. It may show us how we view ourselves or, more likely, the way we appear to others. It could also be a little bit of both.

Cats and dogs can both represent strong sensory powers and telepathic abilities as well as faithfulness, loyalty, and disciplined behavior. Despite this, there is always a certain amount of unpredictability in an animal which needs to be taken into consideration, for they can turn vicious and attack under certain conditions—so can the average person.

Creatures and people in our dreams **almost always** represent traits, qualities, and tendencies in **ourselves**, but occasionally these can represent a negative and possibly treacherous quality in a person or situation you are presently dealing with. **This can be a warning**. However, in such a case, these animal qualities would most likely be symbolized as a pet belonging to the person in question. Otherwise, consider it **your** trait.

FLOCK OF WILD ANIMALS:
This could represent group instincts, group action, cooperation, group power, an over abundance of some quality or trait, doing something in excess, or a type of people or things "flocking" around you. Consider whether or not you are attracting this kind of people or events to

you. What is the flock action and how do you feel about it?

NOTE: Many qualities which are good in moderation have the potential to become misused and distorted when done to excess. Animal natures can refer to this sort of situation, where the trait itself is good but becomes obnoxious when misapplied or multiplied.

FLOCK OF DOMESTICATED ANIMALS:
Group of ideas, feelings, beliefs, energies needing to be herded, led, directed, guided, watched over and/or protected from outside influences or negativity. This may be a flock of unchecked animal instincts, depending on the type of animal and the dream action.

HERD:
May represent herd instincts (symbolized by the type of animal), race consciousness, mass hysteria, going along with the crowd, or group activity as in *flock*.

RUNNING ANIMALS:
May represent our physical fears, emotions, or things we would like to run away from.

YOUNG ANIMALS OR CHILDREN:
Usually symbolize untrained, undisciplined, or undeveloped qualities, often in the process of growth and development.

NOTE: Young animals sometimes symbolize children.

Pets & Domesticated Animals

DOMESTICATED ANIMALS:
In general can represent partly-trained aspects of ourselves or our attempts to teach, train, and control our animal natures.

PETS:
Especially *your* pet, can represent a pet project, pet peeve, or even pet indulgences. Of course your pet can also represent...your pet! Dreams can warn you of a health problem or other difficulty your pet may be experiencing long before it becomes apparent to you. If you want to be sure about which is which, you can program your subconscious mind so that your animal will always play itself in dreams—then any pet animal can represent your pet qualities.

OVERSIZED:
Animal or oversized part would indicate a special emphasis on the quality represented by that animal and part.

Restraints

Trying to *rope, bridle,* or *collar* an animal may indicate the amount of effort needed to control and discipline ourselves or our tempers, or the trait represented by that particular creature. An animal already collared, bridled, or restrained would indicate that we have at least a partial control.

BRIDLE:
A controlling device. When in place it can indicate the amount of control already gained. The act of bridling or an attempt to bridle may symbolize a need for more control or discipline on your part.

COLLAR:
May be decorative, identifying, or both. Can show ownership but not control unless a rope, chain, or leash is attached.

LEASH:
Control device for animal tendencies. May denote a lack of control if not held firmly in your hand, or may indicate a need for more control, depending on the dream action and feeling.

REINS:
Would be pretty much the same as a leash. Who is in control?

RIDING:

Can show the amount of your control over the animal's actions and would symbolize your mastery in the area represented by that type of animal.

ANIMALS RUNNING FREE:

Could indicate a lack of control or may indicate freedom, depending on the feeling and action.

SADDLE:

A means of sitting on top of your animal instincts. The amount of control would be shown by dream action.

Owner Action

BATHING:

May imply a need to clean up your act, clear up the condition, or need to get the "bugs," (offensiveness and negativity) cleansed.

BRANDING:

May show ownership or how we have branded ourselves or others. Can also indicate possession and possessiveness.

BRUSHING OR COMBING:

Would indicate giving your animal quality the needed love, care, and grooming, or attempt to keep those traits in good shape. It may also be loving, encouraging those attributes in yourself, making the most of your faults or talents, getting the kinks out.

FEEDING:

Nourishing, encouraging, expanding, growing in the depicted characteristics. If this is a trait you wish to expand, this would be a good sign; if it is a negative condition such as an uncontrolled temper, this could be a warning of what you are doing to yourself.

FENCING:

Is your animal fenced in? This could indicate some control over the quality is needed or may say that you feel fenced in and restricted in the area represented by the animal. Play around with the idea to see if the fence is a protection, restriction, or problem.

SHEARING, TRIMMING:

Could have several meanings. May suggest a need to curtail, shape up, clean up the qualities or habits symbolized, or to get yourself more presentable, depending on the purpose of the trimming. May represent making the most of the animal quality as in making a profit, or could be "getting skinned by another," "fleeced" by someone, or someone fleecing you.

There is also the possibility that this is a symbol for you to "trim down" your weight in general or trim off some of the excesses of the animal traits. Maybe you are coming on too strong, or some quality is a bit overdone.

WHIPPING:

This may show an attempt to whip yourself into shape, to exercise more control, or a need to discipline yourself in the area of the symbolized quality. Look at the feelings connected with this to determine whether you are "beating yourself to death" over something, or whether you are in real need of disciplinary action.

Shelters

BARNS:

Can symbolise a place or state of animal consciousness where animal characteristics are kept, fed, protected, or neglected. It can be a shelter or a confinement or it may, in your mind, be strongly connected with childhood work, play, or even sex experimentation, depending upon your feelings and associations connected with the dream.

The same idea would extend to other animal shelters.

DOG HOUSE:

Can be pun on being in trouble; out of harmony with a mate or friend; being punished or being ostracized.

CAT HOUSE:

Also has a well-known pun attached to it which we may need to recognize. Puns are often extremely revealing as to our real feelings and insights about ourselves. This could refer to "catting around" or, if you have cats and a house for them to play in, it may refer to playfulness. Maybe you need to be more playful!

PIG PEN:

Another word with double meaning. We usually associate this with sloppy habits, insensitivity, carelessness, filth, and so on. Pigs are often equated with greediness and generally repulsive, unacceptable behavior. *Pig pen* may also bring to mind the story of the Prodigal Son, life on the farm, or some other memory. What does *pig pen* mean to you? Ask the question and let the answer pop into your mind.

BLIND:

This could insinuate that you are being blind to something; being in a blind spot where you can't see; seeking protection so you cannot be seen; hiding, subterfuge, a deliberate act by someone to conceal; preying on another.

ZOO:

May depict limited freedom, captivity, or confinement of the physical nature; natural instincts, qualities, talents, and abilities of the type symbolized by the kind of animal(s) seen in the zoo.

Cats

Cats are intuitive, instinctive, aloof, detached, psychic, sexy, independent, sometimes uncaring, sneaky, proud, curious, sensuous, relaxed, uncooperative, capricious, and playful. They can represent any or all of these qualities as well as that of "fraidy cat" or "catty." They may sym-

bolize hidden fears or friendly, loving memories, depending on the experience and associations of the dreamer. For example, there is a lovely, dignified minister's wife and grandmother who at the mere sight of a tiny, defenseless kitten will scream in terror! She has no memory of any cat problems in her present life, but she does have a past-life recall of being fed to the lions in long-ago Rome! To her a cat of any size represents fear, horror, and painful death. How do you feel about cats? Remember, your feelings color all the definitions offered here.

Consider carefully the action in the dream along with your personal feelings and associations with cats to determine which untrained or partially trained instinct of yours it represents.

ALLEY CAT:

This could signify a nocturnal nature, intuition, catting around, psychic ability, sexual prowess and activity, promiscuity, lack of morals, and general lack of class and good taste.

CAT CLAWS:

Potential to wound others, even in play. Need to be more careful with words and actions.

CAT HAVING KITTENS:

Would indicate increases in your catty qualities, favorable or not. Like begets like.

CAT, NAPPING:

Can be a pun on taking cat-naps—possibly this would be good for you. May mean sleeping or being unaware of your cat-abilities, qualities, cat nature, or intuition.

CAT, WAKING:

Awareness or awakening of the catty nature, possibly of psychic, intuitive powers.

GROUP OF CATS:

Like attracts like. May indicate how your own catty characteristics affect others and brings out those same aspects in them, or that you draw catty people to you.

KITTENS:
Can be little catty traits that will grow bigger; may represent your new-born psychic abilities or some other cat trait.

LITTER BOX:
Can be a pun on littering, or a catty way to go.

Empty Litter Box: No place to "go." No available outlet for catty emotions to be released.

PLAYFUL CAT:
Can say you need to let your playful instincts loose, or perhaps you play too much, depending on the action and feelings in the dream. This might represent how you play around with your catty nature or qualities.

Toying With Mouse: Represents teasing, terrorizing, taunting; using your size, position, or influence as a way to hurt and manipulate others or force them into obedience. Playing or toying with people's feelings and emotions and enjoying it. Tantalizing. It might also allude to how you feel you are being treated.

PUSSY FOOTING:
Soft approach, soft touch, handling with care, or may represent trying not to be seen or heard; secretiveness.

SHOW CAT:
Or *fancy breed* can symbolize a real pride in your catty behavior, a desire to show off in a "catty" way, or an indication that you believe it is the smart, perhaps feminine way to be. Indicative of proud ownership of cat-like characteristics.

STRANGE CAT:
Catty nature or traits you do not recognize or claim as your own but need to look at. These can be good, bad, or both.

YOUR CAT:
Catty characteristics you recognize and claim as yours, something you know you have.

Dogs

All domesticated animals are, in dream symbolism, partly-trained aspects of ourselves, unless the animal belongs to a another. Then, it can represent traits in that person. Keep these **possibilities** in mind as you interpret *dog*. Careful evaluation must be made as to what exactly the dog symbolizes to you by considering the content and action of the dream, along with your feelings about the dream and the qualities you associate most with the animal.

A big difference may be noted in your associations with a large animal as compared to a small one or a pet (known) compared to a stray (unknown).

Dogs may also represent puns such as, "Putting on the dog," dogging your footsteps, hounding you to do something, or your conscience dogging you.

DOG AS FRIEND:
Represents loyalty, protection, courage, companionship, faithfulness, and any other associations or characteristics in the particular dog. How did you handle these?

DOG AS ENEMY:
If you have been bitten or frightened by a dog, this animal would represent fear, treachery, pain, loss, and any other strong feelings you associate with dogs. Look at how you handle your fears.

DOG FRIEND TURNING UNFRIENDLY:
Can warn of a friend who is or will "turn" on you, betray you, can't be trusted.

DOG AS NUISANCE:
To the local mailman, garbage man, or even neighbor, dogs may mean frustration, an-

noyance, and inconvenience, depending on the person's experiences. Dogs to these people would represent uncontrolled, unwanted feelings of frustration, possibly pent up angers not properly dealt with, depending on dream content.

NEIGHBOR'S DOG:

Neighbor means something close to you so the qualities you associate with the dog are yours—something you have to live with, listen to, or look at. Traits are yours but not recognized as such. (The faults we see in others are the faults we have in ourselves—that is why they annoy us!)

PET DOG:

This can represent a pet peeve, habit, or undisciplined quality in you that you really don't want to give up. Petting or feeding a dog with some special quality would be encouraging the continued growth of that trait.

STRANGE DOG:

Represents animal instincts or traits you do not recognize as yours but need to face up to.

YOUR DOG:

A partly-trained or possibly untrained aspect of yourself which you recognize as yours and are probably attempting to train or control. Need to look at the special characteristics you feel your dog has and list these for future references. Recurring dreams will show your progress in this area from time to time, *if you are working on these*.

Dog Actions

BARKING:

May represent your habit of barking at people instead talking kindly, or of "barking" orders; much unnecessary barking about the conditions around you; annoying others; general grumpiness, noisiness, or fussiness.

BITING:

May imply "biting other people's heads off," "snapping" at others, or biting off more than you can chew.

BITING THE HAND THAT FEEDS:

Possibly an aspect or tendency to bite or snip—whether mentally, physically or emotionally—the person who serves you or cares for you. Lack of respect, gratitude, or love.

If it is *your dog* this may say you do not love, care, or respect yourself enough. You may be your own worst critic, your own worst enemy.

BURYING A BONE:

This may be a pun on trying to hide something from others—could be a bad habit or anything you do not want seen. May be a pun on "burying the bone" you have "picked" with others, "burying the hatchet," or burying your grudges. Can be a way of indicating that to bury your hurts and grudges only gets them out of sight and does not eliminate the problem.

CHEWING OR GNAWING:

Can represent something "gnawing at you" or possibly you have been "chewing someone out." May also reflect some area of your life that is being damaged by your lack of discipline or show you how you damage, injure, punish, or hurt yourself. Look closely at the type of object being chewed. Is it something you value? How are you devaluating it? Or, how are you devaluating yourself? Your efforts?

DAMAGING:

May signify the damage your uncontrolled habits are causing yourself and others.

GROWLING:

Over defensiveness, grumpiness, irritability toward others caused, incidentally, by your own fears and insecurities.

PLAYFUL PUPPIES:
Uncontrolled actions, lack of maturity or discipline, or may be a hint for you to be more playful.

WAGGING TAIL:
Expression of love, pleasure, happiness, joy, enthusiasm, approval.

Owner Action

BUYING A DOG:
This could indicate a tendency to "buy" your friends, buy favors and compliments, or may indicate your need to find companionship or even a need to get a dog!

DRESSING DOG:
Effort to cover over unwanted traits or to dress up, conceal, or protect unwanted traits, habits.

FEEDING:
Feeding, encouraging your canine characteristics, possibly indulging in them.

GROOMING:
Act of trying to make your canine habits look better, or efforts to improve the appearance, not the trait itself.

HARNESSING OR LEASHING:
Attempt to control or need to make an effort to discipline self.

PETTING:
May indicate a tendency to feel good about indulging in your canine qualities or animal instincts. This can be an emotional security for you, especially if you are petting your animal after misbehavior.

PUNISHING:
Could symbolize your tendency to punish yourself, portraying how you punish yourself, or the effort needed to train or correct any offensive traits.

SHOWING YOUR DOG:
Indicates the act of showing off or exposing your canine qualities, letting everyone see your basic animal traits, being proud of your animal nature, or could denote a general tendency to show off.

TRAINING:
Act of getting a grip on your offensive habits or aspects. Making an effort to improve or your need to do so if you haven't already.

WASHING:
Act of trying to clean up your act, habits, or your need to do so. Could be getting the "bugs" out of your system.

WALKING:
May be act of exercising, using, strengthening your canine qualities, aspects, or instincts. Do you do this proudly? Defiantly? Protectively? Or is this a hint for *you* to do more walking, get more exercise?

Dog Types

BASSETT, BEAGLE & BLOODHOUNDS:
All known for excellent hunting and scent-following abilities. Beagles are also well-known for their tendency to howl long and loud, which can be *extremely* annoying to others. Hint?

BULL DOG:
Depicts tenacity, determination, inflexibility, possessiveness, bullishness, or guardianship. S/He is both powerful and dependable.

COCKER SPANIEL:
Cocky, spunky, playful attitudes.

CHIHUAHUA:
Tiny, high strung, noisy, generally more for show than anything else.

COLLIE:
Intelligent, a working dog, often a shepherd. Very trainable. Well-known and valued for its gentleness.

FRENCH POODLE:

Mostly associated with show, pomp, wealth, extravagance, over-indulgence, and generally spoiled behavior. Often depicted as owned by wealthy matrons who shower them with affections which would be more wisely spent on human relationships or in other directions. This could be an indicator of misplaced emotions and values.

GERMAN SHEPHERD:

Originally used as war dogs, these are known for their obedience and trainability. Often used as guard dogs, these can be trained to attack or be excellent seeing-eye dogs. May be unpredictable with built-in killer instinct. We give this one a dual meaning: friend that can turn foe; protection or attack. Sometimes faithful but can deviate unexpectedly. Room for doubt or at least caution. If this dog is owned by a friend you trust, this may be a subtle warning—the dog could depict these aspects in him or her.

POINTER:

Could represent one-pointedness or can be pointing out something in the dream which you need to see, do, or correct.

TERRIER:

Generally spunky, a good watchdog, but often too high-strung, excitable, and known for its much barking (yakking, talking, scolding); or, could be pun on terror.

TOP DOG:

Winner or favored to win, most likely to succeed, has the advantage. Part of dual role we often play in dreams of top dog (successful part of you) versus underdog (the fearful, non-confident, deprived, or poor-me aspect of you).

UNDERDOG:

Loser, coming from behind, disadvantaged, or seemingly handicapped. May represent your attitude of being a loser, being picked on, not getting a fair chance. Could point out your need to

stand up for your rights, to have more confidence in yourself, or real need not to give up so soon or so readily. The battle is not yet begun.

NOTE: If you find underdogs in your dreams very often, you probably need to understand how you have created, by your own thoughts and words, your situation and your belief in your inability to cope. There are many good books on this subject.

TOY VARIETIES, ALL KINDS:

Usually these represent a show dog or show-off type of dog associated with play and often prestige, pomp, and glamour. May depict a tendency to show off in miniature ways!

Fish

FISH:

Ancient symbols of Christianity, Christ, Christian beliefs, spiritual ideals or *spiritual food for thought*. May imply being slippery and hard to catch; elusiveness. Can imply "fishy," unusual, hidden danger, or a need for caution, depending on the dream content.

> **Fish Out of Water:** May be a pun on how you feel: being "out of your element," out of place, or being in an extremely uncomfortable situation, in need of help.

CARP:

This type of fish is most likely to imply elusiveness, hidden danger, undesirable kind of spiritual food for thought, or the lowest meaning of fish.

DOLPHIN:

Friendly, playful, highly intelligent and trainable. Known to be telepathic, they may suggest mental telepathy, alpha communications, an ability to commune with nature, the sheer joy of spiritual living, or reaching the heights and depths of spiritual thought and endeavor.

FLYING FISH:
May represent high spiritual ideals.

GOLDFISH:
Because of the gold (spiritual color) these would represent fine spiritual food, spiritual ideas, concepts, ideals, or high goals.

MERMAID:
Half fish, half human; symbol of the combination of human and spiritual, human and divine.

SHELLFISH:
These often symbolize the early stages of unfoldment, confinement, structured ideas and beliefs, limited framework, or our instinctive nature. If you are working on affirmations they may depict your affirmations beginning to take form.

SHARK:
Hidden danger, surprise attack, viciousness.

STARFISH:
Signifies regeneration and healing.

TROPICAL FISH:
Something special, unusual, rare, fine.

WHALE:
May imply a whale of an idea; "spouting off", a whale of a tale, exaggeration, excess, a large dose or overdose of something, more than you can handle, or a huge amount of spiritual food for thought.

Horses

Horses can be a pun on horse sense or even mean horsing around, but generally they represent strong, physical forces, energies, chakras, or tempestuous emotions which can get out of control. The amount of mastery you show in the dream would indicate the degree of dominion you have over these forces.

On the other hand, if you live on a horse farm or work with horses the meaning would vary, as then the horses could indicate your work situation as well as your powers of control over your own forces or those of other people.

HORSE NAMES:
Can be highly significant.

OWNERSHIP:
If you own the horse, the forces or energies are most likely to be yours; if others own the horse this may refer to outside or unknown forces at work in your life.

Horse Actions

BALKING, REARING:
Refusing to go in desired or acceptable manner.

BRIDLING:
Attempt to control or need to master the energy involved.

CURRYING A HORSE:
Loving care of your forces and energies, cultivating a good relationship with your powers.

FALLING OFF:
Loss of control or inability to carry through your plans; rejection of authority.

GROUP OF HORSES:
May imply the power of group force. Note whether they are fenced, free, moving joyfully or fearfully.

Four Horses: Usually refers to the four lower chakras. Color, action, and cooperation are important clues here.

Seven Horses: This often indicates your seven centers, the whole chakra system. Look for amount of cooperation. Is all running smoothly?

LEADING A HORSE:
Guiding, directing, being in control of one's energies and forces.

RACING A HORSE:

This can be a good exercise and development provided it is under control or could say you are pushing yourself too hard, racing against time, or running a good race, depending on the feeling.

RIDING OR SITTING:

Would show your control or lack of it.

RUNNING FREE:

This could represent loss of control or can be a wonderful freedom, depending on the feel of the action.

TRAINING A HORSE:

Act of training, teaching, disciplining your body forces, or could be exerting your will power.

Horse Types

BLACK HORSE:

May represent unknown, mysterious, or even occult forces.

BRIDLED HORSE:

Trained or controlled to some degree.

DARK HORSE:

Usually symbolizes the unknown, chance, taking a gamble, an untested area.

FOAL:

May be a new, untried force or energy emerging.

HIGH HORSE:

Well-known pun for being "on your high horse," pride, arrogance, pomp.

HORSE & BUGGY:

May represent old-fashioned methods, antiquated ways, out-of-date ideas; or, if all else is old-fashioned, may be a glimpse of a past life experience.

HORSE AND RIDER:

Often refers to a message from the higher realms of consciousness. Can also be mentally directed energies.

MARE:

May represent intuitive or psychic forces.

PONY:

Could be playful forces or untried, undeveloped, undisciplined power; a growing force.

RACE HORSE:

One especially bred for speed. Could represent your racing through life, running a good race, or hint to slow your pace.

RED HORSE:

Can represent your energy forces, your temper, or your base chakra.

WHITE HORSE:

May represent purity or purification of your emotions.

WILD HORSE:

Uncontrolled, strong energies.

WORK HORSE:

This can indicate the way you see yourself or may imply your need to work on something.

Other Animals

ALLIGATOR:

Tough hide. Treachery.

ANT EATER:

Usually equated with nosiness because of his long nose. However, he is harmless.

BADGER:

Can be pun on badgering people, aggravating, being persistent to the point of annoyance and frustration. Insisting on one's own way; being vicious.

BEAR:
Represents great strength and power. Can be *overbearing*, pushy; one who uses his power to frighten others into submission or who crushes others with words or actions. Can be very destructive, irate, cross, and menacing; *or* playful, protective, and loving. Known for bad breath, bad temper, and habit of hibernating. Could mean bare facts or forbearance. May also symbolize Russia, Russian, or pun on "rushing."

Teddy Bear: Symbol of security, love, cuddlesomeness.

BEAST:
Usually represents your fears, animal instincts, temper; beastliness; the beast in you; uncontrolled power.

BEAVER:
Good worker, ambitious, intelligent, skillful, persevering, cooperative, and when work is done, playful.

BUCKS:
Big bucks may be a pun on big money. Many bucks, much money. Bucks may also refer to bucking the system, a person, or idea. Might also indicate males, maleness, strength, agility, "passing the buck," or "the buck stops here."

BULL:
Can symbolize a lie or exaggeration, great strength, determination, stubbornness, bullheadedness, unyielding attitudes that hurt one's progress or that of others. Tendency to old habits, staying in a rut, refusal to change, bend, or cooperate. May imply a great ability to see things through to the end when others would have given up. Good stability and holding power. Love of beauty. Zodiacal sign of Taurus.

Winged Bull or Ox: Symbol of St. Luke.

CAMEL:
A camel is a burden-bearer so this could refer to your capacity or potentiality for carrying burdens, possibly indicating that you are carrying more problems and responsibilities than necessary. Camels are also well-known for their long, loud groaning, complaining, and protesting of this burden-bearing, and may portray this quality in you. Camels hold prodigious amounts of water (emotions) for long periods of time which may imply your tendency to cling to emotional hurts, upsets, or feelings, moaning and groaning about these long after the event. This could be a suggestion to forgive and forget, to turn the matter loose. May also imply that you make your own burdens heavier than they need to be or that you take on more responsibility than is necessary. Take a good look to see how much of this fits.

CATTLE:
Probably means animal instincts in general, herd or group energies, thinking, feeling, consciousness, activity. Lack of individuality in thinking, doing.

CENTAUR:
Ancient symbol of humanity.

CHAMELEON:
Changeable, inconsistent, changes its colors with each situation; fades into the background; inconspicuous; often unseen or overlooked.

COW:
Generally peaceful, passive, obedient to authority without questioning. Good provider of milk, lives close to the earth, placid nature, tendency to herd or go along with the rest.

CRAB:
Can mean crabby nature, irritable, moving with the tides of emotion, pincers that can hurt, tendency to hold onto things, possessiveness, perseverance.

CROCODILE:
Falsity, false tears or emotions, untrustworthy. Hidden danger. Could be a warning sign.

DEER:
May represent nature, beauty, grace, gentleness, peace, or can mean "dinner," trophy, or a pun on something that is dear to you. Two deer could be a pun on something being too dear. See *Buck*, this chapter.

DONKEY:
Symbol for stubbornness, lack of cooperation; a beast of burden; hardy but not very bright.

DRAGON:
A mythical animal, a product of the imagination. Often represents your fears and the fact that they are not real, but imaginary ones. It is a religious symbol of false beliefs and resistance to truth, or your beastly aspects and urges. This is also an ancient Chinese symbol of power, a beneficial rain-bringer, and a sign of good fortune. Could be a pun on "draggin'" behind, dragging your feet, being "a drag" or a dragon! In mystical literature a dragon signifies the lower nature which must by slain! See *Serpent*.

ELEPHANT:
Excellence of memory, greatness, power, knowledge, intelligence, and ponderousness. May represent karma (not forgotten).

FAIRIES:
Seeing these in dreams may symbolize your innate ability to actually see or at least be aware of these tiny beings. Perhaps this is a hint to learn more about them, or could be that you are now ready to communicate with them. Seeing fairies, gnomes, and similar creatures in dreams may encourage and expand your unrealized mystical

tendencies and abilities. Possibly you associate these with magic and making dreams come true.

FOX:
Symbolizes that which is sly, clever, quick, tricky, unpredictable; a predator.

FROG:
Ancient symbol for the unclean but may be a prince in disguise, a symbol of magic, fairy tales and witchcraft, or represent the potential to change, to do the unexpected. Can be a pun on being a little frog in a big pond (or feeling that way); could imply jumping from one thing to another or moving in leaps and bounds.

GOAT:
Could be old pun on someone "getting your goat"; antagonism, yours or another's; locking horns with another; opposition, sometimes without reason; using one's head for a battering ram; ramming a point home; clash of ideas; may even depict a "but-in-ski." May represent the sure-footed mountain climber who likes to get to the top.

GOPHER:
May be a pun on "go for" (being errand person for others), being used or manipulated. Could depict the go-getter, go-for-it type person. May indicate you should go for something. Gopher is also an animal which lives underground and ducks into his hole when danger threatens.

GRIFFIN:
Vigilance.

JACKASS:
Could be a pun on how you see yourself or how you are judging yourself.

KANGAROO:
Could represent making quantum leaps into the unknown, or possibly heavy-footed. Big foot?

LAMB:
Innocence, defenselessness, helplessness, gentleness. May indicate vulnerability or pos-

sibility of sacrifice and slaughter. You may need to sacrifice yourself in some way or may feel you are being sacrificed. Check dream content for clues. This could be a warning. See *Sheep*, this chapter.

LION:
Symbol of the tribe of Judah and of kingly qualities of strength, courage, power, leadership, will power, and dominion. These are good qualities as long as they are put to good use. Look at dream action. To tame a lion would show your ability to conquer all the lower instincts in you.

MANDRAKE:
Androgynous powers.

MOLE:
Known for destructiveness, working underground and out of sight until the damage is done. Could be a warning of unseen danger or devastation, possibly something you are doing that is undermining your health, wealth, or happiness in some way.

MONKEY:
Mimicking, mime, imitation; fooling around, monkey business, not taking life seriously; being a copy-cat, using ideas and directions of others instead of your own.

MONSTERS:
These represent fears you don't want to face or confront, yet the fact they are there—usually in a nightmare type scene—shows a strong need for you to face and deal with the problem openly.

Green-eyed monster: Jealousy and/or greed.

MOUSE:
Mousiness, meekness, fear, lack of assertiveness. May represent your feelings of inadequacy or insignificance or could symbolize small problems, minor irritations and annoyances; something

gnawing at you; how you irritate others or how they irritate you. Look at the background area for further clues.

MULE:
Usually symbolizes stubborn qualities but can be your burden-bearing capacities, your long-sufferingness, or even how you see yourself.

OCELOT:
Same as cat, but larger and undomesticated.

PACK RAT:
Represents habit of collecting and holding onto everything, useful or not, and mostly not. Can represent things that "gnaw" on you or may indicate a habit of "borrowing" things and never returning them. See *Rat*, this chapter.

PANTHER:
Same as cat only larger, wild, and undomesticated.

PIG:
Strongly associated with selfishness, greed, gluttony, bad manners, hogging the show or spotlight, habit of over stuffing mentally or physically. Lack of consideration.

RABBIT:
Can be quiet, peaceful, gentle, and nature-loving but may also represent a fast turn-over, quick multiplication, and fast production or reproduction. Rabbit is a well-known symbol for sexual prowess and quick change of partners. It may also symbolize the quiet, undetected nibbling away at your resources, especially if it is in your garden patch.

RACCOON:
Often represents robber, bandit; one who takes but does not give.

RAM:
The sign of Aries; also strong drive to achieve, animal instinct of ramming things through, but-

ting into things or conversations, forcing matters, fighting, pushing, general aggressiveness, and lack of finesse. Also signifies Mars, male, power, war, leadership, strife.

RAT:
Strongly associated with dirt, filth, underhanded habits, stealing, disease, poverty, and squalor. Also one who "squeals" or tattles on another. Unscrupulousness. See *Pack Rat*, this chapter.

RHINOCEROS:
Well-known for unpredictability, aggressiveness, ungovernable temper, and small intellect.

SCORPION:
Sign of sudden death, poison, venomous or stinging remarks, vengeance, hidden or secret actions, sneak attack.

SEAL:
These delightful animals are highly-intelligent and well-known for their ability to play and to applaud themselves. They may represent your need to be a bit more playful and to give yourself fun, credit, and praise more often. These may be a pun on seal of approval or of sealing something.

SERPENT:
Symbol of mind power, wisdom, the creative force, mysticism, clairvoyance, spiritual awareness, or kundalini when dream feelings are positive. Can denote subtlety, lies, and deception; penis; semen; sex; desires; temptations, good and/or evil. Much depends on the serpent action and dreamers feelings. See *Snake*.

Coiled Serpent: Ancient Christ symbol, often denotes the raised kundalini forces, wholeness, oneness with God.

Serpent Biting Tail: Ancient symbol of God, wholeness, oneness, eternity.

Serpent on Head or Headdress: Ancient symbol for the raised kundalini as seen in Egyptian headdress.

Winged Serpent: Mysticism, wisdom; altered states of consciousness, superconsciousness, all the positive attributes of serpent without any negative traits. Symbol of triumph over one's lower self.

SHEEP:
Peaceful, docile, gentle; can be "fleeced" or easily led this way or that. Often unable to care for their own needs. *See Lamb.*

SKUNK:
Can be a real "stinker," peaceful but smelly, repulsive, driving people away, turning people off.

SQUIRREL:
Business, quickness, hustle-bustle, thrifty, saving, hard working.

SLOTH:
Slow-moving animal, passive in nature, nonviolent, ponderous, deliberate, gentle, retiring, generally unmoving. Often used as a symbol of laziness and lack of ambition.

SNAKES:
Generally represent fears, sex play, temptation, sex. Playing with a snake may depict "playing around" with sex or toying with the idea. See *Serpent.*

Snake-in-the-Grass: Old symbol for stealth, sneaking, pulling a fast one.

Snake Pit: Often a pit of writhing snakes is a symbol of the act or need to overcome a problem or temptation. These are strongly associated with initiation rites of ancient Egypt and can be a symbol of the tests we must pass before receiving initiation. This may also be a past-life glimpse.

SPHINX:
Symbolically known as the *Dweller on the Threshold,* it represents fears, illusions, old habits we are loath to relinquish. It may also depict the guardian of all that is sacred, ancient wisdom, secret Egyptian mysteries, and/or a great elemental being on the order of an angel. It is said there is an ancient mystery school located in the immediate area of the great Sphinx.

TIGER:
Go-getter, fast cat, pussy-footing around. Great strength and power of overcoming. See *Cat* for additional meanings.

Paper Tiger: False or ungrounded fear.

TURTLE:
Slow but sure progress; slow pace. May be suggestive of a need to slow down or may suggest that you have to stick your neck out in order to get ahead. Turtles have a tendency to hide or withdraw into their shell when trouble threatens.

WILD BEASTS:
Violent emotional aspects or animal instincts which are totally uncontrolled, untrained, unpredictable.

WOLF:
Associated with traits which are sneaky, crafty, greedy, wily, vicious, deceptive, and untrustworthy.

WORMS:
Creepy crawlers, things that give you the creeps; something creeping up on you.

Night-Crawlers: Something that only comes out in the night time, works under-cover, in the dark. (Actually these worms serve a good purpose, but the symbolism of night crawling in dreams could imply subterfuge.)

UNICORN:
Represents one-pointedness, purity, high ideals, mysticism, virginity, purity, and the higher level of Capricorn.

UNKNOWN, UNNAMED, MYTHICAL CRITTERS:
If friendly, these can typify your own unknown, unexplored mystical or magical tendencies. They may be your link to the fairy kingdom or your key to higher knowledge. They may represent your undeveloped and un-pursued interest in things extra-terrestrial and/or the unexplained. If unfriendly or frightening, they usually represent your unknown, un-faced, unexplored fears which are based on supposition and myth rather than bear/bare facts! A warning to face and examine what you are afraid of and why.

My Own Animal Symbols

My Own Animal Symbols continued...

CHAPTER 13

Background Settings

The background in our dreams is similar to the backdrop of a play in that it sets the tone, the time, the conditions under which the actors play their roles. Most frequently we find ourselves inside of buildings, houses, and rooms which represent particular mental states of consciousness; but occasionally we find ourselves outdoors, perhaps only in the backyard or outer fringes of a certain mental state, or possibly out in the wide open spaces. Wherever we find ourselves, the background is an important ingredient in understanding the purpose of the dream and the specific area of life the dream emphasizes.

Outdoors

There is always the possibility this could be an ESP dream or one saying "everything is out in the open." Nature can represent unmaterialistic thoughts and ideas; but most often outdoor dreams are spiritual in nature, especially when the scene is bright, sunny, clear, clean, peaceful, and beautiful. These scenes usually have us climbing a mountain (moving closer to God), swimming (spiritual activity), fishing (seeking spiritual food), or boating (spiritual journey). This reveals our place on the path of spirituality and gives us an idea of our general progress or lack of it. Messages given here would be of great significance. See *The Many Kinds Of Dreams*.

Indoors

When the activities of the dream take place inside of buildings we are being shown a state of consciousness, ideas, ideals, mental and intellectual concepts. See chapter on *Buildings*.

Ancient, Historic Places

Cities, countries, and lands of long ago along with antique buildings or costumes usually are the framework for a past-life memory or experience. These are mostly concerned with making a connection in your mind as to how events in your ancient past are influencing your current life, or they are presenting a problem/situation which has its roots in another life in order to help you to understand what is happening at deeper levels and to see how this can be resolved. See *Historic Settings*.

Miscellaneous Places

AIRPORT:
Place of high ideals, high-flying ideas, connection point, or point of departure to higher "planes," area of communication and/or transportation. This may also represent the coming and going of high hopes, ideas, ideals, prayers, affirmations, thought-forms, blessings, or curses mentally released which go out, multiply according to their kind, and return to their source—*you!*

BATTLEFIELD:
This is always a place of conflict: old or new, mental, emotional, or physical. Battle may be with yourself! See *Fights, Battles, and Conflicts*.

Familiar: This may be saying you have been here before, have done this many times, have been over this same ground often; that this is an old battle or old stuff which has never been resolved and needs to be settled once and for always. Implies a real need to find a new answer, new way of dealing with this matter.

Old: May say you have fought over this ground, idea, belief, problem many times before or that this is an old problem never completely settled; can show a need to come to terms, make an agreement, bury the hatchet, bring this to a satisfactory conclusion. Notice whether or not you are in modern clothing; this **could** be a past-life problem never solved. See *History*.

New: New worlds to conquer, new situation, new area of conflict, new problem to solve, new settlements or compromises to make.

BEACH:
This could be a spiritual dream, especially if it is peaceful and you are alone or with no more than two other people. Can represent relaxation, refreshment, renewal, cleansing, and psychic stimulation. See *Sea*, this chapter.

BRIDGE:
An important connection, access, a joining, or way to travel. Can be a symbol of crossing over from life to death, a new way of life, moving from one state of consciousness or understanding to another. Often signifies change, area of decision making, leaving the old behind, going on to new and different things, or can be bridging the gap.

Bridge, Covered: Can represent old ways being left or may indicate a secret passage, undercover or subconscious change, hidden or unseen moves. *Cover* may also be protection.

BRIDLE PATH:
Can refer to horses and a passage for the energies they represent; may be pun on bride, bridal path, or path to marriage.

BULL RING:
Area of man against beast or struggle between your animal nature and higher nature.

CAMPUS:
Area of learning, growing mentally, expanding your horizons, giving and receiving knowledge.

CARNIVAL:
Area of fun and games, presence, deception, farce, make believe.

CITY:
Center of activity; congregation of many kinds of people, ideas, beliefs, cultures, customs, interests, and desires. Many choices and options; practical, money making, business area.

> **Downtown:** Business center, hustle, bustle, hurried center of many activities and material concerns. Focus point of ideas.

> **Ghetto:** Area of negative thinking, poverty consciousness, belief in crime, disease, ignorance, and ugliness; feeling of deprivation and hopelessness; living at the lowest level possible physically, mentally, and spiritually.

> **New Town or City:** Whole new state of consciousness, new ideas, concepts, and innovations.

> **Out of Town:** Can be out of your element, unfamiliar territory, out of touch, uncertainty.

Park: Area of peace, refreshment, rest, respite, renewal, getting away from it all if only for a moment, meditation, or spiritual background.

Suburbs: Area of less frenzied activity, a slightly slower pace, greater affluence, yet still a melting pot of ideas and cultures.

CLIFFS:
This may represent a fear of falling, failure, the edge of danger, end of the line, far as you can go in that direction, or a warning you may be headed for a fall.

DARK:
Anytime you find yourself in a dark or dimly-lit place you are being warned that you are not enlightened in this area or this situation. This implies you do not know all the facts, that there is more to this matter than you can see, a real need to get some light on the subject before going on. The lack of light is a very significant symbol.

Dark Point: Place or corner in your dream often showing an area where you are basically unenlightened. It may depict a point of fear, something you don't want to look at or deal with, yet that which must be faced sooner or later.

DEAD END:
End of the road, need for choosing a new path, making decisions, choices, turning your life around.

DESERT:
Area of wilderness; barren, dry; no people, no help, no support; feeling alone; destitute and empty. No visible means of support or help. Or, it can be a place of rare beauty, depending on your associations. Can be a quiet rest area giving you time to meditate, contemplate, and reevaluate. Jesus and almost all of the prophets of the Bible spent some time in the desert (alone time) in preparation for their life work. It seems to be a necessary step in our evolution. It may be an empty spot in your life or a wonderful experience.

EARTH:
Soil, land, solid footing, material level, practical concerns, foundation, place to plant or build.

EGYPT:
Ancient symbol of bondage, limitation, lack, and slavery on one hand; a representation of ancient temples, mysticism, initiations, magic, and mystery on the other.

FARM:
Place where one can get in touch with the earth, where seed ideas can be planted; can be place of peace and quiet or hard work depending on your feelings and associations.

FIELD:
Can be field of endeavor, going "far afield," or may be an area of planting and growing, sowing and reaping. Could be wide open country, space, and sense of freedom. To some this would be an area of hard work, or a place of peacefulness, slower pace, less tension, a simple life. Might be area where you used to live. See *Homes* under *Buildings*.

FLOOD:
Could be a flood of emotions, feelings; a sense of being overwhelmed with emotions or with too many heavy responsibilities; being overworked, overcome; or, may be ESP warning of an actual flood.

FOOTBALL FIELD:
A place of game-playing, much strutting about, showing off, area of two opposing groups struggling for supremacy. Competition—not cooperation—is emphasized.

FOREIGN COUNTRY:
An area that is strange, new, different, foreign to your way of thinking and doing. Unknown, untried, unfamiliar. A challenge.

FOREST:
Profundity of life, growth, peace, plenty. Can imply mysticism, getting back to nature, nature's cathedral, or could be you can't see the forest for the trees.

GARDEN:
Usually a place of peace, quiet, and beauty. If there is an abundance of flowers, foods, and herbs it may depict prosperity and harmony. Can be a place of repose indicating your need for rest or a place to plant the seeds of that which you most want to manifest. May denote the persistence needed in keeping the weeds or unwanted thoughts out of your mental garden. See chapter on *Gardens.*

GRAVEYARD:
Final resting place for old ideas, personalities, discarded aspects of ourselves. Can represent a place where a loved one was laid or depict a sense of loss and mourning. To some it can be place of fear of the unknown.

HIGH PLACE:
Often represents a higher point of view, a more spiritual outlook. Can be high point of exaltation or your point of fear, of challenge. May depict being closer to God.

HOME TOWN:
Can be a wonderful, happy place or a dreaded one, depending on your experiences and associations there.

JUNGLE:
Profundity of life, growth, peace, nature at its best. May also be considered to be a primitive area, wild, untamed, unpredictable, and dangerous, depending on your outlook.

JUNK YARD:
Place of old, unwanted things; odds and ends, out of date items, worn out bits and pieces; often symbolic of old memories, hopes, and dreams.

LAKE:
Often background for a spiritual dream. Portrays peace, quiet, tranquility, and spiritual refreshment unless muddy or wind-whipped. See *Sea,* this chapter; also chapter on *Water.*

LIGHT:
Moving toward the light or reaching in any way to turn on or bring in more light is usually showing what you need to do, not what has already been done. This symbolizes moving toward greater enlightenment and/or your spiritual source. A well-lighted place is always a good sign that you have the needed information to work with, and the action may guide you as to what direction you need to take. You may need to consider the type of light: bright, dim, blinking, blinding, and so on. A bright light moving toward you is most likely a high spiritual being.

MARSHES:
Treacherous footing, uncertain ground, hidden fears, area of that which is unknown, unsure, insecure, unstable. Most of the problem is due to the water (emotions) mixed with the land (material facts), depicting the emotional instability as the basis of the difficulty.

MOON: ☾
This is an ancient symbol of the subconscious mind, cycles, feelings, sympathy, domesticity, natural instincts, receptivity, feminine nature, past memories, dreams, sensitivity.

MOONLIGHT:
Symbol of the reflection of God's light (sun). May indicate how much light we are reflecting.

MOUNTAIN:
These almost always indicate a spiritual dream. They designate higher concepts, being close to God, an exalted state of consciousness, high ideas, ideals, and motives. Mountains also represent free, clear thinking, an uncluttered mind, heights of abstract thought; or, they could represent barriers and obstacles to be overcome.

Climbing a Mountain: Symbol of moving closer to God, being on the spiritual path, seeking a better way of life, desire to know, struggle for spiritual attainment, overcoming obstacles.

Crest of a Hill: High point in our lives, place where we can see and be seen, higher viewpoint, higher state of consciousness, feeling close to God.

Mountain Pass: Path or way through barriers or challenges; highway to heaven.

Mountain Range: Can be heights you hope to attain or barriers to where you want to go.

Mountain Top: Represents high attainment, "being there," a high state of consciousness, or possibly superconsciousness.

Snow-capped: Can be cold, abstract principles, lofty ideals, heights of abstract thought, or wisdom. Ice may also imply frozen assets, ideas not presently being used or perhaps presently inaccessible.

OCEAN:
Ocean or seas can represent psychic currents, emotions, mood swings (tides), our unconscious state, or subconscious mind. See *Sea*, this chapter; also chapter on *Water*.

PLAINS:
Biblical symbol for the level of the common people; low spots as compared to mountains and spiritual heights; low states of consciousness, materialism.

PLATEAU:
High state of consciousness, temporary resting place before moving on higher.

PRIVATE PROPERTY:
Usually means off-limits, out of bounds, a place where you should not be; perhaps treading on another's ground, belief, project, feelings or invading the rights or privacy of someone.

QUICKSAND:
Uncertain footing (understanding or support), dangerous ground, no basis on which to make a stand, no support, no firm belief to uphold you. You can fall on your face or get in over your head. There is a watery base to quicksand which suggests an emotional mess you are caught in. Dream may be picturing how you feel and are floundering in this situation and pointing to your need to make some firm (solid) decisions, to literally get a grip on yourself and your emotions before going any further. You need a good understanding and some strong standards on which to base further action. See *Marshes*, this chapter.

RAINBOW:
Always a symbol of God's grace, forgiveness, protection; God's promises to His children. A sign of blessing, goodness; heavenly stamp of approval.

RAYS, STREAMS OF LIGHT:
A symbol of God's light, guidance, protection, or the presence of an enlightened being.

RENO:
Area known for gambling, high stakes, taking chances, getting divorced from a person or situation.

RIVER OR STREAM:
Portrays a flow of emotion, ideas, information; a spiritual flow, being "in the flow," or a part of the flow. Can indicate being "tuned in." This is often a source of spiritual refreshment and spiritual activities symbolized by swimming, boating, or walking in/on them.

RIVER BANK:
Can represent something you "banked on," depended upon for security and support; could be a bank as a barrier, handicap, wall, edge, limit, or boundary of something, or may be a bit of all of these.

ROCKY OUTCROPS:
Hard places, rough spots, hard knocks, stumbling blocks in your path.

SAILING ON THE RIVER:
Often this shows us our spiritual journey, the progress we are making, and how things are going in general. A small boat may show you going it alone or even struggling. The larger and better the boat or ship, the greater your progress—unless, of course, there are problems.

SANDY BOTTOM:
No support, loose foundation, insecure, unstable ground, uncertain footing.

SEA:
Area of emotions, deep feelings, unmanifested thoughts, hopes, wishes, prayers, and affirmations. The condition of the sea gives you a clue to the state of your emotions. The pounding of the waves, the coming and going of tides often symbolizes our own moods, cycles, emotional upheavals, the ups and downs we go through in life. Then it could be a pun on being "all at sea" about something. See *Water*.

Crystal Clear and Pure: Symbol of your spiritual state or if you are swimming in it, of your spiritual activities.

SEASHORE:
Place where your emotions (sea) and material facts (land) meet. A good place to unwind and think things through, keeping the sea and land in proper perspective. The seashore is an excellent place for spiritual renewal, and your dream may indicate a need to refresh your mind and body as well as your spirit.

Walking Along the Shore: May depict quietly thinking things over, getting your life in order, relaxing, becoming one with nature, spiritual refreshment, peace.

SEASONS:
Pay attention to the time of year. Often this is like a clock, signaling the time-frame for the dream events.

SMALL TOWN:
Boxed in, limited thinking, small talk, gossip, nosiness that can be critical and unkind or quick to lend a helping hand. There can be lack of privacy and limited opportunities or this can be a safe place, friendly, loving and familiar, depending on the experience of the dreamer.

STATE:
May represent state of mind, place of being, situation you would like to be in (or out of), a place where you used to be, a vacation state (of mind), a state of affairs, or state of consciousness. If you are in a specific state of the country the name of the state or city may lend further meaning, or the memories associated with that may be significant.

STILL WATERS:
Often symbolic of deep peace, protection, and spiritual renewal. "He leadeth me beside the still waters."

SUN:
Source of light, dynamo of radiant energy; ancient symbol for God, enlightenment, spiritual blessings poured on you.

Sun Bath: Soaking up spiritual light, knowledge, wisdom, truth.

Sun, Coming Through the Clouds: Symbolizes the beginning of spiritual truth and wisdom.

Sun-filled Rooms: Spiritual enlightenment pouring in (to your state of consciousness). Often this is prelude to a lucid experience.

Sunlight Shining In: God's love, light, and wisdom pouring into your state of conscious, or can depict an enlightened state of consciousness. Often bright, sunny dreams are spiritual in nature and can be preludes to lucid dreaming.

Sun-lit Area: Area of enlightenment, illumination, closeness to God, understanding.

Sun's Rays: Sign of illumination, blessings, and/or approval of the place or person the ray touches.

Sunrise: Special time when God's blessings are poured out on all beings; time of prayer and meditation; new day, new opportunities, new start, new conditions. Promise of better things to come, blessings, or call to worship.

Sunset: End of the day, a cycle, an era, or condition. Time of receiving special blessings, thanksgiving, worship, completion, period of rest and renewal, evaluation.

SWIMMING POOL; CLEAR:
As long as the water is clear and clean, this is an area of spiritual activity such as prayer, meditation, devotion, forgiveness, loving kindness, service given to others, working on spiritual disciplines, or your need to start doing these things. Note your progress or lack of it and whether you are swimming well or floundering. Could also say you are busily immersed in spiritual work.

SWIMMING POOL, MURKY:
Muddy or murky water represents your emotions, so there is a pool of emotions to be dealt with in some way. You could be up to your ears with emotions (yours or another's), be in over your head, or struggling to stay on top of an emotional or unclear situation.

SYMPHONY:
Place of culture, art, harmony, cooperation, beauty, creative people, and uplifting music which can inspire, expand, renew, refine, and refresh us physically, mentally, emotionally, and spiritually.

TRUCK STOP:
May be rest spot, chance to refuel and recharge. May also be a busy, active place with many kinds of people, ideas, small talk, tale-swapping, exchange, give and take, comraderie, communications on all levels.

VACATION SITE:
This could indicate a need for you to rest up, slow down, play a bit more, or even say you need a vacation from what you are doing. May also signify a more relaxed and easy-going state of mind is needed.

VALLEY:
Low spot, usually filled with towns and people, often representative of low ideals, low thinking, lower natures, materialism, race consciousness,

lack of insight, conventionality, average, goal-lessness, depression, the blues, the pits!

VOLCANO:
Symbol of extreme turmoil within, emotions boiling inside, your temper ready to explode. Could be you can't stomach something. Problem needs to be dealt with before it literally eats you up or you blow up, lose control.

WEST:
Going or being out west usually implies an area of great freedom of body and mind, new ideas, places, adventure, plenty of space and liberty to do your own thing, new things to do and try.

WILDERNESS:
Implies a wild area, untried, no paths, no broken trails, a new area to be explored and understood, a new way to go.

WOODS:
To many, going into the woods is the act of get-ting close to nature and all its wonders. Trees radiate peace, loving-kindness, and wisdom when we are relaxed and "tuned in." It is a wonderful, refreshing, and renewing place to be. For others the woods may mean, "You can't see the forest for the trees," or it can be an area where one is unable to see his way clear, a place where one can only take one step at a time. It might even be a fearful place for some. Pause to think a moment on what a forest means to you and what it is symbolizing in your dream.

My Own Background Symbols

CHAPTER 14

Battles, Conflicts, and Fights

Peace is not an absence of conflict...it is knowing how to deal with it.
— *Virginia Satir*

In dreams we may find ourselves in active conflict with another; it may be a verbal battle, a mental clash, or a physical fight. We may be surprised to find we are fighting ourselves! Since all dream people are aspects of ourselves unless specifically programmed otherwise, this type of dream is indicative of the inner conflicts within ourselves. At times one part of us wants one thing while another part wants something else. Often this is a clash between the conscious mind (what we think we want) and the subconscious (what we have been trained to believe). The superconscious may be involved also.

Please note: ***Anytime there is a conflict of opinion between the conscious mind and the subconscious, the subconscious mind wins!*** For example, if you want to lose weight but your subconscious has been programmed to "clean up your plate" or never waste food (which means you have to eat everything in the 'frig), then you are in for a real battle. As long as you exert your will power (conscious mind), you can diet and even lose a few pounds; but as soon as you relax your will, the subconscious resumes control and you promptly gain it all back. The subconscious training overrides all other ideas the moment the will power rests. The only way to win this battle is to re-program the subconscious mind.

Conflicts in dreams dramatize these discords so that you can literally see the problem and take the necessary steps to correct it.

Another type of battle concerns the conscious mind and the superconscious. In this case, your superconscious mind (High Self, God-self, or guardian angel) has your soul-purpose in mind and is guiding you along those lines. The struggle begins when you consciously decide to go in a different direction. You may be about to choose a career which goes counter to what, deep down in your heart, you really want to do. You may feel you haven't the money, education, or whatever to follow your desires and so accept something less. Perhaps someone has said you can't or shouldn't do it or that you "ought to do" something else (their choice), and you let them talk you into a decision not right for you. In such cases there is no such thing as reprogramming your superconscious. It will always be there, urging you on to your rightful purpose; and when you over-ride these deep feelings (your conscience), you find yourself feeling guilty. Eventually you have to break away from "convention," other people's opinions, and expectations to do your own thing, or the duel to the death is on. You are literally saying to yourself in the combat dream, "One of us has got to go!"

As a general rule we aren't aware of these inner disagreements until our dreams point them out, bringing these deep feelings out into the open to be resolved.

Battles which concern your superconscious may be shown as the good guys fighting the bad guys—white hats and all—or could be symbolized by black outfits versus white ones, cops and robbers, or any symbol which would represent to you the good versus the bad, or right against wrong.

A fighting dream may also be saying to you that you are your own worst enemy! People with great gobs of suppressed anger tend to fight and thrash about all night and usually have a high rate of nightmares.

Background Clues

The background setting can give you a clue as to where the problem is. For instance, a combat in your home would point to dissatisfaction in the marriage or family relationship; conflict in a bank would indicate difficulty with financial decisions; while battles at your place of work can show upset with your employer, working conditions or career choice. The *real* you may want to change careers, but the programmed you thinks you can't quit for some important reason. It is up to you to get in touch with the excuses you make to yourself and others in order to find your right place in the world. If your career fails to give you a sense of accomplishment and feelings of happiness, you know you are in the wrong place and need to make some changes. Why spend the rest of your precious life at something which does not make you happy? Life is meant to be joyous!

Whatever the problem, recalling your feelings, thoughts, and emotions together with the background setting of the dream will help you decide what the dream is trying to convey to you.

Bedroom Battles

This would have to do with conflicting ideas about marriage, sex, or both. "Sex is dirty" is the most common belief to be slain here, but that may not be your particular hang-up. Maybe you just don't want to be married!

Consider whether you could be having problems in the area of rest, relaxation, sleep, or anything else you equate with your bedroom, such as privacy, your personal space, or lifestyle. Check all possibilities. If you are still unsure, ask for more dreams on the subject to clarify the situation.

If the bedroom battle is one with your mate, there is a good possibility that the difficulty is in your relationship and could signify a battle of wills. More likely, however, it is a problem based on your inner concept of who and what you are or what your rights are. Your self-esteem may be at fault, since there is no jealousy when one is totally confident in one's own self-worth, and true love is completely without strings.

Basically, our mates tend to reflect to us the problems and weaknesses we have within ourselves. What you dislike most in your partner is what you hate most in yourself. The problem is we cannot see our own faults and tend to put the blame on others without stopping to look more deeply within. Dreams help us see the truth about ourselves.

Dining Difficulties

This could be a literal "Battle of the Bulge" you are fighting with food in general and the emotional problems behind overeating (or under), especially if you are having problems in that area, or it may be a battle with a certain kind of food which your body cannot tolerate. The dream may be dramatizing the inner battles which ensue when you partake of this particular kind of food or drink. Possibly there is an allergy involved or a temporary intolerance caused by stress or other factors. Perhaps the trouble is in the way the food for thought is/was presented/served.

Kitchen Conflicts

These may depict a problem with food for thought—an idea or concept you cannot accept. Then there is always the possibility the dream is saying, "I hate to cook!"

WEAPONS:
The desire to kill is basically from a desire to annihilate something we feel is the cause of our problem. This is usually symbolized as a person, group, or animal which represents the despised trait in yourself. Understand, ***all anger is self-anger!***

This is a basic truth, so if you are angry look within yourself. What trait, attitude, or habit do you despise in the person or animal you wish to kill? Or, ask yourself in what way have you allowed yourself to be pushed or manipulated into a situation which upset you? Strive to find the real reason behind your anger.

IF YOU HAVE BEEN CAUGHT IN A WAR:
Weapons and fighting may be a re-living or re-thinking of the meaning of war, hate, greed, death, and all that comes with acts of violence. May imply a need to forgive yourself and all others involved in this.

BOMBS, GRENADES:
These imply explosive situations. The larger and more powerful the bomb, the greater the anger, hate, guilt, prejudice, or frustration needing to be released. This can be a warning of inner anger and pressures about to explode into violence.

GUNS:
Hand guns symbolize explosions of anger, malice, hate, greed, and frustrations. They depict emotional blow-ups, explosive temper, or sharp retorts and angry words. These are mostly aimed at the "other person," who is actually an aspect or trait in yourself which is symbolized by that particular person. See chapter on *People*.

RIFLES, LARGE GUNS:
These imply greater anger, intensity, and strong urges to kill off this aspect of yourself which has been projected onto others. Again, the person, race, group, or animal represents unrecognized traits within yourself which need to be understood.

HEAVY ARTILLERY:
These can imply a heavy problem, hate, karma, anger, or frustration. May depict the extra-strong measures needed to rectify the situation.

KILLING:
May imply you have killed an aspect of yourself. This could be a hope, a dream, an ideal, or you may have slain the opposing or hated part of yourself and won your battle.

> **Killing a Baby:** This usually symbolizes killing a project, idea, or ideal which was or is important or dear to you. *See Baby under People.*

KNIVES OR SCISSORS:
Can be a sex symbol or may say, "Cut it out!" Note what it is you desire to cut.

MODERN WAR WEAPONS:
These are too numerous to list, but most of these are concerned with large-scale killing of many people, races, problems, or aspects of yourself. Destroying large areas of consciousness, possibly race-consciousness ideas, concepts, or belief systems. This implies great frustration and anger within self and desire to wipe out a vast area or part of yourself or your thinking. This could denote a great need to release pent-up anger before it explodes into violence.

SHIELD:
Protection, defense, or may imply trying to dodge the issue.

SHOOTING SELF:
Putting an end to your bad habits or unwanted aspects of yourself. (Possible need for you to do this.) May imply you are killing yourself in some way, shooting yourself down, or that you are your own worst enemy.

SHOOTING SOMEONE ELSE:
Usually refers to "putting someone down" with words of malice, gossip, or lies. Could be an aspect of yourself or a mirror of your actions to others.

SPEARS:
Going after something with vengeance or one-pointedness. Can represent a primitive or old-fashioned method or suggest the conflict goes back to a former lifetime. Can also represent the spinal spirit-fire called kundalini or be a sex symbol, depending upon the dream.

Sacred Spear: Can represent Spiritual power.

SWORDS:
Symbols of destruction, aggression, ambition, force, courage, war, strife, cutting loose, dividing, separating; may be the sword that hangs by a thread (over your head), a former life struggle, or be a pun on, "Cut that out!" Can also symbolize decisiveness and will power, and can be used for knighting another.

Magic Sword: Spiritual power to accomplish the impossible; contact with spiritual forces; the "force" is with you.

Two-Edged Sword: Cuts both ways—the damage you intend for another may descend upon you. Can be dual awareness, duality, or the warrior being warred upon.

All conflicts between dream people show conflicts within yourself being played out for you to see and understand. Take a good look at the background, the rooms, the people symbols, action, and your feelings. Consider these carefully and use all the clues you can, for these conflict dreams are telling you something vitally important about yourself.

My Own Conflict Symbols

CHAPTER 15

Birds

Birds in general are symbols of joy, song, light-heartedness, freedom, flexibility, a state of love, joy, ecstasy, music, or harmony. They may also symbolize the spirit or the spiritual part of us and may symbolize the soul and its ability to soar to great heights.

A Flock of Birds: Can represent group instincts, group action, cooperation, or an abundance of one or more of the above traits. Can be a hint that "birds of a feather flock together," showing what you are attracting to you by your thoughts and actions. Consider the bird meaning, the flock action, and how you feel about these.

BIRD CAGE:
Limitation or protection of your bird-like qualities such as joy and freedom.

Caged Birds: Although they may still sing happily, they are limited in action and lack the freedom of their brothers. This could be a hint to be joyous wherever you are or may show you an aspect of yourself which feels caged or cramped. May represent sudden loss of freedom, the way you feel about your love life or its condition, or can imply "jail bird," depending on the feeling of the dream.

BIRD FEED:
Can indicate feeding or nourishing your higher, spiritual qualities if the action is right, especially if you feel happy in the act of feeding them or they are responding in a joyous manner; but this

may also portray "small change," as in money, income, payment. This can represent insufficient rewards or indicate that your efforts are skimpy and inadequate, depending on the dream content, or may imply small changes in your life.

BIRD FLIGHT:
Would represent freedom, ability to rise above a situation, detachment from the physical plane, viewing things from a higher level, ideas, ideals, hopes, wishes; or, on the puny side, could represent the "flighty" aspect of you, the "flight of ideas," or your need to rise to higher levels in your thinking.

BIRD HOUSE:
This would imply a joyous state of consciousness, sense of happiness, joy, freedom, and harmony or your need to cultivate these, especially if you are building the bird house.

BIRD NEST:
Symbolic of a high, safe place, refuge, home of spiritual qualities. May also denote nesting, putting away money, saving, building security, having something to "fall back on," independence.

Nest building: May refer to getting a nest (home) of your own or your need to work on your independence and security.

BIRD SONG:
Expression of joy and harmony, singing praises, giving thanks, emoting love and happiness, possibly saying you need to do this more often.

BIRD WING:

May represent freedom of mind or body, "wings of prayer," protection, or ability to rise above a problem.

HIGH PERCH:

This can be a dangerous or conspicuous place or may indicate the high place you have chosen for yourself or your ideals. Might imply that you are acting high and mighty.

ROOST:

Often represents thoughts, deeds, ideas, words, or prayers you have sent out now coming home to roost—the "reap what you have sown" concept. Note the kind of birds or whatever it is that has come home to roost.

Specific Birds

BAT:

Might be a pun on acting a bit "batty," crazy, erratic, unpredictable, or may symbolize being "blind as a bat," not seeing what is right under your nose, or "batting around" with an active night life. Bats are generally considered repulsive to all but their own kind, but they are also well-known for their sonar hearing which could represent intuition, keen hearing, good listening, and ability to tune in to higher vibrations.

BIG BIRD:

A cartoon character associated with teaching children good morals, thoughtful behavior, lessons of life.

BIRDS OF PREY:

While these would symbolize freedom of movement and high flying, they would also have the trait of preying on others. If this does not fit, try "praying" for others!

BLUE BIRD:

Traditional symbol of happiness, joy of spirit, spiritual ideals.

BLUE JAY:

Mostly noisy, cocky, raucous, with irritating, thieving habits, tending to take from other birds. May symbolize your behavior as perceived by others or depict something which you are allowing to rob you of spiritual joy and attainment.

BUZZARD:

Scavenger, symbol of death, decay, and ugliness to most people. Yet, even this bird serves a useful purpose.

CANARY:

Known for their joyous singing, happiness, harmony, especially in their *free* state. Caged would inhibit freedom.

CHICKEN:

Usually associated with being afraid, "chicken hearted," lacking the courage and will power to buck the system or the established pecking order. Could symbolize your acceptance of the status quo, of being "hen pecked" or picked on, and/or your willingness or quickness to pick on others. You may pass the buck rather than making a stand for what you believe to be right and fair or live on "chicken feed." Perhaps you are in danger of losing your head or are being generally thoughtless.

HENS:

Tendency to cluck or brag about little things; possibly represents small talk, gossip, hen party, smallness of your mental scope, a habit of picking on someone, or just general hen-pecking.

ROOSTER:

One who likes to crow; cocky, noisy, ostentatious showoff with no regard for others and not too bright.

> **Banty Rooster:** Small, but with highly combative traits; bold, ruthless, he will tackle anything, any size, anytime, anywhere.

Rooster Crowing: Symbol of bragging, exaggerating, self-glorification, blowing your own horn. This can also be a biblical symbol of denial or the dawn of resurrection.

CONDOR:
Large and high flying, found mostly on the west coast of USA; often represents vision, high ideals, high goals, high flying, or ability to rise above the physical level to get a more spiritual view. Ironically, this is an endangered species in more ways than one.

CRANE:
This may be a pun on craning your neck, or may be portraying flexibility of the neck or will.

CROW:
Known for intelligence but also for his thieving, preying (possible pun for "praying"), and often annoying habits.

DOVE:
Well-known symbol of peace, harmony, and innocence.

> **White Dove** often signifies the Holy Spirit, a special message or blessing to receiver. It is also a symbol of one who has given up all thought of war, hate, or revenge and is totally peaceful in attitude and action. One with a will to do only that which is good, kind, helpful; pledged to complete harmlessness and peace.

DUCK:
Often associated with "sitting duck," fair game, vulnerable position, setting yourself up or being set up for the kill, but may also represent ducking the issue, the situation, or some responsibility. Could imply you are "taking to _____ like a duck takes to water."

EAGLE:
Often represents the USA, but also symbolizes high ideals, loftiness, superiority, supremacy, clear insight, power, dignity, attainment, the highest one can reach.

Golden Eagle: Spiritual wisdom

White Eagle: Pure wisdom.

Winged Eagle: Is sometimes a symbol of St. John.

GOOSE:
Skittish, silly, non-thinking, absent-minded.

HAWK:
While this is a bird of prey in our society, in ancient wisdom he is a symbol of trained wisdom, intuition, vigilance, and accuracy. A very good spiritual symbol.

LOVE BIRDS:
Would definitely symbolize being in love or the state of your affections.

MOCKING BIRD:
Well-known for mocking or copying songs of other birds and weaving them into a song of his own. A very clever, cocky, and independent bird who wants what he wants when he wants it and doesn't mind demanding or insisting on his rights.

OSTRICH:
Well-known for hiding his head in the sand whenever trouble threatens. Represents foolishness and inability or disinclination to face reality; total lack of insight, deliberately choosing not to see, face, confront, or be aware of a person or situation.

OWL:
Usually symbolizes wisdom, knowledge, intelligence, and ability to remain silent.

PARAKEET:
Friendly, intelligent, trainable as a companion, and can talk to some degree but doesn't sing much. Sometimes considered a love bird and could symbolize the need to be more loving to your mate.

PEACOCK:
Portrays pride, pomposity, vanity, strutting, parading, self-importance, and self-interest.

PHOENIX:
Mythical bird which can be consumed by fire and rise above the ashes, renewing itself completely. Transformation for the better. Excellent symbol of purification of the body, mind, and/or soul. Depicts your ability to transform yourself or your situation. Represents metamorphosis, transformation, transmutation, transfiguration, reincarnation, immortality, spiritual rebirth and renewal. A powerful symbol.

PIGEON:
Can be a messenger, stool pigeon, tattle-tale, gossip, or even one who catches the blame for something done by others. This is also a city bird who is considered obnoxious by some and a friendly beggar by others.

RAVEN:
Represents evil, the lower aspect of the love nature, selfish desire.

ROBIN:
Harbinger of spring, new starts, new growth to come. Could be showing you a time frame, especially in an ESP dream, or could imply a spring-like mood or situation.

SEAGULL:
Generally associated with oceans and other large bodies of water, he is a welcome bug-eater and crop saver; therefore can be a symbol of faith and answered prayer.

> **Jonathon Livingston Seagull:** Has become a symbol of daring, of willingness to try new things, to go beyond the socially accepted boundaries to try the untried, the new, and the unusual. He represents the courage to be different and the power to do his own thing, regardless of the opinions of others. He may represent your desire or need to do the same.

SONG BIRDS:
Especially represent joy, love, music, harmony, and light-heartedness.

SPIRIT BIRDS:
The dove, raven, thunderbird, eagle, and phoenix all can represent messengers of the Gods.

STORK:
A common symbol of the pending arrival of a baby bird, animal, or human.

SWAN:
Perfection, beauty, poise, serenity, grace, the higher nature, High Self, or Holy Spirit.

TALKING BIRDS:
May suggest that discussion in a matter is needed or, if they talk incessantly, could imply an overly-talkative aspect of you, or imply that you talk too much and say too little.

THUNDERBIRD:
Equal to the eagle in spirit and power to many, he is also a strong Indian tribal symbol of high ideals.

TURKEY:
Known as an unthinking, foolish, inept bird but still symbolizes thanksgiving in general and holidays. This could represent a time reference

such as harvest season, autumn, November, Thanksgiving day or possibly Christmas.

VULTURE:
Scavenger, symbol of death, decay, greed, deception, destruction, evil in general.

My Own Bird Symbols

CHAPTER 16

The Body and Its Parts

From ancient times the various parts of our bodies have been symbolically linked with definite meanings. These correlations are well-known and understood at the subconscious level of our minds, even though we no longer have a conscious knowledge of them.

Skeleton

Body framework, general ability to be straight, to stand up for one's rights; courage, strength, stability, and mobility. One's general attitude toward life can be easily ascertained by the way he stands and walks.

Muscle System

Supports the skeleton and aids in its movement and is symbolic of the connecting links throughout the body which hold the whole together. When muscles refuse to work in certain areas, it is a clear message from the body-mind that we do not want to do this particular kind of work or participate in the activity required by its use.

Nervous System

Coordinates with muscle system and represents our message centers, intercommunications, the body alarm system, our inner wiring and electrical circuits, the ability to give and receive messages from many levels of existence. A breakdown here can immobilize one or many parts of the body.

Skin

Suit for the soul, outer limits of the body. Skin may represent sensitivity, touch, feelings, vulnerability, the bare facts, a basic situation, or "skin tight."

BIRTHMARK:
Dreamed or real, this is a soul mark—a reminder of something we must do or never do again, a stain on the soul, a commitment, mark, or brand of significance.

BROKEN BLOOD VESSELS:
Submerged anger.

NUDITY:
Implies feeling exposed, unprotected, and vulnerable, or a problem in that area. See chapter on *Nudity*.

OVERSIZED PARTS:
This would give special emphasis to that body part, making it extra-important or possibly saying that the part is overworked, overused, misused, or possibly swollen.

Head

The head represents the mind, intellect, thinking, ideas, will, pride, ego, mental powers, logic, leadership, aggressiveness, the execution of ideas, being head of a group, organization, plot, idea, or scheme.

BOWED HEAD:

Sign of humility, servitude, acknowledgement, greeting, gratitude, reverence, prayer, honoring another.

Head Held High: Haughtiness, pride, arrogance, ego, rebelliousness, willfulness, dominance.

BRAIN:

Intellect, physical act of thinking, material ideas; a need to see or perceive in order to believe.

BROW:

Intellect, mind, broad-mindedness, brow chakra, mysticism, intuition, and clairvoyance.

CROWN:

Top of head, crown chakra, pituitary gland, highest type of thinking, intuition, abstract mind.

EARS:

The ability to listen, hear, understand and cooperate.

Good Ears: Good hearing which implies a willingness to listen, learn, obey, cooperate as well as to have understanding, perception, compassion for others and their needs.

Ear Problems: Poor hearing is directly related to an unwillingness to listen, heed, or to obey. Not wanting to know something or turning a deaf ear to another.

SINUS CAVITIES:

These depict our capacity to store or stuff unexpressed feelings and emotions.

Blockage or Drainage: Indicates a very real need to cry, to release the grief, hurt, or pain we have tried to hide, ignore, or deny. Colds and sinus problems are a grown-up, acceptable way of releasing these hurts, especially for people who are too proud to cry.

Face

The face symbolizes facing facts, confronting, courage to face things, admitting the problem, "losing face" or fear of losing it, identity, self-recognition, self-esteem, appearance.

FACELESS:

Nameless, unseen, unobtrusive, low key. May be something you do not want to face or lack of self-esteem. Incognito. Could imply you have lost face.

LOSING FACE:

Act of losing respect, prestige, of being humiliated, embarrassed, or put down. Can be a warning of this happening.

MAKE-UP:

Can be a desire to beautify, add allure, put on a good appearance, or may be a cover-up, a false front, act of hiding the true self, attempt to distract or deceive.

CHEEK:

Can mean cheeky, pushy, and domineering or can represent turning the other cheek, offer of forgiveness, softness, gentility, Christianity.

CHIN:

Will, stubbornness, bullishness, bravado, determination, pride.

Eyes

EYEBROW:

Expressive part of the face.

Raised: Can show questioning, interest, amazement, surprise, or disbelief.

Knitted Brows: Show worry, concern, dislike, disapproval.

EYELID:
Protection of the eye, ability to block or obscure one's field of vision, to open or close awareness, perception.

Open: Looking, seeing, aware, receptive, observant.

Closed: Unreceptive, unwilling to look at something, afraid of what one might see, shutting down, closing off, hiding; refusing to look, know, join, participate, or get involved.

Half-closed: Half-aware, only partially open to something, afraid to look yet wanting to see. Veiled, not wanting others to know you are aware or looking. Trying to appear uninterested, withholding, hiding, subterfuge. Could be flirting, being coy or shy, or may be guilt and shame.

EYES:
Symbol of the windows of the soul. Imply awareness, sight, perception, understanding or may be a pun on "I," ego, self. They also signify our ability to cry and express or release hurt, pain, feelings, sympathies.

Blind: Unwillingness or inability to see, to take a good look at what is going on.

Crossed: Not seeing straight, inability to see clearly or to comprehend intelligently. Getting facts crossed.

Gold-colored: Spiritual insight into the situation, seeing the spiritual side of things, spiritual outlook, psychic insight, possibly clairvoyance.

Looking Away: Implies not wanting to see something, not wanting to know or face.

Out of the Eye: Out of sight, out of mind, beyond comprehension. Could be something going on behind your back or out of your jurisdiction.

Oversized: Implies extra-good vision, seeing everything; could be a pun on "having the big eye" (can't sleep) or seeing too much of something, someone.

Something in the Eye: Can't see your way clear, obstacles in your path, seeing a fault in another, critical perception, something occluding your view, a fault that needs to be plucked out.

Wearing Glasses or Lens: Can be hint that you or the person wearing them needs glasses or assistance in seeing something; may symbolize correcting your "sights" or perception, better understanding needed, a clearer view, a new look.

Dark Glasses: Poor perception, seeing the dark or negative side of things, not wanting to see or to be seen, blinders you are hiding behind, avoiding direct confrontation.

Frames: Framework in which you view things.

Mirror Glasses: Taking a look at yourself, your reflection, how others see you, looking back on yourself.

Rose-Colored Glasses: Seeing the bright, rosy, loving, happy side of things. Good, positive outlook.

Nose

May portray curiosity, inquisitiveness, research or general nosiness; can depict knowingness (my nose knows), intuition, instinct, or be a pun for "no's" or "no-no's."

BROKEN OR INJURED NOSE:
May refer to your sticking your nose where it doesn't belong or imply danger involved in pursuing your present course of action or inquisitiveness. Could imply being "bent out of shape," "out of line," or your nose is "out of joint." Per-

haps you are taking things the wrong way or seeing things in an unfair light.

FINGER POINTING AT YOUR NOSE:
Accusation or threat.

LARGE NOSE:
Double emphasis on the qualities symbolized by nose.

Mouth and Lips

LIP:
Relates to words, speech, talking, kisses, lip service (words spoken but not meant), or giving lip or sharp words to another.

Applying Lipstick: Can be attempt to make one's self more attractive in a purely physical way or symbolize an attempt to make your words more acceptable with a coat of paint. Sugar-coated words. Whitewash.

Stiff Lip: Holding onto courage, trying not to cry, positive thinking, hanging in there.

MOUTH, TONGUE:
Represent the words you speak out or swallow, giving voice to things, and how your words affect those around you. Also swallowing ideas, accepting or rejecting food for thought. Injury to your lips could be warning of damage you are creating with your mouth and a warning to make needed corrections or apologies.

TEETH:
Symbols of the words you speak, how they affect you and those around you.

Braces: Could be symbolic of a physical need for teeth straightening but most likely implying a need to restrict your amount of talk or correct your manner of delivery. You may need to withhold criticism.

Crooked: Symbol of crooked words, circumventing truth, the intent or habit of deceiving.

False: False words, false works, deceit, dishonesty.

Infected: Foul language, dirty mouth, dirty mind, or ESP.

Loose: Loose words, loose thinking, carelessness of expression, inaccuracies, exaggerations, or being loose with the truth.

Losing: Losing control of your words, speaking without thinking, meaningless chatter.

Pulled Out: Strong need to remove the offending words or statements from your vocabulary or speech habits.

Rotting: Symbol (and physical result) of false or foul words. Strong need to clean up your speech habits.

Surgery on Mouth, Teeth: Can represent lessons, discipline, or situations needed to correct a fault, eliminate lies, gossip, criticism, foul language, or useless, careless talk.

Hair

Hair is a symbol of sensitivity, an outward manifestation of your thinking, thoughts, ideas, and attitudes.

BALD:
Dream symbol of losing ideas or not taking time to think things out. No new ideas growing, barrenness of constructive thought, lack of positive thinking.

Baldness also has a connection with monks and other male religious orders or races who shaved their heads as a symbol, a mark of a special vow or state; therefore, baldness can symbolize a religious or moral commitment.

BRAIDED HAIR:
This could be a pun on upbraiding yourself or others, may represent neat, orderly thinking patterns, or could symbolize a set of mind, determination, or a three-fold strength of mind.

16–The Body and Its Parts

BLOW DRYING:
May be a pun on something that blows your mind, "a lot of hot air," clearing out your thoughts, or may be getting some fresh ideas.

COMBING:
Putting thoughts in order; getting your thinking straight, under control; sorting out facts in your mind. Evaluating, weighing, using your power of discrimination. Searching, sorting, and seeking for something elusive.

> **Comb:** Device for straightening out your thoughts, getting the kinks out of your thinking.

COVERED:
Concealed thoughts, plans. Secrets. Under cover.

CURLERS:
Thinking in circles, worry, going over and over a problem without coming to conclusions. Could be a deliberate reshaping of your thinking or a need to do so.

CURLING, WAVING:
This symbolizes deliberately changing your look, your attitude, your thinking. Generally this is trying to affect a style or way of thinking that you feel is fashionable. Often this represents race-consciousness thinking (following a current style or fad, accepting other people's ideas, losing yourself in mass-consciousness thought) rather than thinking things through for yourself. Can be thinking in circles or not thinking at all, but following the crowd. The emphasis is on your *outer appearance*, on being one of the crowd, actually losing your self-identity and personal individualism. Be very clear as to whether you are developing *your own individual style* or are just following a trend. Dream could be warning, "To thine own self be true."

CUTTING:
Trimming, shaping, curtailing, disciplining your thinking; cutting out something, cutting an idea short, trimming your scope of ideas; reshaping your thinking or ambitions; eliminating unwanted thoughts and habits.

DISHEVELED:
Distraught, mixed up, confused, can't think straight. Strong sign of mental disorder.

DYED, TINTED, COLORED:
Thinking is colored, prejudiced, influenced by outside interference, false teachings.

FASTENED:
Shows some control, discipline, guidance, inhibition, or possibly the need of these.

GOLDEN:
Spiritual ideas, ideals held in mind; pure, spiritualized thinking.

GRAY:
Denotes fear, worry, negative thinking.

KINKY:
Kinks in your thinking, not thinking straight or clearly. Many little problems not worked out.

KNOT:
Knot or "not" in your thinking, implying that you think in terms of not enough, not able, not allowed; or, this could depict highly-disciplined thoughts, every item in its place, no loose ends dangling, no nonsense.

KNOTTED, TANGLED:
Confused, mixed up ideas, uncertainties. Indicates a strong need to take time out to correct this.

LONG:
Long thoughts, thinking long and carefully, planning, good concentration ability. If your hair is actually short, this may suggest that you think a long time about the new idea, suggestion, or situation before making a decision.

LOSING HAIR:
Forgetfulness, losing train of thought, ideas, mental agility, losing your "peace" of mind, losing your composure.

MATTED:

Unbalanced mind, uncoordinated thinking, confusion, long-standing mental problem.

OUT OF YOUR HAIR:

Out of mind, out of your thinking. Possible hint to get the matter off your mind.

RED HAIR:

Usually symbolizes anger, a quick temper, hot-headedness, or being burned up about something.

SETTING:

Training or attempting to train your thinking habits; getting your mind under control; disciplined thoughts, plans.

STATIC ELECTRICITY:

Depicts your magnetic personality, how you draw things to you, or magnetism influencing you.

STIFF:

Rigidity of mind, unable or unwilling to change thinking habits or accept new ideas.

STYLING:

Can be taking on a whole new idea, concept, way of thinking, outlook, or new self-image. Can be taking on a race-consciousness idea of how you should look or think.

SUNNING:

Implies letting in the light, allowing God's light to fill your mind and thoughts. Spiritualizing your mind, being yourself, thinking loving thoughts.

UNCOMBED:

Depicts a need to straighten your thinking, think things over, re-evaluate.

WASHING:

Need to cleanse thinking and attitudes, removing the negativity or washing other people's influences out.

WHITE:

Symbol of wisdom, maturity, graciousness, teacher.

WIG:

Falsehood; misleading, deceptive thoughts, ideas, or opinions "bought" from another. Pre-conceived ideas, false impressions, taking on other people's ideas and opinions instead of thinking things through for yourself. Not being true to your own beliefs and thinking. Choosing another person's ideas over your own.

Losing Wig or Hair Piece: May be pun on losing your "peace" of mind, giving someone a "piece" of your mind, or losing it (your composure). Could warn of a partial loss of mind (hair piece), a total loss of mind (wig), or a complete casting off of old ideas.

Neck and Throat

This part of the body has to do with "sticking your neck out," pride, will, taking risks, using your will power to carry things to completion, swallowing or refusing to swallow your pride or other people's ideas.

LARYNX:

Voice box, where you speak the word of authority, put your will power in words. Problems imply misuse of speech—either saying that which was best left unsaid or failing to speak up at the proper time.

STIFF NECK:

False pride, superior attitudes, unbendingness, unwillingness to change or accept new things.

THROAT:

Willfulness, will power, power of your spoken word, speaking up, speaking out, making your wishes known. Can be ability to swallow or refuse to swallow pride or ideas.

Throat chakra: Energy center associated with use of will power.

Sore Throat: Symbol of problems with saying what you think—not saying what should be said or speaking something that is better left unsaid; swallowing pride, ideas, etc.

Back

Back represents strength and ability to carry a load; support, responsibility, dependability.

TURN YOUR BACK:
Rejection, refusing to help or face something, changing direction, turning your life around. Might also indicate a need to back out of something.

DAMAGED OR WRENCHED BACK:
All dreams of illness or injuries have the possibility of an ESP warning, but this could indicate a need to back off, to unload, to ease up in some way. May imply that you are being wrenched by so much responsibility or that you are damaging or limiting your load-carrying abilities by pushing too long or too hard. Think about it.

BACKBONE:
Stamina, resistance; ability to stand up for your rights, to be responsible, assertive, dependable.

CURVED SPINE:
May say you are bent out of shape about something or that to continue as you are will damage your future ability to stand tall or stand up for your rights.

BACK MUSCLES:
Represent strength, power to lift and move. Large muscles often represent great strength and ability.

Shoulders and Arms

SHOULDERS:
Represent taking on responsibilities, bearing burdens, lifting the load of others, hard work, caring.

WINGS:
Usually seen in shoulder area, these represent ability to soar to great heights, spirituality, uplifting thoughts, ability to beam love, good will, peace to others.

ARMS:
Signify your power to do, your ability to reach out.

Bare Arms: Could be a pun on bearing arms or bearing gifts, ability to bear something, bareness, exposure.

Crossed Arms: Defensive posture; a closed, unreceptive attitude.

Elbow: Can depict elbowing your way through, rudeness, or elbow grease and action, willingness to bend.

Wrist: Flexibility.

Hands

Hands symbolize service, working, having a hand in a situation, hand-outs, hand-me-downs, giving, receiving, feeling, touch, and expression. May also be a pun on handiness, lending a hand, and availability.

APPLAUDING:
Encouragement, appreciation, approval.

CLOSED HANDS:
Ungiving, unwilling to help, closed attitude.

DIRTY HANDS:
May be dirty work at hand, a dirty deal, getting your hands dirty, digging in, hard work.

EMPTY HANDS:
Denote emptiness, loneliness, lack, loss, nothing to do, hopelessness, defeat. Dream implies strong need to find a way to serve in order to feel fulfilled.

FIST:
Implies anger, defensiveness, readiness to fight, defend, hold on, or hold out.

FOLDED:
Submission, humility, peace, patience, prayer.

KNUCKLES:
Can refer to hard knocks or knuckling under.

LEFT HAND:
Usually implies receptivity but can depict a wrong turn, especially if it is pointing or directing.

Open Left Hand: Ability or willingness to receive graciously.

Closed Left Hand: Unwilling or unable to receive graciously.

LOVELY:
Gentility, graciousness, loving service to others.

OPEN HANDS:
Open, receptive, ready to give, receive, try, help.

OUT OF YOUR HAND:
Could be loss, something slipping through your fingers, or a situation that is taken out of your hands.

RIGHT HAND:
Giving, service, point of control, helping. May also imply something being "right."

ROUGH HANDS:
Lack of gentleness in dealing with others; carelessness.

TOUCHING HAND:
Implies reaching out, keeping in touch with a person or situation, getting in touch with your feelings.

Washing Your Hands: Symbol of letting go, taking no further responsibility in the matter, cleansing, getting things out of your system.

Fingers

Fingers are related to work and service or may point to a person, situation, cause, or result. Injuries to them can denote a hurt, a restraint, or an inability to perform well in the area symbolized by that finger.

FOREFINGER:
Considered to be the finger of authority, direction, judgment, or accusation. Can either make a point or point to solution.

LITTLE FINGER:
Represents mental power, intellect, memory, diplomacy, power of communication, and expression of words.

MIDDLE FINGER:
Prudence, practicality, caution, hard work, responsibility, solitude.

RING FINGER:
Known as the finger of success, popularity, creativity, and art as well as being the "marriage finger."

Ring Finger, Left Hand: Symbol of marriage, vows, promises, and commitments.

Rash Under Ring: Implies irritation with the commitment or the relationship in general.

THUMB:
Means of identification or of getting a grip on things. A symbol of power and holding ability, but could be pun on "thumbing" for help or imply you are all thumbs. You can thumb your

nose at a person or situation; you may express approval (thumbs up) or disapproval (thumbs down); or, someone may turn you down.

Palms

The palm is a symbol of giving, receiving, asking, begging, openness.

OUTSTRETCHED, DOWN:
Symbol of giving, helping, greeting, healing, or blessing.

OUTSTRETCHED, UP:
Victory, praise, plea, devotion, or could mean halt.

LEFT:
Receiving (this may differ if one is left-handed).

RIGHT:
Giving.

PALMS TOGETHER:
Prayer, contemplation, oneness, togetherness.

UP, EMPTY:
Represents oneness, asking, begging, receptiveness.

UP, FILLED:
Presenting, giving, offering.

Chest

The chest area as a whole is symbolic of one's feelings, the ebb and flow of emotions, tenderest sentiments, secret longings, hopes, goals, desires, freedom, sensitivity, and receptiveness.

LUNGS:
Signify the breath of life, the ability to breathe freely and deeply; freedom, independence, self-assurance. Fear and tensions close down the ability to breathe freely.

BREAST:
Nurturing, feeding, loving, protectiveness, mothering nature, warmth, sexy feelings, or may be a sex symbol.

HEART:
Love, emotion, feeling for others, compassion, caring, desire to love and be loved; center of things, heart of the matter; concerns, desires, faith, hope.

Blood: Life forces, vital life-supporting essences. Problems result when blood circulation is impeded in any way. There is much to consider here in the way of "being in the flow." Look to see where circulation is blocked or how you are blocking your flow.

Bleeding: Danger, loss of life forces. Note who or what is draining you or how you are spending your life force.

Old or Dried Blood: Symbol of old karma or karmic debts.

Blood Vessels: Symbol of the circulation of hopes, ideas, energies, enzymes, enthusiasm, body fluids, and life forces throughout the body.

Broken Blood Vessels: Submerged anger.

Heart Trouble: Caused by withheld, unreleased, unexpressed love, pent-up emotions, feeling unloved. Strong need or warning here to let love flow freely *to you* as well as *from you* to others. May also be ESP warning of impending trouble.

High Blood Pressure: Feeling under pressure, pushed, tense, unloved, love not returned, stressed. (Stress is result of our expectations—we tend to expect too much of ourselves or others, then feel frustrated when these goals are not reached.) To eliminate stress reduce your expectations, make them more reachable!

This could be an *ESP warning* of impending danger. Be sure to check out all possibilities.

Open-heart Surgery: This can be an ESP warning of an impending problem, or may imply opening your heart!

SOLAR PLEXUS:

Represents your feeling nature, sensitivity, intuition, gut-level feelings and knowingness. This is a sensitive spot where one automatically reacts to shock or stress. It is also the home of the solar plexus chakra as well as an area where you can leave or enter the body.

STOMACH:

The stomach symbolizes ingesting and digesting ideas, knowledge, food for thought; how you "stomach" things; gut-level feelings.

CRAMPS:

An idea or situation that cramps your style; something you strongly disagree with or want to reject. What is upsetting?

UPSET STOMACH:

Upsetting situation, something you can't stomach, something that doesn't set well which you don't think you can handle or would like to reject completely.

VOMITING:

Complete rejection. Refusal to stomach an idea, person, or situation.

INTESTINES:

Symbol of fortitude, discrimination, digesting, and the assimilation of food-for-thought ideas.

Elimination System

The elimination system is symbolic of the ability to discard or throw off any thoughts, ideas, suggestions, or knowledge not compatible with your current belief system. Things which one can't stomach, digest, assimilate, or use—whether physical, mental, or emotional—are rejected or eliminated. This is often a process of filtering out what is usable and eliminating the rest.

ELIMINATING IN A PUBLIC PLACE:

A common problem in dreams, this may depict feelings of a lack of privacy in one's affairs or could denote a need for a public confession, explanation, apology; a cleansing or releasing of negative emotions or some clearing the air, so to speak. This is similar to being unable to find a bathroom—no private way of releasing thoughts, feelings, and pent-up frustrations, no easy way to forgive; or, dream can be saying you need to get this matter cleaned up in a public— not private—manner. Possibly venting your feelings and letting everyone involved know *exactly* how you feel is exactly what is needed!

KIDNEYS:

Symbolize the filtering of emotions and ideas; applying judgment, balance, equality; the cleansing and releasing of all that is not wanted or no longer needed.

BLADDER:

Symbol of releasing fluids, especially old, no-longer-needed feelings and emotions. Signifies holding back or letting go, finding the right time and appropriate place to release. Problems occur when we hold back our feelings or cling to problems and emotions long after the proper elimination time has passed. (This would include grief.)

Loss of Control: Since this is liquid, may imply being unable to control our emotional output as to time and place; or, when a proper outlet can't be found, the dream is indicating a need to find the time or place to unload the emotional buildup before all control is lost. Dream can be warning to get help before you "lose it!"

BOWELS:
Symbol of the elimination of waste, ideas, concerns, physical matters which need release from our lives, minds, thinking patterns, and belief systems. See *Bathrooms*, also *Diapers* under *Clothing*.

CONSTIPATION:
Implies holding on, failing to release our concerns; worrying about problems and situations we cannot change; failure to take effective action in dealing with our difficulties; failure to let go, forgive, or forget.

> **Diarrhea:** Rapid rejection, a desire to get something out of the system *fast*. Possibly too fast, not taking time to analyze the situation or learn from it, not wanting to deal with the problem at all. Results can be catastrophic!

> **Extra Large Bowel Movement:** This implies you have a lot to "unload," much forgiveness, releasing, and letting go to be done by you. Unless you strongly feel you have already done this, dream is saying this needs to be done.

> **Loss of Control, Mess:** This would imply looking at the mess you have made, a dire need to clean up the problem, having to deal with the unpleasant situation *you have created* with your own thoughts and actions, the bitter fruits of your labors. Could indicate *lack* of labor, interest, planning, preventative action, responsibility, and the results of this. This can also be the result of the thought-forms sent out when one frequently uses the four-letter word which begins with "sh" and ends with "it!" We really reap what we sow!

Hips

Hips relate to mobility, adaptability, freedom, going places, and getting things done; or, sitting down.

LAP:
Can be lap of luxury; things dropped in your lap—could be opportunities or problems. Dream emphasis on an empty lap may depict a feeling of lack, loss, loneliness, nobody there. Problems may be dropped in your lap when you don't "stand up" for your rights!

BODY HAIR:
Sensitivity, possibly sensuality.

Reproductive Organs

Symbols of sex, desire, gratification, passion, regeneration, creative expression, and love. These organs are closely related to our creative capacities and our ability or inability to bring forth children (creations of mind or body).

ABUSE:
Misuse or excessive use of sex organs directs the creative energies to the baser levels and lowers one's creative drive and ability. Strong sex urges are actually potential spiritual and healing energies.

REMOVAL:
To have all or parts removed may symbolize cutting off your creative drive, instincts, and capacities or greatly curtailing your ability to create. This could be cutting off your spiritual outlets as well.

PENIS:
Can symbolize the ability to inject or eject a creative idea or seed-thought into a receptive area. Of course it is also a sex symbol which stands for sex or desire for it, depending on the dream content. Anything preventing proper erection or ejaculation may show lack of desire to express creativity or give love to another. Could indicate a mental or emotional blockage which needs to be faced.

VAGINA:

Can signify a channel of creativity or may be the traditional sex symbol.

Blocked: Can symbolize lack of sexual desire, an actual mental or emotional block about sex, or could say one's creativity is blocked, no way to be creative, no outlet for creative or sexual urges.

WOMB:

May represent reception of seed ideas, cradle of receptivity, fertility, ability to produce something new and wonderful; can represent a creative mind, a new project being formed; could show the state of health or actual pregnancy of that organ.

Thighs and Legs

Thighs and legs denote the ability to stand up for your rights, mobility, agility, strength, and power to move.

WEAK, CRIPPLED:

Unable or unwilling to stand up for yourself, to make a stand; excuse for not making a stand. Lack of courage.

KNEES:

Ability to use what you know, to apply knowledge, maturity in relationships, ability to bend and bow to circumstances when necessary, flexibility, humility.

Knee-Cap and Calf: Ability to utilize experiences.

Kneeling: Showing reverence, awe, worship, honor, humility, subservience, or could be a hint to get on your knees and pray!"

THIGHS:

Goals, accomplishing, the strength and power to go and do or stand for something.

Feet

Feet represent foundation, belief, understanding, your ability to stand up for your rights or to put your foot down. May also imply taking the next step, stepping in the right direction, watching your step, one step at a time.

COLD FEET:

Symbol of lack of courage, outright fear, or just having second thoughts about a decision. May imply a need to reconsider.

ANKLE:

Flexibility; knowing and using what you know.

ARCH:

Support or lack of it.

Fallen Arches: Misconception, incorrect understanding, breakdown of your belief system; might indicate lack of expected or hoped-for support from others; may strongly state that you are not supporting yourself. May imply that you can't or won't stand the weight (responsibility), or bending under the strain.

BAREFOOT:

Basic understanding, bare facts, in touch with the earth, with basics, both feet on the ground, well grounded in the facts. If you can't stand being barefoot, this could indicate a situation you "can't stand" or that you are unprepared.

HEEL:

Vulnerable point, weak spot, susceptibility. Could symbolize a "heel"— one who walks on others, takes unfair advantage, or may imply "heeling" (obeying, following in the heels another). May imply how you put your foot down or be a pun on healing.

SOLE:

May represent sensitivity, foundation, bottom line, being in touch with the earth or basics.

Might be a pun on your soul and what you are doing to it. May also refer to the condition of your understanding (feet).

TOES:
Toes relate to the way you move and walk through life, your grace, poise, mobility, and balance. They symbolize the details and extensions of your understanding, the little things. Toes may represent the minor details of life and how you deal with them.

Big Toe: The big toe represents balance and mobility. This can be a pun on "toeing the mark" or having an "educated toe." A sore or injury affects the whole body.

My Own Body Symbols

My Own Body Symbols continued...

CHAPTER **17**

Bugs

Bugs often represent small annoyances, irritations, and frustrations—the little things which
can distract us from our purpose and upset or
undermine our serenity if we don't find a way to
make peace with these minor issues. Bugs can
signify where and how we allow other people,
things, or situations to "bug" us; or, they may
symbolize our most disagreeable aspects, pointing out our irritating habits and indicating just
how we "bug" others. We must decide whether
we are the source or the recipient, or if the situation is a little bit of both. Notice the kind of pest,
the background, the action, and your feelings to
decide.

The key word here is **small**. We frequently give
too much of our time and energies in allowing
little things to bother us when we really need to
either overlook it altogether or make a decision
to confront and deal with the matter in a positive and effective way. However, the animals or
bugs in dreams also represent our **qualities**, so
be sure to look at both possibilities.

Background

Take a thoughtful look at **where** the bugs are:

A BUILDING:
If the bug action is in a building, look at the kind
of building to indicate the specific area or state
of consciousness this involves. (See chapter on
Buildings.)

YOUR HOME:
This tells you the problem is "where you live,"
either physically or mentally. It may be your own
thoughts, feelings, or problems bugging you,
especially if action takes place in your living
room; or, it may be a person, thing, or situation
in relation to your home.

YOUR WORK:
This suggests the annoyances are in your place
of work, having to do with work conditions,
situations, people, or even pollutions in the area.

YOUR BODY:
Could be a symbol of some "bug" you have
caught or is about to get into your system, or
may depict a minor physical problem which is
calling for your attention.

YOUR HEAD:
Little mental aggravations, irritating thoughts, little things you are allowing to "bug" you mentally. Could be nagging suspicions, small, negative
ideas.

Bug Action

BUGS BITING YOU:
This is "getting you where you live" or really
"getting under your skin." Showing need to
either end or control the source of irritation, take
some positive action.

BUGS CRAWLING:

This could be creeping up on you in small increments. Small annoyances or disturbances which need to be recognized and halted before going any further.

BUGS FLYING:

Something in the air. Can be literal, such as a kind of pollution in the air, or may be a mental irritation and a need to look for answers to the problem before it gets to you. Could be ESP warning the house is "bugged" electronically or is physically infested.

EXTERMINATORS:

May be a call for taking strong action to eliminate the problem, calling in outside help, making sure of the results.

SPRAYING BUGS:

Can symbolize the need to get rid of this, to eliminate the source of trouble, take control.

SWATTING BUGS:

Armed for battle, ready to fight, cope, control, defend, deal, settle, or your need to do this.

Bug Types

ANT:

Perseverance, diligence, good work habits, a one-track mind which is on work. Can be workaholic.

BED BUGS:

Related totally with beds and sleeping, these would most likely represent irritations that creep up on you when you are asleep, unaware, unknowing, not realizing the damage until it is already done. Look for subterfuge.

BEE:

Busy, busyness, business, hard worker, one who works himself to death. Can be a "stinger," a pun on "be-ing," or beingness, "to be or not to be."

Bumble Bee:

Aerodynamically this critter should not be able to fly, yet he does; so he could symbolize one's ability to do the impossible, or he may just be a pun on bumbling!

BEETLE:

Ordinary beetles tend to eat and destroy our plants and crops. They then could symbolize the destructive forces at work in our lives, especially in our seed-thoughts and affirmations. Beetles may be a pun on the popular singing group or, if *Egyptian scarab,* they would take on a more mystical meaning of death and resurrection.

BUTTERFLY:

Symbol for Gemini, light-heartedness, and beauty. Can represent freedom, joy, flight of the spirit, or flight of the soul; may be flightiness, instability, scattered energies, changeability, and superficiality; may portray metamorphosis—the ability to change and transform one's attitudes and ideas or change oneself from one way of being to another. May denote constantly changing, flitting from one thing or person to another.

CATERPILLAR:

May imply creeping along through life at a slow pace or say, "Crawl now—fly later," implying your ability to change from one thing to another, your capacity to rise to new heights, to transform yourself, to become a new being. Could symbolize your readiness to change yourself or your lifestyle, or to have completely new (or renewing) experiences. Potential for change, transformation.

CICADA:

Ancient symbol of death, resurrection, and transformation because of their 17-year cycle. May also represent cycles or circumstances which recur at regular intervals, going underground (hiding or hibernating) only to return in even greater force.

COCOON:

This can represent taking a position which is safe but very confining or a process one has to go through in order to bring about change, to become transformed, liberated, free. *Cocoon* also symbolizes death, rebirth, and reincarnation.

DRAGONFLY:
Mostly associated with water and summertime, it can symbolize a trip to a lake or beach, flying over water, or may represent nature spirits, mysticism, Summer Solstice, the fairy kingdom. Could be a minor version of the winged dragon, winged or plumed serpent, but not as powerful.

FLY:
A real pest, one that won't go away. Points to your need to deal with this or it will keep coming back to annoy you. Possibly saying you "buzz around" all day, irritating others, and/or don't get anything done!

FLEA:
Hops around from one thing to another. Could be a pun on your activities, including desk-hopping or bed-hopping.

GRASSHOPPER:
Hopping from place to place, fiddling around, irresponsibility, flighty, unproductive, procrastinating.

HORNETS:
Plenty of trouble, danger; may be angry thoughts returning to their owner; temper, hate, vengeance, revenge, stinging remarks, sometimes death.

JUNE BUG:
Symbol of erratic, unpredictable behavior; bumbling, bumping into things; crazy as a June bug!

LOCUST:
See Cicadas.

MOSQUITO:
Annoying in sound and presence but also drains our blood (energies) and leaves an irritated spot.

Could represent irritations and a draining of our resources in small ways.

MOTH:
Small but destructive. Damage not usually seen until it is much too late. Can be a warning at small irritations eating away at your ideas and attitudes. Holes in your thinking?

PRAYING MANTIS:
Actually a helpful insect, this could be interpreted as **preying on** others or as **praying for** others.

ROACH:
Equates with dirt, contamination, uncleanliness, neglect, carelessness, lack of pride or self-worth.

SCORPION:
Represents the sting of death, the poison of gossip, stinging remarks, vengeance, will to wound.

SCARAB:
Ancient symbol of wisdom, light, truth, fertility, body strength, regeneration, and resurrection. Sometimes used as a symbol of initiation.

SPIDER:
Highly creative creature, spinning marvelous web patterns (traps) to catch his prey. His bite can be very irritating—one may react for days afterward.

Web: May depict the weaving together of ideas to make a whole, the construction of a thought pattern, the out-picturing of something held in mind, or a symbol of an archtypal pattern. Could imply the elaborate plots and plans we make and how we can get "caught up" in them. There is always a possibility of someone else plotting or spinning a "web of deception."

May depict the weaving of ideas, the out-picturing of something held in mind, or represent an archtype pattern, the inner-connectedness of all persons, all things.

TERMITES:
Slow destruction; a threat to home and family; secret, hidden, undermining influences; ulterior motives which are a threat to your foundations. Could be something eating away at your hopes, dreams, health, or possessions.

TICK:
Getting "ticked off?"

WASP:
Sting of death, stinging remarks, temper, poisonous venom, anger, painful annoyances, waspinenss, nasty disposition, will to kill.

My Own Bug Symbols

CHAPTER 18

Buildings and Parts of Buildings

Man is the master of thought, the molder of character and the maker and shaper of condition, environment and destiny.

— *James Allen*

Buildings

Buildings represent varied states of consciousness, awareness, associations, and general belief systems. The type of building would define that particular state of consciousness. The yard around the building would depict the outer extensions of that particular type of influence.

OCCUPYING:
The building you are occupying would represent your present state of mind.

LEAVING:
This may mean a state of consciousness you are leaving permanently or be a state you are coming from, symbolizing the type of beliefs, standards, or precepts you are using in analyzing and working out your present situation.

GOING THROUGH MANY BUILDINGS:
This would indicate your exploration of different kinds of thinking, ideas, ideals, concepts, attitudes, mores, and philosophies portrayed by the type of building or architecture.

If you are a **builder, architect, construction worker**, or any variation of these, buildings may have an entirely different meaning: they could refer to your job, your working conditions, or both. Then again, they may symbolize your thinking as suggested above. Consider both possibilities.

Building Conditions

DECAYING BUILDINGS:
Would indicate negative thoughts and beliefs, old ideas no longer appropriate, negligence, lack of interest, decline of a once-active, intelligent mind or may show you your crumbling belief in whatever the building represents.

LARGE BUILDING:
Large or expanded state of consciousness, big enough to include many people and ideas, large concepts, ideas for the good of all rather than small, selfish interests. May represent universal consciousness.

NEW BUILDING:
A new idea, understanding, concept, mental state, awareness, state of consciousness.

NEXT DOOR:
Something which is "next to you," close by, can't be ignored, must be dealt with, understood.

OLD-FASHIONED BUILDINGS:

Old ideas, concepts, and beliefs which are now out-of-date and in need of renovating or re-evaluating, especially if they are somewhat run-down and battered in appearance. Old buildings about to collapse could warn of a state of mind or consciousness about to break down.

OLD, FINE, ANTIQUE BUILDINGS:

When in good condition these represent basic, fundamental principles and ideas which have stood the test of time. Old state of consciousness.

OLD, DECAYING BUILDINGS:

Depict dejection, negativity, mental instability, and depravity; old, unusable ideas and beliefs held in mind; lack of activity or interest in the area of thought symbolized by type of building.

OLD, DULL, GRAY BUILDINGS:

Can represent negative states of thinking.

SWAYING BUILDINGS:

These portray instability, uncertainty, vacillation, or indecision in that area of mind or type of belief.

UNFINISHED:

Undeveloped, still being constructed; whole new concept, beliefs, or awareness now taking shape.

VACANT:

Empty, unaware, uncertain, unconscious, unsure, undecided, no opinion as yet, empty headed, thoughtless.

WEATHER BEATEN:

Old, time worn, stalwart; an area where you have had many experiences; consciousness that you have weathered the storm and stood the tests of time. Add this feeling to the type of building to get the complete picture.

Building Activities

BURNING BUILDINGS:

Would imply that you are extremely angry, frustrated, and all "fired up" or "burned up"

about a matter symbolized by the type of building on fire. If this does not fit your feelings, consider the possibility of an ESP dream. Fire may also represent a purification of that particular state of consciousness, especially when the fire is inside the building and you are entirely unperturbed at the sight of the fire.

CLEANING:

A good possibility you have a need to clean-up your thinking in this area.

CONSTRUCTING:

A new house would indicate that you are in the process of building a new, different state of consciousness, a new manifestation of your thinking and learning abilities, or new beliefs being assimilated and taking shape.

Laying a New Foundation: Depicts the laying of a new basis of understanding on which to build.

Remodeling: Could indicate the process of making changes in your present belief system.

Demolishing Buildings: Implies a complete destruction of old beliefs and thought patterns, making way for something new and presumably better. If it is your house, this could be a pun on "breaking up housekeeping" or breaking up your home.

Restoring, Painting, Renovating: Would represent your efforts to keep up with new knowledge and trends of thinking, to keep up with progress, so to speak, or can be pointing to your need to update your ideas in this area. May represent changing your mind, getting a new outlook, adding new dimensions, or a new understanding within the old framework.

Whitewashing: May indicate an attempt to cover up the old beliefs in order to look different or more up-to-date, when in fact nothing is really changed, just coated. Can say you are only kidding yourself or pretending to change. May indicate an attempt to cover up something you don't want seen.

LOOKING OUT FROM A BUILDING:
Would be seeing things from that particular perspective.

Building Environment

NEIGHBORHOOD:
The neighborhood suggests the surrounding conditions and various influences, activities, annoyances, or circumstances and their effects on the building or state of consciousness. These may be supporting influences or obstacles to overcome. This can also signify "in the area of..."

YARD:
The area immediately surrounding a building represents the environment, the extension of the consciousness and influences represented by the building; mitigating circumstances. Being outdoors it may also bring in a greater sense of openness and a more spiritual quality of mind, especially if the sun is shining.

Any intrusion by unwanted people or things would represent an invasion of privacy, time, space, or lifestyle and your need to do something about this.

FRONT YARD:
More public in nature, open to the eyes of the world; open to criticism, praise, and public opinion.

BACK YARD:
Private or semi-private, much less open to view and public opinion.

SLUMS:
Area of negative thinking, old, useless ideas and beliefs, crumbling concepts, poverty consciousness.

Floors & Levels of Buildings

The different floors would represent various levels of that particular state of consciousness.

MAIN FLOOR:
Symbolizes the conscious level of mind or may allude to the main event or main center of attraction.

BASEMENT AND SUB-LEVELS:
Depict your subconscious levels.

UPPER LEVELS:
Represent the higher levels of mind.

TOP FLOOR:
Depicts the super-conscious mind or the highest level you can reach.

SEVEN FLOORS:
May represent the seven body chakras or the seven levels of our beingness.

Types of Buildings

Buildings represent established patterns of thinking, beliefs, concepts, attitudes, and opinions ingrained in our minds.

Public buildings often represent public opinion and race-consciousness thinking. You need to establish whether these are publicly or privately owned and whether this is a place where you are living, working, visiting or *where you used to live*. (See *Houses*.) Add all of these together along with the dream action to get the full picture.

**ACCOUNTING OR
BOOKKEEPING BUILDINGS:**
These would represent the area of accountability; how you measure up, positive and negative; the sum-total of what you have said, done, created, and achieved; giving an accounting of

yourself, weighing and measuring your life, your standards.

AIRPORT TERMINAL:
Place of high ideals; mixture of many ideas and concepts from many areas blending together, constantly making new combinations. Point of departure to higher planes. Messages and communications from higher planes; much activity.

ANTIQUE:
Fine, old, antique buildings, especially when they are in good condition, represent the basic, fundamental principles and ideas that have stood the test of time.

APARTMENT:
A temporary state of mind, liable to change or rearrangement. Many things, ideas coming and going.

ARENA:
Place where you play part of spectator, judge or where you can be the center of attention.

ART CENTER:
Area of beauty, culture, fine art, and creativity of all kinds. Consciousness of your own creativeness and the importance of beauty and art in life.

BANK:
Area of financial matters, material things; saving, investment of time, money, resources, prosperity in general; things of value or your sense of values. May be a place to borrow or withdraw from your resources or place of exchange.

BAR:
Can represent a social gathering place, a singles place-to-meet, a happy place, a low dive, a disreputable state, low morals and animalistic be-havior, a place to avoid, a "no-no," a way of unwinding or of escape.

BARN:
Area of animal instincts, lower levels of consciousness; or, if you have happy (or unhappy) memories of barns, it would represent that state of consciousness.

A fire here would indicate your need for purification in this area. If you own such a barn it could be an ESP warning.

BEAUTY PARLOR:
Consciousness of beauty and glamour or the lack of these. Area of make-up, cover up, artificiality, desire to please or impress others, often by deceptive means. This may also represent transformation, rehabilitation, restoration, and renovation. May depict a whole new outlook or state of consciousness about oneself.

BOOKSTORE:
Place to "buy" all kinds of knowledge, ideas, concepts; can be place of learning, enlightenment, or getting answers. Often a source of information exchange.

BRIDGE:
Area of decision making, crossing from one state of consciousness to another, leaving the old behind, going on to new and different things, or could imply bridging the gap.

> **Covered Bridge:** Could imply secret crossings, a discreet or secret change or decision. May be a subconscious change.

BROADCASTING STATIONS:
Place of public communications, news and messages given and received; entertainment, teaching, advertising; a wide variety of knowledge, information, and misinformation given and received.

CABIN:
Small, humble, primitive, possibly self-made. Can represent a self-made or self-reliant person

with highly original and independent ideas. This may depict humility and simplicity or even poverty, depending on your feelings.

CASTLE:
Consciousness of prosperity, plenty, your highest good, the finer things in life, your hopes and dreams, unless you have other associations with castles. First of all it represents whatever it means to you, personally.

CHURCH, CATHEDRAL:
The building you see as a church in dreams can represent the sum-total of your present spiritual beliefs, ideals, and morals you have built; your spiritual life, philosophy, or state of mind, especially if you are comfortable and happy with your chosen church. It may symbolize religious rhetoric or dogma, old, discarded beliefs and impressions, depending on your feelings. Consider type of church, its name, state of repair or disintegration, your feelings about it, and the activities going on in or around it.

Inside Church, Happy: Feeling of belonging, in harmony with God's laws, protection, safety, security, at-one-ment; at home with your present spiritual beliefs.

Inside Church, Unhappy: May show you have outgrown your particular religious training and are no longer happy within this framework. May feel cramped, trapped, restricted. You may need to find a new belief system that works for you and feels good to you.

Outside Church: May imply you are feeling unforgiven, excommunicated, outside of God's grace, out of touch with God or with your early religious beliefs, out of harmony with yourself; possible need to forgive yourself and others as well, unless you feel good about being outside.

Church Altar: Traditionally a place of protection, prayer, worship, devotion, communion, and forgiveness but can be a point of decision or a pun on altering or changing.

Church Censor: This pot for burning incense is to cleanse and raise the vibrations of the church. Can be a hint for you to do the same; may be a pun on censorship and criticism; could refer to your censoring as in cleansing, blotting out, erasing, removing, or omitting something from your life or belief system.

CITY:
Conglomeration of buildings, states of consciousness, ideas, ideals, concepts, desires, needs, lifestyles.

CONCERT HALL:
Area where music, harmony, cooperation, beauty, and upliftment are practiced; area of helpful influences as long as the music is peaceful.

CONDOMINIUM:
Blend of independence and togetherness. Group-consciousness opinions with minor individual variations within the framework.

COLLEGE, UNIVERSITY, GRADUATE SCHOOL:
Place of higher learning, specialized training, advanced thinking, new ideas, concepts, and theories; place to experiment and try new things; great exchange of ideas, knowledge, and new information; also social concepts and cultural changes.

COLLEGE CAMPUS:

Extension of college influences which reach out and filter into surrounding areas, as well as social and spiritual influences.

COLLEGE DORMITORY:

State of higher learning where you have to live with it day and night or are learning to live with it, not just know about it.

COMMUNICATIONS BLDG:

Area of education, communication, dissemination of ideas, teaching, understanding, accuracy in thought and word.

CORNER HOUSE:

To some a corner house is more prestigious, but it is also on the edge of the block, more exposed to view, at the crossroads; could represent being on the outer edge of things or be a place of decision making.

COURTHOUSE:

Judgment, justice, legal matters of all kinds, dispensation of the law; could represent the reaping of what has been sown or the weighing of matters in one's mind.

DEPARTMENT STORE:

Area of material, monetary, practical affairs having to do with the buying and selling of goods, making and spending money, financial affairs, attitudes, emotions, glamour, appearances, manipulations, deals, making favorable impressions, profit and loss, accountability and balance.

DRUG STORE:

Source of healing remedies, miscellany of ideas; can be local meeting place.

DEFENSE PLANT:

May be a pun on living in a defensive state of consciousness or of working on defenses/defensiveness in some way.

FACTORY:

Run of the mill ideas, repetitious thinking and doing, putting out same old stuff, doing the same things day after day. Predictable, unchanging, stable but boring.

FARMHOUSE:

Simple life or hard work; can mean pleasantness or hardship, depending on dreamer's experiences. Could represent a practical state of mind, good horse sense, unpretentious state.

FOOTBALL ARENA:

Place of cooperation or chaos; area of opposition of two different schools of thought; competition, victory or defeat, no half-way measures.

FORT:

Defense, possibly a consciousness of having to defend yourself constantly or to always have to be on guard against attack. Time to make peace.

GARAGE:

Can be a place to store your car or in some cases a place to store all one's old odds and ends with no room left for the car. Could be a hint to clean up the clutter in your life or a suggestion that you have the tools you need to do the job. Since *car* represents body it can be a kind of glorified dog house, an extension of your beliefs, or the outer fringes of your consciousness.

GAS STATION:

Since the car represents the physical body or preferred lifestyle, this would be a place to refuel, refill yourself or where you get fulfilled. Place to check up, tune up, take care of minor repairs. Might be saying that you need a physical check-up or a pause that refreshes. This may be a place where you can serve or fill the needs of others.

Service Station: This can symbolize your area of service, how you serve others, or be some kind of pun on serving.

GIFT SHOP:
Place where you can show or sell your gifts. May symbolize the many gifts you have to offer others, types of gifts, or possibly your need to give to others.

GYM:
Represents activity, exercise, working-out, keeping in shape, using and perfecting our abilities, sharpening our talents, applying what we know, or the "games we play."

Gym Spectator: Watching, looking at your lifestyle, evaluating, judging yourself, assessing your performance, seeing how you play the game of life.

HARDWARE STORE:
Wide array of home or self-improvement articles, ideas, do-it-yourself kits. May indicate your need to work on or seek out some self-improvement course, or may be pun on the "hardwear" you are giving your body or mind.

HEALTH FOOD STORE:
Good, wholesome food for thought; healthful, helpful ideas and concepts; conscious concerns about your state of health and well-being.

HOSPITAL:
Area of sickness and healing, death and dying, courage, compassion, loving service given to others, life, death, transformation, renewal; time and place to re-evaluate life in its deepest sense.

HOTEL, MOTEL:
Temporary, transient state, attitude, feeling—a phase you are going through, or may symbolize constant activity with much coming and going of ideas. Could depict business or sexual ac-

tivities, depending on the dreamer's associations and feelings.

INDUSTRIAL BUILDINGS:
Industriousness, ambition, desire to produce and achieve on a material level. Business, physical, and financial concerns.

JAIL:
Consciousness of being boxed in, limited, restricted, punished, ostracized, unable to follow your heart's desires, longing for freedom, and need to break out of whatever kind of fear, belief, or thinking that is holding/limiting you.

LIBRARY:
Center of information, learning, knowledge, ideas; consciousness of much knowledge available to you.

MALL:
Material, monetary, practical, functional state of consciousness having to do with making and spending money, acquiring the comforts and material pleasures of life. See *Department Store*, this section.

MENTAL INSTITUTION:
Area of mental disturbance.

Inside: May indicate a need for rest or some kind of help.

Outside: Can indicate feeling left out, out of it, unwanted, ignored, excluded, ostracized, neglected, shunned, set apart. May indicate you are nearing a mental breakdown, close to being institutionalized, needing rest and/or help.

MUSEUM:
Area where old and interesting items and memorabilia of all kinds are kept on display, where they can be seen, remembered, honored. Could be symbolic of your mind and memories of the past which you keep out in the open where

you can see, feel, and review them from time to time.

NURSING HOME:
Consciousness of no longer being able to care for yourself, losing your grip on life, needing help, preparation for death.

OFFICE BUILDING:
Overall consciousness of accountability, management, and planning. Indicates a larger scope in thinking, doing things in a *big way*, a great work to be accomplished; planning and concerns for many people; big business, big deals, big money, big responsibility. Includes the possibility of producing something good for mankind...or great greed.

> **Office:** For most of us this is the consciousness of a job to do, work to be done, business affairs, accounting, discipline, order, and organization. May include frustrations or problems at work. Often it is the main center of activity within a larger building:

> **Accounting Office:** Area of debts and credits, accounting for your words and actions; profit, loss, and ability to pay; balancing, possibly paying karma.

> **Your Office:** May represent your place in the business world.

OUT HOUSES:
These are off-shoots from the main building or idea and as such would depict variations of that concept. For example, the outhouse which served as bathroom would refer to the elimination of something symbolized by the main building. A woodshed may allude to punishment (or whatever you associate with woodshed) in relation to the main house, and so on. May symbolize plain, basic, simple, practical, functional, utilitarian, realistic states of consciousness.

PARSONAGE:
Consciousness of one's ministry to others; desire to serve and uplift; life of service and devotion; prayer, healing, and concern for others; forgiveness, understanding, loving-kindness; practicing what you preach.

POST OFFICE:
Area of public communication; message center; place of accepting, receiving, sorting, and sending messages. May symbolize telepathy, clairvoyance, or your own ability to receive messages from sources outside yourself.

PUBLIC BUILDING:
Consciousness of public opinion, "what will people say"; race consciousness ideas and beliefs; a state of consciousness you do not own or accept as your own, do not claim, do not feel responsible for, or think of as being beyond your control.

PYRAMID:
Mostly associated with Egypt, ancient mystery schools, and wisdom. May depict a firm foundation, long-lastingness, stability, high vibrations, spiritual powers, initiations, and possibly past-life memories. Could imply pyramid schemes for making money, chain letters, and so on.

RESTAURANT:
Food for thought, new ideas, new combinations of old ideas being served, variety of thoughts to choose from. Opening up to new concepts, sharing food for thought, or giving your mental sustenance to others. Position of feeding many or of being served by many.

> **Varieties of Food** or restaurant types may give further clues as to the type of ideas or concepts involved.

SCHOOL:
Attitudes of learning or opportunities for knowledge, experience, growth, expansion of consciousness, mind improvement. Type of school from kindergarten on up would indicate the level of learning. See *College*, also *Classrooms* in this chapter.

SHOPPING CENTER:

Place to shop for new ideas, attitudes, experiences; consciousness of many new ideas and opportunities to choose from; area of desires, self-indulgence, buying ideas for self or others, or may be a glamour consciousness.

SKYSCRAPER:

Possibly would represent a high line of thinking, high ideals, wide range of thought, great vistas of imagination and foresight, far seeing abilities, possibly an ability to be a prophet.

STORE:

A consciousness of your supply or lack of supply of material, mental, or emotional needs.

Clothing Store: New attitudes to buy or try-on for size.

Food Store: Food for thought, new ideas to feed the mind.

TEMPLE:

May represent your physical body, the care you give it, and its condition; or, can be your spiritual state of consciousness, spiritual thinking, spiritual growth, prayer, meditation, blessings, spiritual condition. See Church.

TENT:

Temporary state of mind; changeable, impermanent, insecure, unstable, mobile. Can depict living close to Mother Nature or communion with nature spirits, depending on your associations with tents.

In Tents: May be pun on intense!

WINDMILL:

This can represent the power of the mind and/or of the emotions. The color of the mill would be important. See Wind under Weather.

Homes, Houses, and Rooms

HOUSES:

Houses generally represent more personalized states of consciousness.

Other People's Houses: May symbolize their belief system or state of consciousness, especially when you have a need to know where a person is "coming from" or the basis upon which he is thinking and performing in order to better understand a current situation.

Surrounding Neighborhood: This can depict the general states of consciousness and beliefs which are close to you, a part of you, and influencing you but not where you "stay" mentally. See Neighborhood, also Yard,.

House Next Door: Anything next door implies close to you, bordering on your present state of consciousness. This is usually an extension of your own thinking that you do not yet own or accept as yours; nevertheless, it is part of your thinking and beliefs which you need to recognize and accept.

Looking At New Houses: Looking at newer ideas and states of consciousness that you like better than what you have now. Possibly you have outgrown your present state or beliefs and are ready for some mind expansion. This may also designate mental growth taking place of which you are not yet aware.

Moving Into a Larger House: This implies you have expanded your awareness, talents, understanding, and thinking; have widened your horizons and accepted new ideas.

HOMES:

Your Home: Represents where you live mentally and emotionally, the area of the thoughts you entertain most constantly, the framework of your whole belief system built from early childhood. It represents where you belong, your base, roots, tradition, security, and your usual state of consciousness. It symbolizes the sum-total of all you have been taught to believe.

As you learn and grow, accept new teachings and ideas, your consciousness expands. This is often symbolized by new rooms being added or discovered *as long as the new ideas fit within the existing framework of your old belief system*.

When the new cannot coexist within the old, a new house to represent the new thinking must be found or built. This is where we start building or looking at new houses. We may have several different sets of beliefs and houses in the various areas of our lives.

If you don't own a car, your home *can* represent your physical body and its condition.

HOME ACTIONS:
Your Home Burning: Extreme irritation of mind, emotionally fired up, or all burned up about something; strong need to control your temper and/or change the situation before it destroys you. Dream suggests the act of inner purification or your need to purify your consciousness. Could be a warning of danger or possible ESP sign.

Cleaning Home: This would signify cleansing of old thought patterns and making changes in your usual way of thinking, believing, and perceiving things.

Flooded: Emotionally overcome, overwhelmed, inundated.

Going Home: Usually signifies going back to God (your real home), back to spiritual truths; may represent a return to your usual habits or old ways of thinking and believing.

Lightning Struck: A new truth or idea which suddenly illumines and changes permanently one's way of thinking.

Moving Out: Leaving behind old beliefs, concepts, dogmas, prejudices, limitations.

Torn Down: A state of consciousness which no longer exists.

HOME TYPES:
Manor, Mansion: Consciousness of wealth and abundance of all things. Above-average intelligence; graciousness; many rooms, many areas of ideas, interests, and abilities. This may include spiritual wealth of ideas as well.

New Home (Yours): Would represent a whole new attitude and outlook, new state of consciousness you have just gained or moved into. Can be a whole new awareness, new talent, or new understanding.

Old Home, You Living In It: Can indicate your whole belief system is getting old or out of date, especially if it is looking old and run down in the dream. Possibly the whole neighborhood is run-down. This would indicate a need to update and renovate your ideas.

Old Home You No Longer Occupy: This portrays a place where you used to live mentally. Old ideas, beliefs, ways of perceiving things which are no longer yours but which you may fall back into or return to from time to time.

Often this depicts a state of mind or memories of how you used to think or feel when you lived or visited there. This is a very important symbol to understand, as it tells you that something that has happened in the last day or so or a situation you now find yourself involved in is similar in thought and feeling to the way it was when you lived in the old home. For example: if you felt stifled or inhibited in the old home, your new home, job, relationship, situation, or whatever makes you feel similarly stifled and limited. This can be a warning or a simple statement that, "This is how you *really* feel about this matter."

Parent's Home: This has many possibilities. It may represent the place where you were loved and cared for or where you were misunderstood and neglected, according to your associations. It can be a state of childhood dreams and memories, childish conceptions, innocence, freedom, or a sense of security, having someone strong being responsible for you, or possibly a sickly or very unhappy time.

It can symbolize the state of your relationship with your parents, family bonds, or family memories of all kinds as a whole or a particular event which stands out in your mind. It may denote the general belief system and patterns of thinking taught at an early age or your feelings of being limited, deprived, and restricted by overbearing parents. Think carefully what your parent's home means to you and write this out for future reference.

To visit your parent's home in dreams is to go back to that state of consciousness, that feeling, those memories. This may be because something currently happening in your life recalls these feelings to mind or may be a wish to return to an old, safe, secure feeling you once knew.

Where You Used to Live: It matters not whether this was *your* home, that of your parents, your grandparents, an apartment, or vacation spot. It is *any place you have lived*, however temporarily. This implies that the situation, relationship, or circumstances in which you now find yourself are the same as those you experienced "where you used to live." See *Old home*, this chapter.

ROOMS:
Rooms in houses represent individualized areas of your consciousness or concern.

Attic: Higher levels of mind, super-consciousness, High Self.

Back room: Back of your mind.

Basement: Subconscious mind, lower levels of mind.

Bathroom: Place to cleanse, release, relieve, let go of all that is no longer useful. Represents cleansing of ideas, emotions, problems, old hurts, old habits. A room to refresh and renew. Can also depict need for privacy.

Can't Find: no place "to go," no acceptable way to release or cleanse your emotions, no way to get things "out of your system." This depicts the urgency of your present need to unload your hurts, fears, or worries. Can mean your body or soul is desperately needing the release of tears, forgiveness, or whatever. This can be on a physical level, an emotional need, or quite often both.

Commode: Signifies the release of old feelings, emotions, ideas, prejudices, problems; getting things out of your system, letting go. See *Elimination System* under *Body.*

Stopped Up Commode: Real blockage in your ability to let go, express your thoughts and feelings, release your hurts.

Urine: Emotions and feelings of any kind.

Feces: Old ideas, habits, beliefs, prejudices, problems, thought forms, or materialism which need/s to be eliminated.

Locked Bathroom: Implies you have locked or blocked all acceptable ways to release. Your urgency is depicting your urgent need to tell yourself it is okay to cry or to express your needs and feelings.

Shower: Place for cleansing and forgiveness, getting a fresh new start, feeling clean and good, washing away the old. Clear water can represent spiritual cleansing.

Tub: Place for cleansing and new start as in *shower.*

Tub Stopped Up: May represent your inability (so far) to let go of your problems and emotions, a symbol that your cleansing is not yet complete, something is blocked.

Tub Overflowing: Emotions overflowing, need for immediate action on your part.

Bedroom: Area of rest, sex, marriage, integration, retreat, rest, dreams, sleep, quiet space, privacy.

Small Bedroom: May indicate feeling cramped by your mate or that you don't allow yourself enough space, rest, quiet time. Possibly you are in a situation that feels restricted, fenced-in, limited. You may need more privacy, quiet, space, or alone time.

Your Bedroom: Your private space, where you belong, your place in the world, your own little world; retreat, privacy, or place to pray and meditate.

Board Room: Place where plans are discussed and decisions made. Can be a pun on "bored."

Class Room: Learning situation, place of knowledge, wisdom, information, understanding, education; lessons we are learning in the school of life, possibly need to learn. May be a pun on class, classy, or "out of your class."

Conference Room: Place to plan, discuss, confer, confront, or defend our ideas, ideals, plans, and projects.

Den: Family room, family situation, togetherness, game playing.

Dining Room: Area of consumption of food for thought, digestion of ideas; possible discussion and evaluation of ideas. Can be leftovers, same old stuff warmed-over, or wonderful new ideas.

Royal Dining Room: Suggests God's abundance, wealth of ideas, all good things within the dreamer's reach or being served for the asking.

Dormitory: Suggests area of learning along with others, exchange of ideas and cultures.

Family Room: See *Den*, this chapter

Front Room: Up front, exposed, open, in full view, readily accessible, not hidden.

Game Room: Area of playing games with ourselves and others. Competition. Can be fun and games or playing parts, not being our real selves.

Hall: Area of changes, going from one state of consciousness to another, moving through different areas of thought or belief. Can depict a channel, process of channeling, or the Hall of Learning.

Large Hall: Can be a pun on a large "haul" you are making, an overhaul in your life, or a large change.

Long Hall: May mean the "long haul," a long way to go; much change in store; going through many, many stages; taking many steps.

Hidden Room(s): Unexplored or unknown areas of consciousness, beliefs, understanding, abilities, hidden talents, hidden knowledge; unexplored areas of mind or ideas.

Kitchen: Place of food or thought preparation, storage, or disposal. Also of gathering, mixing, and even digesting of ideas. Also represents the heart of the home, the center of activity.

Laundry Room: A place to clean up your act, your attitudes, wash away yesterday's problems, refreshing, restoring, making the best of what you have.

Library: Area of learning, study, information readily available to you, within your consciousness. An *upstairs* library may represent higher knowledge, infinite wisdom, cosmic consciousness.

Living Room: Area of daily mental activities, thoughts, and attitudes; your basic beliefs about yourself, who and what you are. The quality of thoughts are symbolized by the type of furnishings.

Beautiful Furnishings: Lovely thoughts, positive attitudes, prayers, loving-kindness, caringness.

Shabby Furnishings: Dirty words, unkind thoughts, careless habits; sloppy, unloving, or negative thinking.

New Rooms: Building new rooms or discovering them indicates newly formed or realized talents, abilities, qualities, or awareness you didn't know you had. Mental expansion and growth. Can be unexplored areas of your mind.

Nursery: Area for your new project, ideal, or idea to grow in; a special place in your mind or heart. A nurturing place.

Office: Can be your work room, where you plan, organize, get things done in a business-like manner, take responsibility, give and receive orders, figure up the costs.

Projection Room: Symbol of your need or ability to project an idea or an ideal, your capacity to visualize, to plan ahead.

Reception Room: A place to receive or be received, meeting point for introduction to new concepts.

Rest Room: May refer to a place or a need of resting or of giving yourself time or room to rest, relax, unload your problems, emotions, burdens. See *Bathroom*, this chapter.

Room Within a Room: May represent inner sanctum, secret closet, prayer or meditation room; an inner, sacred part of yourself where others cannot go.

Sewing Room: Place of creativity, of putting things together in your mind, mending old attitudes, or problems.

Storage Room: Spot for putting away ideas, concepts or problems we do not care to look at or put to use at present but don't want to throw away either.

Study: Can represent a place of study or imply the need to study and apply yourself more.

Sun-Filled Rooms: Spiritual enlightenment pouring in, good understanding in this area, or a spiritual place.

Utility Room: May refer to your basic needs and functions, or may be pun on utilizing what you have.

Waiting Room: Consciousness of waiting for something to happen, or possibly a need to wait and not act now.

Your Room: Your own private space, your personal state of consciousness; your inner thoughts and feelings, hopes and wishes; your retreat; your place in the world, where you belong. It may also represent your place in society, business world, or your established identity. See *Bedroom, Yours,* this chapter.

Parts of Buildings

These would represent particular areas or components in your beliefs and general state of consciousness.

ARCHES:
Support.

ARCHWAY:
An opening with no barriers, doors, or gates. Free, easy passage, total freedom to come and go.

ALTER:
Symbol of religion, devotion, worship, prayer, piety, meditation, answers to prayer, decision making. See *Church.*

ATTIC:
Upper levels of mind, highest state, superconsciousness, or your High Self.

BASEMENT:
Represents your foundation, basis, or your subconscious mind.

BELLS:
Doorbells, phones, alarms, any kind of bell ringing in dreams serves to draw your attention to whatever is said or done next—it is a point of emphasis. An alarm bell could simply depict something you need to be alarmed about.

Church Bells: May depict harmony, call to worship, prayer, or devotion; a reminder of your religious heritage; a call to return to church. Can be a happy sound of wedding bells and good news, a warning or toll of death and mourning.

Telephone Bell: Message for you to give or receive.

Other Bells: Can be warnings, signals, attention-grabbers.

BLOCKS:
These may indicate building blocks or stumbling blocks, mental blocks, blockages and limitations to our progress. They often represent our present lesson, the specific limiting fear or idea which we must work through before moving on.

BRICKS:
Can mean same as blocks but usually indicate small, individual thoughts, ideas, hardened thought forms. We often build a situation or condition one brick (thought) at a time. Bricks can imply the hard shell or veneer we put on the outside of our consciousness, the walls we build.

Dark Red Bricks: May represent karmic conditions we have built and now have to live with.

Yellow Brick: Old symbol of self-knowledge, recognition of one's own dominion over material things.

CEILING:
Your mentality in general and its condition.

Plaster Falling: Possible need for a new way of thinking or may be a warning that you are under too much pressure and may "fall apart."

Splitting, Cracking: May say you are cracking-up; could indicate faulty logic, misconceptions; might denote mental expansion.

CHIMNEY:

Place to safely vent or let off steam, smoke, fire. Could represent the flow of kundalini, agni yoga, the fire of purification and burning away of the dross, or may be symbolic of inspiration. Can depict a channel of energies or the channeling process, depending on the feeling and action of the dream.

CLOSET:

Place to store your ideas, emotions, feelings, attitudes, memories, talents, fears, hurts, pet peeves, and old problems you don't want to see. A place to hide your true feelings or the truth about a matter. Can represent storage or denial. Note what items you are stuffing in or taking out. You could be pulling out old memories which need to be reviewed, understood, forgiven and cleansed. Could imply "Go into your closet and pray," depicting a place of prayer, devotion, meditation, or act of being alone with God.

CORNER:

Being in a corner may depict "cornered," stuck, rejected, trapped, no way out.

CUBICLE:

Limit, protection, safety, privacy, structure, boundary; a nook within the larger area of the building.

DOOR:

May represent an open or shut mind, your freedom to come and go, entrance, exit, escape, opening, accessibility, or opportunity. Note who opens or shuts the gate or door.

Back Door: Hidden, subtle, secret, private, escape.

Closed: Unwillingness to enter, unreceptive attitude, or need to knock, ask, try, let your wishes be known.

Double Doors: Double opportunity or double-trouble, might be a multiple choice.

Front Door: Available, out in the open, in plain sight, reachable.

Golden Door: Spiritual opportunity or opening.

Glass Doors: May represent ability to see ahead, see into the future, view what lies ahead.

Locked or Nailed Shut: Inaccessible, closed, not for you.

Many Doors: Multiple choices, many opportunities.

New Door: New opportunity, chance, way, path.

No Door: No chance, no way to get there from here. Try elsewhere.

Open: Available, ready for you, wide open opportunity, way to go, or can be openness to receive.

Revolving Doors: Could represent going in circles, multiple chances, choices that go nowhere, ever-changing possibilities, or a pun on evolving situation.

Storm Doors: Extra protection. May signify a need for you to take extra precautions, use extreme care with this opportunity, or can be a sure thing. Possibly you need to seek extra help in this situation.

DOORKNOB:

Means of opening up to opportunities; involves your reaching out, making a move, helping yourself.

DOOR KNOCKER:
Implies asking for admittance, knocking, seeking, prayer activity, persistence, "going for it," action.

DRAWBRIDGE:
Protection or defense from intruders or unwanted situations.

ELECTRIC WIRES:
Carriers of currents of energy, thought, or even body currents. Implies your connection to the power source, ability to make things go, channeling energies, or may represent the state of your nervous system.

PLUGS:
Ability to plug-in, tune-in, make connections to power source.

SWITCH:
Control of power flow, ability to direct or control amount of power.

ELEVATOR:
Way up or down.

Down: Can warn that your situation or action is degrading, you are putting yourself down or allowing another to do so.

Up: Someone may be lifting you up in prayer or you may have a need to lift up your sights, pray, meditate, elevate your thoughts, aim for greater heights, think highly of yourself.

FENCE:
Protection, support, boundary, limitation. May be a pun on offense.

FLOOR:
Foundation, principle, basis; where you make a stand.

New: New foundation, understanding, principle.

Rotting Floor: Poor foundation or basis, won't hold up, need for more research and understanding in this area.

Sinking or Uneven Floor: A poor foundation, need for a better understanding.

Slanting Floor: You may have the wrong slant on things, or this could indicate a bias in your thinking; prejudice in the area represented by the building, room, or both.

FIREPLACE:
Source of warmth, comfort, burning desire, can be heart of the home or situation. Can represent the fires of purification, inner cleansing, inspiration, love and warmth given out. Dead or low-burning fire can mean low energy level, disinterest, discouragement, or disheartenment.

Sparks from Fire: Sparks can be scattered bits of anger flying about which could cause trouble. Can also denote the Spark of Divinity in us and as such can be light given out, inspiration, enthusiasm, the creative spark of genius, sparks of ideas, the ability to give love, light, and warmth to others, or the need to do so.

FOUNDATION:
Basis, footing, basic ideas and understanding that hold the whole belief system together. If it crumbles, the whole house goes. A crack in the foundation can be a warning.

FRAMEWORK:
Basic teachings, beliefs, ideas we have been taught from childhood which we use as an outline in which to fit all our new ideas and teachings. It is a frame of reference, a balancing point.

FRONT OF BUILDING:
Image, projection of consciousness, outer appearances.

False front: False or misleading image, pretense, false impressions deliberately made.

FURNACE:
Same as *fireplace*, or may represent the condition of your heart or of your stomach. Fire burning low can indicate low energy or even disheartenment.

New furnace: Taking new heart in the situation, new interest and enthusiasm.

Old: Worn out, disheartened, disillusioned, heart isn't in it, little or no energy and enthusiasm, or a heart problem.

GATE:
Way through or around obstacles, opportunity. See *Door*.

GLASS:
Represents a see-through object, barrier, or protection. Lets in the light, allows you to view what is beyond. Obvious separation. Sometimes signifies border between planes of existence. We can see but not touch.

Broken Glass: Broken barriers, potentially dangerous situation; can be a break-through or a tough break.

KEY:
Access, dominion, opportunity, control, key to success, ownership and responsibility.

Crossed Keys: Ancient symbol for the disciple Peter; may also represent the "keys to the kingdom" or hidden doctrine, secret, esoteric teachings.

Golden Key: Key to spiritual riches, spiritual dominion, growth.

Heavy Key: Heavy responsibility.

Large Key: Great amount of control, responsibility, dominion.

Lost Key: Lost or given up control of self, situation, responsibility, or opportunity.

Many Keys: Multiple responsibilities.

LAMPS, LIGHTS:
Representative of enlightenment, awareness, insights, perception.

LEDGE:
Outer edge, as far as you can go. You may feel you are literally out on a limb or ledge.

LOCK:
Security, protection, safety measure.

Big Lock: Extra security, doubly-protected.

MAIL BOX:
Receptacle for receiving information. Can imply an important message or messages coming, or if full it can say messages (in dreams or otherwise) have come to you but have not yet been read or heeded. Condition of box may indicate your receptivity to messages **or** your ability to be a channel.

Full Mail Box: Messages sent but not received, opened, valued, accepted, digested, or heeded. Advice not taken; can be a warning or ESP of much interest, many messages coming your way.

House Mailbox: Receptacle for personal messages coming to you.

Rural, Road-side Box: Receptacle for both sending and receiving personal messages. May be channel for sending and receiving messages, ESP, or whatever.

MAIN FLOOR:
Conscious level of mind or main area of concern.

PADDED WALLS:
Protection, possibly from yourself, your own words and actions; imprisoned; out of touch, sight, sound.

PATIO:
An extension of what main building represents with more openness; receptive state of consciousness. May be a combination of mental and spiritual states.

PILLARS:
Support, backing, upholding, dependability, durability. Can be the pillars (strong or supporting beliefs) of the mind. If colored, black represents the negative side and white the positive. Together these represent the balance or polarity of both. If you stand between them, look to see if you are balanced between the two or stand more to one side than another.

Two Pillars: These often represent the higher mind and the lower mind working together. To stand between these would show good balance.

PORCH:
On the edge of the type of consciousness represented by the building. Could be outer limits or openness.

RAFTERS:
Support and foundation for roof, mentality, ideals; the mental framework you hang ideas on.

RAILING:
Support, protection, balance, safety, limit; also a barrier.

ROOF:
Protection of your consciousness, mentality, beliefs, habits, mores, traditions. May depict your mental state, ideals, or a high point in your consciousness.

Leaking Roof: Can be a chink in your armor, protection, or defenses; a sign of something "getting through to you"; distraction, annoyance, interference, unwanted influences. Can be emotional problems, hurts, unshed tears, or fears seeping in affecting, obscuring, tarnishing, or coloring your mentality, implying a need to repair, confront, or resolve this situation. May be an intrusion of another's thoughts, emotions, or will power.

New Roof: Whole new attitude, new ideals, new sense of protection.

Roof Falling In: Can symbolize ideals crashing down or be a warning of this. May imply a tendency to "wait until the roof falls in" on you before you make a move.

Roofless: No limitations, you can go as high as you please, or can be pun for ruthless.

SHUTTERS:
Denotes a way to shut out people, ideas, and enlightenment or to limit visibility and perception.

Opening: Opening your mind to the light, to new ideas.

Closed: Implies not wanting to see or face a situation.

SIDEWALK:
Hard path, hard way to go; or, may be solid footing, sure, convenient, or public way to go.

No Sidewalk: No path, no easy access, no way to get there.

Private: Your own way, your own particular path to follow.

Public: Way most people go, a race consciousness path, or may say "Everybody does it."

STAIRS:
Steps, footing; steps we take; one step at a time; a step in the right direction.

Bottom Step: Can represent the first step up in life or may depict the bottom level, bottom line, last step downward.

Coming Down: Represents moving away from God, moving down to subconscious levels, or may be lowering yourself.

Going Up: Moving closer to God, meditation, prayer, communion, moving on up in the world, raising your consciousness, moving to higher levels of mind, a step up, or taking steps in the right direction.

Missing Step: May say you have missed an important step in whatever you are preparing to do, or possibly you have to do some "high stepping" to reach your goal.

Spiral: Usually represents meditation or beginning of astral travel.

Top Step: Highest level, high as you can go at this time.

SUN PORCH OR DECK:
Your place in the sun.

TOWER, TURRET:
Higher consciousness, a higher viewpoint, lofty ideas and ideals, overview, foresight, far-seeing abilities; or, can represent setting yourself up

higher than others, false presumptions, or a false sense of security.

TUNNEL OR CAVE:
May be a dark passage, a reference to "tunnel vision," or suggest going through a mountain or obstacle rather than around it. Suggests subconscious areas of mind, may represent something like the light at the end of the tunnel, seeing the end of a difficulty, or tunneling your way through a difficult situation.

UPSTAIRS:
Higher levels of consciousness.

WALL OR FENCE:
Obstacle, limitation, boundary, or protection. Walls can represent your mental limits, barriers, prejudices, obstinacy, fixed thinking, or old habit patterns which obstruct your thinking and understanding abilities. If the walls were hindrances in your dream, this indicates they need to be removed in order for you to be able to perceive new and better ways or to learn new things.

Breaking Down Walls: Breaking through barriers, obstacles, and limitations; overcoming blockages.

WALLPAPER:
Out where all the world can see, highly visible, something you can't hide; a cover-up of past "designs" or mistakes, old patterns; a new look, renovation of old ideas and attitudes, or "letting it all hang out."

WELL:
Your individual supply, source of pure spirit.

WIDOW'S WALK:
Traditionally a place of hope, worry, concern, watching, waiting; unsure of the outcome.

WINDOW:
Represents your point of view, the way you look at the world, perception, clear-seeing, understanding, insight, outlook.

Clean, Clear: Clear perception of the situation.

Curtained: Obstructed view, clouded, veiled, filtered, only partially clear.

Dirty: Perception clouded by negative emotions, doubt, fear, prejudice, misunderstanding, or emotional blockage which is obscuring your view.

Frame: Ability to perceive is limited by your "frame of mind." Possibly you are blocking something.

Looking in the Window: Looking within yourself, soul searching.

Looking Out: Pausing to think, to dream, to be open to new ideas or guidance; daydreaming, getting some new perspective, a different view of things.

Picture Window: Implies perfection, seeing things as you would like them to be, to picture what you want.

Stained Glass: Could represent spiritual rays, healing lights, prayer, devotion, beauty, spiritual enlightenment, church, and feelings associated with church. If one color predominates it may indicate the color you need for healing, or the color itself could indicate a quality you need to cultivate. (See chapter on *Color*.)

My Own Building Symbols

CHAPTER **19**

Clothing

Clothing represents your idea of how you look to others, your outer appearance, attitudes; type of ideas and emotions that you feel, "put on," act out. It may imply your sense of protection, style, fashion or your total self-esteem. For the best interpretation, recall what you associate with the particular type of clothing, outfit, or costume seen in the dream and go from there.

Example: Jeans may be work clothing to some but depict relaxation and recreation to others. Some clothes are sexy, some are dressy, some are business-like. Clothing may be of mixed styles such as boots you wear for horseback riding worn with a shirt you associate with going dancing and a business suit worn over that. In this case, take the associations from each part and put them all together. This combination may say that under your business-like exterior you are really a sportsman (or woman) at heart, or may say, "I'd rather be dancing!"

BIZARRE OUTFIT:
May be saying that you feel ridiculous in the situation you are now in, depict an absurd attitude you are taking, or emphasize a particular part of the body.

LACK OF CLOTHING:
Can indicate a feeling of great vulnerability in the area represented by the part of your body exposed. See *The Body and Its Parts*.

NUDITY:
Indicates a feeling of defenselessness, a lack of protection, a fear of being exposed to public view or criticism, being unprepared for a situation, or shows your concern about having your deeds or misdeeds revealed. It can be a pun on "getting down to the bare facts," may simply say you have no encumbering prejudices or attitudes to get in your way or that you have no opinion or attitude one way or another. See chapter on *Nudity*.

Generally speaking, it is not **what** is done but the **way** it is done—the **attitude** behind the action—which makes the big difference in your spiritual growth. It is better to refrain from giving altogether than to give grudgingly. Your clothing in dreams reflects your attitudes and feelings and is therefore quite important in your dream interpretation.

Clothing Descriptions

BEAUTIFUL, EXPENSIVE:
May represent beautiful attitudes, love, kindness, graciousness, compassion, and general purity of thought. Might also indicate a desire to show off, make an impression, or depict an exaggerated sense of self-worth, a super-star.

FAMILY CLOTHING:
Need to clean up family matters, attitudes, problems, misunderstandings, or hurts.

FAVORITE CLOTHES:
Ideas and beliefs we feel comfortable with; that which is suitable, tested, known, familiar, and usable.

FORMAL:

Refinement, good taste, graciousness of attitude. Could be an attitude you "put on" for special occasions only! May represent pride, an attitude of showing off, pretense, snobbery, aloofness, and lack of real warmth. May be the outer appearance of "having it all," of luxury, aristocracy, prosperity; choice of the good things in life.

ILL-FITTING CLOTHES:

Attitudes which do not fit with your overall lifestyle and beliefs or present understanding. Something unsuitable for you.

> **Too Large:** May hint you need to "grow into" these attitudes, especially if you like the clothing. If you dislike it, then it is definitely not right for you.

> **Too Small:** May indicate that you have outgrown these ideas and attitudes and need to find something more "your size."

NEW CLOTHING:

Would represent putting on new attitudes, having a new understanding, taking a new look, seeing things in a different way, new perceptions, new slant, changes in your thinking-feeling nature.

OLD CLOTHING:

Could depict old attitudes and ideas that need to be updated, replaced; no longer "suitable" for you. You may tend to cling to the old or the past too much for your own growth.

OLD-FASHIONED CLOTHES:

In a modern setting this would indicate out-of-date attitudes that no longer apply to modern situations and New Age thinking. May represent archaic ideas and beliefs or may indicate that you are living too much in the past. This might also represent a past lifetime if everything else in

the dream is also antiquated, or it may indicate a karmic situation.

OTHER'S CLOTHING:

Need to cleanse your attitudes, prejudices, or hard feelings about this person or this aspect of you.

USED CLOTHES:

This could imply you are taking on other people's attitudes, opinions, and prejudices and not thinking things out for yourself, not making your own decisions, doing your "own thing."

YOUR CLOTHES:

Cleansing of your personal attitudes, prejudices, habits, patterns, feelings, hurts.

Condition of Clothing

DIRTY:

May symbolize a "dirty mind" or negative thinking. Obvious need for a cleansing of thoughts and attitudes.

HANGING ON THE LINE:

May mean putting your ideas, hopes, or wishes "on the line"; making a positive statement; can be airing out your attitudes and feelings, hanging out the family linen (for all the world to see), getting things out in the open, letting everybody know how you feel about a matter. May imply your "hang-ups" or "hanging in there."

> **Taking Clothing Off the Line:** Getting rid of hang-ups.

> **Folding:** Would be putting things in order, into their right places.

TORN, RIPPED:

Some flaws in our thinking, lack of cohesiveness, repairs needed in the way we think and feel, unsuitable, unusable, or shabby attitudes.

Things We Do with Clothing

BORROWING:
Borrowing ideas, beliefs, or attitudes of others.

BUYING NEW:
Finding new ideas, beliefs, and attitudes we like and feel comfortable with. Updating our thinking in general.

IRONING:
Act of ironing things out in your mind, smoothing out your relationships with others, working out the kinks, straightening out your attitudes, eliminating the "rough spots" in your life and affairs. Notice the kind of things you are ironing and check the symbolism of these.

HANGING ON CLOTHES HANGERS:
This could denote our "hang-ups" or may be setting our things in order.

MENDING:
Act of repairing or our need to make restitution, correct our outlook, position, or make amends for something said or done. Mending the holes or flaws in your thinking.

OUTGROWN CLOTHES:
Outgrown ideas and beliefs.

PACKING:
Getting it all together, or can be unsettled, ready for a change, ready to go.

> **Suitcase:** Receptacle for "getting it all together," especially your attitudes. May also say it's "in the bag," or can symbolize vacation, travel, freedom, mobility, changes.

STEALING:
Stealing another's ideas and taking them for your own.

TAKING OFF:
Eliminating cumbersome attitudes, getting down to the bare necessities, getting to personal feelings.

TRYING ON:
Trying out new ideas and attitudes to see if they fit with our lifestyle and outlook.

WASHING:
Implies a need to clean up your act, cleanse your attitudes in some area. You may need to forgive yourself or another or get rid of the emotions and prejudices ingrained in the article or in the part of your body it covers. Whose clothes are you washing?

Hats

Represent the attitudes you show others most, your mental outlook, your various jobs, talents (many hats), personalities, and aspects of yourself; how you cover up or display what your really think, how you protect your ideas.

There are many, many kinds of hats. If the hat in your dream is the one you use for a particular kind of job, then it would symbolize your attitude about that job. If it is one you wear for other special occasions, it would denote your attitude about that. Hats may also denote a type of work or position, like a captain's hat.

TRYING ON:
Trying out new ideas and outlooks, new ways of perceiving things. Often has to do with being confronted with a new situation or idea and your trying to find a suitable stand or position for dealing with it. Looking for an attitude or handle that suits you and feels comfortable.

A HAT YOU DON'T OWN:
Would be symbolic of an attitude or feeling that you associate with that specific kind of hat which you may have but don't "own" or admit.

A HAT INCONGRUENT WITH YOUR OUTFIT:
May suggest that your attitude is unrealistic in some way.

KINDS OF HATS:

Beanie: Skull cap; often indicative of brains, mind, intellect, ability to use your head, or can be a special, spiritual hat worn for prayer and devotion.

Bonnet: Can be old-fashioned, out of date, or may depict tunnel vision.

Cowboy Hat: Many of these are worn by people who never came near a cow. Could refer to race consciousness, a put-on, or a go-along-with-the-crowd idea or outlook.

Fancy Hat: Indicative of worldly attitudes, artificiality, pomp, social climbing, showing off, desire to be seen.

Hard Hat: Can represent hard-headedness and fixed thinking, or may imply danger and a need for you to protect yourself. Could imply you need to be on your guard.

Helmet: Protection, possibly saying you do not want to see, hear, or participate in some matter. Can imply you do not want anyone to get too close, especially if you wear armor with it, or may represent your fear of getting hurt and the mental barriers you raise to protect yourself.

High Hat, Top Hat: Can represent dignity, pomp, and special occasions or be haughty, holier-than-thou, "putting on the dog" type attitudes, or can be an incongruent attitude when worn with informal clothing. Could be a pun on being ridiculous.

Many Hats: Many attitudes, abilities, interests, talents, or expertise in many fields. Many aspects of yourself, ability to change from one idea, area, expertise to another with ease or as needed to suit each occasion. May be great versatility but also could be instability, insincerity, or irresponsibility.

New Hats: Trying on or "buying" new attitudes or beliefs.

Someone Else's Hat: Using another's ideas, attitudes, or prejudices; not thinking things out for yourself.

Straw Hat: Light, summery; may depict a light-hearted, care-free attitude.

Uniform Hats: Can refer to war-like attitudes or may mean conformity, getting in line with everyone else, taking orders from others, no original thinking going on.

Shoes

Shoes symbolize beliefs, basis of understanding, the foundations on which you stand and the protection of these. They can denote barriers to understanding, stiffness and inflexibility, or the support of your beliefs depending on the type of shoes and how they feel on your feet. Some feel best when barefoot, others prefer sandals, tennis shoes, heavy, supportive shoes or boots. Consider your own preferences, associations, and feelings about the kind of shoe before deciding its meaning for you.

BAREFOOT:
Can designate playful attitudes, feeling sure-footed, free, uninhibited, relaxed, joyous, natural, unaffected, having a good grip; feeling or understanding of a situation or being in close touch with the earth. Or barefoot can mean poverty, discomfort, embarrassment, lack of mobility, being inhibited and unable to move. Can denote a total lack of understanding or protection.

BUYING NEW SHOES:
New understanding or beliefs which can be helpful or inhibiting. Note fit, color, kind, and your personal associations with that type of shoe.

HEEL:
Could be a pun on acting like a heel or on healing. Heel is also traditional weak point (Achilles heel). Might mean heel as in submission.

High Heels: Fancy, feminine, dressy, sexy; impractical for some, a necessity for others.

Low Heels: Can mean practicality, sure-footed, comfortable, down-to-earth, sensible, or unfeminine.

LOSING SHOES:

May imply loss of understanding in a matter, not comprehending the situation or person involved; losing freedom, power to move, protection of your rights, beliefs, or understanding, especially if you feel uncomfortable without shoes. To those who enjoy being barefoot it may imply freedom, being in touch with the situation, basics, facts.

REMOVING SHOES:

Taking off all barriers to understanding, getting a better feel of the situation, putting both feet on the ground; good foundation.

SOLE OF SHOE:

Can be a symbol for soul; may mean sole as in being the only one or soul as a spiritual basis of understanding.

TYING SHOES:

Putting it all together, tying up loose ends, getting a firm grip on your understanding, or a working grasp of the situation.

KINDS OF SHOES

Ballet Slippers: Understanding the principles of balance, grace, beauty of movement, poise, harmony with others.

Boots: Extra strong and tough exterior to protect one's beliefs. Can represent impenetrable barriers, hiding, or over-protecting one's understanding. Sometimes this can be an outer symbol of inner tender-heartedness with a tough coat for security.

Boots, Dress: Same as shoes.

Boots, Heavy: Solid protection, ruggedness, power to do a job, readiness for anything.

Clogs: May be pun on clogged understanding or loose ideals and beliefs you don't stick with.

Gym Shoes, All Kinds: Firm but flexible foundation, easy going, agility, mobility, comfortable to live with outlook; playful attitudes.

House-slippers: Comfortable understanding; relaxed, informal attitudes you can live with.

Large Shoes: Room to grow, space to move or expand, much learning or understanding necessary to fill the shoes, or could be totally unsuitable. Could imply a broad base of understanding or learning to live up to bigger, greater concepts.

Misfit Shoes: Mis-understanding!

Mocassins: Following or belief in the Indian way of life, moving gently on the earth, respecting earth, trees, nature, and all beings. Walking softly, peacefully. Standing tall.

Muddy Shoes: Memories, emotions, and old beliefs still clinging to your understanding like barnacles. Need to cleanse these.

New Shoes: New, better outlook, understanding, concepts.

Nurses Shoes: Understanding based on service, helpfulness, healing, compassion for others.

Old Shoes: Old, comfortable beliefs and understandings you hate to part with. If ratty-looking may imply a need for some new concepts.

Sandals: Light, easy, comfortable, open understanding, not much support or hindrance. Can be light-footedness, dress up, or party-type understanding; sufficient and comfortable for some or frivolous and unnecessary to others.

Tight Shoes: Attitudes which do not fit the situation, tight squeeze, painful predicament, unbearable, unsuitable.

Miscellaneous Clothing

APRON, WOMAN'S:
Woman's work.

Apron, Variations: A carpenter's apron or other strictly (or used-to-be) male-type aprons would of course refer to doing a man's job.

ARMOR:
Tough outer coat, defense, impenetrable barrier, outer protection of our existing attitudes; may depict resistance, hard feelings, hardness, or immovability of ideas and attitudes.

BATHING SUIT:
Attitude for play, spiritual activity, "strutting your stuff," or tanning your hide.

BELT:
May refer to "tightening your belt," preparing for what is to come, belting it out, getting "belted," hardships, restrictions.

BIKINI:
Basic minimum of protection, maximum exposure.

BLOUSE:
These emphasize the chest, the heart, feelings you have under cover.

BRA:
Upliftment, protection, projection, putting up a "good front," sexy attitudes held in check, maternal or nurturing feelings.

Padded: False front, exaggeration, pretense, padding the truth.

Braless: No control, no discipline, sexy, "hanging loose."

CAPE, CLOAK:
Can be cloak of pride, mystery, attitude you hide behind.

CHILDREN'S CLOTHING:
Childish attitudes or behavior patterns.

COAT:
Protection or cover-up for attitudes and beliefs.

Fur Coat: May imply sensitivity and sensuousness; can imply you are touchy about your attitudes and beliefs or represent the animal attitudes you put on for protection.

Overcoat: Protection, cover-up for your ideas and more personal beliefs. In some cases this can represent your physical body.

Old: Old beliefs no longer applicable or worthy of you. May also represent the physical body which we lay aside at death like an old garment we no longer wish to wear, and as such represent death if it is tossed aside.

Rain Coat: Protection from emotions, unpleasant conditions

COSTUME:
Falsity, playfulness, a light-hearted attitude; a false impression, false pride, putting on an act, hiding the truth.

COVERALL:
Covers all, protects all, hides all. Also refers to dirty work, job to be done.

DIAPERS:
Babyish attitudes, actions, and emotions. Dependency on others, messy situations,

preparation for coming changes, need for a change, or need to grow up.

Changing Diapers: A need to clean up or change childish habits and attitudes or to change your attitude regarding your new project, idea, or ideal.

Messy Diapers: This implies a need to clean up your act, clean the mess you have created by childish attitudes or habits, restore peace and harmony, undo the harm done. See *Elimination System* under *The Body and Its Parts.*

DRESS:
Feminine attire and outlook. May also mean intuitive, receptive, passive, gentle, or possibly feminine wile.

EMBLEM:
Can be marks or rewards for service given, climbing to a higher rank, leadership abilities acquired, or can be a purely ornamental or social-climbing device, something meant to impress others of your worth or credibility. Can say, "money talks."

GIRDLE:
Represents attitudes that bind, limit, restrain, and restrict. May be the pain we suffer in order to "people please" or beliefs which are uncomfortable to live with but can be stretched. May depict support or the lack of it.

GLOVES:
How you handle things, getting a handle on something, working things out; may represent a hard job if they are work gloves or handling things in a childish manner if mittens. Look at the type of glove for further meaning.

HAND-ME-DOWNS:
Using someone else's attitudes and ideas, not your own.

HEADBAND:
Can denote control of thinking, discipline; may signify rebellion, or may symbolize a particular tribe or group connection.

HOSE:
Flexibility of understanding, using what you know to best advantage.

HOUSECOAT:
Quick cover-up of personal feelings, attitudes, privacy; or, if worn continuously, may depict sloppiness, laziness, carelessness, or a low in self-esteem.

JEANS:
Non-conformist, free-style, "I don't care" attitude, especially if they are old and faded. (This may not apply to fancy name brands.) Easy-going style, live and let-live outlook. It some cases jeans may stand for rebellion, poverty, dirty jobs, or just plain hard work.

Cut-off Jeans: Adapting, making do with what you have on hand, cutting things off short.

Fancy Name-Brand Jeans: One-up-man-ship, show-off, snobbish attitudes, or may be an attempt to keep up with the crowd. Dressing to be accepted by snobs and those judging others by outward appearances and labels only.

JUMP SUIT:
Ready for work or play, capable, prepared for all contingencies or emergencies.

KNIT CLOTHING:
Flexible attitudes.

LACY CLOTHING:

May be pun on being able to see right through you or another, an apparent situation, or may be an elaborate "put-on."

LINEN:

Expensive tastes; beautiful, natural, untainted attitudes.

MATERNITY CLOTHES:

Motherly attitudes, expectancy, protection, nurturing, room to grow and expand.

MONK'S ROBE:

Spiritual attitudes, devotion, service, love, ancient wisdom, humility, compassion, spiritual learning.

MITTENS:

Childish attitudes toward work or service.

NEGLIGEE:

Sexy ideas, desire to attract or interest, "see-through" attitudes, suggestiveness, or could be a pun on negligence.

OVERALLS:

Can refer to "country hick," sloppy attitudes, or slick new fashion depending on clothing type and dream feelings.

PAJAMAS, NIGHTGOWN:

May represent your attitudes on rest, sleep, night life, sex (or lack of it), dreaming, sleepiness, unawareness, feelings of disinterest, or inability to cope.

PANTIES:

Strictly feminine outlook and feelings, female point of view, very personal attitudes; could be a pun on "getting to the bottom" of things; can be symbol of sexy feelings and ideas or feminine wile.

Removing Panties: Can be very sexy ideas or using sex as a come-on, weapon, wedge, excuse, or way out of a situation.

PANTS, TROUSERS, SLACKS:

Refers to intellectual, masculine opinions, attitudes, ideas, rights, and the protection and preservation of these such as being the boss, authority figure, having control; manly or macho ideas in general. Removing these may mean giving up authority or could refer to sexy ideas.

Pants, Female Version: These depict the growing trend of equality of the sexes, attitudes of freedom, independence, capability, equality of ability and mentality, lack of subordination to male authority. Can denote females asserting their intellect, authority, and equality, balancing their male-female qualities, or need to do this.

Trying On: Implies considering these but not yet buying or accepting the idea.

Wearing: Implies becoming more independent, free, self-sufficient in attitude, outlook, and position. Using independence, ability, and right to equal opportunities.

PLAY CLOTHES:

These would depict your attitudes about play, fun, relaxation. Can say you play too much or not enough.

PURSE:

Symbol of material possessions, values, security, purchasing power, and prosperity or the lack of it.

SARONG:

A loose, easy-to-wear or remove outlook. May represent loose attitudes or may be pun on, "'S a rong (wrong) idea."

SOCKS:

Could be a pun on socks as hard knocks you give or get, or may represent warmth and flexibility of understanding.

SKIRT, FULL:

May imply fullness of ideas, full of compassion, abundance, or may be a pun on skirting around the situation, skirting the issue, or hiding behind a full skirt.

SKIRT, TIGHT:
Provocative, sexy ideas, tight spot, limited movement, or exaggerated, emphasized moves.

SPORT COAT:
May depict shouldering responsibility, feeling and concern for others, but may also be just for show or fashion.

STREET CLOTHES:
May symbolize your attitudes about everyday matters, life in general.

SUIT:
Suitable state or attitude. Possible pun on suitor.

Jump Suit: Ready-for-anything attitude, ready to jump into a situation or relationship.

Knit Suit: Both suitable and flexible.

SUPERMAN SUIT:
Alludes to your above-average talents, ideas, abilities you may not realize you have.

SWEATER:
Informal, casual, relaxed, flexible, and comfortable ideas and feelings.

TIE:
Can represent any kind of ties we have with others: physical, mental, emotional, even karmic ties.

TIGHT CLOTHING:
May portray a stingy attitude, a sexy, provocative one, or restrictiveness.

TUXEDO:
See *Formal,* this chapter.

UNDERWEAR:
Personal attitudes, intimate feelings, things close to you, what you keep hidden from others; basic,

underlying beliefs, attitudes, affirmations, which may or may not support your lifestyle. Could be getting down to the bare facts or may allude to sexy ideas, private thoughts not known by others.

UNIFORMS:
These can symbolize your work, the group you are presently associated with, or allude to uniformity of ideas, conforming to group ideas, being one of the crowd.

Army, Navy, Etc.: War-like attitudes and ideas, defensive outlook, macho ideals; might also be strict discipline, no-nonsense approach.

Nurse: Ideas of health, hygiene, service, and/or compassion for others.

Police: Law enforcement, attitudes of right and wrong, guilt, judgment, punishment, discipline, authority, karma, and getting caught.

Servant: Ideas of servitude, being used, unappreciated, underpaid, unworthiness, lack of authority.

Waitress: Attitudes of service, food for thought, conformity to demands of others.

VEIL:
Symbol for something hidden or half-hidden—knowledge, ideas, feelings, motives, intentions, secrets. Veils can imply shyness, modesty, mystique, flirtation, temptation, enticement, or lack of confidence, a tendency to stay in the background or behind the scenes. May be sex, secretiveness, subtleness, undercover, deliberate illusion, delusion, or deception. If veil covers the eyes can imply inability to see clearly, not wanting to be seen, or an attitude which veils our understanding.

Hat Veil: Would imply hidden thoughts, intentions, motives; emotions deliberately withheld.

Blue Veil: Sadness

Pink Veil: Love.

Red Veil: May say you are "seeing red," angry.

Torn Down or Removed: Finding or uncovering new knowledge and understanding, better perception, increasing awareness, access to greater wisdom.

White Veil: May be virginity, preparation for or symbol of high spiritual communion, communication from High Self or Holy Spirit.

VEST:
This emphasizes or covers the heart, feelings, compassion for others. See if it matches rest of clothing.

WALLET, BILLFOLD:
Symbol of material success or lack of it; also your sense of values. See chapter on *Valuables*.

WEDDING GARMENTS:
Attitude of giving or offering yourself to another in love, pledging love and devotion to each other or possibly to God. Long-range commitment.

WHITE HOODED ROBE:
This can symbolize several things:

Ghost Costume: Prank, party, play, or pretense.

Klu Klux Clan: Thin white robes of sheet weight and feeling. Mood or feelings of righteous indignation, self-righteousness, vengeance, anger, prejudice, small-mindedness; possibly an ugly, vicious mood. Feeling and purpose would be less than kindly toward the intended victim.

White Brotherhood: Soft, thick, hooded robes, feeling of holiness and loving-kindness. Donning these may indicate preparation for initiation and possible joining with the brotherhood. Wearing the robes may imply that you have been accepted for initiation or that you have become one of the brotherhood. A holy, awed, honored feeling would corroborate this.

WOOL CLOTHING:
May represent warmth and compassionate feelings or may be pun on "pulling the wool over your eyes."

WORK CLOTHES:
Your attitudes about your work, job, career.

WORN-OUT CLOTHING:
Indicative of old attitudes which no longer suffice; unsuitable, need to be replaced.

My Own Clothing Symbols

CHAPTER 20

Colors In Dreams and Auras

Colors are indicative of our emotions, each hue having a different meaning taken from the actual observations of clairvoyants who long ago noted the correspondence between certain feelings and the resultant colors visible in the aura. These have filtered into our language in expressions such as, "green with jealousy," "seeing red," "having the blues," and so on.

COLORS WE WEAR:
These affect our bodies, our minds, our moods. Bright, clear colors help us to feel more joyous and light-hearted and can actually counteract depression. Blacks, dark grays, and browns and dull, muddy colors tend to depress us, while the green tones are healing.

BRIGHT, CLEAR COLORS:
These are positive in nature and action, pure and clear, unsullied by ulterior motives.

PASTELS:
Show immaturity or weakness in the area signified by the color.

DARK OR MUDDY COLORS:
Reveal the negative qualities of doubt, fear, hate, anger, greed, and so on. Wearing these colors will intensify these feelings.

EXTREMELY VIVID COLORS:
In comparison to the usual color range in dreams, these are usually indicative of the astral planes and can imply an impending lucid state.

Color Meanings

BLACK:
Usually denotes the unknown, mysterious, darkness, death, mourning, hate, or malice, especially when associated with fear or uncertainty. However, if the feeling in the dream is one of joy or happiness, it would probable imply unmanifested spiritual gifts or qualities.

BLUE:
Blue, Clear: Represents truth, wisdom, heaven, eternity, spiritual feelings, aspirations, devotion, contemplation, tranquillity, truth-seeking, loyalty, or "true blue."

Deep, Rich Blue: Awakened spiritual forces, one who has found his/her life's work and is immersed in it. Attainment of spiritual goals, serenity.

Light Blue: Struggling religious aspirations, a beginner on the path of righteousness. Immature spiritual qualities starting to develop.

Blue Green: Combination of healing green and spiritual blue, often denotes a spiritual teacher, healer; being trustworthy, helpful and peaceful in nature.

Blue Violet: High spiritual qualities, devoted, inspired, rich in spiritual truth, trustworthy, honorable; often a spiritual leader of some kind in a quiet, unobtrusive way.

Blue Gray: Religious feelings tinged with fear.

Muddy/Murky Blue: Spiritual aspirations mixed with negativity, depression; emotionally "down," having the blues.

BRASS:
Strongly associated with the false, base, and deceitful, or brassy, bold, and ostentatious.

BROWN:
Brown, Clear: Earthy, worldly, physically oriented, practical, materialistic.

Light Brown, Tan: Mixture of brown (negativity and earthiness) and white (purity). Pure and noble ideals tinged with doubt, depression, and earthy reasoning (I'm ONLY human) or (I MUST be realistic!)

Dark, Dull Brown: Depression, lack of ambition, inaction.

Greenish Brown: Greed, jealousy, negativity.

Gray-brown: Selfishness, negativity.

Muddy Brown: Selfishness, confusion, negative attitude.

Reddish Brown: A rich brown implying power to achieve material things, natural money-maker.

Dark Red Brown: Avarice, greed.

GOLD:
Spiritual rewards, refinement, attainment, God's love and approval; also the enhancement of whatever it surrounds.

Golden Stars: Indicate high, spiritual ideals.

Golden Thread: Brotherly love, continuous caring and affection, loving connection.

GREEN:
Clear, Leaf Green: Denotes Spring, good healthy growth, healing, hope, victory, rest, balance, peace, and serenity. (Green thumb people are natural healers.)

Dark Leaf Green: Similar to clear green described above but with added maturity, mellowing; slower paced, more filled with wisdom, compassion, patience, grace.

Light Green: Spring green, new growth, healing, youth, vigor, health, vitality, exuberance of youth.

Pale Green: Sympathy, immaturity.

Blue Green: Helpful, trustworthy, devoted, often a spiritual teacher-healer or minister.

Brownish Green: Materialism, greed, jealousy.

Gray Green: Envy; possible deceit, raspiness, and fear.

Moss Green: Much the same as clear green with a touch of maturity, wisdom, and patience added.

Olive Drab: Drab and dull and tends to slow everything down. It is often associated with work uniforms and uniformity of attitudes.

Yellow Green: Deceit, cowardice, sign of the liar (the yellow streak).

GRAY:
Fear, fright, depression, ill health due to prolonged thoughts of fear held in mind. Also means unclear, not well defined. Gray may also symbolize a balance between black and white.

IVORY:
Superiority, royalty, purity tinged with a bit of negativity—not quite pure. May be ivory tower type of detachment.

ORANGE:

Friendliness, courtesy, sociability, out-goingness, extroversion. May represent the fruits of the spirit.

Light Orange: Same as above but not as strong, less mature, more timid in nature.

Dark Orange: Same as orange but with greater maturity, more reserve, perhaps more materialistic and less trusting.

Brownish Orange: Tendency to be lazy, self-indulgent; low morals, low intellect, or both.

Red Orange: Pride, abundant energy.

Yellow Orange: Self-control, thoughtfulness, consideration, strong intellect, active mind.

PEACH:

Love-wisdom combination, a New Age color.

PINK:

Love, joy, happiness, affection, kindness. Can symbolize being in love.

Light Pink: Immaturity of the love nature; baby pink.

Deep Pink: Greater depth and maturity of the love nature.

PURPLE:

Symbol of royalty, of oneness with God, devotion, healing abilities, loving-kindness, compassion, spiritual powers developed.

Pale: Same as above but not as developed. Promise of things to come, beginning of true Godliness.

Deep Purple: Symbol of oneness with God, deep devotion, loving kindness, love-wisdom, deep compassion, powerful healing abilities, great spiritual powers; a Magi.

RED:

Clear Red: Raw energy, force, vigor, aggressiveness, action; power to love, hate, conquer, go, do, and be.

Light Red: Same as clear red with less force, less maturity.

Deep, Clear Red: Same as clear red with more reserve, caution, and maturity, yet still strong and vigorous.

Brownish Red: (Dark red-brown as in dried blood) Anger, negative or misused energy, old karma, old or dried blood.

Burgundy: (Rich red-brown) Symbol of prosperity, success, wealth, plenty, power to do, be, and have.

Orange Red: Social energy, outgoingness; may be mixed with pride and much energy.

Pinkish Red Violet: Passion, sex.

Rose, Deep Pink: Love energy, loving-kindness, deep affection, Christ love.

Scarlet: Courage, loyalty.

Wine: Combination of red and blue, energy and devotion. Question is, devotion to what? If dull in color (warning), may be self-centered, negative, or sensual with a tendency toward a nervous breakdown. If clear, may be spiritually devoted.

SILVER:

Reflection of God's light, justice, and purity; may symbolize moon or mercury and excellent protective energies.

VIOLET:

High spirituality, religious aspiration, devotion, affection, love, gentleness, peacefulness.

Pinkish Lavender: Spiritual love, affection, tenderness, compassion, devotion, gentleness, goodness. These qualities are present but not yet fully developed unless deep in color.

WHITE:
Purity, perfection, holiness. May also represent "white wash."

Off-white: Fresh, clean, almost pure, close to perfection but tinged with some worldliness.

YELLOW:
Intellectual prowess and agility, acumen, well-being.

Golden: Wisdom

Muddy Yellow: Poor health, negative thinking, confusion.

Yellow Green: Deceit, dishonesty, cowardice, liar.

Yellow Orange: Strong use of intellect. Socially inclined.

Yellow Streak or Stripe: Cowardice.

Color Combinations

BLACK AND WHITE:
This often implies good and evil, right or wrong, yin and yang, both sides of the issue, the balance of forces and the power inherent in this balance and control.

CHECKERED COLORS:
Can imply a checkered career or mentality, questionable tactics, combination of feelings and energies going on in the area. May be saying, "Check this out," or "Double check" this.

PLAID:
May represent mixed or opposing ideas, directions, or attitudes designated by color, or could be this is the pattern of things.

SPOTTED:
Usually means impure or maybe mixed-up. May represent stains of misdeeds and how they color your aura, attitude, or both.

STRIPES, CROSSWISE:
May indicate something "rubbing you the wrong way," a discordant energy, "going against the grain," or possibly going around and around.

STRIPES, LENGTHWISE:
May be parallel ideas or emotions, or represent the ups and downs of things.

STRIPES, MIXED:
Could be mixed emotions, energies, or feelings.

My Own Color Symbols

CHAPTER 21

Death and Dying

A dream of death can be an expression of a desire to see someone dead, to see them out of the way, or it can depict the death of a relationship, the death of some aspect of yourself, or the demise of some habit of yours which you have been trying to eliminate. Only rarely is it an ESP warning of an actual event, but it can be.

Death of Yourself

To see yourself in dreams is equivalent to having your conscious mind viewing your ego, an aspect of you, a quallility, characteristic, habit, or strong belief belonging to you.

To kill or injure this "self" can signify the death of this part of yourself and can be good news, especially if it is an undesirable trait. On the other hand, it is also possible to cause the death of a good and positive quality in yourself, in which case the dream would be a warning.

Most often a dream of death simply symbolizes the death of your old self, an old habit, or old way of thinking you have been trying to overcome. It may be a message for you to let go of the old, outmoded image of yourself to make room for the new one; as such, it is often a sign of the end of the old and the begining of a new you. The dead person may be seen as yourself or can be portrayed by a person whom you feel has that particular habit or fault. See the chapter on *People*.

One needs to carefully search within to see just what is involved. The feeling of anything from nonchalance through mild pleasure and outright joy, as opposed to regret and sadness, can assure you the death is a symbolic one and there is no reason for alarm.

If you feel regret or apprehension about the death, it is fairly certain this is a warning of the death of a good quality or talent you have allowed to die through neglect or misuse. Or, it can denote a health hazard and possible death resulting from poor health habits and bodily abuses. Carefully check the dream content and feeling before deciding.

On the other hand, if you are in poor health this may be advising you to take precautions or else! There is always the possibility of an actual notice of impending ill health or imminent death, so a death dream should be considered as a possible ESP message. The death of the body can occur, but it is not necessary or unavoidable. Never neglect the health aspect. If in doubt get a medical checkup, especially if you have had similar dreams.

BEATING YOURSELF (OR ANOTHER) TO DEATH:

This can be advising that you are doing just that to yourself by your habits. Can be through overwork, overeating, excessive drinking, smoking, or any of many bodily abuses. Look carefully to see just how you are beating yourself.

KILLING YOURSELF:

This can refer to a bad habit, quality, or characteristic you need to "kill" or imply that you are killing yourself unwittingly by these habits, mental or physical. Be aware of what you are doing. If you are trying to eliminate an unwanted aspect of yourself, this could be an encouraging sign. If not, what part of you are you killing off? Is this good? How do you feel about this in your dream? Consider both the details and your feelings in the dream to correctly understand the message.

SEEING YOURSELF DEAD:

If this dream has a sense of finality or foreboding, it could well be a warning, particularly if this is followed or accompanied with the urge to put your life and affairs in order and make peace with friends and family. This feeling would be more like an acquiescence or acceptance of the inevitable.

SEEING YOURSELF BURIED:

Could be a pun on how you are burying yourself in your work or that you feel inundated by some work or events in your life just now. Check out all possibilities and feelings.

Not many people have this warning because most of us have been thoroughly trained to believe there is only *one* life, and they fear to let go of it. In reality, dying is simply leaving the physical body just as you do when you drift off to sleep, and life goes on in the spiritual body. This is actually a joyous event, like graduation day.

Death of Other People

Since we all decide (on spiritual levels) just when, how, and where we will permanently depart from our bodies, it is not at all unusual for a loved one to come to you in a dream and tell you plainly or symbolically that they are planning to leave their physical body soon. If this person is extremely close to you, the first message or two may be symbolic in form until you have had some time to get used to the idea. Then the message will be repeated in plainer forms. You may have several warnings, giving you ample time to adjust.

In my own life, three people very dear to my heart have come to me in dreams and told me quite plainly of their plans to depart. In each case, the warning came at least nine months ahead. Others report as much as a year's advance notice.

Types of Notices

Your loved one may appear in a dream and simply say, "I'm leaving!", but this is not common. Usually it is much more subtle. They may walk toward a waiting airplane without any luggage, or they may climb into a car made in the year of their birth and drive off (even if they can't drive a car). They may just slowly walk away from you and disappear, leaving you with a sense of never seeing them again. Possibly you will see the person happily conversing with people you know have passed on, totally leaving you out of the conversation. This may happen several times. It is their subtle way of saying that they have business elsewhere, that it is time for them to "move on" and it is up to you to accept this.

How to Cope

When loved ones begin their inner preparations to leave the earth plane (very few are consciously aware of this), there are often many little things to be worked out in the relationship between you and them. Matters which require forgiveness on either side will come to mind, usually through dreams. It is important for both of you to make amends, work out your unresolved problems or misunderstanding, and be aware of the need to complete your relationship in a peaceful, loving manner.

One of the hardest things to do is to consciously release the one you love (done as a prayer of relinquishment), for it is definitely possible for us to hold on to a dear one long after their departure time and prolong their suffering by not giving them our *loving permission to go*. This release *is* important to their peace of mind and yours.

Long, lingering, painful illnesses are often prolonged because of minor problems not mended which the loved one hopes to resolve before leaving. Your cooperation is needed, so be aware of this important dream work.

Death Symbols

BURIAL:
This can symbolize the end, the finish, release, a final letting-go of a person, situation, relationship, habit, problem, or whatever.

CASKET:
Symbol of death, of yourself, an aspect of yourself, an old habit or problem, or of another person. This can imply dead but not buried. In ancient times a casket was simply a box with a lid used for many purposes.

> **Carrying Casket:** Can denote carrying your grief around with you, carrying the burden or blame for another's death, or allowing a death to affect your life, to be a permanent burden. Inability to let go of the past.

CLOCK, STOPPED:
Can imply time is running out, there is no time left, or the end of time.

DEATH:
In general terms implies a drastic change in one's consciousness, awareness, lifestyle, direction.

DEATH OF AN ANIMAL:
If it is not your pet it is most likely the ending of an animal instinct or quality you had. See chapter on *Animals*.

DEATH OF A BABY:
This is usually the death or end of an idea, ideal, hope, project, or responsibility which you have "dropped" or neglected. See *Baby* under *People*.

DEATH OF A BIRD:
Most likely the death of a high ideal or hope you held.

DEATH OF A FRIEND:
There is always the possibility that this is an ESP warning, but consider the possibility of an aspect of yourself which this person would represent.

DEATH OF AN UNKNOWN PERSON:
This is the most frequently used symbol for the elimination of a bad habit or aspect of you, probably one you didn't know you had.

LARGE SCALE DEATH OR DESTRUCTION:
May be an ESP warning of a coming event or could be symbolic of the death or destruction of a project or venture involving many people, such as a large business venture.

This could be a precognition of something that cannot be changed—such as the sinking of the Titanic—but can be avoided (many people dreamed of this event and canceled their reservations), one that can be changed through prayer, or one that is unchangeable and unavoidable. (Unchangeable events are usually extra strong, clear, and vivid.) See *Visions* under *The Many Kinds of Dreams*.

FUNERAL:
Implies a gathering of friends and aspects of yourself to celebrate or mourn your change in consciousness. Not necessarily a physical death.

OLD MAN WITH A SCYTHE (SICKLE):
Common symbol of death, the end, or completion of a cycle.

Scene of Death and Dying

BAR:
Could be the death of a drinking habit or warn that drinking can be the death of you.

CHURCH, TEMPLE:
May symbolize a spiritual death, an initiation, a change to a higher state of consciousness.

HOME:
Can be your state of consciousness, where you live mentally; could be a family break-up.

HOSPITAL:
Can relate to an actual physical problem or accident.

WORK AREA:
Could be a pun saying, "Your work (habits) will be the death of you," or imply the death of that particular job, position, or business.

Communicating With the Dead

Many people have had the dream experience of meeting and talking to people we think of as "dead." This is quite commonplace, since their spiritual bodies are on the same (astral) plane where you and I travel every night; so it is perfectly natural that you should run into them from time to time. This is a frequent occurrence in dreams and nothing to be alarmed about. It is possible, in dreams or in prayer, to ask forgiveness or give it, and to work out matters we were not ready or able to resolve before their departure. Or, we can simply have a nice visit. Don't be surprised to find that months or even years after a death, a dream may point out something which has not yet been forgiven, released, or worked out between you. This may seem minor to you but can be a blockage to the progress of your loved one, so it's best to take the matter seriously and take time to cooperate in whatever seems necessary.

EXAMPLE: Ten long years after my husband's death, I found through a dream that I hadn't yet made my peace with the circumstances surrounding it! So, I closed my eyes, reviewed the happenings, and deliberately forgave myself and all the others involved until I felt at peace about it. Simple, but effective.

Be aware that you can mentally communicate with a loved one anytime. It's never too late to ask forgiveness or to tell them that you still love them. They *do* get the message and often reply in your dreams.

Talking to the so-called dead may also be your clue to remember that you "must be dreaming" and therefore be your chance to become lucid within the dream. Watch for this.

Teachings from Beyond

Occasionally you may receive teachings through dreams from one who has passed on. This can continue over a long period and be highly enlightening.

You may also receive messages from "On High" commenting on your spiritual progress, as Arthur Ford did in a near-death experience where he was told he had "failed to accomplish what he knew he had to finish." He confesses, "There was a purpose for me, it seemed, and I had not fulfilled it. There was a plan for my life and I had misread the blueprint. They are going to send me back, I thought, and I didn't like it" (Ford and Bro, 1968).

My Own Death Symbols

My Own Death Symbols continued...

CHAPTER 22

ESP or Precognitive Dreams

The majority of people seem to believe that *all* dreams are ESP in nature. This is partly due to the clarity of ESP dreams as compared to the symbolic dream, which is so often dismissed as silly and promptly forgotten. Precognitive dreams are generally clear, logical, and have a persistence about them which makes a deep impression on the dreamer who senses their importance and mulls over the scenes in his mind. Then, a day or so later when the event actually happens, the dream is even more vividly impressed; and its memory and importance are deeply etched in mind.

Unfortunately, the experience of having fateful or tragic precognitive dreams—even when they happen infrequently—tends to make the dreamer repress his dream memories so as not to be the receiver of bad news.

As we mentioned before, this attitude can greatly decrease the frequency of your dreams or stop the dream-recall process completely. If you suspect this has happened to you, you need to re-program you mind by affirming "I really *do* want to remember my dreams, but please omit warnings of death..." or whatever it is you prefer not to deal with. Remember, you are in full control and you can tell your subconscious mind just exactly what you want and how you want it. On the other hand, now that you understand the purpose of dreams a bit better, you may be ready to accept whatever messages come to you, in which case you would only want to state that you now want to **remember all your dreams**.

Recognizing the ESP Dream

The question most frequently asked about these is, "How can one tell a psychic dream from a symbolic one?" There are several things to look for: the lack of symbolism, the logical sequence of events, the clarity of the dream, and the feeling of urgency.

LACK OF SYMBOLISM:
The people are dressed mainly in the kind of clothes they usually wear; the cars, houses, streets, and so forth are much as you would expect to see them on any ordinary day. You and others are basically engaged in doing plain, everyday activities. In other words, the whole background of the dream seems to be normal and familiar.

SEQUENCE OF EVENTS:
These follow a reasonable course. You may see or experience something which is quite within the realm of possibility, unlike the symbolic dream where things tend to jump from one scene to another.

CLARITY:
Images are fairly sharp and clear, not fuzzy or vague. Colors and details are clearly defined and often brighter than usual.

FEELING OF URGENCY:
Your feelings about this can be an important clue, as there is often a sense of either great importance or urgency about the dream as you

wake. In fact, it is not at all unusual to have a dream of this type wake you out of a sound sleep.

If it is a happy event and your feelings on waking are joyous, all is well and good. If it is a tragic or unhappy one and your feelings match, it can be a warning of things to come. Anytime your feelings are totally opposite to what you would normally expect them to be, you should suspect a symbolic dream rather than a predictive one.

RECURRING ESP SYMBOLS:

After keeping records of your ESP dreams for awhile, you may find a particular symbol or clue which repeats itself in each precognitive dream. Learn to recognize this as your personal trademark of the predictive dream.

Occasionally psychic dreams are a mixture of ESP and symbolism, but don't worry—you will soon learn to get the "feel" of the precognitive dream and easily know it from the symbolic one. The more you work with your dreams, the better you become; just like anything else, practice makes perfect!

Usually we get only a glimpse of a coming event, but occasionally we will remember all of it. Whatever the dream is showing you, it is good to remember that at this point *it is only a possibility*, a *warning* of what can and probably will happen *if* you don't do something to change it.

A Chance to Change Things

One of the reasons for the precognitive dream is to bring a possible danger to our conscious attention and to give us a chance to do something about it. For example, if you dream of having a blowout which results in wrecking your car, don't panic—go out and check your tires! Replace the worn one. It can be as simple as that. The dream is merely warning you of what *may* happen *if* your old tire isn't replaced. It is *not* a *dire*

prediction of unavoidable tragedy, nor is it meant to be.

Always check out your dreams on the physical level first and on the symbolic level second. Sometimes the dream is relevant on both levels and can even be meaningful on all three levels: physical, mental, and spiritual.

TIMING

Writing the date of each dream can be of utmost importance in ESP dreams as it helps you to get a clear idea of just how much time elapses between your precognitive warnings and the actual happening; the timing varies greatly from person to person. Some folks dream of events to come on the morning of the very day they happen, while others receive their warnings days, months, or even years ahead.

COMING TOWARD YOU:

In general, objects or people coming toward you in a dream imply events coming into your life in the near future.

Big disasters such as the sinking of the Titanic, John F. Kennedy's assassination, an earthquake, or anything which affects the lives of many people are often picked up by many, many dreamers. Some will listen and heed the warning while others will say, "It's only a dream!"

My Own ESP Symbols

My Own ESP Symbols continued...

CHAPTER 23

Examinations and Tests

He who has conquered fear has conquered failure.

— *James Allen*

We frequently have dreams of taking examinations or tests of some kind. These have to do with our self-esteem and confidence or our lack of it. Often we are being shown our fears of not making the grade, not measuring up to other people's expectations, not being accepted, not passing the test, not being prepared, or feelings of not being good enough.

A little bit of consternation—which prompts us to work harder or to study more—can be a good thing, but repeated dreams of tests and exams indicates a basic lack of confidence in ourselves which needs mending. This low esteem is often the main cause of our failures. Our dreams consistently try to show us where we need to work on ourselves.

Unprepared

We often feel unprepared or incapable of handling the circumstances that face us. Indications of this include losing our books, papers, pen, and so forth, or missing the bus or being unable to find the school or classroom. Sometimes we can't even find our *own* room. Obviously, we are just not ready or willing to take the test or face the situation. Feelings of stress may accompany these dreams.

Fear of Failure

The fear of failure is a common problem in all of us, and our dreams of being unprepared are just showing us how we really feel about ourselves. We fear we won't measure up to someone else's standards. We must have awareness of a situation before we can correct it, so dreams point this out; but it is up to us to make the necessary changes. Remember what we have said about goals—*your goals* as opposed to *other people's goals* and *their expectations* of you. Often this is the crux of the examination dream.

Your Biggest Test

Your most important test is in learning to decide your own goals, standards, hopes, plans, dreams, and wishes for yourself; to become absolutely clear about what *you want* in your life and, once decided, *standing up for what you believe*. Measuring up to your own standards is what really matters.

Once this is done there will be no more examination dreams, for the need has been met and conquered.

Spiritual Levels

Occasionally testing dreams are on a spiritual level and may be partial remembrances of tests or even initiations into higher realms. In these the setting would be calm and serene, most likely occurring either outdoors or in a cathedral or temple-like setting and would be accompanied by feelings of peace, devotion, and joy.

My Own Examination Symbols

CHAPTER 24

Foods

Food in dreams usually refers to food for thought, ideas, new teachings, new concepts, new beliefs. They are ideas you take in and digest mentally.

DIFFICULTY:
Difficulty with a particular type of food can indicate an allergy or some other physical problem your body is experiencing with that specific food or diet; or, a certain food/herb may be emphasized (enlarged) because you have a specific need of it. So be wise, consider all the possibilities, and don't forget your own associations with the particular kind of food.

FOOD COMBINATIONS:
Combinations such as turkey and dressing, cheese and crackers, and so on can symbolize the interdependence and inter-relationships of ideas and things, the complementary interactions between two entirely different thoughts and beliefs.

Actions With Food

BACK BURNER:
Ideas we want to let simmer awhile before swallowing.

BANQUET:
Plenty of food for thought, but all are served the same ideas.

BUFFET:
Wide variety of ideas, concepts, philosophies offered with the freedom to pick and choose what suits you best.

CHOKING:
Oten is a pun indicating our reluctance or inability to "swallow" the information or concept offered.

COOKING FOOD:
Preparing, working with ideas, finding uses for them, integrating them into your thinking and life pattern.

DISHES AND TABLES:
Relate to food for thought and how you are handling or ignoring it.

FASTING:
May mean an actual abstinence from all food for a period of time or just the omission of one particular kind of nourishment. Can symbolize living in a state of purity, refraining from negative thoughts, rejecting evil. May be discipline, religious preparation. Could be a refusal to accept any new ideas.

FREEZING FOOD:
Halting all emotional flow connected with the food idea. Shutting out all feelings; can indicate hardening of the heart or mind about the matter. May also imply putting the food-for-thought away for an indefinite period of time.

MICROWAVING:

Can be a pun on fast foods, instant everything, speeded-up preparations, exciting ideas.

MIXING FOODS:

Combining several ideas into one whole, or may be getting things all mixed up.

NO FOOD AVAILABLE:

Lack of nourishment or support mentally, physically, emotionally, or spiritually. No way to grow, nothing for the mind to feed upon. Strong need for real nourishment on one or more levels of being. Consider whether you are nourishing and loving to yourself or denying self. This may also apply to empty, meaningless thoughts and ideas or negative, poverty-conscious thinking.

OFFER OF FOOD
YOU DON'T USUALLY EAT:

May indicate your need for this particular food.

REFUSED:

Ideas and teachings rejected by some aspect of the dreamer.

SPILLED:

Could be wasted ideas or lessons; may indicate where your diet is unbalanced or depict a need to eliminate that article from your diet.

STORING FOOD:

Putting away in memory for future use when we will be ready or hungry for it or ready to re-evaluate.

THROWING FOOD AWAY:

Can be refusal, or may say you need to eliminate this item out of your diet.

UPSET STOMACH:

May mean you cannot "stomach" a situation or idea, or may imply what that particular food does to you.

WASHING DISHES:

Cleaning out old ideas, beliefs; preparing for new.

Kinds of Food

APPLE:

Often represents forbidden fruit, seeing both good and evil, having faith in the worst as well as the best, of being "double-minded" rather than single-minded. Can also be fruit of the spirit or a healthy food you need to eat.

BACON:

Can mean supplies, staples, provisions, earning a living, or may denote a forbidden food.

BANANA:

May be a needed element in your diet (high in phosphorous, easy to digest), especially when shown with other foods or in a kitchen or dining area. However, this can also be a phallic symbol representing a repressed urge for love, sex, and/or a strong need for close companionship with the opposite sex. (People who stifle their sensuality or loathe to face and admit their sexual urges, thinking "sex is dirty," are much more likely to have subtle sex symbols such as bananas.) Look at what you are doing with the bananas and your feelings about them.

> **Bunch of Bananas:** Would show a powerful need to deal openly with one's basic sexual desires, urges, and bodily demands. It's time to take a close, objective look at one's "sex is dirty" beliefs. See Sex, *Pregnancy and Birth.*

BEANS:

Could be staples, basics, or pun on "don't know beans."

BEEF:

Can mean "beefing it up," exaggeration, complaining, or a lot of bull. See *Steak,* this chapter.

BEETS:

Can be pun on being "beat," "heart beats," or karmic fruits (dark red).

BEER:
Something to please, placate, soothe, relax; may be a means of escape or a substitute to appease a hidden hunger.

BOTTLED DRINK:
May indicate bottled emotions, things bottled up inside you, keeping the lid on your feelings.

BREAD:
Bread of life, sustenance, daily needs, money, wages.

BUTTER:
Suggests buttering up, smoothing, flattery, or may be a luxury.

CAKE:
Rewards, sweet things in life, added luxury, love, or benefit, something extra, or may be a pun on "piece of cake," easy, sure thing, can't lose.

> **Icing:** The extras, something special, the best part, the added touch of love or beauty. Icing color adds an additional quality. See chapter on *Color*.

CANDY:
Reward or temptation. May represent the sweet things in life.

CANNED GOODS:
Ideas put away for future use, not to be digested now, or can be bottled hurts, emotions.

CHEESE:
Can be wholesome ideas or pun on smile (for the camera...or just to put on a happy face).

CHERRIES:
Happiness, joy.

CHILI:
Hot stuff, controversial subjects, temperamental topics. Something too hot to handle, or may be chilly reception.

CLAMS:
Could be a spiritual food, a pun on clamming-up, a gourmet delight, or may be memories associated with clams.

COFFEE:
May imply a bitter drink, dregs, blues, negativity, brooding, worldly ideas, gossip, small talk, or can be warm hospitality, stimulation, awakening of mind, ideas.

> **Coffee Poured On You:** Could indicate someone "dumping" on you.

> **Oversized Coffee Cup or Pot**: Could imply you drink too much, too large an amount.

> **Substitute Ingredient in Coffee Pot:** Suggestion for you to use that ingredient in place of coffee, a dietary hint.

CORN:
May be kernels of truth, ancient wisdom, corny idea.

> **Corn Husk:** Emptiness, untruth.

> **Grinding Corn:** Working out your own spiritual truth or philosophy.

COVERED DISH:
Food for thought prepared in advance; prepared statement, speech; also under cover, covert, protected.

CRUMBS:
Could be a crumbling situation, rejects, leftovers, unwanted, not your best, or a "crumby deal."

CRUST:
That which holds all ingredients together, basis or form for a dish, that which makes it attractive and easy to "handle," or can be a pun on having "a lot of crust."

No Crust: You have all the ingredients or ideas but it doesn't yet "hang together," won't make a cohesive whole. This can be a lack of form, say you "can't handle" it, or that you don't "have it all together."

DATES:
Can be food you need, refer to a special date, be a pun on dating, or imply dates on your calendar.

DESSERT:
Something extra, special treat, climax; just desserts, rewards; the sweet things in life.

DIET COLA OR DIET FOOD:
Accepting diet food or drink can indicate a need to diet or at least cut down on calories. Refusing this or knocking it over may say it is time to end the diet.

EGG:
Creative force, oneness, wholeness, or can be a seed idea.

FAST FOOD:
Preconceived ideas, quick wit, fast thinking but not necessarily well-prepared or well-thought-out ideas and suggestions. Consider the source.

FEAST:
Lots of food for thought, plenty of variety, many good ideas to try out.

FISH:
Spiritual food.

> **Sole:** May be pun on your soul, solely, only, singly, uniquely, or food for the soul.

FOREIGN FOODS:
Unusual, different ideas and customs, foreign to your usual thinking.

FRESH FOODS:
New ideas, concepts, teachings, beliefs.

FROZEN FOODS:
These represent assets, ideas, talents, or feelings which are frozen, inaccessible, unusable in their present state. Dream points to a need to "thaw out" the qualities represented by the foods and put them to good use.

FRUIT:
Implies results of what you have planted: harvest, fruits of the spirit, love, joy, peace, patience; or, could denote forbidden fruit.

GARBAGE:
That which needs to be thrown out, rotten ideas.

GARLIC:
Associated with healing, cold prevention, relief of high blood pressure, also with offensive breath! Can be strong ideas and opinions that offend others. Are you coming on too strong?

GRAPES:
Often represent harvest, fruits of our labors, rewards coming, fruitfulness, prosperity, wealth.

GROCERY:
Area of buying food for thought, going after new information, ideas, feeding the mind, refilling. If you are buying junk food, dream may be saying you are filling your mind with junk or race-consciousness ideas of little value.

> **Bagged Groceries:** Getting it all together, in the bag, getting a grip on new ideas.

GUM:
Can be pun on a "sticky situation" or "gumming up the works."

Chewing Gum: Often represents characters who are cheap, shallow, sleazy, or not very bright. Or may be chewing on the same idea over and over and over.

HALF-BAKED:
Not well-prepared, not ready, unfinished, not well thought out.

HAM:
Forbidden food, piggishness, tendency to over-react, hamming it up, squealing.

HEALTH FOODS:
Healthy, helpful, positive, uplifting, encouraging, and healing food for thought. Could also be a dietary hint.

HERBS:
Often associated with healing broths or teas as well as good flavor and zest for life. A special herb may indicate a physical need for that particular one. (Most herbs have specific healing properties too numerous to mention here but can be found in any good herb book. Herbs can be a symbol for a vegetarian diet or healing properties in general. See *Herbs* under *Gardens*.

HONEY:
Soothing, sweet reward, luxurious extras.

HONEYDEW MELON:
Could indicate a good, healthy food you need or can be a pun on "Honey, do this...honey, do that..."

ICE CREAM:
Type of dessert, but may say "I scream."

INGREDIENTS:
Facts, ideas, teachings, parts that make the whole.

JELLO OR JELLY:
Can signify uncertainty, flexibility, wobbly, unsettled, or wishy-washy.

JUNK FOOD:
Wrong food for thought, erroneous beliefs held, need to get some truth, some spiritual food or literature.

LAMB:
Innocence, purity of ideas, gentleness, self-sacrificial thoughts.

LEAVENING:
Uplifting ideas, prayers, loving thoughts, balancing, helping; possible pun on leveling.

LEFT-OVERS:
Old ideas not yet used or dealt with, same old stuff, nothing new.

LETTUCE:
Money or pun on "let us." Also a pacifying vegetable which tends to soothe jangled nerves.

MAIN COURSE:
Main idea, crux of the matter, basic concept.

MEAT:
Main or most important part, the meat of the matter; or, if you are vegetarian, it can be most repellent part, animalistic in nature and outlook, worldly, to be avoided.

MILK:
May denote milk of human kindness, food for the immature, nourishment for the young, wholesomeness.

Goat Milk: Can be milk of kindness or may be a diet suggestion.

NUTS:
Seed ideas, great potential for growth, an idea in a nutshell.

OIL:
May be the oil of human kindness, cooperation, harmony, or removing friction.

OLIVE:
Represents peace, holy land, wholeness.

OLIVE OIL:
Healing balm.

ONIONS:
Bitter fruit, strong flavor or seasoning, strong opinions which impress or offend.

ORANGE JUICE:
Depicts one of the fruits of the spirit with special emphasis on friendliness, courtesy, graciousness, warmth, loving kindness, reaching out to others in love.

> **In Coffee Pot:** Substitute orange juice for coffee!

PEANUTS:
Can mean small profit, something not worth your time, pittance.

PEAR:
Can be pun on pair or prepare.

PEAS:
Can be a food you need in your diet, or may be a pun on peace!

PEPPER:
Zest, hot stuff, enthusiasm, too hot to handle, a little bit goes a long way; too much may imply you are overly-enthusiastic or tend to overemphasize things. Could depict peppery temperament.

PLUM:
Reward, best part, prize.

POMEGRANATE:
Female symbol representing passivity, receptivity, and fecundity.

PUDDING:
May be rewards, a rich dessert, your "rich desserts" (a pun on what you deserve), or pun on "proof of the pudding is in the eating." Possibly you have to try the rich idea for yourself.

RAISIN:
May mean "all dried up," your health, wealth, sources, or whatever dried up or drying out. Can be pun on what you are raising.

SACRAMENTS:
Bread and wine, holy food; holy, uplifting ideas, inspiration, love. Possible symbol of preparation for initiation.

> **Bread:** Bible reading, devotions, songs, praises, thanksgiving, holy thoughts, daily sustenance.

> **Wine:** Symbol of the Holy Spirit. Unless blessed, this too can have "evil spirits," as does whiskey or any other alcoholic beverage.

SAGE:
Pun on wisdom, also healing herb.

SALAD:
Combination of fresh ideas and concepts good for you.

SALT:
Zest for life, flavor, accent, spark, enthusiasm.

SOFT DRINK:
Can be bottled or canned emotions and feelings held back, unadmitted, unresolved.

SOUP:
Combination of many ingredients and ideas, usually considered to be healing in nature.

SPICE:

Spice of life; ideas which liven things up, give zest to living; hope, joy, enthusiasm, inspiration, fun, variety, zing, change of routine.

STEAK:

May symbolize good eating, prosperity, living it up, rewards, good times, or may be a pun on what is at stake, investment, interest, part you play, price you pay.

SUGAR:

May represent junk food or the sweet things in life. Sweet smell of success, rewards.

TEA:

Refreshing ideas, mild stimulation, soothing, healing, or may be "tea and sympathy," hospitality offered, friendly gesture, caringness.

UNLEAVENED BREAD:

Hasty preparation, special celebration of release from bondage, reminder.

VEGETABLES:

Ideas which are productive, nourishing, will feed you and others.

WATER:

Spiritual refreshment.

WHEAT:

Sacred life essence.

WHISKEY:

Ancient symbol of evil spirits based on actual clairvoyant sightings of the entities that hang around and attach themselves to the alcoholic fumes, the bottle, the person, or the place where these drinks are served. Often these entities or spirits attach themselves to the habitual drinker, actually urging him to drink more. Whiskey can also be a means of oblivion, escape from reality, a stimulant (temporarily), and a depressant.

WIENERS:

May be a pun on sex play, toying with the idea of sex, playing around with it; can be phallic symbol.

YEAST:

Increase, upliftment.

My Own Food Symbols

CHAPTER 25

Games and Sports

Games can represent the "game of life" or the games people play with one another and whether or not they play according to the rules. Games have to do with learning the rules, talents, skills, aims, goals, competition, showmanship, practice, training, accuracy, winning or losing, and how we play the game. This includes harmony and cooperation or the lack of it, teamwork, fairness, and good sportsmanship. Miscellaneous sport events where one team plays against another could represent two opposing "schools of thought" or may imply that things are "teaming up" against you.

Naturally, some games will have entirely different meanings to those who earn their living in the sports field as well as those who are actively engaged in a particular sport or closely connected with those who are. Your own feelings and associations are always of primary importance in interpreting your symbols.

Important Factors to Consider

Which one of the following are you?

COACH:
One who organizes, coaches, coaxes, teaches, preaches, yells, encourages, or criticizes; vociferously tells everyone what to do and how to do it.

PARTICIPANT:
Actively playing, totally involved in the action.

REFEREE, UMPIRE:
One who calls the shots, makes the judgments, keeps order, makes everyone play by the rules. Can be loud, abusive, and intrusive or just, fair, and helpful.

SITTING ON THE SIDELINES:
On the edge of things, passively but not actively involved. Semi-involved onlooker.

SPECTATOR:
Casual or not so casual onlooker; sitting, not participating, not using your own talents, potentials, or abilities; not making any progress. Could be watching as a learning and perceiving process prior to taking action or making decisions, or may be a pun on looking before leaping into a situation. Can say you prefer to watch and possibly criticize the actions of others rather than be personally involved.

WIN, LOSE, OR DRAW:
Winning or losing can be a comment on how you are playing the game of life or on what is actually happening in your present situation. The dream may show just how you see yourself and your abilities, or it may indicate your strong belief in being a winner or a loser.

To Lose: May show a need to re-think your present actions or situation. Possibly you need to change your tactics or attitudes, make a new start, or get out of the situation altogether. The cards may be "stacked" against you, or perhaps someone is not playing fairly.

Cheating: This could be an ESP warning about someone else, or it could be an aspect of yourself. We sometimes cheat or shortchange ourselves in an effort to win quickly. You know it's **how** you play the game that counts!

Remember that in many cases, all the people in the dream represent different and possibly opposing aspects of you. (See chapters on *People* and *Battles*.) Occasionally, conflicting teams may represent opposing aspects in yourself or totally different ideas, factors, or groups at odds in some area of your life. This could be in any group endeavor where there are differences of opinion including your job, your religious beliefs, education, and so forth. Or, it could be contradictory ideas, beliefs, or feelings within your consciousness.

The Games

AEROBICS:
Can be games you play with your body or a hint to work out and get yourself into better shape.

ARCHERY:
Represents your aims in life, ability to hit the target, to achieve your goals, having something to "shoot at," ideals.

BALL:
This can be a toy representing fun, relaxation, and playful attitudes or activities, particularly if your present situation seems to be all work and no play. Or, it may be a pun on being "on the ball," "on the mark," getting things rolling, or possibly "batting around" an idea.

Ball Coming To You: This implies your turn, your opportunity to perform, your responsibility, your chance.

Ball Coming To You a Second Time: Implies getting a second chance, another try. Possibly many opportunities coming your way.

Beside Goal: This may say, "You can't lose"; easy win, sure thing, being in sight of the goal, or within easy reach. Encouragement to keep going.

Overhand Throw: Can be hard, fast, strong, possibly a deliberate aim to fool or foil another.

Throw Falling Short: Implies missing your aim, not enough effort or accuracy on your part, less than your best.

Underhand Throw: Can be easy-going, soft-peddling, a more gentle approach, half-hearted, not your best shot, or a pun on an underhanded play or deal.

BASEBALL:
This could include the idea of hitting a home run, making a hit with others, getting home (home to God or back to your basic religious beliefs), or it may represent winning approval of yourself or others, doing what you like best or do best. It can be a hint to "strike out on your own" or to play in your own field. There is also the basic idea of **how** you play the game, fairness, teamwork, and cooperation or the lack of it.

BASKETBALL:
Seeking and obtaining goals with the cooperation of others. Emphasis on teamwork. Might also symbolize the blocking and thwarting efforts made by you, your teammates, or by others. Could indicate that you, or aspects of you, are standing in the way of your own progress or goals.

BRIDGE:
Mental game which involves bluffing, out-bidding, outwitting, and out-maneuvering others. It often suggests gossip and can be a symbol of so-

cial climbing, arrogance, or trying to appear stylish. This may be showing you your general attitude in dealing with others, how you handle life in general, or the mental games you play.

BICYCLING:
Keeping in balance, moving under your own power, self-motivation.

Unicycle: Very fine balance, takes real skill and practice, may imply that you need a delicate balance in the situation you are now going through.

BOOMERANG:
May symbolize getting back what you have sent out, reaping what you have sown.

BOWLING:
Implies strikes and hits for success. Could be pun on a striking performance or may say you have to put others down in order to feel successful.

Gutter Ball: Getting in a rut, down a beaten path, can't change direction once started. Could be hint you are in a rut and need to make some changes.

CARDS:
Playing card games implies taking chances, being controlled by luck, or blaming things on luck as opposed to taking responsibility for your actions and affairs. This could say you love to gamble or that you tend to take too many chances. Card playing may also denote one who has little or no interest in the deeper issues of life, one who is just passing the time away—not doing anything of real importance. Cards may signify your wheeling and dealing in life.

CHECKERS AND CHESS:
This takes strategy, matching wits, good use of intellect, planning ahead. Could be a hint to plan your life or your "next move" more carefully.

CLUE:
This could be a pun on finding or receiving clues as to how to solve a problem. What "clues" did you find in your dream?

DEALING:
This may indicate how you feel fate is dealing with you, how you deal with your fate or with other people (no cheating), and making a deal (good or bad).

Dropping Cards: May indicate a need to drop the "deal" or that you are making a bad deal/decision/bargain, agreeing to an unfair deal, or could imply the possibility of a "stacked deck," manipulations, double-dealing.

DICE:
Game of fate, taking chances, leaving your life to chance. Can imply a need to take dominion of life and affairs, learn to master your fate.

Die: May be a pun on death, dying, killing yourself, taking unnecessary chances with your life.

FISHING:
Often represents seeking spiritual food or perhaps the need to do this. Could also be fishing around for ideas or opportunities.

FOOTBALL:
Cooperation or chaos, making passes, blocking and interfering with the efforts of others, rough or foul play, carrying the ball, taking initiative, making your goals, hard way to go.

FRISBEE:
This would most likely symbolize a friendly give and take situation or relationship with no strong sense of competition or antagonism as in some other games.

GAMBLING, CASINO GAMES:
This implies gambles you are taking in life, the chances you take, the risks you are running. This could be a warning that what you are about to

do will be a gamble or possibly a greater risk than you can afford to take. Look closely at the action and feeling of the dream.

GOLF:
This could indicate a need to play, relax, and get away from it all, or may be a pun on your "driving range," how hard you drive yourself or others. Could be you take many swings but never reach your goal...or maybe you are just putting along...or even cheating a little here and there. How *do* you play the game? This could be a bad pun of gulf.

HOCKEY:
Teamwork, attaining and protecting goals, and "putting one over" on your opponent. Many hard knocks, moving at high speed.

HOP SCOTCH:
Hopping around from this to that, skipping things, not staying in one place long, childish or immature activity.

HUNTING:
May symbolize search for yourself or for a better way of life, or may show a hidden desire to hurt, maim, and kill. This may represent a desire to kill out your animal nature, if that fits.

JOGGING:
Can mean pacing yourself, running at the right speed and distance for you, doing a good job, taking care of yourself; but could be hint that you need to jog for your health.

JUMP ROPE:
May imply jumping at the commands or demands of others, getting the jump on someone, or a need to have a good workout, toughen up, get yourself in better shape.

MONOPOLY:
Most likely this is a pun on how you monopolize others or how someone is trying to monopolize you. Can be showing you the way you do business or be a warning as to the intentions of those around you, depending on the action of the dream.

POKER:
Game of bluff, chance; could lose your shirt, can indicate that you are taking a gamble or risk in some way or you may be "poking" into something.

POOL:
Can be a game of relaxation and fun, or can be chance-taking for fun or money. Could be a pun on your need to pool your efforts, funds, or skills in some project.

PUZZLE:
This may represent a puzzling situation, a thing untried, unknown, unfamiliar, unfinished, one that needs to be turned over in your mind to see all sides of it or how it "fits together." Can be a problem you have to solve, a mental challenge, possibly a hint that you don't have all the facts, pieces, or parts to solve this.

Crossword Puzzle: Can be a pun on cross words thought or spoken which you may need to "work on" in some way, or it can relate to a mental challenge being put before you.

Jigsaw Puzzle: Same general meaning as puzzle, but check to see if you have all the pieces. Missing parts could indicate that you do not have all the facts you need to make a good decision or to complete something which may be puzzling you.

RACQUETBALL:
Good symbol for action and reaction, ricochet effects of our actions; can show need for fast reflexes in your situation or be a pun on "What's your racket?"

RACING:
Life in the fast lane, moving too fast, going around in circles, trying to get ahead, spinning your wheels, playing a dangerous game.

Autos: Can be test of car and driver, body and soul. Implies a fast lifestyle and gambling with sudden death.

Foot: Test of self, moving on your own power, making the most of all your abilities, doing things the hard way, making it all on your own.

Horse: Test of horses (emotions) and your control over them. May refer to your chakras or energy fields and how you use these.

SKATES:
May imply you are skating on thin ice.

SKIING:
Test of mental and muscle strength; agility and balance. Can be pitting yourself against yourself, trying to improve or better your own record. Moving and maneuvering under your own power.

SOLITAIRE:
May be a pun on being alone, making it on your own, working things out all by yourself, being independent, or could be a hint for you to make time for solitude, find out what you can do alone. This may also symbolize competition with yourself and/or testing your own abilities, or possibly point out how you are cheating yourself!

SKIPPING:
This may indicate your need to take a more light-hearted, joyful approach to life and its affairs or could be a warning that you are skipping something important, depending on the feeling of the dream.

SWIMMING:
Usually this is spiritual activity such as prayer, meditation, service to others, drive for spiritual achievements; but may imply you need to "get into the swim" of things or suggest this as a good exercise for you. Can imply that you are "getting in over your head" in some way.

TARGET PRACTICE:
Taking pot shots at other's expense (criticisms), or can be symbol of working on your aims.

TENNIS, PING PONG:
Going back and forth over the same territory over and over. May mean fun and games, endless repetition, or action and reaction.

Tennis Racquet: Can be a pun on "it's a racket," racketeering, or a shady deal of some kind.

TRIVIA:
Probably a pun on your getting involved in things that are trivial in nature, following trivial pursuits in life, a hint that you are not taking your life seriously or making the most of your opportunities.

VIDEO GAMES:
Sharpening your wits and mental reflexes, playing mental games, testing your physical and mental abilities.

WRESTLING:
Can be grappling, struggling with life, ideas, or your work.

My Own Game Symbols

My Own Game Symbols continued...

CHAPTER 26

Gardens

A man's mind is like a garden which may be intelligently cultivated or allowed to run wild. But whether cultivated or neglected, it must, and will, bring forth.

— *James Allen*

A garden represents the fertile soil of your mind in which you plant and grow ideas and seed-thoughts. As Edgar Cayce says, "Thoughts are things" and "Mind is the builder." The ideas you hold in mind produce the events and situations in your life. A garden can be a symbol of your soul, your mind, your thoughts, your job, your ministry, or your flock (any group of people within your sphere of influence: friends, family, students, co-workers, etc.).

A garden may also be the Garden of Prayer where you plant your hopes, dreams, and prayers for yourself and others. Just as a garden can produce both weeds and flowers unless diligently cared for, our minds also need continuous vigilance and cultivation and persistent weeding.

The Soil

Earth is the basis for growth, fertility, fecundity; a starting place, foundation, bottom line; physical level, practicality, or being "down to earth." As such, it is symbolic of the fertility of our minds to produce that which is sown. "As a man thinketh, so is he."

BARREN GROUND:
Nothing growing, nothing doing, no comfort, help, beauty, support, or sustenance. Unused opportunities, wasteland.

GRASS:
Part of garden, part of fertility of mind; depicts healing, growth, balance, or can be an allusion to surface conditions.

> **Mowing:** Represents discipline, shaping, curtailing, trimming your thought patterns.

MUD, MIRE:
Slippery footing or emotional barrier you don't want to move through. Mud on anything implies emotional problems or difficulties clinging to the situation represented by the article. May say the emotional trauma has to be cleared away before the problem can be intelligently handled.

Garden Props

ARBOR:
Structure, form, outline, discipline, support, or framework for our ideas.

COLD FRAME:
Area of extra care, protection, and nurturing.

FENCE:

Protection or limitation, can be a supporting device for growth. Protection from intrusion or strong wind, a boundary. May symbolize need for privacy, retreat from the world, or indicate this is *my space*. Can limit or support your view of the world.

FLOWER POTS:

Both a protection and a restriction to the growth of whatever is planted. The protection is needed in early stages of development but later becomes a boundary which limits further growth and development.

> **Pot-Bound:** When the plant becomes pot-bound, it must either break out of the pot or have its growth thwarted. Many of us reach this stage not once but many times in our lives, being forced to make a decision to either remain bound or break away from old, safe, familiar customs and belief systems (especially religious dogma) and move on to wider horizons and a richer, fuller life.

GREENHOUSE:

A place to give special care to tender, growing things, symbolizing extra protection and attention to the growth and development of whatever is planted. This could imply a need to carefully nourish your new project, seed-thought, or affirmation. May indicate food-for-thought items, a touch-of-beauty, spiritual ideals, or possibly the fruit of your labors growing.

HANGING POTS:

Could depict hang-ups or individualized thought-patterns and ideas you are cultivating, or affirmations or ideas you are cultivating. These may portray isolated items in your mind not presently connected with the rest of your thinking, or perhaps these ideas, beliefs, and concepts are "pot-bound"— limited in scope with no room for growth and expansion—left "hanging there," so to speak.

LAWN MOWER:

Instrument of discipline for the weeds of negative thinking and a means of curtailing and keeping one's thoughts "in line," under control; regular care.

STAKES:

Supports, anchors, supportive measures, something to cling to.

TRELLIS:

Type of physical support or framework to grow on, lean on, cling to, or wrap around. Our basic belief system is a type of framework.

Gardening Actions

DIGGING:

Getting at the root of the matter.

FERTILIZING:

Giving the best possible conditions for growth; act of loving care.

GARDENER'S ACTIONS:

These indicate the care or neglect given to your thinking, creative ideas, talents, and potentials.

HARVESTING:

Reaping what you have sown mentally, physically, and emotionally.

HOEING, CULTIVATING:

Cleaning out weeds, negative thoughts; keeping mind open, loose, pliable, ideal for growth.

PLANTING SEEDS:

Would imply new sowing; new ideas, prayers, affirmations, decrees, thoughts, habits, or talents we want to encourage. May symbolize repeating positive seed-thoughts in your mind. (Negative thoughts take root also.)

PLOWING, SOIL CARE:

Relates to our mental preparations, prayer, meditation, study, and efforts to improve ourselves.

Plow Under: Wipe out, removing old growth to make way for the new, a type of cleansing, forgiving, letting go, and preparing the mind for the coming new seeds and plants. May signal the end of one cycle and beginning of another.

PRUNING:

Shaping, disciplining, exercising control over the size, shape, and form of your new ideas, affirmations, habits; cutting out dead ends, removing faults. Dream may imply a need to eliminate something from your habitual thinking or may imply that you are making cutting remarks, cutting people down, cutting them off short; or, this could be a pun for "Cut that out!"

PULLING WEEDS:

Equivalent to routing-out wrong thinking, bad habits, or negative ideas.

TRANSPLANTING:

Moving ideas out into the open or forefront of your mind. Could be replacing negative ideas with positive ones.

WATERING PLANTS:

Act of nourishing and encouraging the growth of your planted seed-thoughts.

WEEDING:

Banishing all unwanted, negative, unloving thoughts from the garden of our minds, not allowing them room to take root. Dream may be reminding us to do this more diligently.

Garden Miscellaneous

FORMAL GARDEN:

Sign of well-disciplined thought patterns, constant watchfulness, and elimination of weed-thoughts; continuous care and attention to detail.

INSECT-RIDDEN:

Allowing negative, nasty thoughts to eat, gnaw, and riddle your plants, plans, ideas, prayers, affirmations.

NEGLECTED PLANTS:

Unused or neglected talents, ideas, ideals, gifts; lack of discipline, watchfulness, and nurture for your seed-thoughts and good intentions. Strong hint to start cultivating good thinking habits.

POISONS:

This can depict your attempts to rid yourself of things (or people) that "bug you" by poisonous words, thoughts, or deeds which affect everything in your radius in a negative, withering way. (Radiating your hate or anger in all directions.) Implies a need to find loving solutions which uplift rather than harm and to watch the tenure of your thoughts.

ROCK GARDEN:

Unchanging truth (rock) and beauty (flowers).

ROOF GARDEN:

Planting your ideas and ideals high above the material level.

STRAIGHT ROWS:

Implies neat, orderly, logical, disciplined thinking.

Seeds and Bulbs

Seeds in dreams portray unplanted, undeveloped possibilities capable of tremendous growth and expansion which we can grow and nurture in the fertile soil of our minds. They symbolize an undeveloped quality or talent, the power of an idea, a new beginning, a potential for good or evil.

ACORN:

Symbol of durability and strength; small beginnings, ideas, goals, or events which have great potential for growth or to exert a powerful influence in the lives of others.

BULBS:

These are like seed ideas which grow, only they are larger and much slower growing. May stay dormant a long time, then show up unexpectedly.

MUSTARD SEED:
Biblical symbol of faith.

NUTS:
Seed ideas with greatest potential for growth. May symbolise an idea or concept "in a nutshell."

SPROUTS:
Ideas, thoughts, or affirmations you have planted which are now coming into manifestation, becoming visible on the physical plane.

Flowers

Flowers depict beautiful, loving thoughts, kindness, caring, joy, compassion, gentleness, grace, and abundance. They are an expression of love, joy, beauty, freedom, happiness, and healing. (Recent studies indicate healing qualities in the blossoms of flowers as well as of herbs.) Flowers may also be "time tellers," as many blossoms are closely associated with a particular season. These can be important clues, especially in ESP dreams.

FLOWERS IN BUD:
Promise of good things to come, eventual fruits of your labors.

FLOWERS IN POTS:
Contained, restrained, restricted, limited in growth. Symbolic of being "pot-bound" in your thinking, unable to go or grow beyond a certain point. Limited, thwarted, strong need to break loose.

FLORAL BOUQUET:
Bouquets given or received represent respect, affection, approval, friendship, admiration, love, and rewards. Flowers also emanate healing energies.

FLORAL BRANCHES:
These depict all the qualities of a floral bouquet plus the added strength and grace of the tree, as well as the characteristics symbolized by the type of tree.

FLORAL GIFTS IN GENERAL:
Consider the qualities symbolized by the type of flowers, the color meaning, and the idea represented by the gift to find the fullest interpretation.

FLOWER BUDS:
Can be talents or qualities, symbolized by the type of plant, which are taking shape, ready to open, coming to their peak of perfection. May imply hopes, affirmations, prayers, or goals as well, especially when these are flowers in general and not a specific variety.

NEGLECTED FLOWERS:
Unused, uncared-for hopes, dreams, talents, or potentials.

Floral Time Tellers

SPRING; EARLY:
Crocus, daffodils, tulips, rockcress, violets, dandelions.

LATE SPRING:
Dogwoods, lilacs, redbuds, fruit trees, peonies.

SUMMER:
Roses, phlox, daisies; many, many more.

FALL:
Chrysanthemums, asters, trees, and shrubs with colorful foliage, falling leaves.

WINTER:
Mistletoe, holly, bare branches.

Plants and Flowers

Plants symbolize full or partially-grown ideas which we plant in our minds; new ideas, beliefs, concepts, affirmations, prayers, positive statements, decrees.

ACACIA:
Portrays eternal love, immortal love.

AGERATUM, PURPLE:
Peace, gentleness, quiet devotion, steadfastness.

ALYSSUM:
Grace, gentleness, artistry, delicacy.

AMARANTH:
Symbol of immortality, life everlasting.

ANEMONE:
Resurrection, transformation.

ASTERS, HARDY FALL:
Colorful stars, symbols of God's grace, love, and blessings freely given to all.

BABY'S BREATH:
Sweet, gentle, innocent, harmless.

BACHELOR BUTTONS:
Old symbol for celibacy.

CACTUS:
Sticky situation, a need to handle with care, a delicate touch, barriers for self-protection; stiff, unbending plant or mental activity; very slow to change; hard to reach or to get in touch with. You can get stuck with this idea or attitude.

CARNATIONS:
Symbol of light-heartedness, joy, vitality, and sometimes bachelorhood. However, on Mother's Day red carnations are used to indicate a living mother, while white ones indicate she no longer lives.

CHRYSANTHEMUMS:
Symbol of autumn, end of summer, harvest, abundance, prosperity, spirit of gratitude, humility, and thanksgiving or can be a pun on keeping "mum."

COLUMBINE:
Gentleness and enlightenment; its seven petals symbolize the seven gifts of the spirit.

CLOVER, RED:
Symbol of plenitude, faith, love, and healing.

CLOVER, WHITE:
Depicts good luck, faith, hope, and love that spring eternal. Blessings for the humble; carefree days.

COSMOS:
Shouts of joy and praise, happiness, gay spirits, love overflowing.

CROCUS:
Harbingers of spring, first blooms of the season, sign of growth, new beginnings, hope.

DAFFODILS:
Cheerful harbingers announcing the joys of resurrection and of spring. Gay, colorful joy-bringers.

DAISY:
Freshness, newness, simplicity, refreshment, innocence, cleanliness. Bright, cheery, sunny.

DELPHINIUM:
Chants of praise, adoration, devotion; constant prayers rising to God. Inspiration and blessings radiated to all.

FERN:
Peaceful acceptance, grace, serenity, gentility, and quietude.

FORGET-ME-NOT:
Friendship, caring, loving thoughts.

FUSCHIA:
Astral bells, angel bells, harmony, healing for those who grieve.

GERANIUMS:
Positive attitudes, strength of purpose, steadfastness and cheer.

GLADIOLAS:
Can be a pun on gladness of heart.

GOLDENROD:
This is a weed to many but is also a symbol of spiritual discipline. It is sometimes the cause of hayfever and allergies, so could be a warning depending on the dream.

IMMORTELLES:
Flower of the soul.

IMPATIENS:
Colorful symbol of patience, steadfastness, loving kindness.

IRIS:
Symbol of power.

JASMINE:
Peace, goodwill, healing.

LARKSPURS:
"Little spires" of aspiration, joy, gratitude, and loving emanations.

LAVENDER:
Aspiration, ancient wisdom, holiness, constancy in prayer, steady upliftment, and blessings for all.

LILY:
Faith, grace; pure, holy thoughts; abstract thinking; the wine cup, grail, chalice; faith; chakras, crown chakra; new life, resurrection, or spiritual healing powers bestowed upon the dreamer.

   White Lily: Purity, virginity.

   Seven White Lilies: All seven chakras open and purified.

LOTUS:
Represents opening of the chakras, especially the crown chakra; opening to God ideas, expanding awareness, beauty of the soul. If in bud stage this would show the promise of opening.

MAGIC LILIES:
Magic, also joy and laughter.

MARIGOLDS:
Gaily colored soldiers boldly protecting their area. Blossoms symbolize friendliness, cheer, courage, and joyful service rendered to the plant kingdom.

MISTLETOE:
Parasitic thoughts, ideas that drain and kill it's host—you! Can be a symbol of death, but it also depicts tiny pearls of love and service and was a religious symbol of the Druids.

MORNING GLORY:
Herald of the dawn, symbol of morning prayers said and daily blessings received.

NARCISSUS:
Self-reflection, also egotism, self-love, vanity.

NASTURTIUM:
Depict songs of the devas, trumpets of the fairies, cheerful gladiators protecting their area with their circular green shields, serving with joy and gladness.

ORCHID:
A delicate plant requiring special care and conditions, symbol of gentleness, delicacy, or of very special occasions, usually linked with love and

romance but also beauty and sensuality. Could be linked with your feelings the first time you gave or received an orchid.

PANSIES:
Gentle thoughts and friendly faces.

PEONIES:
Well-developed thoughts, possibly rooted in the past. These also are symbolic of Memorial Day.

PETUNIA:
Peace, harmony, serenity, upliftment of body and soul.

PODS:
Containers for multitudes of "seed" ideas; thoughts that grow, multiply, and bring forth after their kind.

POPPIES:
Symbol of forgetfulness, happy dreams.

REEDS:
Symbol of mind bending to spirit.

ROSE:
Symbol of Christ love, spiritual love, Christ consciousness, beauty.

> **Fragrance:** Same as rose (above), also a symbol that a high spiritual being is near you.
>
> **Pink Rose:** Love, affection, kindness, compassion, aspiration, brotherly love.
>
> **Red Rose:** Human love, personal love, desire, being in love.
>
> **White Rose:** Pure love, unconditional love, brotherly or cosmic love. Agape.

SNAPDRAGON:
Symbol of the mouth, jaw, communicating, and mental telepathy.

STAR OF BETHLEHEM:
Purity.

SUNFLOWER:
Traditionally follows the sun, follows God's light, depicts nature in its fullness; abundance, sunshine, sunny disposition, prosperity.

THISTLE:
Symbol of trial, hardship, and difficulties.

THORNY PLANTS:
Severity, hardship.

TULIPS:
"Two lips" announcing spring and the joy of living; they represent faith, hope, and charity.

VERBENA:
Peace.

VIOLETS:
Symbol of shyness, humility, quiet joy, tender thoughts, gentle love.

WATER LILY:
Fruit of peaceful emotions.

WATER HYACINTH:
Can be beautiful but is presently associated with creeping, choking, polluting streams or essential life forces, so may imply negative thinking.

WEEDS:
Negative thoughts of all kinds which can choke out the fine and beautiful in you, stunting your spiritual growth. May also be a pun on marijuana which can also harm spiritual growth.

> **Pulling Weeds:** Act of removing the unwanted ideas, or may symbolize your need to do this.

WILDFLOWERS:
God's blessings sprinkled generously over all.

ZINNIAS:
Joys of summer, symbol of beauty and abundance, of friendship, joy, and laughter.

Herbs

Herbs symbolize healthful, healing, soothing remedial thoughts, ideas, and prayers. To dream of a specific herb may be an indication that your body has a need for this particular herb. A gift of herbs may represent the gift of healing.

ROSEMARY:
Remembrance and friendship.

RUE:
Sorrow, despair.

SAGE:
Wisdom, prudence.

THYME:
Peace. May also be a pun on time.

Vegetables

Vegetables symbolize ideas that will feed and nourish you and others; productive ideas.

BEANS:
May be a pun saying, "You don't know beans" about it or may depict a very productive idea. Could be a pun on "using your bean."

CORN KERNELS:
Symbol of kernels of truth.

CORN, PLANTS:
Can be pun on "corny" or mean potential for truth. Corn may represent psychic currents or energies, too.

ONIONS:
Bitter fruit, karma, strong ideas and opinions that can be offensive to others.

PEAS:
Can be a food you need in your diet or may be a pun on peace.

Vines

BRAMBLES:
Stickers, hang-ups, things we get "stuck" on or stuck with.

CLIMBING VINES:
Represents ambitious thoughts, ideas, or memories that cling. Can say, "Hang in there." May depict clinging to others, someone or something for support, non-self sufficiency.

> **Mass of Climbing Vines:** Can be mass confusion.

GRAPE VINES:
Symbol of rewards, prosperity, spiritual fruits.

> **Vineyard:** Symbol of earthly riches, rewards, the fruits of your labor, prosperity, blessings.

POISON IVY:
Poisonous thoughts that cling like hate and revenge, resentment, jealousy; irritating thoughts or memories. Possible pun on poisonous conditions or something to be avoided.

Shrubs

BURNING BUSH, ACTUAL:
Symbol of the beginning of spiritual awakening in you. May symbolize your spiritual purification and preparation or your need for this, with the promise of a great spiritual awakening to come.

> **Burning Bush, Plant:** May represent your need to prepare for a coming spiritual awakening or say that your awakening is imminent. If you are already on the path, it may imply an initiation, a new awakening, or a new cycle of awareness and growth to come.

FLOWERING SHRUBS:
Sign of abundance, profusion, beauty, happiness, prosperity, God's love for you.

HEDGE:
This can be a border, limit, boundary, or protection; or, may denote hedging, dodging, delaying tactics, avoiding involvement in some way.

LAUREL:
Symbol of victory.

LILAC:
Symbol of first love.

THORN BUSH:
Place of big hang-ups, base desires you can be caught up in; getting caught, caught-up, something you can get stuck on or stuck with. May also represent severity.

Trees

A tree often represents the "Tree of Knowledge," the fruits of your labors, or the absence of them. Notice whether or not the tree is healthy and growing in a balanced way, as it can depict your spiritual life and its state. May denote your belief system, your vitality, your state of health, or may be a pun on the family tree and its ties.

FLOWERING TREES:
Trees often signify the state of your spiritual growth and development. Flowering would be sign of inner beauty, good growth, abundance, and promise of eventual fruits of your spiritual labors.

FOREST, MANY TREES:
Can be a pun on "Can't see the trees for the forest." If it feels good it may mean peace, quiet, stillness, the serenity of nature, possibly your need to find a quiet place and be still for awhile.

FRUIT TREES IN FRUIT:
Representative of the fruits of your labors in particular, also your talents and good deeds. Look at the kind and condition of the fruits you have planted.

Rotten Fruit: Warning of what you have sown.

ROOTS:
These can symbolize the roots or rootedness of one's belief system, one's connection with the earth, the universe, and all things, or the cause/root of a matter. May also depict one's family ties, roots, and bonds. Roots may represent a reaching into the past, karmic roots, or connections of many lives and experiences. Note the kind of soil or neighborhood.

UPROOTED TREE:
Out of balance, torn from its physical connections or foundations, ungrounded, disconnected. Can imply your belief system is uprooted, may show the condition of your present spiritual state, or depict broken family connections. May be a warning of a major upset.

UPSIDE DOWN TREE:
Roots in the air or branches in or on the ground can say that you or your beliefs are "rooted" in heavenly things, in the spiritual realms. Good symbol.

Tree Types

APPLE:
Ancient symbol of fertility, also of temptation and your ability to bear fruit.

CEDAR:
Biblical plant renowned for its strength and endurance.

CHERRY TREE:
Delicate beauty, fragile loveliness, grace, gentility, and serenity. These can be inspirational as well.

CHRISTMAS TREE:
Represents the Christ spirit, lovingness, Christianity, the Christmas season, the Christ in you.

DOGWOOD:
Beauty, grace, simplicity, gentleness, delicate strength.

EUCALYPTUS:
Gentle healing powers, strength, durability, wisdom, caringness.

FIG TREE:
Can represent the tree of life, the power of generation and regeneration, an overbearing abundance if alive. When cut down it depicts the end of one generation and the beginning of another.

FIR TREES:
Often associated with the idea and meaning represented by Christmas tree, or can represent strong, straight, towering spiritual growth.

FRANKINCENSE:
Wisdom, centering, devotion, and prayers; transmuting things from physical to spiritual.

MAPLE:
Friendly philosopher, warmth, openness, humility, contentment. A colorful character.

OAK TREE:
Noted for strength, endurance, steadfastness, power, wisdom, solidarity, majesty.

OLIVE TREE:
Ancient symbol of the holy land, peace, love, and the path of healing and regeneration.

ORANGE TREES:
Can represent the fruits of your labors.

> **Orange Blossoms:** Traditional symbol for a wedding but may represent the mystical, spiritual marriage rather than a physical one.

PALM TREE OR BRANCH:
Victory, unfolding of spiritual forces.

PINE:
Represents peaceful forces, psychic energies, healing, calmness, serenity, love, growth, or can mean sadness (pining away).

POMEGRANATE:
Tree of many, many seeds. Symbol of production, reproduction, sex, and fertility.

REDWOOD TREE:
Ancient wisdom, brotherhood, lofty ideals, truth, dignity, strength, endurance, peace, and solitude.

SASSAFRAS:
Stateliness, healing and purifying qualities.

WEEPING WILLOW:
Mourning, remorse, tears and sorrow of death, self-pity, or can be grace, beauty, flexibility, gentleness in motion.

YEW:
Strength and sinew, but can be a pun on you!

Leaves

Leaves in general can be a pun on leaving or departing, especially if the leaves are blowing away from you.

FRESH GREEN LEAVES:
Represent new growth, new starts or potential, new chance at life. Fresh green growth in general can be a symbol of healing or healing forces at work in a situation.

AUTUMN LEAVES, FALLING:
These represent old memories, ideas, thought-forms, concepts, or teachings which have passed their prime or usefulness. Ready or needing to be cast aside. May designate the end of a season or cycle, a slowing down, oncoming time of harvest and/or rest. Change.

DEAD LEAVES:
Dead or dying ideas, thoughts; old memories, wastes, left-overs from another time which need

to be cast aside, cleared, and cleansed. Physical, mental, or emotional cast-offs, body dross, things which need to be eliminated or returned to the Source.

RAKING:
Gathering up, cleaning up, cleaning and clearing your mind of unnecessary burdens.

BURNING LEAVES:
Act of purifying, transforming, eliminating the old (ideas, memories, etc.). Finishing, completion, end of the matter.

My Own Garden Symbols

CHAPTER 27

Historic Settings: Our Past Lives in Review

Nature decrees that when the creature can no longer fulfill its purpose, it should be removed from this sphere of activity and given a fresh start.
— Manley Hall

Ancient Scenes

From time to time you may find yourself in a dream setting that appears to be straight out of the pages of history or perhaps a motion picture backdrop. The buildings, the streets, the people are all typical of a scene in ancient Rome, Egypt, or maybe the wild West. You may find yourself in an Arabian tent, a straw hut, or a fine Grecian palace.

Your first reaction may be sheer unbelief, or perhaps you would dismiss it as a silly dream. Not so. Whether you believe in reincarnation or not, you may have glimpses of former lifetimes now and then—not to convince you that you have lived before and will do so again, but to help you understand a circumstance that existed **then** and to understand how that situation relates to the problem you are struggling to work through **now**.

Ancient Themes

The theme that repeats itself most in these dreams is one of failure to forgive, trust, or love another in a previous lifetime; and this hatred, distrust, or unforgiveness has been a recurring block in all your subsequent relationships with that person (the real source of instant hate or dislike). Therefore, your dream may depict the original cause of the trouble, which may have happened many centuries before, so that you may understand, forgive, and make peace. You may want to pay particular attention to the dream action, for it may be a recurring theme woven through many dreams.

Old-fashioned clothing in a modern setting would most likely depict an out-of-date attitude and not a past life recall, unless the circumstances were such that you felt the clothing represented a particular attitude held in that time period.

Modern clothing in an old-fashioned setting may simply say that you are out of date, out of sync, or could be ahead of your time.

The Tie That Binds

Old wisdom teachings tell us that hate and love are extremely strong bonds; while a loving attitude toward everyone is our ultimate goal, hate is the karmic tie that pulls us back into earthly lifetimes again and again until at last we have learned to obey Christ's command to "Love one another, even as I have loved you."

God is a loving Father who gives us many, many chances to make right our wrong-doing, and this is what reincarnation is really all about. For those who doubt, references to reincarnation can be found in the Bible if one cares to look. (Matt. 16:13, 17:10 or John 1:21, to name a few.)

So...when you find yourself in a Roman toga or a Hawaiian hula skirt, pay attention! Often the people you meet in these past life episodes are people who are very close to you in your present life. Some—loving and supporting—are old loves, while others are old hates to be overcome now.

Don't be at all surprised if the old hate in your life turns out to be your partner in marriage; this happens quite frequently. One of you wronged the other—one of you never forgave, and now you two are fighting that battle once again, or at least struggling to make amends. A love that can also forgive is all-important.

Even when two people part in hurt and anger, there is a need to eventually make peace to avoid having to go through it all yet another time. Unforgiveness causes karma!

As always, your dreams are giving you insights, guidance, and the understanding necessary to help you solve your present problems. They use the symbols that work best for you.

My Own Historic Symbols

CHAPTER 28

Household Furniture, Musical Instruments, and Tools

Furniture

Furniture in dreams represents the thought-forms your mind creates as it thinks. Your ideas literally take form and shape in your mind, becoming solidified thoughts and beliefs which then stand as clear symbols of the state of your mind, your consciousness, ideas, beliefs, memories, customs, and habits.

Notice what condition the furniture is in, whether new or old, shabby or beautiful, broken down or in good shape.

Types of Furniture

ANTIQUES:
If these are beautiful and well cared-for they represent fine, high ideals, beliefs, and principles which have stood the test of time; held and cherished with good reason. Antiques may also represent family heirlooms, both physical and mental, such as beliefs, values, ties, pride, and memories. Antiques may also depict the things you treasure, or may be past life indicators—symbols of another lifestyle.

BABY FURNITURE:
Would depict childish, immature ideas or ideas based on a new project or concept you have just given birth to. Could be wishful thinking (desire for a family) or an ESP symbol of what is to come.

BEAUTIFUL FURNISHINGS:
Loving, gentle, compassionate, understanding, caring thoughts, prayers, and ideas. Forgiving attitudes.

BROKEN DOWN FURNITURE:
Concepts which are no longer useful or relevant, possibly broken from misuse which would imply a need to renovate and update your thinking in the area you find it. This could also denote negative thinking, a worried or mentally unstable mind.

CLUTTERED:
Signifies sloppy, undisciplined thinking habits; an obvious need to sort things out, throw out the unusable, find a right place for everything, put some order into your thinking and feeling habits.

FOREIGN:
Furniture from other lands and cultures can depict ideas that are foreign to you, different from your usual thinking or basic beliefs. Note whether you accept or reject these.

MODERN FURNITURE:
These would naturally depict new, modern ideas and concepts. This may be very good, forward thinking or possibly something you have not really thought through yet; could be untried ideas.

NEW FURNITURE:
New ideas, formed or possibly still forming.

OLD FASHIONED FURNITURE:

If these are in good shape they would portray good, solid, old ideas still relevant today. Basic, unchanging, having stood the test of time; but may also represent old-fashioned, out-of-date, questionable values, things no longer appropriate, not what they once were, or behind-the-times thinking, especially if these are not in tip-top condition or are no longer serving a useful purpose.

TRADITIONAL:

These would symbolize traditions, long-held beliefs which are slow to give way to new ones. Traditional values change slowly, are considered to be solid, valuable, unquestionable, stable. May depict good taste, desire for only the time-tested ideas and beliefs, safe ground, being in line with the accepted beliefs and traditions of those around you.

Furnishings

AFGHAN:

Personal security, warmth.

ASHTRAY:

Repository for ashes of old habits, grievances, ideas; also oblique reference to smoking habits.

Broken Ashtray: Broken smoking habit.

BAR:

May be a pun on barring your way, barring others from something, or may depict desire for strong drink or social amenities, depending on your feelings.

Beverage Bar: Can be a place to serve refreshment, physical or spiritual, or may be a hint that alcoholic drinks are barring you from something.

Breakfast or Snack Bar: Can depict nourishing foods, family togetherness, or could say snacks are barring you from something.

Exercise Bar: May be a hint to exercise your body more, exercise your mind, or may symbolize a barrier.

BED:

May represent rest, dreams, sex, privacy, sleep, or marital situation. Can say, "You made your bed...now you have to lie in it."

Double Bed: Often symbolizes the marital state and your relationship with your partner in particular, as well as other ideas listed under *Bed*.

Four-poster: Refers to the four corners or stabilizing qualities that hold the marriage together. May represent the basis and foundation of the marriage, or could be old-fashioned ideas about love and marriage.

Hide-a-bed: Temporary situation, makeshift situation, hidden sex or relationships, drop-in affairs, kiss and tell affairs, or desire to hide these.

Single Bed: Denotes the single life, aloneness, privacy, things pertaining to you alone, being "on your own," independence, singleness of purpose.

Twin Beds: If you are in a marital relationship sleeping in a double bed, a dream of twin beds may denote a separation, a parting of the ways, a distance coming between you, or thoughts along that line.

Making a Bed: Can be a pun on having to lie in the bed you have made, coping with a situation you have created. Could be making up your mind about a marriage or deciding not to get back into that situation again. May depict the act of righting an upset or marital misunderstanding, smoothing out the wrinkles or rough spots in a marriage or partnership. A double bed usually indicates a marriage or partnership; a single bed often signifies living alone or going it alone.

Mattress: Can denote the foundation of a relationship.

Water Bed: May imply instability, an emotional foundation, latest fad, or greater comfort, depending on your feeling.

Water Bed You Don't Own: If you don't own a water bed, this may symbolize an emotional situation, fluctuations, repercussions, emotional reactions, ups and downs, lack of a firm commitment or solid foundation in your relationships with yourself or with others.

BEDSPREAD:
Depicts the outer appearance, cover-up, of your private life, sex life, or marriage.

BELLS:
When bells of any kind ring in a dream it is to call your attention to that particular part of the dream. There is something important for you to see or hear.

Silver Bells: Mysticism.

BIBLE:
Holy Word, spiritual laws, inspiration, truth, comfort, knowledge, God's promises, ten commandments, way of life, possibly your basic belief system, or may be a hint to turn to the Bible more often.

Bible Verse: Whether given as chapter and verse number or quoted verbatim, it would indicate a need to think about the words and idea revealed. Can be a personal message to you.

BLANKET:
Often depicts security, can be a "cover up."

No Blanket: Could imply insecurity, feeling unsure of yourself.

BOOKS:
Knowledge, information, opinions, fixed ideas (already in print), ideas, rules, laws, history, facts, fiction, escape, fantasy, education, a group of related ideas, or may depict knowledge to be sought by you. See *Magazines*, this chapter.

Law Books: Depict law, mores, precedents, regulations, rules, codes of conduct. May imply a need to learn this.

Manual: Directions, instructions needed to do-it-yourself.

Many Books: May say you are reading too much.

Old Books: May mean out-of-date material and information, or could symbolize ancient wisdom.

Phone Book: Means of looking up, locating, making contact with old friends or new; getting help or information.

BOOKMARK:
Marks your place, may be a pun on "keeping your place" or imply "making your mark in the world" or in the field covered by the book. A large marker may say you will leave a big mark.

BRIC-A-BRAC:
Ornamental but unnecessary odds and ends, something you could do without, catch-all or dust-catcher.

BROOM:
Symbol of cleanliness, neatness, household chores, or a need to clean. Might be a pun on making a clean sweep. Clearing out your mind.

CABINET:
Place to store unused food-for-thought or ideas.

CALCULATOR:
May signify the calculating properties of our minds. Calculating thoughts, schemes, plans, computations.

CANDLE

Candle, Lit: Symbol of enlightenment, light source, worship, devotion, vigilance, church, warmth, romance, or a romantic setting, softness, friendliness, charm.

Candle, Unlit: Potential not being used.

Candleholder: Holder of light for others.

Golden: Holder of spiritual light.

CARPET:

Decorative covering of the basics, your foundation; could depict a cover up, represent what you stand upon or walk. Carpet can be *you* being walked on. See *Rugs*.

Wet or Damaged Carpet: May say your "stand" is all wet or that your basis, belief, or foundation is faulty or based on emotion. Note whose home or carpet.

CHAIN:

May represent a chain of thought, links (physical, mental, karmic or emotional), a thing or action which leads to or links with another, or a chain reaction. Could depict security, safety, or captivity, depending on the dream action and feeling.

CHAIR:

Depicts your seat, your place, your rights, your position; could indicate a need for more rest or say you are sitting too much and not accomplishing anything.

Boss' Chair: Seat of authority.

Giving Up Your Seat: Giving up your place.

Lounge Chair: May be your idea of rest, relaxation, or laziness, lack of ambition, negligence. Could be an invitation to take it easy.

Rocking Chair: Vacillating back and forth, undecided, or may be your idea of comfort and relaxation.

Straight Back Chair: This would depict strict discipline, a straight-backed or stiff-necked attitude, a lack of ease and luxury, or perhaps a tendency toward or need for strong self-discipline, depending on the feeling.

Throne: Seat of dominion, authority, ownership, leadership, responsibility or sign of being in charge of your life and affairs, unless someone else is sitting on it! May also be a pun for commode!

CHEST OF DRAWERS:

May be a container for your attitudes, ideas, memories, knowledge, even talents. Might also refer to your feelings, chest, lungs, getting things "off of your chest", or may represent your heart and things stored in your heart or coming from the heart.

CHRISTMAS TREE:

Represents your Christ consciousness, Christ-like way of life, Christ-like ideals, also your Christmas spirit.

Christmas Lights Shining: Christ light shining in you.

Christmas Lights Not Turned On: Not using your potential, not letting your light shine.

CLOCK:

Consciousness of time passing by; indication of an important moment in time; could be the time of your life, or a hint to watch your timing.

Alarm Clock: This can be a pun on something to be alarmed about, especially when ringing. It would imply being aware, alert, prepared, concerned. Of course it can also represent time and possibly allude to how you are spending it.

Racing Clock: Symbolizes how time flies, time running out, little time left, or possibly hint you are wasting your time in some way.

Stopped: End of time, time running out, "ticker" stopped, death, end, no time left.

Ticking: Consciousness of time passing by, life goes on, or may be feeling of life passing you by.

COBWEB:
Represents confusion, uncertainty, mental or physical inaction. Need to clean house!

COMPUTER:
Represents your mind, brain, intellect, mental activities, memory, subconscious information and belief systems, old or new ideas and concepts, stored information, old and new ways of doing things; games to play, new areas to explore, room for mental expansion.

Disk: Place to store memories, beliefs, ideas, facts, information, attitudes, and emotions, or games you play.

Erased Disk: Old memories, beliefs gone.

CORNUCOPIA:
Symbol of abundance, prosperity, God's bounty.

COUCH OR LOVESEAT:
Togetherness, lovingness, closeness, harmony, or just lounging around.

CRADLE:
Resting place for new creations; can imply expectancy, nourishment, caring, protection, unfoldment of a new start, baby, project, or idea.

DESK:
Center of mental activity, study, concentration, computation, contemplation, work, plans, creativity, writing, communicating, accounting, unfinished business; your particular area of concern, responsibility, duty, area of expertise; working out problems; your job or your career.

ELECTRICAL CORDS:
Channels of power, carriers of useful energies; implies your ability to plug into extra power, bring in extra energy when needed; your connection to a power source, whether or not you stay plugged in.

ELECTRICAL EQUIPMENT:
An object capable of high-powered action, able to accomplish things more quickly and (usually) more efficiently. Could symbolize help or power from other people, other sources.

ELECTRICAL SWITCH:
Control panel; ability to regulate the power, turning it on or off, up or down as needed.

ERASER:
Can be a hint to erase, eradicate something from your mind, feelings, or actions. Possible need to let something go, clear it out of your mind, or eliminate a bad habit.

FERN STAND:
Could be a pun on making a firm stand or be a "standard" of beauty.

FIGURINE:
Small aspect of yourself, thinking small, demeaning or belittling yourself, underestimating yourself and your abilities, not measuring up

to your own standards, or not seeing yourself and your actions in the right perspective. Note what the model or figurine represents: this could denote your male, intellectual self you put down or the female, intuitive self. If the figure is a sportsman, warrior, or whatever, take this aspect of yourself into consideration also.

FILE CABINET:
Memory bank, storage of information, keeping your facts straight. May depict things you file away in mind or unnecessary details and memories you rummage through.

Open Drawers: Openness to giving or receiving new information.

Closed Drawers: May indicate privacy or unwillingness to share, give, or receive new ideas, information.

Locked: Can imply something the owner does not want revealed to others or does not want to look at. Can depict a closed mind, things locked inside one's heart.

FLASHLIGHT:
Depicts your ability or need to bring light into a situation, to direct a flow of light in a specific direction, to enlighten.

FLOWERS, BOUQUETS:
Beauty, graciousness, loving kindness in the home, loving thoughts, gentleness, harmony, honor.

FREEZER:
Your frozen assets or emotions, unused potentials, ideas, projects set aside for later on, not being presently used. May indicate a cold or chilly aspect or attitude in you. Taking things out of the freezer may imply a need to thaw out your unused potentials or your personal attitudes.

Thawing Ice or Objects: Depicts a softer attitude, a melting of harsh beliefs, letting down the barriers to your deepest feelings.

FURNACE:
Often depicts heart of the home, the love that keeps everyone warm and comfortable.

HOSE:
Depicts ability to channel, guide, direct, and focus energy, emotions, feelings, or life-giving substance into a situation or area.

IRON, IRONING BOARD:
Symbolic of ironing things out in your mind, smoothing out relationships, soothing rumpled emotions, straightening out the kinks mentally and emotionally.

KITCHEN SINK:
Center of activities surrounding food for thought. Area of selection and rejection, cleansing, cutting, culling, and preparation of ideas and concepts.

Waste Disposal: May denote what we waste or dispose of or imply how much we waste.

LAMP:
Instrument or channel of light or illumination which can be turned off or on at will. To turn off would be to shut out the light or the flow.

LAMPS, LIGHTS:
Generally denotes enlightenment. Notice the degree of light or darkness and the area involved, since you can be very knowledgeable in some areas and totally unaware in others.

Light Bulb: Symbolic of an idea, sudden inspiration, and illumination.

Moving Toward the Light: This may symbolize your need to move toward more light or show your progress and direction in becoming enlightened, depending on the feeling in the dream.

Moving Away: May be warning you are moving in the wrong direction, that something you have chosen is a step toward darkness.

Spotlight: May simply say that the spotlight, or attention, is focused on you or that you feel that everyone is looking at you.

Turning Off Lights: Can imply shutting out your source of enlightenment, refusing to "see the light," not wanting to know, understand, or look at the situation.

LETTERS, PAPERS:
These can be expressions of one's personal ideas, attitudes, opinions, hopes, dreams, thoughts, beliefs, concerns, purpose, decisions, intentions, or will. May also be information or messages to you. Could also be letter of learning, e.g. Ph.D.

Blank: An opportunity to express your ideas, or indication of having no idea or opinion in a matter.

Letter Unopened: Messages sent but not read, heard, accepted, digested, or heeded. Advice or information ignored.

Taking Notes: Collecting your thoughts, ideas, insights; getting your facts together.

Typing: Organizing your thoughts and feelings, putting your ideas together, expressing your talents, creativity,

Printed: Ideas solidified, finalized, ready to give to the world; also printed matter ready for you to read or study, accept or reject.

LINENS:
A fine linen cloth usually is associated with wealth, luxury, good taste, simplicity, aristocracy, and the good things in life.

MAGAZINES:
These represent one's special area of interest, goals, attitudes, concerns, hobby, career, or expertise.

MENDING:
May denote correcting a number of things: attitudes, situations, or circumstances where you need to make amends.

MIRROR:
Self-reflection, or may imply a need to reflect upon yourself: who you are, what you are thinking and doing, how you see yourself, taking a good look at yourself. May say, "Know thyself" or, "To thine own self be true." Could be a reflection of your lifestyle.

Breaking a Mirror: Old symbol for seven years bad luck, but can imply breaking an old image of yourself, putting an end to some personal trait or habit. Could say, "I don't want to look at (or face) this!"

Broken, Cracked Mirror: This depicts a poor or distorted self-image, a bizarre, warped, or broken image, a broken pattern, or may be showing many facets or reflections of you. Could symbolize a split personality or a split image, many factions, aspects of one's self.

Fogged Mirror: May indicate foggy vision, a hazy concept about who or what you are, lack of clarity in purpose or perception of yourself, your life, your situation.

MOP:
May indicate a need to clean up a situation.

NAIL FILE:
Symbol of pruning, smoothing, eliminating the rough edges of your being.

NEWSPAPER:

May represent the latest news items, local gossip, current and global events, plus advertisements designed to lure the unwary into greater acquisitiveness and self-centered concepts. Most likely, however, it symbolizes current public opinion, prejudice, race-consciousness ideas and attitudes, as well as large doses of worldly, materialistic thinking.

PENCIL:

May illustrate making a point, a pointed remark, making your mark in the world, possibly a need to put things in writing, or even depict a talent for writing.

Pencil Sharpener: Preparation for work, sharpening up your act or your wits, or may be grinding things to pieces.

PICTURES:

This may seem like a meaningless detail, but every picture or symbol in your home makes a mental imprint in your mind and has a subtle but persistent influence on all those in the home, whether in the dream world or the real one. Take a good look at the kind of picture and the story or impression it makes. Recall your feelings about it in the dream for best interpretation. Can be a pun on "picture" this or that, or picture yourself here.

Picture Frame: May depict your frame of mind concerning the person or situation pictured.

A Golden Frame: Would indicate high esteem.

Picture of Another: This may show how you see another person or may be an aspect of yourself you need to examine more closely.

Picture of Yourself: This may say, "Take a good look at yourself," or, "This is how you see yourself"; may imply self-examination needed or look at what you are doing or creating.

Taking a Picture (Photo): Act of capturing or recording a person or event, getting a clear picture, focusing your attention, creating a permanent memory, getting a good understanding or grasp of a situation.

PILLOWS:

Symbol of comfort, luxury, relaxation, and ease. May indicate laziness or depict a need to take it easy on yourself.

RADIO:

ESP, awareness, receptivity, intuition, telepathy.

Playing: This implies you are tuned in, alert, listening, receptive, getting the message.

Turned Off: Indicates you have the ability to receive but for some reason you aren't tuned in; not listening.

REFRIGERATOR:

Implies a place to store food for thought for future use, being unwilling or unable to consume it now, or something to snack on, getting it a little bit at a time. This can be a place to cool off heated ideas or indicate a frigidity or coldness in you, an attitude of being chilly toward others; emotionless, lack of warmth, need to thaw out.

RUGS,:

These can be things of pride and beauty which enhance the looks of your home, can be a cover-up for flaws or protection of your floor, foundation, basis of your beliefs. They can also represent a part of you that gets "walked on" as long as you allow it, for none can walk on you unless you lie down first! This may depict your idea of being used and abused, a lack of respect from others, and general self-deprecation. It may be time to put a stop to being "walked upon." See *Carpet*.

SCALES:
Balance, justice, karma, harmony, fairness, weighing and measuring. Unbalanced scales may indicate an injustice.

SCISSORS:
May indicate something which needs to be cut out of your life; may say, "Cut it out!" or show your ability to cut things or people our of your life; separation, division.

SEWING MACHINE:
Denotes your ability to be creative, to put things together in a new way, to patch up or mend things, to use your abilities in a creative way.

SHELVES:
Levels of your mind where you store ideas, memories, concepts, mementos, and junk.

STAMP:
Rubber stamps represent repetition, doing or saying the same things over and over.

STOVE:
Way to warm things up, put the heat on, get things going; cooking up new ideas, hot ideas, combining ideas into new concoctions and variations; may say, "Now you're cooking!" or perhaps you are putting things on the "back burner" of your mind. You may be simmering with anger, getting ready to boil over, or perhaps you are "boiling mad" about something.

Stove may also represent the idea of "slaving over a hot stove" or a hot situation, a feeling of being a slave to the stove, chores and/or family—a situation you may need to stop and think about.

SWING:
This usually represents vacillation, going back and forth over an idea, not making up your mind, indecisiveness.

TABLE:
A convenient piece of furniture used for dining or to lay things out, to play games, to place things, or to face things. Its more exact meaning may come from the type of table.

Bridge: Area of game playing, gossip, social gatherings, hospitality, friendly competition; possibly a pun on bridging the gap or laying your cards on the table.

Buffet: Symbol of plenty, wide variety, freedom of choice. Implies helping yourself, serving yourself, making choices, deciding, results are up to you. No one to serve you, this is something you must do for yourself or do without.

Coffee: Informal dining, sharing, togetherness, coziness, friendly hospitality, relaxation, and comraderie.

Conference: Can mean confrontation, agreement and disagreement, business affairs, talking it over, facing the facts, seeing another point of view, compromise, working out differences.

Drafting: Planning, designing, plotting a course, moving with a purpose, creativity, putting it all together (often by yourself), under your own power.

Dining: Area of sharing ideas and food for thought with friends and family.

Kitchen: Table talk, food for thought, family matters and discussions, or need for these. Coziness, confidence, personal matters.

Poker: Area of game playing, chance taking, competition; can be fun and games or deadly serious.

Pool: Pretty much the same as poker table but may be a pun on pooling your efforts, or depict family entertainment.

Restaurant Tables: Can indicate different circles or areas, thought and effort within a given area. Putting separate tables together may depict a combination of efforts, ideas, and abilities, a joining together, cooperative efforts.

Round Table: Equal rights and opportunities for all, equality, oneness, evenness, cooperation, and sharing. There is also an overtone of Knights of the Round Table here which implies fairness, honesty, loyalty, and chivalry.

Work Table: Obviously a place where you face up to the tasks to be done or make an effort to get things done. May represent the work that is set before you to do.

TAPE RECORDER:
Ability to remember and record things exactly as they happened. Photographic memory.

TELEPHONE:
An instrument of communication. If it is dusty may be a hint to communicate more, get in touch with others, let your feelings and ideas be known.

Busy Line: No one can get through to you; implies lack of openness, unwillingness to listen to someone or to the intuitive messages coming to you.

Plugged In: Shows you are ready and able to communicate.

Ringing: Often an indication of a message coming to you in reality or an important message in the dream. Pay special attention to whatever is said or done next.

Unplugged: Not receiving, out of touch, unwilling or unable to communicate, give, or receive messages.

TELEVISION:
This may represent family entertainment, a source of information of all kinds; can be a diversion, a method of relaxing, or instruction. Can depict clairvoyant, telepathic, psychic, or clairaudient abilities, being tuned in and receiving, or if turned off can say you are capable but not using all your abilities.

TOASTER:
May symbolize new ideas and food for thought popping out of your mind. Of course it may also be a way of warming things up.

THREE-LEGGED STOOL:
Firm foundation.

Musical Instruments

Stand for the ability to harmonize with others, to make beautiful music, to uplift yourself or others when properly used. Can imply being in (or out of) tune with the Universe. If you are playing an instrument in your dream which you cannot actually play, this may indicate a talent you have for that particular instrument.

This may also be a symbol for being instrumental in doing, preventing, creating, or you may be an instrument for another person, idea, concept to come through. You may be a channel for healing, writing, encouraging, enlightening, or whatever needs to come through you.

DRUMS, DRUMMER:
Can be "marching to a different drummer," following your own beat, doing your own thing, getting into the rhythm and flow of things, taking a beating, drumming up business, beating your own drum.

HARP:
Symbol of heavenly harmony, spiritual upliftment, gentle, soothing music, healing and idyllic situations; but can be a pun on harping at others.

FIDDLE:

Can be harmony or fiddling around.

PIANO:

This usually stands for harmony but can be discord as well. Can denote a need for harmony in the home, family, or in whatever situation the piano is placed.

TRUMPETS:

Often represent declarations of truth but may have other meanings for you.

VIOLINS:

Frequently associated with romantic places, candlelight dinners, and luxury as well as beautiful, soothing music. May also represent throbbing, happy, gypsy rhythms, or may be sadness or a sob story.

Tools

Generally, tools are instruments to work with—something you use to get a job done—or may represent you being used as a tool or instrument in achieving some task or purpose. You might even be a tool for God. These can also depict preparation for your life work, what you have to work with, your unused potential, talents; or, it may be a do-it-yourself kit.

RUSTY TOOLS:

Imply your need to sharpen and polish your talents and abilities, possibly take a refresher course.

UNUSED TOOLS:

Imply unused talents, knowledge, abilities.

SPECIFIC TOOLS:

Electric Saw: Power to cut through the problem quickly, ability to get right to the point or target. See *Saw*.

Hammer: Driving a point home, hammering away at something or someone, getting things together, nailing it down, constructive work or achievement, or may be beating up on yourself or on your state of consciousness.

Ladder: Means of ascending and descending, coming and going, climbing to great heights, reaching for a goal or higher levels; may be lifting yourself or others up, climbing up in the world. Can be rising up in meditation or prayer, an altered state of consciousness, or a higher level of awareness.

Monkey Wrench: Often a symbol for fouling up the works, quitting, monkeying around, being irresponsible.

Sandpaper: An instrument for smoothing things over, leveling out the rough spots, making things easier to handle; soothing, smoothing, polishing, refining; making things more beautiful, more acceptable or workable. Can be a hint for you to smooth some thing(s) in your life or relationships.

Saw: A cutting, severing instrument; you could cut things in two, cut it to fit, or may imply you need to "cut it out." Might be a pun on something you saw or are seeing.

Screwdriver: Ordinarily an implement for tightening or loosening things, it can be an instrument for minor repairs. But in modern terminology it can mean messing things up, "screwing around," fooling around, or having sex (not making love—just sex).

T-Square: May symbolize imbalance and a need to get back "in line." Can be a measuring device or a way to check out or find a new angle.

Vise: Signifies getting a really firm grip, not letting go until you are finished, hanging in there despite pressure or pull from others. Could be a pun on vice.

TRUNK:
Area where one keeps old memories, ideals, hopes, dreams, old emotions, hurts, and probably unforgivenesses. If you are taking things out and looking at them it is likely these are matters you have not dealt with and the time has come to get them out in the open, to forgive, forget, make amends, and bring matters to a peaceful completion. Don't leave these things dangling.

VACUUM CLEANER:
Represents ability and probably the need to clean up your act, yourself, your emotions, attitudes, or your affairs, to get things in order in the area of the room depicted in your dream. May be your whole house (state of consciousness) is in need of cleaning. *Vacuum* may also stand for cleansing power.

> **To Empty Bag:** Getting rid of all your negativity.

VASE:
This is usually a receptacle for flowers and/or a thing of beauty in itself. In early Christian symbolism it represented the container for the soul or a symbol of the soul.

VCR:
Implies recording, remembering past events with absolute clarity, ability to take these out and review them over and over. Could say you live or indulge too much in past memories.

WASHING MACHINE:
Implies a need to clean up your emotions and attitudes.

My Own Household Symbols

CHAPTER 29

Illness and Injury

Dreams can reveal that illness does have a purpose and is not merely pathological.

— *Meredith Sabini*

An avid interest in dreams has caused me to read any and all articles on dreams. One of the most interesting new concepts comes from a Russian doctor, Vasili Kasatkin, who is head of a scientific research group at the Neurological Surgical Institute in Leningrad. Constantly analyzing the dreams of the ill, he declares (Gris and Dick 1978), "It is very clear that dreams are sentries watching over our health while we sleep...Brain tumors, mental illness, diseases of the heart, lung and stomach are **commonly depicted in dreams** from **two weeks** to a **year before the person knows he is ill!** [emphasis added]" He recommends, "See your doctor and give him full details of any dream that keeps recurring. Dreams that repeat themselves are early warning signals of serious illnesses." He goes on to say that "although the doctor may not be skilled at interpreting dreams...a recurring dream will draw his attention to a particular area of the body that should be investigated medically."

Single dreams of a physical problem may be caused by passing events, but it is the recurring dream of a physical or mental problem we need most to heed as an important warning.

Dr. Kasatkin explains that injuries or wounds to a certain area can indicate a disease or illness of that part; for example, wounds to the chest area are indicative of heart, lung, or chest problems and so on.

To follow this theme further we find that Norman Cousins, in his well-known book called *Anatomy Of An Illness,* says, "What you believe and feel can have an effect on your health." He reported that a public announcement to a football crowd stating several people had become ill with food poisoning was immediately followed by mass retching and fainting in the crowd. Then, when these same fans learned that the report was erroneous, the symptoms immediately cleared up!

This is an excellent example of mass hysteria or *race consciousness.* Emotions **can** cause physical reactions in the body. Long-held negative emotions can actually make us ill. Conversely, positive thoughts and feelings can be highly therapeutic. Forgiveness, love, good will, kindness, hope, joy, and best of all laughter are wonderful cures.

In other dream research, broken furnaces have symbolized stomach disease, faulty wiring has portrayed nerve disorders, houses have represented the bone structure, and automobiles have depicted parts of the body such as headlights representing the eyes, and so on. The main key seems to be in watching for the **recurring** dream and the **repeated** symbols.

Carl Jung, commenting on dreams and diagnosis, said, "It looks as if it were a poet who had been at work rather than a rational doctor who would speak of infections, fever, toxins, et cetera" (Jung 1961).

Cause and Cure

Tradition says, "There was in India, a school of philosophers who led a life of such absolute purity that they commonly reached the age of one hundred and fifty years. To fall sick was looked upon by them as an unpardonable disgrace, for it was considered to indicate a violation of spiritual law."

It has been said, too, that to be dissatisfied or unhappy about one's lifestyle is to cause dis-ease. We are here to overcome our problems and challenges, not to be subservient to them...or to other people. Failure to do this results in anger, frustration, and general malcontent.

In direct connection to this dissatisfaction, many of our illnesses and injuries are self-created by means of the "I can't" attitude. We can't *see* our way clear to solve the dilemma (eye problems), we can't *stomach* the circumstances (stomach and digestive organs), or we lack the courage to *stand up* and declare our rights (feet and leg difficulties). So, rather than lose face, we create an illness or injury sufficient to excuse ourselves from the scene or to punish ourselves for not finding a way to overcome the situation! This is the *basic underlying cause* of disease.

Your dreams try to help you become aware of what you are creating before the situation manifests as an injury or disease in your body. It takes *real courage* to stand up to authority figures, but once done it is worth the effort. When we avoid this, the same type of problem will lift its ugly head again and again until one day you will say, "Enough! I've had it! I won't put up with this any longer!" Then you will do what you should have done long ago.

CURE: First, the courage to stand up, face, and solve your problem firmly and intelligently.

Second, see the whole matter as a lesson necessary for your soul growth. (Remember, nothing happens by accident.)

Third, be willing to forgive yourself for any mistakes you feel you have made, and forgive those around you as well.

Last, make it a point to do the kind of things which make you truly happy. (To work at a job you hate or where conditions are upsetting can definitely make you ill!) Strive toward goals that suit *you* and take time to play and relax often. (If your job won't let you, *change it!*)

Be justly proud of your accomplishments and successes. Give yourself a hearty portion of love—so much love that it spills over into the lives of those around you.

Types of Illness and Injury

ACCIDENTS:
To see this in a dream can be a warning that you are an accident looking for a place to happen, implying there is something out of balance or going wrong, which at this stage can be corrected.

BANDAGES:
Denote a feeling or need to cover up your wounds or tender places, to protect yourself, and/or a necessity to give yourself the time and space to heal. This may be telling you that your hurt was greater than you thought.

BIRTH DEFECTS:
This is usually a condition the soul has chosen to work through in order to learn some specific lesson.

BIRTH MARK:
We are told that birthmarks are marks of the soul—a reminder of something we must accomplish or that must be avoided but not forgot-

ten. It can be a karmic retribution from a lifetime of too much pride in one's appearance.

BLOOD:
Your life forces, energies, vitality.

Bleeding: This may indicate the heavy price you are paying for your actions, or indicate you are pouring your very life into this situation/project/person. Could suggest a person or situation which is literally bleeding you to death. Blood loss may also mean creating karma in some way.

Bright Red Blood: Can represent your life forces or a life or death situation. What are you pouring your life forces into? Is it worth the cost?

Dark Red Blood: Indicates old wounds, old karma, possibly bad karma you are currently creating by your present action.

Internal Bleeding: May symbolize inner pain, injury, loss of vital forces, valuable energies wasted, or an ESP warning of an inner problem.

BOIL:
Infection, irritation, suppressed anger coming to a head or to the surface to be released. The larger the boil, the greater amount of suppressed emotions are involved. Need to release this in a controlled manner or emotions may explode.

BROKEN BONES:
This can be a warning of a problem developing in the bone structure—it would be wise to check with a doctor. Of course it could also be an ESP warning of a danger which can be avoided.

CANCER:
Research has found this directly linked to grief (held in mind), self-pity, and unforgiveness. Dr. Carl Simonton has proven that positive affirmations (right thinking) can reverse and dissolve cancer. Dream can be a warning to change your

negative thinking *before* it creates a cancer in you!

CRUTCH:
We lean on crutches. This could portray your need or tendency to lean on others or use some situation as a crutch or excuse to do or not do something. Could be you are being used as a prop.

FALLS:
To dream of this may be simply saying, "You are headed for a fall," or something you are involved in may fall through. Always consider ESP possibilities.

Falling On Your Face: Can be a pun showing you how you see yourself (as falling flat or losing face), or could be a warning that your present plans may fall through.

FEVER:
A fever in dreams says literally, "You are all burned up about something." Take care of this before it "gets to you!"

INJURIES:
Dream injuries may simply tell you that you are really hurt by recent happenings and need some time to heal. They can also say you are being too hard on yourself or be an outpicturing of thoughts such as "I could kick myself for..." or, "I hate myself for..." or, "I'm so mad at myself...", all of which can lead to injuries. You *are* what you think!!! Also keep in mind the possibility of ESP warnings.

ILLNESS:
The basic metaphysical truth behind every illness is self-pity. You can see your way clear to do what you want, can't find an easy solution to a problem, or are not brave enough to stand up for yourself, so you catch a cold or bog down in a pity-party. This is a confrontation avoidance move. If you can't get it by strength of will, you'll try sympathy. Half the battle is understanding

this principle! The other half is learning to take a stand for what you need. A dream of illness can be pointing this out, showing you what you are creating. It can be telling you that you are literally making yourself sick over a situation. Need to make amends before any real damage is done. Love and forgiveness are nature's best healing medicines.

INFECTION:
Mental poisons affecting the body. Get out that bottle of forgiveness-for-all-including-yourself and some of those I'm-gonna-stand-up-for-my-rights-or-else pills, and **do something** about the problem.

MIGRAINE:
A type of mental battle, a clash of wills; when you can't see any way of winning, migraine results. Dream warning would be for you to understand the problem and take some **positive action**. Illness is running away.

RASH:
Dreams of this depict submerged anger, frustration, irritation, aggravation, annoyances. If itchy, can be an inner itch to go somewhere or do something. Try to find the source of your irritation and correct it before these feelings manifest themselves as an actual fact.

SCARS:
A mark or symbol of pain held onto, an inability to let go, old wounds, unforgiveness. A dream scar can say you need to forgive this or it will scar your life.

TUMORS:
Could imply an actual growth or can be the harbinger warning you of hates or grudges held onto and growing in your mind, which can eventually manifest as a physical growth.

WARTS:
A type of self-punishment, self-chastisement, an unforgiveness of self. Note the area and its meaning. (A wart on the nose, for instance, is a typical symbol of a witch!)

My Own Illness Symbols

CHAPTER 30

Jewelry, Gems, and Crystals

Calmness of mind is one of the beautiful jewels of wisdom.
— *James Allen*

Gems and Jewelry in dreams can denote several things. First of all, the jewels in themselves are valuable; second, these stones exert individual, meaningful vibrations and influences; third, the jewelry we wear often serves to emphasize the particular part of the body they adorn; and last, there is symbolism attached to the type of jewelry.

Jewels in your dreams may symbolize special talents, gifts, or rewards you have earned. At times they may represent spiritual gifts that are beginning to unfold and shine forth, or they may depict your values in general.

Dreams try to show you something about these gifts and talents of which you are unaware. A point to remember is that regardless of who has them, if they are in *your* dream they represent *your* talents—accepted or not yet claimed, as the case may be. If you are wearing them, they represent gifts you "own" while those held by others depict gifts you have not yet discovered or claimed as your own. Pay special attention as to what is being done with them and by what aspect of yourself.

Jewelry

Dime-store variety jewelry may represent false or superficial values, worldly things that look good but have no real value. May imply something not worth the effort. Genuine jewels with real gold and silver, especially when given as gifts, may represent spiritual rewards coming to you or may represent new talents and gifts coming to you.

ANKH, OR CRUX ANSATA:
Shaped like a cross with a loop or circle on top, this is an ancient Egyptian symbol of eternal life. More recently it has been known as a symbol of love as well, possibly because of its similarity to the glyph for Venus. "Mirror of Venus."

BRACELETS:
These place emphasis on the arms and wrists, accenting the meaning of *arm* (power to do) and what you are doing with your power, arms, wrists, and hands.

> **Charm Bracelets:** These may denote many charms that you have in your possession, imply that you should turn on the charm, show your charms more, or hint that you could be more charming.

CROWN:

A crown depicts royalty, dominion, and mastery over self. Also, responsibility as to the right rulership over whatever is in your domain and all parts of your "kingdom," be it inner, outer, or both.

> **Crown Circlet, or Tiara:** Jewelry worn here lies on the crown of the head which is also known as the *crown chakra*. It may serve to emphasize the fact that your crown chakra is open or opening and, if the jewelry is right, sparkling.

EARRINGS:

These accent your hearing, whether or not you are really listening or turning a "deaf ear," and who and what you are listening to. Is it gossip and hearsay or truth? If truth, this may be a symbol of clairaudience developing, especially if there are diamonds in your earrings.

GOLD OR GOLDEN JEWELRY:

These represent spiritual gifts.

LOCKET:

This may accent either the heart area or the throat chakra depending on its location, or could be a pun on, "Lock it."

NECKLACES:

Since these are worn about the neck, they can represent a "string of ideas"; may emphasize the quality of your voice, possibly a talent for song or speech; or, they could accent your throat chakra, which represents your will power and its use as well as the use of your spoken words in connection with your will.

Gemstones worn over the heart area may accent your heart and its feelings or the radiations from your heart. They also help stimulate the heart chakra into greater activity, love, and compassion.

> **Chain Necklace:** Can be a chain of events having to do with the use or misuse of your will power or your spoken words.

> **Golden Necklace:** May imply loving, spiritual words being spoken, or may imply your need to practice this—to speak golden words of love and wisdom.

> **Pearl Necklace:** Can refer to pearls of wisdom and the ability to speak them.

PINS:

Wherever these are found, the keynote would be on that part of the body and the talents and abilities associated with it. For example, the heart would mean loving, compassionate qualities or riches of the heart which you can share with others.

RINGS:

These place an emphasis on the fingers and hands. You can do many creative things with your hands, so they could easily relate to creative abilities and talents connected with the use of your hands, or the accent may be on a particular finger. See *The Body and Its Parts*.

> **Loss of Ring:** May indicate a broken or unkept vow.

> **Damaged:** Implies a problem with keeping the agreement.

> **Ring, Plain:** Often signifies a commitment such as a marriage or may stand for a circle, a cycle, unendingness, eternal love, no beginning and no ending, or can be a symbol for God.

> **Ring with Jewel:** The type of jewel would add its meaning to that of the plain ring.

> **Wedding Ring:** Symbol of marriage bond, but may also represent other bonds or binding agreements—something you are wedded to like a job, career, or project.

> **Lost:** Possible symbol of the love bond being broken, love lost, marriage split.

On Wrong Hand: Implies something wrong with the marriage, an uncertainty or insecurity. Can be a pun for, "On the other hand..."

Rash or Sores Under Wedding Ring: Implies an irritation, frustration, or unhappiness in the marital relationship—someone is getting "sore" about this or it's becoming unbearable.

WATCH:
While we consider this jewelry, its main keynote would be time and its passage unless the watch is decorated with gems. Then you would have to add the meaning of the gem with both time and your power to do, serve, give, or whatever. Could be a pun saying watch out, be alert, aware, or someone is watching.

Antique Watch: Old time, old concepts, old ways of thinking, feeling, judging, measuring. Old-fashioned ideas out of synchronization with modern times.

Barred Watch: (Bars across the crystal) Behind bars, doing time, time barriers, bar(ely) enough time.

Borrowed Watch or Clock: Borrowed time.

Drooping Watch: (Salvadore Dali style) Time warp, time lag, time dragging on and on, endless time.

Dropped Watch: Time slipping through your fingers, passing you by, getting out of hand.

Lost Watch: Lost time, losing touch with time, time out of mind, time out to do something.

Two Watches: Could say two people watching or be a pun on double-time or two-timing.

Wrong Watch: Wrong time, bad time or timing, hard time, mistaken time, or misunderstanding about the appointed time.

Gemstones

Paramhansa Yogananda said "Pearls and other jewels as well as metals and plants, applied directly to the human skin, exercise an electromagnetic influence over the physical cells" (Yogananda 1972).

In *Gems and Stones* Edgar Cayce said, "Vibratory forces arising from certain stones and metals collaborate with similar forces originating within individuals to permit them to attune to the Creative Forces of the Universe. In this way men may receive and transmit healing vibrations, spiritualize their desires, or obtain 'food' for soul development, to mention a few possibilities" (Cayce 1960).

AGATE:
Symbolic of the spiritual love of all things good, and also associated with the *third eye*, or brow chakra. This is reputed to help your receptivity.

AMETHYST:
Emblem of piety and dignity, love, devotion, truth, passion, suffering, and hope. It is more recently associated with the seventh ray, ritual, magic, ceremony, meditation, transformation, humility, and calming the mind. It is an excellent healing stone.

AZURITE, OR LAPIS LINGUIS:
Said to help people to contact higher realms, higher sources of activity or vibrations. This stone is said to help in meditation and in developing one's psychic abilities.

BERYL:
Associated with safety, quick intellect, and receptivity.

BLOODSTONE OR HELIOTROPE:

Acts as a blood purifier; it detoxifies and is reputed to help check hemorrhages. An excellent healing stone.

CARNELIAN:
Good for grounding of energies and blood purification.

CITRINE QUARTZ:
This is associated with the solar plexus, attunement, and drawing to you things that you need.

CRYSTAL:
These are symbolic of purity, clarity and one-pointedness. They have the quality of magnifying and focusing energies, of which the mind is one. They increase the clarity of mind and aid in maintaining concentration, lucidity, and emotional stability. Because crystals amplify one's thoughts, they are often used in healing and in mental telepathy. The Atlantians were reputed to wear these about the head to help them tune-in to higher energies.

DIAMONDS:
Diamonds in dreams symbolize success, wealth, happiness, and victory as well as the power to bind men and women together in happy wedlock. Diamonds also represent clear, sparkling, pure ideas, clarity and general beauty of the soul. A diamond, wherever it is worn, would tend to magnify the qualities in that area of the wearer. They aid greatly in attunement.

EMERALD:
Famous for its beauty and healing qualities, this is a symbol of faith and hope.

GARNET:
Healing and protection.

JADE:
Excellent healing stone, especially in digestive areas.

LAPIS LAZULI:
Tends to make one more sensitive to higher vibrations, mental and spiritual influences. Aids in making attunement to higher levels and gives strength to body and mind. Was used by Egyptians to treat eye problems.

MALACHITE:
All-purpose healing stone and symbol of love and friendship.

MOONSTONE:
Good to soothe, heal, and balance the emotions; a symbol of hope, said to bring peace of mind; a link with the mystical and with *second sight*.

OPAL:
Known as *the gem of the gods,* this is reputed to be the stone of love, hope, and achievement.

PEARL:
Traditional symbol of wisdom, perfection, beauty. It may also depict a seed-thought, seed idea, the point about which the wholeness of truth is formed; the irritant, illness, or problem which is transformed into wisdom and beauty. This may, therefore, symbolize the process of transformation in us from pain or problem to truth and beauty. The pearl is a good healing stone and a symbol of purity, truth, wisdom, and understanding.

PERIDOT:
Stone is said to relax nervous tension and generally rejuvenate the body. In dreams, this may indicate a need to rest, relax, and recharge either by wearing the stone or taking a few days off.

RUBY:
Good physical and mental health, valor, strength; ability to concentrate; the quality of contentment.

ROSE QUARTZ:

Known for healing the wounds of the heart, it brings inner peace and self-fulfillment and helps the heart chakra.

SELENITE:

Good for mental clarity and helps with telepathy.

TURQUOISE:

American Indians use this stone for healing, grounding, and protection from snake bite. It has a soothing and calming quality.

My Own Gem Symbols

CHAPTER 31

Kitchen Utensils

Dishes, pots, pans, silverware, and so forth would mostly pertain to food for thought, teachings, concepts, and what you do with these. For greater understanding, think to your most recent class, lecture, or discussion in which a new concept was presented. Your dream will give you the truth about this idea and the degree of your receptivity or lack of it.

If you are a teacher of **any** kind or like to share your knowledge with others, the dishes and your handling of these in dreams can give you helpful insights as to how you are "dishing out" the information.

There is another side to this, however. Sometimes a kitchen—the sink, stove, pots, and pans—can represent to a person, especially a housewife, the idea of being a servant or slave in her own household. There may be feelings of anger and frustration associated with these dreams, which would be shown in the handling of the food and utensils—the pots and pans especially—so be aware of all these possibilities.

If you are burning food or pans, you are most likely "all burned up" about something in your life, possibly represented by the stove or the food burned. You need to look carefully to see if it was a new idea, project, concept, situation, something that was said, or whether it was the whole concept of feeling like a servant that is burning in you.

Things that sizzle, dishes that are too hot to handle, or items that burn your fingers are all variations on the theme of frustration, irritation, and being all burned up. Look at the dream details to help you pinpoint the real cause of your anger.

Please bear in mind that dishes and eating utensils may refer to diet or to mental, physical, or spiritual food.

BASKET:
Means of getting a group of many miscellaneous ideas together and out in the open in an easy-to-handle manner. It is offered but not pushed on anyone. Very good symbol for one who wants to present ideas in a gentle, thoughtful manner. See *Containers*, this chapter.

BLENDER:
Ability to blend ideas into a harmonious whole or to make a mess of things.

BOTTLE, CAPPED:
Can refer to bottling up your emotions and true feelings, your pent-up emotions, or an emotional issue.

BOTTLE, OPEN:
Could be pouring or readiness to pour out compassion, knowledge, love, or milk of human kindness, depending on the action and feeling.

BOWL:
Container or receptacle for food for thought, new ideas offered but not yet accepted. Can imply availability, gift, offering, yours for the taking. See *Containers*.

CAN:
Could be a pun on can do, I can or can't, or may represent unused possibilities.

CAN OPENER:
Ability to open up a new concept, a new "can of worms," well-preserved ideas for self or others, or may be your ability to say, "I can."

COFFEE POT:
Often associated with hospitality and sharing of knowledge, ideas, hopes, dreams, concerns. People tend to share over coffee. May represent neighborliness, comfort, friendship, companionship. Gossip may also be associated with this, also compassion and helpfulness. There can be much love poured along with the coffee and a listening ear.

CONTAINERS:
Hold, mix, serve, show, offer, or get it all together or keep things in separate sections. These can contain ideas, concepts, traditions, or temptations offered. Implies availability, gift, yours-for-the-taking. See *Bowl*.

COOKING UTENSILS:
Generally connected with food (idea) combination and preparation to make it more interesting and palatable.

CUP:
Container of ideas, ideals, and feelings. This can be the cup of kindness poured out or in, your cup of joy, kindness, bitterness, or sorrow. Can show sharing, measuring, and your ability or inability to swallow things.

Bottomless Cup:
Can signify an unending situation, or may say, "This isn't working" or that something's not "fulfilling." If you are pouring something out for another person, this may be your signal that they will never get enough, or that for some reason you cannot fill their request.

Broken Cup:
May signify that you feel unable to serve, unqualified, inadequate, not up to the situation, or may be feelings of poverty, guilt, low self-esteem, possibly all of these.

Broken Cup Handle:
May indicate your feelings of being unable to "handle" a situation or not knowing how to "handle" this emotion (liquid), or could represent your feelings of poverty, inadequacy, or inability to serve others graciously.

Round Bottomed:
This cup—once filled—cannot be set down again until every drop has been swallowed, the task finished, or the promise kept. May say, "Think twice!"

Running Over:
Can be your cup of joy that is running over or your cup of sorrow, depending on your feelings. Who is pouring out what to whom? Could be you need to pour out your feelings, or may say you've over-done—poured, emoted, or overflowed enough.

DISHES:
These deal with the preparation and serving up of ideas and the presentation of concepts. They are containers and holders of ideas and attitudes. Note how you serve these to others or how they present dishes to you. This could also be a pun on what you are dishing out or how you dish it out to others.

Antique Dishes:
Can imply old-fashioned ideas or an old-fashioned or traditional way of presenting things. Could imply traditional

beliefs, concepts, habits, and customs or may symbolize reluctance to try new things.

Broken Dishes: Feeling of poverty, lack, inadequacy, inability to serve or to meet expected requirements. Can be low self-esteem or possibly carelessness. *See Broken Cup.*

Fancy: Putting your best foot forward, doing your best, making the best-possible presentation, trying to make a good impression, careful preparation and planning.

Empty: Open, ready to receive.

Everyday Dishes: This may refer to our actual day-to-day routine, our actual diet (which possibly needs changing in some way), or the everyday thoughts we feed upon—the things we see, hear, and read which nourish or pollute our minds.

Loaded with Food: Plenty to think about, many ideas to choose from, much to digest.

Modern Dishes: May suggest new, untried, non-traditional, New Age, or unusual ideas and concepts.

Scraping Dishes: Getting rid of the old, throwing out the unwanted, unused, inapplicable, making way for the next step.

Washing Dishes: Care, cleansing, preparation, and planning for the next idea or next presentation.

Dishes You Missed Washing: Things overlooked, problems, difficulties, emotions, or old ideas not cleared, cleansed, worked out, dealt with, and completed. If you and another person were washing dishes together, it may be something you haven't settled, clarified, or worked out between you.

DRAINER:
Can be draining off excessive emotions involved in a situation or a need to drain off emotional aspects of the "food ideas" you are working with.

FORK:
May be pun on "fork it over," turn it over and see the other side, or can be an extension of your reach. Might refer to your diet or eating habits—you may overindulge or be too picky with food or the ideas presented.

FULL POT:
All the ideas you can hold, all you can handle. If the pot is bubbling over, dream may imply that you are bubbling over with enthusiasm, ideas, or may indicate you have more than you can handle.

GLASSES:
May be ideas or emotions offered to you or imply that you are "drinking it all in," swallowing things whole. Could be a drink to your health or your undoing, may suggest you drink too much of something (large glass) or not enough (small glass).

KITCHEN SCALES:
May represent a balanced diet or your need for one, could depict a need to weigh and measure your words or ideas before serving them to others. Balance, diplomacy, tact, fairness.

KNIFE:
May be pun on "cutting up," a need to inject more humor, or could be mincing your words, cutting remarks, malicious gossip, dividing, separating, cutting things down to size, picking through ideas, cutting out the unwanted.

Electric Knife: Could be power to cut through to the truth of a situation quickly, or can be you are too quick to make cutting (re)marks. May say, "Cut that out, fast!"

MIXER:
This can be a perfect blending of ingredients to make your ideas more palatable—you could be making mush out of them! Action may indicate you are getting your facts all "mixed up," possibly mixing ideas and emotions. If the person

doing the mixing is one of your programed-to-play-themselves people, this may say s/he is mixing up the facts.

POP CORN POPPER:
This may represent your ability to "pop up" with myriads of ideas on a moment's notice, a multiplicity of ideas, or kernels of truth popping into your awareness.

MEASURING CUPS OR SPOONS:
Can imply care and precision taken or needed in preparing your speech or ideas, careful mixing of ingredients in a situation, giving exact words, possibly taking care not to over-do or exaggerate.

MICROWAVE:
Fast food, quick thinking and doing; could represent "haste makes waste" or even prepackaged "junk food," depending on your associations with it. May depict new ideas, new and better ways of doing things, New Age concepts.

PITCHER:
Symbol of outpouring of ideas, knowledge, feelings, of sharing, the pouring out of yourself, emptying yourself for others, giving freely.

POTS AND PANS:
Can represent your attitudes in many ways. Can be "panning" others' words or deeds, may show your attitude toward the food you prepare physically or mentally for self or others.

Dented Pans: Reveal hidden anger and frustration with the ideas or people you serve, the service you give, or your situation in general. Maybe you are in the wrong job?

Handle Broken or Missing: Can be a pun saying you have no way to handle this, can't handle the situation or idea, can't get a good grip on things, feeling unable to cope.

PRESSURE COOKER:
This can easily represent the pressure you put on yourself, pressures building up in your mind or body, the feeling of being under pressure, pent up emotions, stress. Can be a warning that you are about to explode or a symbol of your blood pressure rising. May show a need to gauge the pressure building in you, to let off steam immediately or take the risk of blowing up unexpectedly. This could be an explosion of uncontrolled anger or can take the form of a heart attack.

SINK:
The heart of the kitchen, center of activities in the area of food preparation and service to family and friends. Could be a place you hate or enjoy, a symbol of chores, or be a pun on that "sinking feeling."

No Sink: May imply your heart has gone out of kitchen work or service. You may need to find another way to serve that suits you better or find a better attitude toward what you do. This may imply you have no enthusiasm for the ideas you have to work with, or could be a pun for "everything but the kitchen sink."

SPOON:
Excellent symbol for stirring things up, spooning it out, tasting to see if the dish is good, spoon feeding others, or measuring things out in small doses; swallowing ideas.

SIFTER:
May indicate a need to "sift through" those new ideas, sort things out in your mind, taking care not to swallow things whole.

STRAINER:
May refer to something being a strain on you, straining to learn or accomplish, sorting things out, draining off excess emotional contents, getting emotions out of the way of reason, or sorting/separating things out in your mind.

TEA KETTLE:
Often a sign of instant hospitality, desire to be of service to others, giving freely.

Kettle Whistling, Steaming: This would imply readiness, preparedness to do what needs to be done; may also depict being "all steamed up," ready to boil over, tempest in a teapot," emotional upheaval that is ready to go. It can be poured out peacefully, or if ignored can burn out.

TOASTER:
May represent ideas popping up, the bread of life, or quick thinking.

Burned Toast: Being all burned up about a small matter.

TOOTHPICK:
Being "picky," picking on others, picking at the faults, impediments, and flaws in others.

TRAY:
Getting it all together, serving, service, giving or having things handed to you on a (silver) tray.

WASTE DISPOSAL:
Getting rid of the garbage, the left-overs, the unwanted or unusable things in life.

My Own Kitchen Symbols

CHAPTER 32

Metals

These could represent your personal mettle, strength, and stability in facing up to life's situations; symbols of endurance and flexibility or the lack of these.

ALLOYS:
Combination of qualities which make for greater strength.

ALUMINUM:
Light and strong but may break rather than bend.

BRASS PLATE:
A gold look-alike which in symbolism represents that which is deceptive, false, untrue, a facade or pretense, not all that it appears to be.

BRASS, SOLID:
Biblically this represents the false as compared to gold, but in modern usage may depict solidity, quality, well built, possibly antique and valuable. Could be a pun on brazenness.

BRONZE:
Earthy, elastic, durable; holds onto details.

COPPER:
Malleable, impressionable, durable; said to repel arthritis.

GOLD:
Often represents spiritual gifts, grace, rewards, powerful truth, God's gifts to you. Could be a golden opportunity or represent purity of spirit.

Giving Golden Objects: Giving of your spiritual gifts, talents, wisdom.

Paint, Cover, Gild: Can symbolize the act of spiritualizing, bringing spiritual life to something or someone, or may be an attempt to cover up something—to make it appear better than it really is.

Receiving These: Receiving God's gifts, accepting your spiritual rewards.

GOLD PLATE:
Not what it seems to be. A false front, attempt to deceive, "put on," a fake or facade, yet has some value. Can represent a thin veneer—beautiful on the outside but not much underneath.

IRON:
Hard, strong, enduring but will break rather than bend. Often used as a symbol of will power and strength. Inflexibility.

Wrought Iron: Strong, hard, permanent, unbending, usually set in concrete, immovable, unchanging, but can rust out if not well cared for. Inflexibility.

Iron Horse: Old name for railroad engine; would imply power and strength harnessed and set on a definite course of action. Horses are often symbolic of your emotions, and since these engines run on steam it may imply strong emotions are running things in your life.

LEAD:

May indicate that you are easily led, molded, or formed into the shape others desire. Possible need to be more aware of the molding and manipulating of others. Could also say, "Get the lead out," implying that you are dragging your feet in some area. Then, could be you have a "lead foot" or a heavy hand in doing things. See what fits.

PEWTER:

Much the same in meaning as *alloy* but with the added connotation of being old, antique, valued, or valueless depending on your assessment.

PLATINUM:

Extremely hard. Bends only under extreme pressure. Durable, dependable, valuable.

QUICK SILVER, MERCURY:

May be a reference to quickness, fast thinking, changeability, adaptability, and hard to pin down; something that slips through your fingers, elusive, evasive, difficult to grasp or understand. Could be warning of an elusive, unpredictable situation.

SILVER:

Precious metal, loved and admired by many. May represent sterling traits of character, good taste, the finer things in life. Can denote justice, purity, or an ability to reflect God's light in your life.

SILVER PLATE:

Stronger than silver but not as lasting or as valuable. Can be a put on, a front, pretense, facade, or misconception. May portray sterling qualities on the outside but not much underneath. May not "ring true."

STEEL:

Durable, strong yet flexible, stainless, dependable; can be the courage of your convictions, or may be a pun on something being a "steal."

TIN:

Flexible, won't hold much weight, bends at the slightest touch, can't stand the hard knocks, not too dependable.

My Own Metals Symbols

CHAPTER 33

Names in Dreams

Men do not attract that which they want, but that which they are.
— *James Allen*

The names of the people you meet in your dreams may be puns or definite clues as to the real nature of the person. Some names may stand for characteristics and qualities, while others may describe the motives behind the person's facade or actions. A name can be a label—a description of a person, place, attitude, or state of consciousness. It may be associated with a particular person, characteristic, talent, fault, feeling, or experience. Remember, most people in your dreams are aspects of yourself.

Names may also be a link, a password, a key to power, privilege, or a desire held in mind. For example, to mention the name of an influential person can get everyone's attention, can open doors you could not otherwise enter. If you dream of *famous people* or their names, consider the possible meaning of the names and/or the characteristics of the famous person's qualities. See chapter on *People*.

Below are some suggestions as to how these can work out, but *always* consider *your own associations* first.

Names

ANGELA:
This usually brings associations of angelic beings or perfect behavior, being an angel, unless you know a person by that name who is a real stinker.

Then it may mean stinker to you. Go with your own feelings and personal associations.

ALICE:
Could be a symbol of fairyland, wonderland, or other-worlds, out-of-reality, unless of course you have other associations with an Alice you know.

BARBARA OR BARB:
Can be a pun on barbaric behavior, barbed remarks, or the qualities you associate with a known person of that name.

CARPENTER:
Brings to mind one who builds, constructs useful articles.

CHEETHAM:
Sly little pun on cheating or being cheated.

COWARD:
Fearful, afraid to try anything new or different.

CROUCH:
Attempt to hide, deceive, betray.

DODGE:
Who or what are you dodging, avoiding?

DOOLITTLE:
Can be a pun on your own behavior, doing as little as possible, or if you are over-doing it may say the opposite.

DUGAN:
Do it again?

DUNN:
Can refer to a debt or bill to pay, may be pun on Ken B. Dunn, Will B. Dunn, or others types of getting things done.

FAIRFAX:
Pun on being fair with the facts, could refer to your not being fair enough or not having all the facts, or possibly a need to get all the facts in order to be fair.

FOX:
Can be a pun saying this person is foxy, sly, tricky and may try to fool you.

GAIL:
Can be a pun on weather or on talking too much (full of hot air), long winded.

GARNER:
Means to gather, collect, put together facts or parts.

GODMAN:
May be a strong indication of your need to recognize the God in you and behave like a God-man in all you say and do.

GOODMAN:
This may imply that you really are a good person but you do not see this in yourself—dream is pointing this out. Possibly alludes to your feeling that you are not good enough and your need to recognize your own worth.

HOPE:
May be portrayal of hoping, keeping the faith, don't give up hope.

KING OR KINGMAN:
Could refer to kingly or authoritative qualities; may be one who tries to lord it over you or your own lording behavior.

KLINGER:
Pun on one who clings to others or, if you are a TV devotee (to M.A.S.H), this name may be associated with ridiculous behavior and attitudes.

LINCOLN:
Usually associated with honesty, honor, fairness, justice, humility, leadership, compassion. Any or all of these.

MOODY:
Can refer to your own moods, emotional ups and downs, possible tendency to be depressed or morose.

NAPOLEON:
Often associated with boldness, pompousness, and/or defeat.

POWERS:
Reference to the powers you have and how you use or abuse them.

MR. SPOCK:
May depict wisdom, superior intellect, detachment, unemotional thinking, unfamiliar habit patterns, or a being from another planet or lifestyle.

ROBIN:
Could be a pun on robbin' others or thieving tendencies.

SEYMORE:
Maybe you need to see more of what is going on around you, or could be you are being too nosy.

SLICK:
May be pun on someone trying to pull a slick or sly maneuver, or one who thinks he is slick or sleek.

SLIM:
Possible pun on your weight.

SHEPHERD:
May depict one who tends to aid and protect others, or could be this aspect of you.

TURNER:
Can be a pun on turning things around or turn her around.

WENDY:
Can be a pun on much speaking, long-winded conversations or monologues.

WILL (WILLIAM):
Associated mainly with the use of the will.

WISEMAN:
Would indicate the wise man in you, or may be a symbol of one who is guiding you.

WIZARD:
May represent your subconscious, a genie, or a guide.

WORDSWORTH:
What are your words worth?

WRIGHT:
Can refer to Mr. Right Guy (or gal) for you, or may symbolize the right time, person, place, or whatever.

My Own Name Symbols

CHAPTER 34

Nightmares

The soul attracts that which it secretly harbors: that which it loves, and also, that which it fears.

— *J. Allen*

Fifty percent of dreams are said to be nightmares. Actually, this varies greatly with the individual, for those who are natural problem-solvers seldom have nightmares...and solving problems is what nightmares are really all about.

Modern researchers claim there is a definite relationship between our problems (physical, mental, or emotional), our nightmares, and our physical health or the lack of it.

Who Has Them?

Those who experience nightmares most are people who have a fear or a problem they don't want to face up to or prefer to run away from, in the hope it will go away all by itself. Not only do our problems not go away when ignored, they are often symbolized by nightmares which will most certainly become recurring nightmares if not dealt with—as if once isn't bad enough!

Dr. Ernest Hartman, a psychiatrist at Tufts University School of Medicine in Boston, has made an in-depth study of nightmares and has found that certain personality types are far more prone to have nightmares than others (Welles 1986). These people tend to be more open, vulnerable, and sensitive in nature. Dr. Hartman claims that once one can determine the theme or pattern in their dreams, it is easier for them to

work through the problem areas in their waking life.

Why?

Nightmares seem to occur most when a person—often gentle and sensitive but also fearful—is allowing someone else to manipulate or dominate him and is unwilling or unable to change this.

The nightmare background is always dark and menacing, the figures are large and threatening, often taking on the form of an animal or monster. These evoke a feeling of fear—even terror—and we feel utterly helpless. Invariably we try to scream, run, or escape in some way only to find ourselves unable to do so. The action of the nightmare simply restates what we are trying to do—run away from our problems—and the dream is telling us *you can't run away from this!*

"If nightmares are a response to an external threat, then dealing with that external threat will reduce the nightmares," says Dr. Milton Kramer, head of the Sleep Disorder Center at the Veteran's Administration Hospital in Cincinnati, Ohio (Welles 1986). We must learn to stop running away in our dreams and begin to confront our monsters with questions of, "Who are you? What do you want?" or, "I won't let you do that to me!" Such questioning is often all we need to do to turn the dragon into a mouse. It has been found by psychologists that if we can handle the problem in our dreams, we can then resolve the issue in our daily life.

Children's Nightmares

Children have more nightmares than adults because they "feel more vulnerable and helpless and have more fears," according to Dr. Hartman (Welles 1986). Dr. Patricia Garfield tells us, "A child who has persistent dreams of drowning, getting lost or killed, or of suicide may have a serious emotional disturbance" (Garfield 1984). A child who can't remember any dreams may be depressed or suppressing a traumatic experience.

When a child dreams of a bogeyman, it is because he feels threatened by something or someone he can't put a name or a face to. Usually it is some authority figure, such as a father who is an alcoholic and possibly mistreats him, or a mother with a violent temper, or even a brother who gives him a hard way to go; but it is still someone he is *supposed to love!* Herein lies the problem.

He can't bring himself to say he is afraid of his "loving" mother, for this goes against all his programming. Children are supposed to love their parents! So, his real fear is clothed in mythical images. The dream is telling him he has a fear he must deal with, but his training won't let him face this openly. He is not ready to admit, even to himself, who this monster is. He needs help because his fear is very real, but most likely he will be told to "forget it, it's only a dream!"

Whenever a child dreams of being chased by a monster, it is a sure sign he is feeling threatened in some way and needs some love, understanding, and reassurance. It is important that he be helped to understand the real cause of his problem and to be shown how he can solve it.

The monster is not always a family member—he may represent threats from other children, a teacher, relative, stranger, neighbor, a family argument, or even a scary movie. Whatever the cause, it is best dealt with as soon as possible in a gentle, loving, and understanding manner.

MONSTER MASH:
If the cause is obscure, he needs to be taught and encouraged to stand up to the next monster he meets in a dream. (He can call his strongest friends to come and help him if he wants to.) Assure him he can't be hurt in a dream, so there is really nothing to fear. You might explain that to work out a problem in a dream is to also overcome that fear or problem in real life. Advise your child to stop and ask his tormentor, "Who are you, and what do you want?" Tell him to either conquer his molester or make him a friend, asking for a gift to seal the friendship. Let this be something of a game he can play, an important game.

PROPERTY LOSS OR DAMAGE:
When a child feels or fears that something precious to him is threatened in his dream, it is often symbolized as some favorite possession being lost or damaged in some way. Here again is a signal for help and reassurance.

INJURIES AND DEATH:
Injuries sustained in dreams often indicate that the child has been emotionally traumatized in some way and needs some tender, loving care and understanding so that he may heal. There is one exception to this. Sometimes the nightmare is really a past life remembrance of some terrifying event. A recurring dream of drowning or being killed in battle is quite common, and a little careful questioning on your part about the type of clothing he was wearing, the kind of buildings, and other background information can help you decide whether it is a present-day nightmare or a traumatic memory of another lifetime. In either case, the child needs some grownup help and understanding to sup-

port him in working through—not avoiding—these frightening experiences which tend to recur until the matter is resolved in some way.

RECURRING NIGHTMARES:

These simply state that the problem has not been overcome, that the inner fear still exists and needs to be dealt with in a positive way. This is especially true for nightmares dealing with death or injury.

Adult Nightmares

The same situation holds true for adults. Your nightmares, too, are caused by your fear and/or some conflict between you and the authority figure you hesitate to confront. It can be a parent, relative, boss, teacher, situation, or whatever. Or, it can be a clash between the **real** you and the **persona**, the facade you put on for people to see—the make-believe you. This battle between the two you's would be more likely to show up as dreams of conflict, but the possibility exists for some neat nightmares.

YOUR PROBLEM IS YOUR TEACHER:

All too often, we teach and are taught how to avoid anything which is ugly, painful, distasteful, or upsetting to us. One of the most important things we need to learn is that our problems actually serve as beacons of light or as magnifying glasses, emphasizing or pointing out our most crippling fears, our most restrictive attitudes, prejudices, and misconceptions which are holding up our progress—things we really must face up to and overcome if we are to grow.

We need to understand that our problems represent the **lesson we need to learn**. We are all in the process of becoming wiser, better, and more God-like. The difficulties we face are like the gateway through which we must pass in order to proceed. Our problems are actually our teachers.

BEING CHASED:

This symbolizes the futile effort to escape from a situation you do not want to face. The worst thing you can do is to wake up to avoid seeing what the dream is trying to tell you. The best thing you could do would be to stop running, face your enemy, and demand to know who s/he is and what s/he wants. Try to work out your problem on the spot; make peace and if possible ask for a gift from your enemy. Remember, to work out your difficulty in a dream is to pave the way to work out these issues in your life.

TRAPPED:

This type of nightmare experience can imply feeling trapped in your job, your marriage, or some other situation. It may symbolize needing more space, more alone time or privacy to meet your deep, inner needs. It is important that you honor this need and **make space for yourself**.

NUDITY:

In general, being nude in public refers to your fears of being exposed in public. In can symbolize vulnerability and fears of being found out, ridiculed, disgraced. See chapter on *Nudity*.

POLICEMEN:

A sheriff, policeman, detective, or "the Law" in nightmares would represent a fear of being caught in doing something you feel is wrong.

FALLING:

Falling in nightmare dreams may be nothing more that the remembrance of returning to our bodies as we have discussed earlier, especially if this occurs just before awakening; but when this happens in the middle of a dream it can symbolize losing your position in life, heading for a fall, plans or a project about to fall through, or a feeling that you are in a precarious position, vulnerable, or insecure.

GENERAL FEARS:

Whether in school or at work, nightmares can indicate a fear of failure, a fear of your teacher or boss whom you hesitate to confront. If you are married, the monster could be your mate or in-laws who dictate what you must or must not do. Generally, anyone who curtails your natural right to freedom of expression in any way is subject to suspicion in your efforts to detect the villain behind the dragon in your dreams.

SHADOWS:

Often a vague, shadowy form is indicative of some obscure, unformed fear that actually has no basis in fact. It is quite possible to be afraid of a hypothetical event that may never happen, yet it can be a real threat to you until you face it squarely and see it for what it really is. This may take some mental probing on your part, but it is important to you or you wouldn't be having the nightmare.

Shadows can also represent a part of you which needs to be recognized, accepted, and integrated into your beingness. It may be the dark side of a special talent you did not know you had or which you have misunderstood or misapplied in some way. If you can remember to do so, try turning on the lights while in your nightmare so as to see who or what this aspect of you really is.

Your Detective Work

You need to ask yourself what person or group is trying to force or manipulate you into *their* goals, ideas, or ideals. Authority figures will hint or even tell you outright that you are a failure because you don't measure up to *their* expectations and goals! (As though your own goals don't count!) Clearly, this is a challenge for you to stand up for *your own goals!*

Powerful people tend to push others into their own molds—what was good for them should be good for everybody, they think—but we all know that doesn't work. We can't all fit into the same mold. Besides, we don't need a world full of clones!

If this is happening in your life, you need to see this for what it really is, and most of all to do something constructive about it. A nightmare is telling you that the situation is crucial, that your lifestyle, independence, freedom, individuality, peace of mind, and your spiritual growth are all at stake. Life is telling you it's time to break through your present barriers, learn your needed lesson, and move on.

YOUR SUSPECT LIST:

Your first task after a nightmare experience is to identify the source of your fear. Where do you feel pressured? What do you fear or whom do you dread most to confront? Perhaps you would be better off to stand up to your boss, mate, Mother-in-Law, big brother, or whomever is pressuring you. They will respect you for it. You would regain your own self-respect as well. If you get fired, realize this may be the best thing that could happen. It may be high time to move on. Since your problem is your teacher, your ogre boss may be teaching or forcing you to stand up for your rights, or s/he may be revealing that you don't need to work under such miserable conditions any more. Your marriage partner may be teaching you never to fear his/her temper again, or that you don't have to depend on someone else for a living—you *can* make it on your own. There is *always* a valuable lesson for you hidden in the depths of the nightmare. Take a good look at both the background and the dream symbolism. If your monster is a bear, and you often think of your boss as a bear or as being overBEARing...see how easy it can be? Dreams are often puny.

They can even be funny, once you get the message.

SOLVING YOUR CASE:
If, after trying all the above, the identity of your bogeyman still eludes you, try sitting down with paper and pen. Write out names of the people, situations, and events that are most annoying, upsetting, or threatening to you—then check your list with the dream symbols. Pay particular attention to your feelings. What did that monster feel like? How did you feel when it came near? When did you last feel like that? (Remember, the dream may exaggerate the situation in order to make a point.)

Analyzing the stresses in your waking life will help eliminate nightmares. In your journal, try writing some of the things you dislike most in your life—things or people who make you feel cramped or restricted, people you wish were not in your life—then check these with your dream symbols. Pick the one that comes closest, that feels most likely to be your problem, but *do not stop here*. Don't flounder in "I don't know who or what." Take what feels most nearly right and start from there. The main thing is to make a start. (If you guessed wrong, you will get a correction.) Calmly and with determination, write out a desirable solution. Decide what you would like to see yourself doing or saying, then *do it!* If you lack the courage to take the direct approach, fear not—there is more than one way to kill a dragon! Read on.

Slaying Your Dragon

Once you have come to a satisfactory although make-believe solution, your next step is to close your eyes for a moment and see this scene taking place just as you have pictured it. Spare no details. Make it clear in your mind. Go over it several times, making it better and better. See yourself confronting the problem and working out a solution which is highly satisfactory to you. Feel the joy and freedom this brings. See everyone concerned agreeing to your proposal...even thanking you for bringing it to their attention. Picture your happy ending *clearly*. Then, when you go to bed, try making this into a dream, seeing it all happening again as you drift off to sleep. This will program your subconscious mind as to just how you want your life to be so that it can cooperate with your plan.

Another approach would be to wake from a nightmare, calm yourself, and go right back to the scene to work out a satisfactory solution on the spot. Your imagery is all important here, and *it works!* Try it sometime—next nightmare.

GRAND FINALE:
Once your mind is made up as to what you want to do and how you want it done, magical things happen. Since we are all highly telepathic, especially during sleep, your nightmare characters receive your message; and whether consciously remembered or not, as you actually make your stand, those who formally opposed you may suddenly accept your proposal—often without a word of protest! There you are, ready for a battle, and there are no warriors! You have won your freedom without a fight!

Preventive Measures

Once you have learned your lesson, the next time someone asks a favor stop and ask yourself, "Do I *really want* to do this?" Be absolutely honest with yourself and your feelings. If your answer is "No," then remember you have a perfect right to say, "Sorry, I have other plans." (You don't have to tell them what your plans are—you may *plan* to sleep late or just relax!) Honor your own needs!

Don't allow yourself to fall for that old "If you love me you will do so and so..." for if they loved *you*, they wouldn't impose on you! So, be brave enough to say, "No thanks," or "I have other plans," because if you don't the "bogeyman will getcha" in your next nightmare.

Of course, it may shock the person who is trying to make your plans *for* you...but that is *their problem!* Your task is to preserve your freedom. God gave you free will, and you have an obligation to maintain it!

Doing things for others because *you want to give* is a wonderful, loving thing. Being manipulated into doing is failing to honor the God-in-you and committing a crime against yourself. Learning to honor your feelings will keep those bad dreams at bay.

Generally speaking, once you start to seriously work with your dreams, trying to understand their import and to apply what you have learned in your life, you won't have nasty dreams—for a nightmare is an ignored warning replayed in a highly dramatic and exaggerated manner in order to *get your attention!*

Nightmares point out a crucial need for you to face your fears and problems and to make a stand for your rights. You deserve the very best. Jesus said, "I came that you might have life more abundantly"— not to be miserable. Part of your problem with experiencing misery is that you don't believe you deserve better. Your dreams are trying to tell you differently.

My Own Nightmare Symbols

CHAPTER 35

Nudity

Finding yourself totally nude in a dream can be a disturbing experience. We often try to dismiss this as silly without stopping to look for a deeper meaning. Actually, this is a fairly common phenomenon and can mean a variety of things, depending on one's feelings about the situation.

Nudity can symbolize a feeling of naivety, gullibility, unpreparedness, or of being uninformed. Most often it depicts being in a situation where you feel exposed, caught unaware, and afraid of having some deed brought to public attention—especially if you are naked in a public place. It can represent feelings of poverty, a lack of protection, love, support, warmth, or of the necessities of life. Any of these would make one feel barren, empty, and exposed to fate, the elements, or the whims of the public. Being naked might also depict feelings of guilt, defenselessness, and susceptibility.

Since clothing usually represents our attitudes, ideas, opinions, and prejudices about things, the lack of clothing could represent a lack of a "proper attitude," the absence of any real caring, not having an opinion in the matter, general indecisiveness, or possibly not having any idea of what to do in the situation.

Nudity can be a pun on getting down to the bare facts, getting to the bottom of things, letting down barriers, dropping all pretenses, or letting go of a situation, depending on the circumstances and feelings in the dream.

Partial Nudity

If only a part of the body is bare, then your dream may be pointing to your feeling of vulnerability in the particular area that is exposed. See *The Body and Its Parts.*

Naked and Uneasy

When you dream of finding yourself nude in a public place and are feeling embarrassed about it, the chances are you are about to be exposed in some way. This may be something you have done privately and want to keep hidden; it could be a mistake, misjudgment, or misdeed you prefer to conceal, something you have done or left undone which you don't want revealed. Often this is just a fear of having misdeeds or hidden behaviors made public, but it could be a warning not to be caught unaware, that you are in a vulnerable position, or that you are about to be exposed.

Naked, But No One Notices

This implies that the situation is inconsequential, except to you. It says in a way that no one will notice but you, implying that your fears are either unnecessary, exaggerated, or unfounded.

Naked and Unconcerned

To be naked in a public place and feel no embarrassment can imply a release of old attitudes and restrictions, a new sense of freedom, a revelation, a shedding of all affectations, a new sense of honesty and openness.

You may have a nude dream where the feeling is one of perfect peace, contentment, and total unconcern about the lack of clothing; this may indicate feeling unencumbered, happy, and carefree. This could portray a new confidence in your self-worth, your abilities, your values, and lifestyle. It could show a clear perception, an uncluttered attitude, a lack of any prejudice or pretense, with everything open and above board. No prejudice, no subterfuge, no need to cover up. Having an open, frank, and honest approach, a sense of justice, freedom, and joy. Nothing is hidden, nothing to hide, and feeling really good about yourself.

Undressing

The act of undressing could, under certain conditions, represent sexual interests or desires but could just as easily be a desire to be free of all encumbrances, to "let the matter drop," to be open and above board with nothing to hide. It may represent taking off attitudes and beliefs that tend to interfere with free movement of thought and deed; removing prejudices, limited ideas, anything that hinders progress.

On the other hand, if you are nude or your loved one is nude or both, then it is quite probable this is a sex dream or one concerning your attitudes about sex, depending on how you feel about the nudity. The dream could be making a comment on how you really feel about sex, your vulnerability in that area, or it could be pointing out the open attitudes you have concerning each other or possibly how much of yourself you feel you have "exposed" to the other. It may indicate how you really feel about that person.

Some Possibilities

CHEST BARE:
This usually symbolizes your emotions, feelings, hopes, and dreams, but could be a pun on getting things off your chest or letting your feelings show, depending on the dream action.

FEET UNCOVERED:
May imply that your basic beliefs are being revealed in a way which is embarrassing to you, or can depict a sense of freedom, depending on the feeling in the dream.

GENITALS EXPOSED:
Could be your sexual activities are being exposed, about to be exposed, or could indicate your fears of having these out in the open.

HANDS:
Can be the disclosure of your deeds or how you have handled a situation.

HEART AREA BARE:
Exposed emotions, vulnerability, or sensitivity of feelings. Affairs of the heart may be divulged—dream may show your fears of having this happen. See *The Body and Its Parts*.

My Own Nudity Symbols

My Own Nudity Symbols continued...

Numbers

CHAPTER 36

Numerology

The ancient art of numerology has its basis in the Jewish *Kaballa*. Its background may go deep into man's early beginnings. We know numerology was taught in the Egyptian and Greek mystery schools and that it is reputed to have originated in Atlantis. Whatever its historical background, it is still being taught today and, regardless of whether or not you have studied this, the basic information is stored in the race-conscious mind. Therefore, whenever these symbols appear in our dreams, they still retain the ancient meanings which, at some level of our being, we understand. So, unless you have some **strong** personal associations with one or more of these numbers, it would be best for you to use the meanings listed below to interpret your dreams.

To begin with, it is necessary to take any number of more than one digit and add together all the components until they are reduced to one digit, with a few exceptions listed below.

For example, the number 257 is treated as:

$$2 + 5 + 7 = 14$$

Fourteen is reduced again to make a single digit:

$$1 + 4 = 5$$

Five is then the numerological number, so you look up the meaning of five, not 257.

In the same manner:

$$301 \text{ is } 3 + 0 + 1 = 4$$

Look up the meaning of four.

$$97 \text{ is } 9 + 7 = 16.$$

$$1 + 6 = 7.$$

Look up seven.

$$2{,}349 \text{ is } 2 + 3 + 4 + 9 = 18.$$

$$1 + 8 = 9.$$

Look up nine.

The only exceptions to these rules are the *Master Numbers*: 11, 22, and 33. These we do not usually break down to a single digit. However, there are a few other double numbers listed, as they are considered special in meaning, such as the often-used Biblical reference to "40 days."

The number 38 would be $3 + 8 = 11$.

$$1 + 1 = 2.$$

Look up two.

But, since eleven is a master number, you would also look up eleven.

The single number components are important, so you may want to look these up individually; but bear in mind, the main meaning is found in the final, composite digit.

ZEROS EMPHASIZE A NUMBER:

Zeros give numbers greater strength and meaning. Fifty would be a strong five; three thousand would be a very powerful three.

NUMBERS WITH DASHES:

Dashes in a number, such as a phone number, would be treated as two separate numbers **and** as the total. Look at it both ways.

Example: 242-4396.

242 is 2 + 4 + 2 = 8.

Eight is the power to do or to be.

4396 is 4 + 3 + 9 + 6 = 22.

Twenty-two is master or mastery.

8 + 22 can be the power of mastery, power to be a master or to master the subject in the dream.

Twenty-two can also be a four, which is earth, worldly and/or plain hard work, doing things in a purely physical manner. In that case, the phone number could be read as, "The power to be a master or the power to be worldly and work hard." This is an either/or possibility.

Also, 8 + 22 (2 + 2) = 12. Look up twelve. Consider all the above.

Exceptions

There can be exceptions. **If your mind is focused** on lottery numbers and you dream of what looks like the right combination of letters and numbers, **then** the group of numbers **could** be your winning number—but only if your mind is intent in that direction. Otherwise, use the method shown above. If in doubt try it both ways. This would apply to any type of winning numbers you may be seeking.

Always bear in mind what kind of help or information your heart or mind is seeking, for this is the stuff dreams are made of. Your desires preselect the dream content. Sometimes these are subconscious hopes, wishes, or concerns coming from the depths of your heart. Try to be aware of your innermost desires, for what you seek is what you get!

Number Meanings

0 Timeless, endless, perfect, no beginning and no end, absence of quality, quantity and mass. Absolute freedom from limitation. Sign of infinite and eternal conscious energy, superconsciousness, symbol for God or eternity if seen alone. Behind other numbers it gives added importance, emphasis, and power.

1 First, beginning, basis, original, pioneer, leader.

2 Double weakness or double strength, division, soul, receptivity, subconscious mind.

3 Trinity, great strength, completion, creativity, or your ability to create. May represent the physical, mental, and spiritual (combination).

4 Four corners of the earth, physical, worldly, material matters, four lower chakras or centers, doing things in a material (nonspiritual) manner, doing things the hard way, hard work.

5 Usually means change in the area or matter it is associated with, but can mean freedom or refer to the five senses of man.

6 Perfection, beauty, strength, harmony, completion, or cycle of creation.

7 Seven days of creation, completion, perfection, balanced spiritual forces, seven centers of the body, seven levels, seven planes, victory, Sabbath.

8 Power to do or be, potential of success, wealth, material gain, money, balance.

9 Finish, completion, termination.

10 One plus zero, great strength, new start with the expectancy of success, new round of increase. Consider number one, also.

11 Intuition, mastery, spirituality, enlightenment, capacity to achieve, mastery of the physical plane. Please note: eleven is considered a master number, showing mastery or potential for mastery in a particular area; however, if the potential is not used, it may work as a mere two.

12 Strength of spirit, cosmic order, spiritual completion, divine perfection. May also work as a three.

13 Death and birth, end and beginning, change and transition. May work as a four.

15 This is a number to use to dissolve difficult conditions, such as saying or writing an affirmation or prayer fifteen times; may work as a six.

16 Not a numerology number per se, but we usually associate this with "sweet sixteen"— young, innocent, tender, naive, sweet, vulnerable. Consider a seven.

17 Soul. Consider an eight also.

22 Mastery on all planes, power to achieve and teach, special abilities, power of reason and diplomacy, mastery on the mental plane. When the potential is not used, this number can revert to a four (2 + 2 = 4) and act as such.

26 This number represents earth, the material plane, and is said to be the most karmic of all numbers. It is the sum total of the name *Yod-Heh-Vau-Heh* and is also a form of eight, the power-to-do, so consider it carefully.

33 Spiritual consciousness developed through experiences and the desire for a higher plane of service. A very high potential. Mastery of the spiritual plane, but consider possibility of a six.

40 Time needed to prepare, period of cleansing or testing (as in the biblical forty days and forty nights), period of growth and formation. Can mean "as long as it takes" or, "a very long time." Possibly a strong four.

50 Holy of Holies, a very sacred number, key to God's grace, but consider a strong five.

As always, there can be a few puns thrown in for good measure such as "B4" for before, or "4C" as foresee, so watch for these.

My Own Number Symbols

CHAPTER 37

People

Man is literally what he thinks. His character is the sum of all his thoughts.
— *James Allen*

Dreams seem to represent pieces of ourselves that elude us during our waking hours. The people we meet in dreams are not what they seem to be! A good ninety-five percent of them, familiar to us or not, are aspects ourselves. That gossipy old Mrs. X is not really Mrs. X at all but is the gossipy *part of you* which you are meeting in your dreams!

When you dream of other people, these are almost always parts or *aspects of yourself* which you do not choose to recognize as yours.

Sometimes the people in your dreams are over-dramatized or oversized replicas of yourself or your attitudes, in order to give you a vivid glimpse of the direction in which your thoughts and attitudes are taking you or to bring needed insights as to who and what you are and how you behave.

Often you have to confront these aspects—who may be seen as threatening to you—before you can accept the fact that these character traits do exist in you, especially the less desirous ones. Eventually you can take steps to control, change, or use these qualities.

Conversely, dream people may represent beautiful attributes or talents which you have but do not see in yourself. Your dreams introduce these to you so you can begin to accept the fact that you do have these qualities or skills and in-

tegrate these heretofore unclaimed qualities and characteristics.

People Becoming Other People

Occasionally you will have a person who starts out as hot-tempered Mr. Nasty but later turns into Mr. Niceguy. This kind of dream may be pointing out your need to change one aspect of yourself into another, showing you just how easily this can be done. On the other hand, we may find in dreams that certain events can turn us from niceguy into a terrible terror—a situation we need to carefully scrutinize in order to erase the cause of our irritable behavior patterns.

WHAT'S IN A NAME?

Often you will meet people with telltale names, such as Mr. Cheetham (an obvious pun on cheating) or Mrs. Doolittle (the do-little aspect of you). See chapter on *Names*.

DREAM PEOPLE YOU KNOW:

The *people you know* in your dreams may represent qualities you are aware of but do not own as yours, while *those you don't know* represent qualities or energies you are unaware of having. *Friends you know and like* would depict aspects of yourself which you are familiar and comfortable with, while those you don't care for usually personify features you dislike and do not recognize as being in you. Fritz Perls tells us we often disown certain parts of ourselves, the so-called good as well as the so-called bad, and we tend to bury or deny any thoughts or feelings which are not in line with what we have been taught to believe is appropriate.

PEOPLE YOU DON'T KNOW:

Females: often represent feminine qualities and instincts in us such as intuition, feelings, sensitivity, emotions, softness, gentleness, receptivity, sympathy, caringness, and the ability to let go and cry.

Males: usually depict intellect, action, aggressiveness, self-assertion, will power, fact finding, no-nonsense approach, ability to be strong, to fight or push when necessary (and sometimes when not necessary).

Ideally we should each have a balance of male and female qualities within us. Unfortunately, we are taught to encourage only the masculine or feminine traits, as the case may be, and to suppress, rather than balance, the opposite half; this leads to problems. Our dreams try to show us where this imbalance exists, so note carefully the action and relationship between these. If all goes well, these halves should become good friends (known qualities) and eventually integrate, which may be symbolized by marriage.

Disabled: A disabled male may represent ways in which you are crippling or stifling your masculine qualities. The same holds true for disabled, raped, mistreated females.

Who's Who in Your Dreams

Statistics tell us that ninety-five percent of our dreams are about ourselves; the rest involve other people—usually those in one's immediate family or work environment. This causes a real dilemma. How can we tell which people are giving us needed information about our friends and relatives and which persons are aspects of ourselves?

To answer this we must go back to our computer-like minds once more. To be absolutely clear on who is who in your dreams, it is necessary to program your subconscious mind so that there can be no uncertainty on this issue.

To do this you need to make a *Dreamer's Guest List*. Take an ordinary sheet of notebook paper and make three columns labeled *Name*, *Relationship,* and *Meaning*. Next, decide which members of your family you feel love and responsibility for, and place these on your list as those "playing themselves." Then, quietly go within and tell your subconscious that you *want these people to play themselves only*, repeating this at least three times to make sure the programming is adequately impressed. From time to time you may want to add other people to your Guest List, along with the qualities you most strongly associate with them, as they make appearances in your dreams.

This list can go on and on as you meet new people in dreams and decide what aspect of you they represent, writing down the results for future reference. Meanwhile, you will have a quick check of who is playing whom, which can be a tremendous aid in interpretation. Just remember that people in dreams will *occasionally* play themselves, even when not programmed.

Responsibility

Any person or persons we are responsible for, whether an aging parent, a child, or a group, will appear in our dreams from time to time to help us be aware of their needs or any problems we may need to work out with them. Often, details we overlooked during the busy day are brought to our attention during the night. It can be anything from drug abuse, depression, or an oncoming illness to a slight misunderstanding or

Dreamer's Guest List

NAME	RELATIONSHIP	MEANING
David	son	plays himself
Jenny	daughter	plays herself
Lewis	grandson	plays himself
Mother	Mother	plays herself
Carl	friend	very intelligent, intuitive, psychic, healing abilities.
Martha	close friend & school teacher	good humor, love, laughter, school teacher, joy; teaching, caring aspect
Bob T.	boss	authoritative, conservative, cautious, blunt, brusque.
Charlotte	artist, friend	gentle, loving, kind, happy, artistic, creative
Carol	minister & friend	high IQ, leader, teacher, healer; loving, caring, inspiring.
Jane	co-worker	gossip, criticism, faultfinding, negative, unhappy

hurt feelings that need to be talked out and mended.

Dreams about our family members or close friends can bring us warnings or insights into situations or conditions in their lives in order to give us a better understanding of what they are going through, or that we may be of greater help and support in their time of need.

You Watching You

Occasionally you will find yourself watching your actions from the standpoint of an observer, seeing yourself from various perspectives and in a number of different roles. You may perceive yourself as you think others see you or as being "done unto" by others.

At other times you may find yourself looking at your dream sequences through your own eyes, as yourself—the doer, the one who instigates the action, the eager participator. You may survey things from the position of how you would **like** them to be, and once in a while you may witness from all of these levels. Note carefully, when writing out your dreams, just which modes of perception are used.

Your Shadow

When you see vague, dark people in dreams who may or may not look like you, remember these shadows represent repressed characteristics you have not yet developed or your own undefined and obscure fears which you are loathe to face and overcome. One of the cardinal rules of dreaming is to **confront and conquer fear or danger** in your dreams. If you can remember that all those you meet in dreams are only parts of yourself, then you can call forth the shadow, ask what it represents, and proceed to subjugate your fear—or discover and bring out your repressed talents. See *Shadow* under *Nightmares*.

Three People

When there are exactly three people in your dream, these usually represent the trinity of yourself: the physical, mental, and spiritual; the body, mind, and soul; or the conscious, subconscious, and superconscious levels of your being. Ideally these are all working together, moving in the same direction, but there may be times when they are in disagreement or even in conflict. As mentioned before, whenever there is a disagreement between the conscious mind and the subconscious, the **subconscious always wins**. It is our basic belief system, the way we have been trained to see, think, and act; so a dissension here means it will be necessary to retrain the subconscious mind in order to make any progress. Your dream is pointing out this problem for your edification.

At times you will have an authority figure such as a policeman, judge, minister, spiritual teacher, or person-in-charge who will represent the superconscious part of you or the part we call our God-self or High Self. Be particularly attentive to the words and actions with these. You may even want to put your favorite spiritual person or symbol on your Guest List as depicting your High Self.

Your subconscious mind may be portrayed as a shadow, a servant, or even an automated piece of machinery. All the beings we meet in our dreams, whether people, figurines, dolls, toys, animals, or even shadows are parts of us which we need to recognize, confront, and work on, either to change these for the better or to accept them as our own fine qualities.

For example: a woman named Mary dreamed about the lady next door (something she has to live with). Mary described Mrs. X as finicky, old-fashioned, and insistent that everything of hers be kept clean, neat, and in good repair. Meanwhile, in Mary's yard (extension of her consciousness), there were two trucks being repaired in the middle of her garden. (Mary runs a small nursery, so this is very important to her.) She calls to her son (aspect of herself), "Why are they there?" (Mary is really asking this of herself, since she has not programmed her children otherwise.) He does not answer but uproots her Christmas tree (representing the Christ-in-her or her Christian beliefs as a whole). Next, her whole back yard is flooded with water, which threatens to engulf her house but no one else's home.

After a little questioning, we found that friends and neighbors often use Mary's yard and driveway as a convenient place to repair their cars. Up to now Mary has allowed this. We soon decided Mrs. X is the neat, clean, and tidy aspect of Mary which she has not yet asserted in her life. Her son represents an undisciplined aspect of herself which allows the mess and the intrusion of other people's lifestyles (trucks) to continue, while the uprooted Christmas tree implies that the very roots of Mary's Christianity are deeply disturbed.

Her idea of being a good Christian would not let her refuse her friends' abuse. The flooded backyard that threatens Mary's house is the upcoming flood of emotions building up from this constant infringement, and it threatens Mary's whole state of consciousness (house). As you can see, Mrs. X is not such a bad person after all but represents Mary's inherent ability to insist upon neatness, cleanliness, respect, and dignity. *She* wouldn't allow the mess in *her* yard, and neither should Mary. Mary knows that now, and she also realizes that her Christian beliefs, in this case, were misplaced.

Babies and Toddlers

Babies in dreams may depict a variety of different things to you, but usually a new baby is a new and valuable idea, project, concept, or ideal you have just given birth to, or a responsibility you have accepted. It is "your baby," your "thing to do," your personal project, responsibility, hobby, or concern. It may be a creative idea you plan to put into words, music, or picture. Whatever it is, it is something which you present to the world—a thing uniquely yours—of which you can be proud.

In later dreams you may see yourself feeding and nourishing the child, even watching it grow from dream to dream, viewing the progress you are making with satisfaction. Or, you may—much to your great dismay—find the baby dead or dying and realize that you have sacrificed it in some way or dropped and killed it accidentally. This can be a very disturbing dream until you realize the baby represents your valued project, not a real child, and that the dream is suggesting that it may not be wise to "let the matter drop" or to sacrifice your ideas or ideals for the sake of someone else (which is something we too often do to ourselves). The dream may point

out that you have allowed another person to belittle your hopes and plans to the point of dropping them, or you have permitted them to talk you out of what you really wanted to do with your life or talents. In such a case, the dream would show you are sacrificing more than a baby—you are literally sacrificing a very dear and valued part of yourself, hence the highly significant symbolism of your "baby."

Of course there can always be exceptions. An infant could represent infantile aspects of yourself, or possibly a newly-emerging personality just beginning to become visible. Baby or child could depict the outcome or product of a certain quality or action.

If the infant is actually your own newborn child, this may have a double meaning for you, both symbolic and in reality. You may want to place his/her name on your Guest List for greater clarity.

BABY BAPTISM:
Implies commitment, dedication, a joining with God forces, a blessing, consecration, reverence.

BATHING, CHANGING BABY:
Cleaning up any messes or mistakes you have made, making a new start, taking care of problems.

DROPPING BABY:
Suggests you are dropping a very valuable idea or project. Warning to reconsider this step.

FEEDING BABY:
Feeding, nurturing your ideal or project, taking care of its needs, working on positive goals.

KILLING BABY:
You may be sacrificing your hopes, dreams, project, or ideal which is important to you. Ask yourself if it is worth the cost. Is this really what you want to do?

LOSING BABY:

Losing hope, losing sight of your precious dreams or ideals, perhaps allowing yourself to be talked or ridiculed out of them. Hint to reconsider the situation.

TOO MANY BABIES:

May imply you have taken on too many new ideas, options, goals, projects, problems, or responsibilities at one time.

TWINS:

Two new, important goals or projects.

Children

These are more likely to represent the childish, immature, and undisciplined aspects of yourself, undisciplined thoughts, habits, and activities, especially when these are children in general and not a specific child. Children whose actions are annoying or distressing often indicate qualities, habits, or characteristics in you that are only half grown or partially developed, which you may want to squelch.

PLAYING:

Playing youngsters can represent the world of imagination, the ability to transcend time and space, a carefree and unhampered spirit, abilities to change at a moment's notice—qualities which you may need at this point in your life. Happy, laughing children often designate the carefree, innocent, joyous, and fun-loving qualities of life which you may have been neglecting or suppressing. In this case, your dream could be suggesting that you need to relax and have more fun in your life as a much needed balance.

Your thoughts and ideas are also your creations; therefore children can portray the thoughts, hopes, wishes, and dreams you hold in mind which are growing and developing. (This may

also be symbolized as a pregnancy.) A child might also denote creative talents and abilities not yet developed to their fullest potential. This could be any talent, hobby, or project you are currently pursuing.

Brothers or Sisters as Children

These could portray childish aspects of our siblings (depending on your programing), something very close to you, what you have to "live with," or can mean related events, circumstances, talents, or situations where one thing is connected (related) to another. Look at the talents or qualities associated with your brethren to fully understand the meaning.

Teenagers

A teenager is considered too old to do childish things and too young to do adult things. It is truly an awkward, insecure, untried, unsure, halfway-there, caught-in-the-middle kind of situation which is infuriating, confusing, and upsetting. Teenagers in your dreams may symbolize this neither-nor stage, the feelings and frustrations of being unable to get where you want to go or do what you want to do in your life and career, or the attempt to find a balance between two worlds of thought.

Teens might symbolize your efforts to bridge the gap between two ways of thinking and doing, or between the old and the new.

Friends

A FRIEND OF A FRIEND (OR RELATIVE):

Usually denotes a quality, aspect, characteristic, trait, habit, problem, or hang-up of your friend which you have not yet noticed but need to recognize. Could be warning of a problem.

GROWN-UPS:

Grown-up implies a full-grown, full-blown habit, quality, or characteristic in us, like it or not.

FAMOUS PEOPLE:

Meeting famous people is one of the many ways in which dreams can tell us of talents and abilities we didn't know we had. This is a fairly common event in dreams. Ask yourself, "What is this person famous for?" What talents or qualities do I associate with him/her? Then, realize these talents or qualities are also in you.

FAMOUS PERSON:

Represents the talents, qualities, abilities, possibilities, or faults which you also have.

FICTIONAL CHARACTERS:

The same principles as those of famous people apply here also. "Fictional" makes no difference—they still stand for certain characteristics, possibly qualities you do not believe you have. Look again!

GODS AND GODDESSES:

These, too, appear in dreams as symbols of fine qualities or abilities you may have. Take time to read more about your god or goddess to see what the special talents were. These are yours also, but unrecognized and possibly not fully developed. This is food for thought.

Movie Stars

These often represent fame and fortune. To dream of a star can be a wish or hope of being rich and famous, or may depict your tendency to put on an act, ham it up, make believe, and play roles. Might symbolize your acting abilities. Again, the qualities you associate most with them may be yours, or these may imply you have been behaving like a comedian, tough guy, cop, criminal, alien, or whatever.

CHARACTER ACTORS:

These usually denote the quality, habits, or characteristics they are noted for. John Wayne, for instance, is noted as the tough but good guy. Others are associated with drunkenness, innocence, humor, law and order, beauty, viciousness, mischief, stupidity, bad guys; and so it goes.

ELVIS PRESLEY:

Rags to riches capabilities, originality, ability to do things in your own special style. Might also represent drug abuse, but also fame and fortune.

SEX SYMBOLS:

Many stars are considered sex symbols. As such they may depict your own sex urges, actions, morals, flirtations, or sex appeal.

SPECIAL TALENTS:

Some stars are noted for special talents and may depict that particular talent or ability inherent in you. Think what quality you most associate with that person.

VIOLENCE SYMBOLS:

Be aware that some of the so-called tough guys in many movies are just plain violent in nature and can symbolize the potential for violence in you.

Ordinary People

PEOPLE, MANY:

Many aspects at work in this situation, or could be getting yourself all together; may depict a public opinion.

SHORT PEOPLE:

May be a pun on coming up short, not measuring up to standards.

TALL PEOPLE:

Possibly a "think tall, walk tall and proud" aspect.

PEOPLE IN WORK CLOTHES:

May be reference to the job at hand, your attitudes at work or about work; aspects you have to work with or through.

ACTOR:

Aspect of you who is always on stage, acting up, putting on a show, pretending, over-acting or reacting, dramatizing, showing off, hamming it up. Unrealistic, possibly untrustworthy. Can represent your personality self.

Bit Player: Could denote that you seldom get a word in, tend to take the "bit" and never the lead; could be a hint to step out of your shell and do more with your life and talents.

Bosomy Actress: Putting up a good front, possibly a false front.

Character Player: May imply you are quite a character, or maybe you are out of character; possibly you play so many different characters that you have lost all sense of who you really are.

Sex Symbol: Actor, Actress: Aspect of you preoccupied with sex.

Understudy: One who is always studying but never gets on stage, meaning you never apply what you have learned.

ALIEN:
Aspect unfamiliar, unrecognized; something different, unusual, unorthodox, unknown, new, untried; possibly genius ability.

ANGELS:
There are many of these. They may represent your guardian angel, Solar Angel, your High Self, God-self, your conscience, a guiding angel, or an answer to your prayers. Some of the most well-known angels are Archangels:

Raphael: Angel of the East, sunrise, air sylphs, Spring Equinox, healing, supercon-

scious mind. He is most often seen holding the Holy Grail, but sometimes a fish and staff.

Gabriel: Known as the Angel of Love, he is the angel of South, of Christmas, Winter Solstice, rain, and water sprites. He is usually symbolized holding seven white lilies.

Michael: Angel of the West, of the sun, of purification, fire salamanders, Autumn Equinox, he is pictured with the sword and the scales, known as the Dragon Slayer.

Uriel: Angel of the North, of Nature Spirits, beauty, growth, and the Summer Solstice; usually seen amid flowers.

ATTENDANT:
Helper, assistant, aide, guide, servant.

AUDIENCE:
May signify the public, public opinion, or passive aspects of you.

BOGEYMAN:
Symbol of your fears. Often a cover-up for an authority figure who is giving you a hard time.

BOOKKEEPER:
Part of you that is keeping the records straight, trying to balance the books, pay old debts to bring balance into your life.

BOSS:
Authority figure. Can represent your High Self if he is one you can admire, or may symbolize limitation, fear, hard work, lack of freedom or originality.

Fear: of Boss: Fear of authority persons, of what people will say or think. Need to ask yourself who you allow to run (ruin) your life, to dictate what you can and can't do.

CAPTAIN:
Authority figure. Highest meaning is control over all aspects (crew) of yourself on the ship of life.

CARDBOARD PEOPLE:

Pretense, false impressions, make believe, someone not what they seem to be, unreliable, dummies, a life-like appearance but only an appearance—not real.

CHEER LEADER:

Aspect of you which is cheerful, encouraging, supporting, or may point to the need of this.

CHOIR:

Aspects of yourself in close harmony or a need for more harmony in your life.

CINDERELLA:

Rags to riches, transformation of attitudes, self, lifestyle from poverty to riches.

CLOWN:

Clowning around, not taking life seriously, foolishness, irresponsibility, or this may be a part of you which desires to make others laugh. Could be your talent.

COMEDIAN:

Your sense of humor, fun-loving nature, aspect of you that can laugh at life or at yourself. If this is a stranger to you it may be your own repressed joy and humor you have failed to express.

COP:

See *Policeman*, this chapter.

DADDY:

Same qualities as *father* but closer, less formal; more love, companionship, and understanding indicated.

DARK FIGURES:

May represent vague, unformed fears or can be symbols of your lower, baser self or your subconscious.

DARK-SKINNED PERSON: (Darker than yours)

Indicative of seeing the darkest side of yourself, thinking negatively about who and what you are, putting yourself down, underestimating your abilities.

DETECTIVE:

The inquiring, investigating, curious, searching part of you. May represent the subconscious mind or soul-memory.

DEVIL:

A negative aspect of yourself; hate, discord, greed, fear, jealousy, false conceptions; any destructive tendency.

DOCTOR:

The healing aspect of yourself, your healing talents, ability to help and serve others, compassion, knowledge, authority, capability, respectability, wise counsel. This may depict your High Self, God-self, or your guardian angel.

> **Dr. Ruth:** Self-appointed sex expert

DRUNK:

An aspect of you that drinks too much, may have a drinking problem, very low self-esteem, or both.

DUMMY:

Tendency to sit back and let others manipulate or use you, inability to stand up for yourself, speak your piece, or do your own thing. Might denote harsh judgment of yourself, such as calling yourself dumb, or feeling you are of little or no use.

FACELESS PERSON:

Person, situation, or aspect of yourself you do not want to face or confront.

FAIRY:

Mystical, magical aspect of you in tune with angels, God-forces, earth, environment, oneness.

FALSE FACE:

See *Mask*, this chapter.

FATHER:

Depicts authority, responsibility, discipline, maybe punishment, leader, man of the house;

also any qualities you associate with fathers in general or your father in particular.

FOREIGNER:
An idea, attitude, or aspect that seems foreign or different to your usual way of thinking and feeling.

FRIEND:
An aspect of yourself you have accepted to a certain degree.

>**Friend of a Friend:** A friend of your friend in dreams is usually an important aspect or quality of that friend of which you are unaware but need to notice.

>**New Friend:** An aspect of you which you have now acknowledged and befriended. Action between you shows the amount and kind of relationship now attained.

GARDENER:
Caretaker; responsible for growth, plants, things in his care. Can be symbol of a teacher or minister.

GENIE:
A mythical creature who represents the creative power of the mind, productivity of mind, dominion of mind over matter. Your creative mind power at your service.

GIANT:
May be your High Self, your God-presence, or may say this aspect, habit, or quality of you is bigger, stronger, greater, better (or worse) than you realize. Could be a pun for think big.

>**Giant Sleeping:** May be undeveloped states of mind, unused powers or potentials, unawareness of your God-power.

GHOST:
Thought-form or thought projection you have created by your own thinking which may now be haunting you. Could be old memories or fears haunting you.

GLEE CLUB:
Symbol of harmony or need to harmonize your relationships with others. May be group harmony and uplifting qualities which help others. Joyousness.

GROUP OF MEN:
All the male, masculine, intellectual aspects of you.

GROUP OF WOMEN:
Feminine, intuitive, receptive, sensitive aspects of you.

GUARD:
Security, authority; prepared or need to be on guard.

GUY:
Could be a pun for guide or guidance.

INDIAN:
Reverence for the earth, spiritual, mystical, at one with the forces of nature, peaceful, attuned unless you feel otherwise about Indians. Then it may depict the savage in you. Indians may represent guides for some.

INGRATES:
People (aspects of you) who don't appreciate or value you, your talents, abilities, or ministrations.

JUDGE:
Your Higher Self, possibly the judgmental qualities in you; pun on using good judgment.

KIN:
May say "in relation to" a matter or depict your relationships with others; similarity of background.

KING:
Ruler; aspect of control, dominion, overcoming; can be self-exaltation, self-delusion, or self-control.

KNAVE:
Can be pun on naive or a person of deceit, deception, false impressions, roguery.

KNIGHT:
Willing to fight for what is right, for truth. One who accepts responsibility, who serves others. May mean self-righteousness, knight in shining armor, or high ideals.

LITTLE MEN:
Literally little men, people with small minds, small ideas, petty peeves.

MAID:
May be a helpful aspect, assisting, aiding, or could represent feelings or attitudes of being "made" to do things; servitude, lack of freedom, feeling overworked and underpaid, unappreciated, looked down upon, unworthy, lack of respect and authority.

MAIL MAN:
Message bearer; may be symbol of telepathy, channeling, giving and receiving messages, delivering the goods, getting the word out. Could be a pun on male-man.

MALE:
Often refers to the masculine, intellectual, outgoing, or even aggressive aspect as opposed to passivity of female.

> **Male Who Turns Female:** Showing the feminine qualities in you, something you need to integrate into your awareness.

MANAGER:
Aspect of management, control, authority; possibly your Higher Self, teacher, or helper.

MASK:
A cover-up, a false face to conceal the real desires, motives, feelings, attitudes we fear to express. Can suggest qualities we would like to express, put on, or possess. Usually a warning to look behind the appearances.

MATE:
May represent the "other half" of you, an integral part, your balancing aspect, sounding board, your mirror, or your opponent.

MEDIUM:
Can be aspect of you which is very sensitive, aware of unseen presences; ideas of persons no longer living or of angels and high spiritual beings. May be a channel for messages from other beings; intuitive, psychic, open. Can be a pun on mediocrity.

MERLIN:
Suggestion of your inner powers to transform, create, heal. The magician in you, your unused potential or greatness.

METHODIST:
A methodical, analytical, practical, no-nonsense aspect of you.

MIDGET:
Undeveloped aspect; growth arrested by sense of lack or limit. Suggestion to think *big!*

MINISTER, BISHOP, PRIEST, POPE, RABBI:
One who exercises spiritual dominion. Your ministering abilities, your spiritual self, High Self, God-self, your spiritual guide or teacher, counselor, adviser, spiritual authority; inspiration, aspiration, Christ-like spirit in you, your conscience, your spiritual beliefs, or the particular religious belief of that person or beliefs as-

sociated with that person or religion. Could also depict pomp and circumstance, self-aggrandizement, ego, self-righteousness, narrow-mindedness, prejudice, greed, pomposity, and holier-than-thou attitudes, depending on your experiences, associations, and feelings in the dream.

Larger: To become larger or taller than a former teacher or ministerial person is a symbol that you have outgrown the concepts or teachings which that person represents. (This may come as a shock; but such a thing is not only possible, it happens all the time.) You can and should outgrow outmoded beliefs.

MOB:
Uncontrolled aspects and feelings.

MONSTER:
The outpicturing of your fears.

MOTHER:
Mothering, nurturing aspect of you; your female authority, discipline, teacher, friend, or unadmitted foe, depending on your true feelings. Almost everyone has some unresolved problems to work out with their parents: their ideas, ideals, beliefs, or disciplines.

MOTHER AND FATHER:
Balanced aspects of you or a need to balance these.

MUSICIAN:
May represent the music-making talents in you, your ability to uplift and inspire others through your music, your ability to harmonize with others, or your need to do this. May be pointing out your need to listen to good music.

NEIGHBOR:
Someone or something you have to live with, work with, or a situation "next to you," a condition you cannot get away from.

OFFICER:
One in charge; depicts authority, discipline, laws, rules, regulations; possibly your High Self or your conscience.

OLDER PERSON:
Often indicates wisdom of the years, knowledge, teacher, or cosmic consciousness. Can imply old as in decrepit.

ORIENTAL:
May be an aspect "foreign to you" or a need to "orient" yourself in the situation.

ORPHAN:
One without parents, without love; feeling of being left out, unwanted, unloved. This may depict how you always feel or just how you feel today. "Give (love) and ye shall receive (love)."

PATIENTS:
May be a pun on having patience or refer to your need or ability to care for and possibly heal others.

PILGRIM:
Aspect of building a new life on a spiritual basis, one with strong religious convictions; may imply strict religious beliefs, courage, strength, and hardiness; may be a pun on being grim.

PIONEER:
Aspect of leadership, finding new and better ways; inventor, innovator, self-starter, and go-getter.

POLICE:
May represent your conscience, your Higher Self, the self-righteous aspect of you, or may be an authority figure, discipline, karma, rescue, the long arm of the law; law abiding in general.

Police Chasing You: Implies guilt, breaking rules, getting caught, punishment, law and order, right and wrong, paying for your crime, your past catching up with you.

POLITICIAN:
May represent unknown talents in leadership, diplomacy, tact, diplomatic service of all kinds, public service and concerns; imply you are playing politics, speaking much and saying little, or whatever else you may associate with politicians good or bad.

PRIEST:
See *Minister*, this chapter.

PRINCE, PRINCESS:
Undeveloped or partially-developed qualities of a ruler. One who is learning to take dominion over his life and affairs, about to come into his spiritual inheritance.

PROSTITUTE:
One who prostitutes or usurps principles. May be a warning not to compromise or prostitute your ideas, ideals, or morals. Can be one who gives sex but not love, or one who sells himself short.

PROWLER:
Subtle, shadowy aspect of you which is lurking about, afraid to come out in the open. Not recognized or accepted as part of yourself.

PURITAN:
Can be an aspect of purity of body and purpose, or be a goody-goody.

QUEEN:
Same as king, only female and with more emphasis on intuition and feeling.

RELATIVES:
Some person or aspect close to you, next to you, or in working relationship you. Could be a person or activity, possibly related to chain of events.

RUSSIAN:
Could be a pun on the rushing aspect of you and a hint to slow down, or may be foreign or have some association only you know about.

SAINT:
Follower of truth, one who sticks to truth principles.

SCHOOL MATE:
Could be a learning partner or a scholastic aspect of you. If it is someone you used to know, add the qualities you associate with that person.

SCOTSMAN:
Could be usual pun on thrifty, saving, or penny-pinching qualities.

SECURITY GUARD:
One who stands guard, protects the person or property of others, makes life more secure. Can be quality of safeguarding or possible pun or warning on a need for more safety, security.

SERVANT:
Aspect of servitude, unworthiness; feeling of lack of respect, lack of prosperity or authority, bad luck, or all work and no play.

SHADOW:
An important aspect of you which you haven't acknowledged, have neglected, or do not recognize. Shadows represent qualities we need most to accept into our awareness for our personal growth. The shadow can become hostile (nightmare) when ignored. Carl Jung says your shadow has a gift to give you—a missing quality, gift, or attitude you need most at this time. Shadows depict all that you have repressed or denied and therefore hold an extremely important position your in dreams.

Shadowy Man: A masculine aspect not yet recognized or integrated.

Shadowy Woman: Feminine aspect of you not yet integrated.

SHEPHERD:
One who watches, guards, and guides his flock of ideas and thoughts, allowing no negative (wolf) ideas to enter.

SOLDIER:

The warrior in you, your fighting qualities, readiness to fight or quarrel; battle-ready, trained to defend, fight, shoot, harm, kill, or do whatever is necessary to obtain or defend yourself or your goals. May represent a belligerent, bellicose nature.

STRANGER:

An aspect of yourself unknown or unrecognized by you.

SURGEON:

Can represent your healing abilities or could imply a strong need to cut something out of your life.

TOURIST:

Transient aspect of yourself, just passing by; can say this is a temporary situation or aspect.

TEACHER:

Your source of knowledge, learning; your Higher Self or guide.

TRICKSTER:

Can be an aspect of you which plays tricks—often the joke is on you! May imply you are not honest with yourself. The trickster can stand between your conscious mind and your subconscious. He represents self-deception and creative possibilities. This one can take many playful forms and in a way is similar to the shadow.

TWINS:

May mean balanced aspects or indicate a need to get yourself together in this situation. Could be two people of the same identity, two sides to a matter, duality, a split personality, being "beside yourself," dual awareness, going in two directions at once, or a pun on double trouble.

UMPIRE:

Aspect of you which judges words, deeds, actions, and makes snap judgments, quick decisions.

VAMPIRE:

A blood-thirsty aspect, one who drains the very life out of you or another, one who psychically draws on another's energies. (People who are self-starters have high vitality and can be targets for those who have no special goals, aims, or purpose.) Vampires do little and are unable to generate enough energy for themselves, so they literally feed off of others, often without either person realizing this. A dream of a vampire may be a warning that you are being drained physically, mentally, emotionally, or all of these. Likely vampires are the sick, the aged, self-pitying people, and the lazy. If you are feeling drained, the vampire dream indicates:

- You are draining your own energies by your negative thinking habits and attitudes and are being warned to change this, or

- You are allowing someone to drain you. If this is the case, you need to carefully consider your activities of the previous day and the people who were around you. At what point did you notice being drained? If you are always drained after being with a particular person, you may have to realize that this person acts like a vampire and then avoid his/her company as much as possible.

VOICE FROM THE REAR:

Voice in the back of your mind, your conscience, intuition, High Self, or guide; or, bit of doubt, having second thoughts, being of two opinions.

WAITRESS:

One who takes orders, serves others; the serving, cooperative aspect of you. Note **how** you serve. Can be low self-esteem, humble work, even taking abuse from others. May be underpaid, overworked aspect of you. Could depict your subconscious mind (your servant) taking your order, prayer, or affirmation in order to serve you, or could be your signal that your prayer is heard and being answered.

WATCHMAN:
Observer. May imply you need to be more watchful, or could say to observe what you are doing or creating.

WEALTHY MALE:
May represent the animus, or male aspect of you, with plenty of everything to offer.

WIDOW, WIDOWER:
Aspect of loneliness, aloneness, without a mate or partner, a longing for companionship.

WISE MAN:
Often represents your own innate wisdom, or can portray the wisdom of your God-self or High Self.

WITCH:
An aspect of your negative thoughts, bewitching yourself into thinking you are less than you really are, or nasty, witchy aspect of you.

YOUNG GIRL:
Depicts undeveloped, immature, innocent, or young and appealing.

YOUNG MAN:
Active, vigorous, prime-conditioned, intellectual part of you.

My Own Guest List

CHAPTER 38

Roads, Paths, Streets, and Signs

Streets

Streets symbolize the path you have chosen to travel, your way of life, your direction, and your goals or lack of them.

Set a new purpose and you may dream of a new path, depicting new patterns of mind, new habits you are forming. Paths may signify the latest lessons we are learning or the heretofore unknown vistas we can now see.

A **RIGHT TURN** in dreams usually indicates a right decision, good direction to travel, while a **LEFT TURN** may symbolize an unwise decision or direction.

ALLEY:
Path of limitation, lack, poverty, disease, and suffering. Dream is pointing out that you have *chosen* this path of less than the best, and you can also choose to change it. It's up to you.

ASKING DIRECTIONS:
Implies a need for help, direction, instruction, or guidance. Since help can never be given, even by angels, without your request, dream may imply that you have a need to ask for help or may be a reminder that help is readily available for the asking.

BACK STREETS:
Out of the lime light, behind the scenes; implies the hidden, obscure, undesirable. A possible setting for low-life or criminal acts.

BRIDGE:
Means of crossing from one state of consciousness or reality to another, symbol of change, new decision, leaving old lifestyle behind, crossing over in mind or body. Could be a symbol of death, as in crossing over to the other side. Might be a pun on bridging the gap.

> **Broken Bridge:** Broken connections. Need for repair. No way to get there from here.

> **Building Bridges:** Reaching out, building links, connections; paving the way for those who follow. Making things easier for others.

BRIDLE PATH:
May be a pun on bride's path, path of marriage; or, since horses represent emotions, may be the path where your emotions lead you, especially if there are many ups and downs, or a path involving learning to be in control of your emotions.

BUMPY ROAD:
Rough going, hard way to go, lots of ups and downs. See *Road*, this chapter.

CITY STREETS:
Imply a fast pace, city sophistication or degradation, many people, mass thinking, race consciousness, going along with the crowd (right or wrong), hurry-scurry, moving with the traffic, noise, stop lights, distractions, confusion, many side streets or side tracks.

COUNTRY ROAD:

Peaceful path, getting close to nature, spiritual progress, unhurried pace. Can be a long, winding road saying you have a long way to go.

CROSSROADS:

Place where choices and decisions must be made, turning point. Could indicate moving "cross ways" of the accepted rules, customs, beliefs, or behaviors.

> **Crossing a Road, Street, or Bridge:** Can indicate making a decision, changing your mind, changing sides in a matter, taking a new direction, crossing the line of old boundaries or old limitations. Can imply seeing things from a different point of view, seeing the "other side" of the story, gaining a new perspective, or may indicate that you need to look at things from a totally different angle.

> **Off the Road:** Off the track, out of line, off course.

CURB:

Small barrier, limit, restriction, or guide line.

DEAD END:

Path to nowhere. No progress possible. End of the line. May imply the end of this road is death. Must re-route. Turn-around point.

DETOUR:

Could imply you "can't get there from here," or may indicate a need to circumvent—to take a different path or attitude, change your tactics or planned course of action. May even warn of a "rough road ahead," proceed with care. Could be a side track.

DIRT ROAD:

Could be a lonely road, not well traveled, rough going, need for care; but the trip may be well worth it.

DIRTY, LITTERED:

Depicts the type of path you have chosen or are considering and the kind of mental, spiritual, and emotional conditions you will find there.

DO NOT ENTER:

Obvious warning this is not for you. Wrong way.

DOWNHILL:

See *Hilly Road*, this chapter.

DRIVEWAY:

Path that leads to home, yours or another's. Can represent path home to God, security, rest, or end of your journey. Time to relax before starting out again.

FAST LANE:

Obvious pun on living life in the fast lane. May be warning that you are moving too fast, need to change pace or tactics.

FREEWAY:

Free and easy road, wide path, no stops or obstructions, no interference, fast pace, good progress. Might imply going along with the crowd, especially if there is a crowd. May be a pun on free ways, free rides, possibly not paying for services rendered.

GRAVEL ROAD:

Rough way to go, tricky underfoot, need to be careful and watchful on this path or find a better way.

GUARD RAIL:

Can be a protection or a barrier. May be the limit as to how far you can go, a pun on guarding yourself, or a warning to be on guard in this area.

HIGH ROAD:

Path to higher levels of being, lofty insights, high ideals, inspiration, great achievements, spiritual growth.

HIGHWAY:

Path of life, way to go, smooth path, many others going along with you, fast pace, main artery; could be moving along with the crowd or with the flow of things.

HILLY ROAD:
Many ups and downs ahead.

> **Downhill:** Can be taking the easy way out or imply an easing up of your difficulties, but may also imply things are going from bad to worse. May be a wrong choice, less than good conditions, your life going downhill, hitting bottom, the lowest possible choice. You could land at the bottom of the heap.

> **Over the Hill:** May be you are "over the hump" and the struggle, ready to ease up awhile, or can be pun or warning that you are past your peak and heading downhill if you continue on the way you are headed.

> **Uphill:** Implies a long, hard struggle to the top.

INTERSTATE:
Same as *freeway*.

LOW ROAD:
Choosing the path of least resistance and lesser accomplishments.

MAIN STREET:
Center of activity, main way to go, the accepted way, the beaten path, race consciousness beliefs and conditioning.

MOUNTAIN ROAD:
Many ups and downs, peaks and hollows; difficult way to go but the experiences are well worth it. Mountain tops are standard symbols of being close to God, peak experiences, difficulties overcome.

MUDDY ROAD:
Many emotional difficulties to "wade" through and overcome. Danger of bogging down. May imply that you need to work on your attitudes and emotions, clear out the emotional backup.

NARROW ROAD:
Can mean limited choices, a feeling of being hemmed in, confined, hampered, crowded, stifled; or, may depict the "straight and narrow."

NO OUTLET:
Warning you can't get there from here, a turn-about point—no use in going on; or, may be a pun implying you have no outlet for your creative urges to be fulfilled or ways to express your emotions, talents, skills, or whatever (which might be symbolized by what you are carrying with you).

NO ROAD:
No clear-cut path to follow, need to make your own way, forge a new path for yourself and others, following your own instincts, doing something that has never been done before, a challenge and a privilege; or, to some, a stopping point.

ONE-WAY STREET:
This may symbolize prejudice, only one way to do it—*my way!* Can denote limited choices that, once made, would commit you to go on with this, or could suggest that "you may have to back out of this one!"

PATH:
Indicates walking, taking life one step at a time, moving at a slower rate, going at your own pace, taking time to be yourself, having deeper learning experiences, getting close to nature and God, or can denote the spiritual path or path you have chosen in life.

PRIVATE ROAD:
Not for just anybody, only for special people, original, different, independent, aloof; can represent your own way to go, a path just right for you, a desire for privacy, peace, and quiet, no need to go along with the crowd.

PUBLIC ROAD:
The way of the crowd, copy cats, race-consciousness path, non-original thinking, "everybody does it," the easy way out.

RAILROAD CROSSING:
Sign of cross purposes, cross currents, danger, "stop, look, and listen," be aware, dangerous crossing.

ROAD:

Path of life with a little less hustle and strain than city streets; a more peaceful way to go, but still a heavily-traveled path, still a hint of going along with the crowd.

ROADBLOCK:

Mental or emotional blocks you have thrown up in your own path, usually out of fear or insecurity. It is easy to think somebody "out there" did it, but you create your own blockages. Take time to rethink your decisions and find out what your blocks are and **why**. Ask your dreams for help.

ROAD MAP:

Represents having a plan of action, a direction or goal to reach, finding the right way for you, guidance.

RUTTED ROAD:

Ruts can be old "tracks" your mind tends to run on through force of habit. Old ways of thinking, habit patterns you automatically follow. It takes some real concentration and will power to break out of these old thinking and behaving ruts, to learn to think along new and better paths.

SHORTCUT:

This may be wise or foolish. If you have truly found a better way to do things, a quicker or more efficient method, this is very good. Dream may be showing you there is a better way or affirming you have already found one. If it feels good, go for it, as the saying goes. On the other hand, if the action and feelings in the dream are negative, your shortcut may be unwise. Use your discretion.

SIDE ROAD:

May imply a side-track from your goal, ideal, or purpose, or may be taking a less-traveled path, a different way to go.

SIDEWALK:

Going at your own pace but taking a hard path, a city path, a crowded path; much noise and distractions, less beauty and peace of mind. Might be pun on side path, getting off-sides, off-center. *Sidewalk* is mostly a race-consciousness path with preconceived ideas and expectations, heavily influenced by the surrounding states of consciousness.

SMOOTH ROAD:

An easier path, at least for awhile; physical ease, lack of stress, or at least a lessening.

STOP SIGN:

Implies a need to bring whatever you are doing to a complete halt. It may mean to stop, look, and think before moving on and may imply danger. Can denote other people or circumstances trying to stop you. Proceed with caution.

MANY STOP SIGNS:

Many stop signals can imply you are going against the grain, a strong need for caution, to stop and look at where you intend to go; or, can denote many barriers and difficulties along your path. Could be many ideas, beliefs, or people trying to stop you from your goal. Strong need to stop, survey the situation, and re-think your plans, decide how to handle the opposition.

RUNNING A STOP SIGN:

Implies ignoring the laws or dangers, living recklessly, failure to stop and consider the consequences.

STREET:

Usually indicates a fairly fast pace, city sophistication, mass thinking, many people going the same way with the same selfish standards, hurry, scurry, worry. Little peace or privacy, many distractions and side streets or side tracks. One can easily get lost in the hustle and bustle and be overwhelmed by mass opinion. Can lose your individuality there.

TUNNEL:

Suggests working your way through the problem, rather than trying to avoid or circumvent it. May imply you can't go around this, you must go through it, or could denote your moving through subconscious levels to find the answer. Can imply tunnel vision—only seeing one way—or one-pointedness which will not allow any distractions.

Light at the End: Implies things will get better soon, not much further to go, it won't be as bad or as long as you thought, better times just ahead.

TURNPIKE:
This is a pay-as-you-go path; you know the price you will have to pay, but it may be worth it. Your choice.

U-TURN:
Symbolic of making a complete turnabout in your life, changing directions, goals, ideas, beliefs, possibly all of these.

No U-Turn: You can't turn back, can't change this.

UNDER CONSTRUCTION:
Rough road ahead, obstacles to overcome, no easy path to follow, difficult travel; possibly making your own way or a new path for others to follow. May imply building new habits, new ideals, new patterns of mind; learning new ways to approach old problems, or possibly taking a path into unknown, unexplored territory. Definitely indicates a new way to go, heading toward virgin land, new growth and development of the mind, and reaching out further than you have gone before. Could be improving old ways, making them clearer and easier for those who follow.

UPHILL:
Implies a long, hard struggle but a climb to the top.

WINDING ROAD:
May be taking the long way around, avoiding the challenges, perhaps not being sure which way to turn, or may be constantly changing directions. Can be a hint that there is a better way to go.

WRONG-WAY SIGN:
Obvious warning this is not for you; you are about to go the wrong way or make a bad decision.

X:
Symbol for railroad crossing, "stop, look, and listen," a sign to stop and listen to your intuition, to see what is going on around you before proceeding. Can be a place where decisions are made, or can depict a need to "X" something out of you mind or life. May be "X" marks the spot or an important crossroad in your life.

YIELD:
Can be your signal to yield in the situation you are now in. Could say cooperation is needed here.

YELLOW BRICK ROAD:
Very old symbol for the path of learning, for taking dominion over your life and affairs, as depicted in the Wizard of Oz story when they followed the yellow brick road to wisdom.

Areas and Neighborhoods

In dreams you may find yourself wandering through the general area of where you used to live (or work) or in a neighborhood which vaguely suggests your old home, hangout, old friends, and memories. This is one way of symbolizing that the feelings you had when you were there are reminiscent of the feelings you are experiencing now, in your present life situation.

Take time to get in touch with those feelings and realize that those same feelings are re-surfacing now so that you (now older and wiser) can recognize where and how they started. You can then begin to isolate the problems involved, understand your feelings, and work through those old hurts—past your point of sorrow, weakness, or pain—to overcome the obstacles that once were so crippling or overwhelming.

This is your chance to make good, to conquer old fears, remove the old blocks, and to accomplish more than you ever dared before.

My Own Road Symbols

CHAPTER 39

Sex, Pregnancy, and Birth

Sex can be a symbol of union, marriage, one-ness, a coming together of opposites, a balanc-ing of your male and female halves, a creative act, or a number of other things including your longing to be whole.

Causes and Sources

There are a number of reasons for sex dreams. Usually these are the direct result of your own thoughts, desires, and wishes which you are well aware of; but at times there can be hidden or suppressed desires you don't care to admit, even to yourself. Sex dreams may be pointing out your secret frustrations with your sex life in general or with your present partner. This can be a warning that something is wrong and needs your attention.

Sex dreams can be a mere statement of fact, tell-ing you of your feelings, desires, and arousal. They may even show you how these are stimu-lated by your food (red meats and heavy spices), strong drink (alcohol), your reading materials, visual excitations, or stimulation from other people in general. This would be especially true if you are on a dedicated spiritual path and would serve as a warning to help you realize what you are creating unwittingly.

Other people's thoughts, hopes, dreams, and wishful thinking may be the cause of your sexy dreams! An admirer's desires or intentions toward you (of which you may be totally un-aware) can affect the tenure of your dreams.

Since everyone is highly telepathic, especially while in the Alpha state, it is not at all unusual to find yourself involved in a sexy dream with someone you do not even care about. You might be shocked to experience an extremely sexy dream and may wake up feeling guilty, wonder-ing what on earth "got into " you. As long as you are sure that your desires do not move in that direction, you can relax and realize that it is merely the outpouring of someone else's strong desire and imagination—not your own. These may come to you as a simple statement of fact to consider, or they could be warnings you need to heed, depending on the person, situation, and your feelings about these.

Your Desires

Most sex dreams are the outpicturing of your own desires, hopes, and wishes or fears and need to be considered in that light. It is essential to be totally honest with yourself, admitting your real feelings, since so often sex dreams are warn-ing of hidden or suppressed feelings which need to be honestly faced and dealt with in a healthy way. Your dream may be pointing out some emotions or feelings you have failed to recog-nize or won't admit having—showing you things you would rather not face.

Your Fears

The sex drive is a strong, often intense emotion which, while needing some form of expression, can also be a source of deep, inner fear. Those who have been badly frightened and/or sexually abused in childhood (even though the event has been suppressed or forgotten on conscious levels) can have what seems to be irrational fears which emerge whenever sex matters arise. Dreams, which may take the form of nightmares, may well be revealing the source or cause of the fears and blockages that were erected as a protective measure long ago. These could even go back to a former lifetime. Certainly if you have any doubts or problems about your sex life, dreams are your best possible source of information. You may want to program a dream which will give you greater insight and understanding.

Some phobias stem from overly severe parental or religious training; but, whatever the source, these anxieties can cause a tremendous blockage of all creative activity and a suppression of all desire, which can be unhealthy on many levels. It is important to be totally honest with yourself about your feelings in sex dreams in order to understand the message and uncover the cause of your fears and conflicts in this area.

POINTED OBJECTS:
When inserted into openings or crevices, these can be a subtle symbol of sex, with the possible exception of a key in a lock. Watch for these, especially if you have problems with sex.

OTHER SUBTLE SEX SYMBOLS:
Rabbits, bananas, snakes, screw driver, knife, pen, pencil, or any object which goes into a hole-like receptacle, like a sword and sheath.

Interpretation

Naturally, the first thing to consider is your own feeling about the dream as you woke. Were you happy? Frustrated? Angry, guilty, comforted, pleased, surprised, what? It would be helpful for you to write out these feelings honestly and fully before going further in your interpretation.

Secondly, take a good look at the background, the people involved, the interplay and action. Who initiates the action? What is your reaction? How did you feel about this? These questions will help you to decide the type of sex dream you had and what message it is trying to convey.

Next, you need to consider the source. If you were surprised or repulsed, the dream quite possibly came from another person's desire toward you, welcome or not. (This happens quite frequently when an amorous male or female thinks strongly and imaginatively about having sex with his or her would-be mate.) Perhaps you need to be aware of the way that person feels about you. The most important point to ponder is, how did you feel about it? You might also consider what you want to do about it.

Dealing with Sexual Energies

For those who do not have a loving partner, dealing with your sexual energies can pose a problem. Repressing these urges is the worst thing you can do to yourself, as this blocks and bottles up energies which eventually find an outlet somewhere—sometimes in a manner you would regret later. It is better to recognize these energies for what they are and then redirect to other outlets such as:

- CREATIVITY: Using sex energies to create from within you a thing of value and/or beauty. Something uniquely yours.

- SPIRITUAL GIFTS: Using sex energies for prayer, healing, devotion, serving or worshipping God, serving humanity. (People with strong sexual urges are potentially powerful healers. Priests and nuns do not take vows of celibacy without good reason. Strong sex desires are actually spiritual desires not yet recognized and harnessed.) It is up to you to decide how you will use those energies.

- LOVE-MAKING: The physical expression of real, deep love. When sex is done in this manner—with true love, compassion, and complete willingness from both partners—there is an exchange of love and a balancing of male-female energies resulting in an uplifting, inspiring, and even spiritual experience. Problems occur when one or the other is unwilling or there is an uneven exchange of love energies. These may show up in your dreams.

- PASSION: Sex for self-gratification, no deep emotions involved, no love exchanged. (Not recommended. Since this act is selfish in nature, there is no lasting satisfaction and the soul is left feeling empty.)

- DREAM SEX: It is both possible and acceptable to make love and have an orgasm in a dream!

In any case, sex dreams are quite normal and nothing to feel guilty about—they just help you keep in touch with your real feelings so that you can make the right decisions.

A person living alone, especially one who works in an area where everyone else is of the same sex, can develop a very real need to converse, touch, and interact with someone of the opposite sex in order to keep in good balance. Your dream may be pointing this out. One simple cure for this would be to join a group, preferably a spiritually-oriented one, where touching and hugging are not only allowed but encouraged in the spirit of true brotherhood.

We need to remember there is a strong connection between sex, creativity, and spirituality. All of these stem from the same center—the difference lies in the direction of our will. Often a strong sex desire stems from an inner urge to merge with God, to become more spiritual, or to reach for a higher state of consciousness, but we fail to recognize this as the source. We may desire to give birth to something worthwhile as our gift to the world, or we may have a deep desire to express love feelings and emotions which have been too long repressed. Creative activities serve to channel the sex drive energies into productive outlets which can benefit everyone, especially you!

Sex desires can be blocked by fear, guilt, ignorance, and a lack of self-worth.

Other Meanings

Sex can be a symbol of being intimately involved in a situation, a simple coming together of opposites, or a touching, grounding, balancing experience. It may also symbolize the possibility of a new "birth" coming from the union of two concepts, two opposite ideas joined, or our male and female energies merging and balancing. Much depends on the feelings, actions, and background of the dream.

Pregnancy in Dreams

ABORTION:
Can be an ESP warning of a coming miscarriage if your present trend of action is continued, or may warn you are about to lose your "baby," ideal, or project through some deliberate action or decision. Possibly this is something which you need to abort, depending on your feelings.

BEING PREGNANT:
This may indicate that you have a creative idea, concept, ideal, or project which is developing within you, or that you are carrying an important unborn idea. Whether you give birth or abort the idea is up to you. Pregnancy usually suggests that your project is one of great value and should be nurtured or cultivated. In relation to this, you may want to pause to consider just what new ideas, urges, or projects you have been contemplating lately and how you can bring these to completion.

Naturally, if you are a young female a pregnancy dream could mean an actual pregnancy. Or, if you are already pregnant, the dream may be telling you something about your condition, your diet, your hopes, fears, or whatever it is you need to know about yourself and your baby. Since "Thoughts are things" and you *do* create your conditions, your dreams may be applauding or deploring the kind of thoughts you are holding in mind during your pregnancy, knowing that they will exert a very definite influence on your unborn child. Your attitudes and feelings affect the type of entity you will attract (before pregnancy occurs) and the actual physical, mental, and emotional growth of that child, once he or she is conceived.

A series of dreams about you and your as-yet unborn child or project may proceed on a regular basis, if you are interested, giving you the help and advice needed to bring about a healthy, normal baby or a well-completed project. You may even learn the sex of your child or grandchild through your dreams.

CONCEPTION AND PREGNANCY:
Can be indicative of a concept or a creative "seed idea" implanted in you which can grow and develop before being born, delivered, or presented to the world. It may be implanted by another, male or female, who has purposefully or even inadvertently given you the "germ" of an idea.

GIVING BIRTH:
The release of your child, creation, gift, or project into the world. It may also represent the culmination of an affirmation, prayer, or desire you have been working on, showing you it is now completed and is manifesting in your world.

Cesarean Birth: This may denote a new project "cut out for you," a creative idea cut and tailored to your particular needs and talents.

Multiple Births: May simply be telling you of an upcoming reality, or may be symbolic of one idea giving birth to many more.

KISSING:
Can be an expression of affection and caringness, a prelude to romance and sex, a stimulation of desire for union. You have to decide who or what you will unite.

LABOR:
Labor pains can be the labor of delivering your new idea, project, or concept to the world or may represent the labor and effort needed to complete your project. It could imply that your "baby" is completed and ready to be presented.

LONGING FOR CHILDREN:
May be just exactly that, or it can symbolize your deep inner creative urges longing and needing to be expressed.

MISCARRIAGE:
This could be a symbol of losing something of value which you have been developing or working on. If you are actually pregnant, this could be a needed warning of an impending event or at least the possibility of the actual occurrence. This might be a pun on the miscarriage of justice or of some other meaningful event.

PETTING:
Can be a show of love and affection. When prolonged, is definitely a stimulation of desires which can lead to sex and union. This does not always portray a purely sexual union but can lead to a balancing of opposites.

STERILITY:
A dream of sterility could indicate your feeling of being unable to be creative or to "produce." Now, since everyone has the ability to be creative in some way, this may imply that you have completely repressed your creative urges to where you think you are unproductive.

STERILIZATION:

This would indicate a happening or situation, habit, or whatever which can completely block or destroy your creative talents and abilities. Warning.

SYMBOLIC BABIES

The same type of dreams may also occur for a symbolic baby or creative project you are bringing into the world by your own efforts. A follow-up series of dreams may show you feeding and nourishing your baby, watching it grow bigger, or letting it drop! See *Babies* under *People*.

UNCOMFORTABLE PREGNANCY:

This may symbolize an uncomfortable idea, project, or situation which must be faced, confronted, and handled eventually.

My Own Sex Symbols

CHAPTER 40

Valuables: Finding or Losing

Finding Valuables

Finding something of value in dreams is symbolic of the discovery of something of value in you. It could be a new understanding, a new vision, a talent you didn't know you had, or the development of some new quality or gift within you.

Valuables may depict rewards for your labors, mental or physical, and your attitudes toward receiving them. For instance, *finding* something of value in your dream and immediately turning it over to someone else may reveal a basic feeling of unworthiness, an inability to accept the good things which are offered to you. You may have an attitude of "I have to work *hard*" for a living or whatever you receive in life, which is another way of saying that you don't feel you deserve to have anything given to you or that you have difficulty in accepting things from others.

Many people have this problem, which is a form of punishment we impose upon ourselves, showing a basic self-deprecation. When you feel unloved, unwanted, unworthy, or all three, your dream will dramatize this situation to point out this low self-esteem so that you can work on it. This could be depicted by losing something nice that was given to you.

On the other hand, finding valuables and happily receiving them would indicate your willingness to accept your good fortune and may also serve notice of many good things coming your way. Should the dream involve something you are planning to do, it could predict the prosperous outcome of your efforts.

Losing Valuables

Losing valuables in dreams indicates the loss, possible loss, or fear of losing something you value such as your home, job, mate, family, love, business, honor, or money. It may indicate the "price you have to pay" for something you have done or are considering doing. It may be a warning against carelessness in the handling of your money or affairs, or it could be an ESP dream.

Take a good look at what is going on in your life and especially what went on the day before. Were you having doubts about something? Are you in the process of making a decision? If the background of your dream was dark or dimly lit, it could be a warning that you do not know all the facts, that you are "in the dark" about this matter and had better seek some enlightenment!

Your dream could warn of a loss because you are unaware of some facts or that someone or something is untrustworthy. Certainly it would be a warning to reconsider the facts, your position, or decision. Need to stop and re-evaluate.

Losing valuables may denote feeling vulnerable, powerless, defenseless, hurt, uneasy, insecure, or devalued in some way.

MISPLACED VALUABLES:

Can imply misplaced values, mislaid sense of values, or sense of right and wrong temporarily misplaced or forgotten.

Miscellaneous Valuables

ANTIQUES:

May mean treasures of the soul, treasures of mind, loving, gracious attitudes and spiritual attributes.

Old, Rare Books or Scrolls: May symbolize ancient wisdom, spiritual gifts, or knowledge. Could also represent past events, memories, akashic records.

BILLFOLD OR WALLET:

Can represent your sense of values as well as the "price you pay," your purchasing power, security, influence, your sense of well-being, your power to go, do, and have, as well as your credit cards, credibility.

Finding: Can depict an unexpected reward.

Losing: Could represent the price you have to pay; a lost sense of values, loss of freedom, identity, capability, power, energy, connections; loss of something you value highly.

BILLS:

Big bills would be prosperity; small ones may be insufficient funds, inadequate remuneration for your efforts.

BROKE:

No money or insufficient funds indicate a feeling of poverty, not good enough, low self-esteem, insecurity, uneasy, unworthy, uncomfortable.

CHANGE:

A handful of change found could be a pun on many changes coming to you, or could be small change, as in not enough to "count," not worth the effort, chicken feed, or insufficient funds.

COINS:

Finding large coins may indicate big money.

Old or Rare Coins: This could be abundance beyond your expectations or possibly an old debt paid.

COUNTERFEIT:

No real value, not worth the effort, a thing that only appears to be worthwhile, not what it seems to be. False premise, needs a closer inspection.

JEWELS OR JEWELRY:

Finding jewels may denote the discovery of gifts or talents formerly unknown to us. Receiving gifts of jewels or jewelry usually implies rewards, God's gifts to us, possibly spiritual rewards for some effort we have been making. See *Jewelry, Gems, and Crystals.*

Losing Jewels: Could imply possibility of losing one or more of our spiritual gifts through lack of use or misuse. Might imply losing a talent or anything we value greatly.

MONEY:

May mean material rewards for the labors of your mind and body, an exchange of energies, or could be karmic gain/debt.

MONEY EXCHANGES, BILL OR STATEMENT:

Implies a debt owed, an accounting of debts or expenses, notice of costs incurred, reminder of payment due, demand for settlement, or can be the price or karma you have to pay for your actions.

Payment: Offering, gift, response, act of good faith, measuring up, being responsive, paying a monetary or karmic debt, atonement, balance, energy exchange, effort to make things right, or may be used as a bribe or enticement.

PIGGY BANK:
Can represent your savings, also sacrifices you have made; could be a pun on putting all your eggs in one place or being piggish about money.

VALUABLE CREATIONS:
Valuables such as various works of art could symbolize creative talents.

VALUABLE PAINTINGS:
Could symbolize a beautiful "frame" of mind, beautiful thoughts, prayers, or memories.

Theft

A dream of having something of value taken from you can denote feeling cheated, violated, attacked, wounded, powerless, angry, abused, hurt, insecure, devalued, fearful, and vulnerable.

To lose valuables in this fashion is a clear warning to be more careful in your dealings and could possibly be an ESP dream. Note the area of the theft both realistically and symbolically, and cover all possibilities.

You may also want to consider whether or not you may be robbing yourself in some way. This could be robbing yourself of time with your family, cheating yourself out of needed sleep or funtime, neglecting your spiritual needs or your creative instincts that need to be expressed, or denying yourself of a lifelong dream.

Look closely at your dream symbols and ask yourself if you are indeed robbing yourself of something important—then try to determine what it is.

Poverty

A dream of poverty can indicate negative attitudes, feelings of lack, or a habit of thinking and talking "poor." Many are not aware of the power of spoken words, especially the things we repeat over and over. These statements eventually materialize into what the Biblical Job describes as, "That which I feared the most, I have brought upon me." Dreams may be showing us, sometimes in an exaggerated fashion, just what we are creating by our thoughts and words.

My Own Value Symbols

CHAPTER 41

Vehicles of Transportation

Vehicles, according to the dictionary, are our means of conveyance from one place to another. Since the soul uses the body in much the same way, moving in and out at will, *vehicles* in general can *represent your lifestyle*.

YOUR AUTOMOBILE:

Your automobile, or whatever means of transportation you use the most, *depicts your body and its condition*. This can also symbolize your self-image, self-esteem, personality, your wheeling and dealing, the way you see yourself, your freedom to come and go, your power to accomplish, your driving desires, your drive for success, or your course of action.

> **Mashed, Bashed, and Dented:** Poor self-esteem, lack of self-worth, the way you really feel about yourself, or can be a symbol of poor health, of damage done to your body. Consider the area of damage and look under *Vehicle Parts*.

YOUR FAVORITE VEHICLE:

This can represent your body and its physical condition, so you need to pay careful attention to any problems, defects, or warnings about these. Check both your body and your auto for possible difficulties.

Your conveyance may at times designate your life work, a pet project, or a vehicle of expression such as a book or song you are writing, a hobby, or concept.

SEVERAL VEHICLES:

Having several vehicles can indicate your many lifestyles, directions, interests, and various ways of expressing yourself, each one symbolic of a different aspect of your life.

ANOTHER PERSON'S VEHICLE:

This can symbolize that person's lifestyle.

The Driver's Seat

Because your conveyance also depicts your lifestyle as a whole, you should be in the driver's seat and in control at all times. Therefore, being in any place other than the driver's seat of your car would depict your not being in full charge of your life—not directing and controlling, but allowing your life to either drift aimlessly or to be driven, controlled, manipulated, or pushed by others as the dream indicates.

In other words, the person driving your car is the person who is presently controlling your life in general. Different types of vehicles would represent different areas of your life. Obviously the family car would symbolize your family affairs. For example, if you dream your mother-in-law is driving the family car, you can bet she is running your life and family affairs, whether you are aware of this or not—your dream is bringing this to your attention so that you can take appropriate action.

FRONT SEAT:

When you are in the front seat of your car but not driving, you have relinquished command to another person or to chance. You can see where you are going but do not have any control.

BACK SEAT:
If you are riding in the back seat of your car, this can imply putting yourself down, taking a back seat to others, allowing others to take over, not using your abilities, or not exerting your rights in your life or career.

A person of the opposite sex getting into the back seat with you could have sexual implications.

RUMBLE SEAT:
This has even less control—you can't even see where you are going, no chance of directing; you don't have good contact with what is going on in your life.

TRAILER:
To ride in the trailer behind your vehicle would indicate following the lead of others with no attempt to direct the proceedings. Going along for the ride.

TRUNK:
Being in the trunk is being totally out of contact with your life, no vision, no goals, no attempt to see your way clear. Could be bound by circumstances and limitations of your own making, especially if it is *your* car. Could show how you feel about your present lifestyle—cramped!

RIDING IN SOMEONE ELSE'S CAR:
Can refer to someone "taking you for a ride," imply that you are "going along for the ride" (no goals of your own), or may imply that you "use" other people for your physical needs.

All of the above would be warnings for you to begin to gain or regain total control over your life and affairs. To progress in a series of dreams from the trailer or back seat to the driver's seat would be a confirmation of your steady progress in getting your life under your control.

Naturally, if your brakes should fail or any part of your car breaks down, this would point out your need to make corrections or exert disciplines in the area symbolized by the faulty part. See *Vehicle Parts*, this chapter.

THE DRIVER:
How you drive your vehicle can depict how you are driving yourself or how you drive others. It can denote your driving desires and ambitions, show what motivates you, or may imply that you are not paying any particular attention to where you are going in life.

DRIVER'S LICENSE:
Implies your permit, right, or privilege to run your own life, to be in control of it.

> **Lost or Taken Away:** Implies losing control over your life.

DRIVING DRUNK:
May imply that alcohol is driving your life!

DRIVING ANOTHER PERSON'S CAR:
May imply you are either exerting control over their life or that you may be taking advantage of them in some way, using them or their talents, ideas, abilities, or energies for your own purposes.

> **Being Driven by Another Person:** May denote when or how you allow other people to "drive," push, or manipulate you.

SOMEONE USING YOUR CAR:
Someone using you, your talents, money, ideas, energies, abilities. May show how others take advantage of you or how you are allowing this to happen.

Vehicle Parts

AIR CONDITIONER:
Could symbolize your lungs, your ability to breathe freely; may be a pun on the condition

of the air you breathe (pollution, smoke, etc.) or the condition of your lungs.

AIR FILTER:
Can symbolize your nose, throat, or lungs. If the filter is dirty this can be a health warning.

BATTERY:
Power, heart, desire, motivation, energy, reserve.

Dead Battery: Could represent a heart problem or a lack of motivating power on your part, or you could be physically run down. It would be wise to have a physical check-up and to test your auto battery as well to be sure.

BRAKES:
Discipline, control, will power, caution, restraint. Could be pun for the breaks in life.

Brake Failure: Points to lack of the use of effective controls over your thoughts and actions. No control, inability to stop the motion of events.

BUMPER:
Bumper can be a buffer zone or type of protection of your lifestyle. May imply the part of you that bears the brunt of things or your way of protecting yourself or others from hurt. Could be your protective barriers.

No Bumper: No protection, vulnerability.

ELECTRICAL SYSTEM:
May symbolize the veins and arteries of the physical body and their ability to operate smoothly, keeping up the life-giving flows of energy to the body; or, could represent your nervous system and its condition.

ENGINE:
Power potential, go power, vitality, energy, drive, motivation, ability to keep going.

Engine Tune-up: Could refer to your car's needs, but most likely indicates your need for physical help, check up, rest, treatment, exercise, or whatever is needed to renew, recharge, restore, and rejuvenate your body.

FENDERS:
This may represent your feelings, ego, outer personality, appearance, vanity, good looks, or your "touchiness."

Dented Fenders: Hurt feelings, damaged ego, poor self-image, letting others see your hurts, wearing your heart on your sleeve.

FUEL PUMP:
Could represent your heart, veins, and arteries, the flow of vitality through your system.

GAS TANK:
May depict your stomach, digestion, ability to refuel when empty; recharging of energies, renewed vitality.

Out of Gas: Out of energy, drive, pep, enthusiasm. Cut off from your source of supply.

HEADLIGHTS:
May denote your ability to see and perceive, the amount of your enlightenment, your ability to pierce the darkness. Can represent your eyes, vision, and insight.

Dim: Can denote imperfect vision or perception; unclear understanding.

Fog Lights: May imply your ability to see through the fog, smog, subterfuge, confusion.

Lights Out: Can denote blindness, inability to perceive, function; may say you cannot see what is going on around you or in front of you. Could imply a tendency to "black out."

IGNITION OR STARTER:
Ability to start and run, being a self-starter, not needing a push from others to get going.

KEY LOST, STOLEN:
No access. Lost dominion or control of your own vehicle. No key to the situation.

LICENSE PLATE:
Your identification, license to operate, permission; legal right or God-given right to life, liberty, and freedom to run your own life.

REAR-VIEW MIRROR:
Hindsight.

SEAT BELTS:
Regulations, limitations, safeguards, rules, protective measures you put on yourself. Can be inhibitions and feeling strapped or tied down.

STEERING WHEEL:
Your control, direction, aims, choices, goals, guidance system, ability to manipulate or maneuver.

> **Locked Wheel:** You may be locked into a situation, unable to control, guide, or direct the way you want to go.

TIRES:
May represent your feet, foundation of your lifestyle, your understanding and ability to use the creative knowledge you have. Might relate to a part of your ego, being a big wheel, your enthusiasm, or the amount of "hot air" you have; wheeling and dealing, or ability to get rolling.

> **Flat Tire:** Indicates lack of comprehension in the situation, no way to go, nothing to fall back on, immobility, your enthusiasm or energy has gone flat.

> **Tire Chains:** Getting a better grip on life, on your understanding, or on the situation at hand.

> **Tires Wearing Thin:** Can be ESP or may be a pun on your patience and/or understanding running out. May be the result of your emotional stress.

TRUNK:
Implies hidden, out of sight, possibly unknown storage space or hiding place.

WHEEL:
This can be wheeling and dealing, being a big wheel, circles, cycles, karma, death and rebirth, the zodiac, the cosmos, or simply the "turn of events."

> **Hub:** Archtypal symbol for creative thought or thought world, creative power center.

> **Hub Cap:** Outer show, decoration, put-on, surface.

> **Middle:** Formative powers

> **Outer:** The manifested thought, material world.

> **Spokes:** Eight spokes often depict channels of energy. Twelve spokes may represent the wheel of astrology and the twelve houses or cycles and seasons of nature.

Vehicle Colors

If your vehicle, whatever kind, is different in your dream from its actual color, then there is an added significance shown by that color. See *Colors in Dreams and Auras*.

BLACK AUTOS:
Often denote conservative, orthodox ways of thinking and acting, an overall unwillingness to change.

The Action

Always take into consideration the possibility of the dream content being literal as to the conditions of your conveyance, a mental or emotional situation, or an ESP warning. Check both your auto and your body when in doubt. Most of all, remember that your associations with these symbols could be far different than mine and *yours are the most important!*

ACCIDENT:
Collision with another automobile in dreams can be a "run in" with another's lifestyle, beliefs, goals, or purposes; it may be symbolic of a "jolting" experience, a shocking situation, injured pride, or a painful encounter. It may denote a coming conflict or confrontation or be a warning that you are on a collision course with a person or group. This could be an indication of a situation which can be detrimental to your health, or just plain ESP.

Accidents can warn of dangerous or careless driving habits or health problems coming from the way you "drive" yourself.

If the other driver is your mate, this may warn of a possible collision of lifestyles or ideals or an impending break-up of the marriage.

AUTO RACING:
Implies a very fast pace, hard driving, pushing for success, but it also implies that you are going around in circles trying to get ahead, getting nowhere; or, this may be a test of both car and driver or body and soul.

BACKING UP:
Implies backing out of a situation or an agreement, going back to something you did before. May be going back over things in your mind, reviewing and re-evaluating. Could be events or problems you need to forgive and forget, cleanse.

BLOWING YOUR HORN:
This usually signifies egotism, bragging, exaggerating, showing off, making your presence known by all; could be lack of consideration for others or making a fool of yourself.

BRAKES FAILING:
Lack of discipline or control over yourself, out of control, no stopping you. Warning that you are about to lose control of your life or situation,

your composure, or your brakes (ESP). Consider all possibilities.

BUYING A NEW CAR:
Can be "buying" a whole new lifestyle, updating your goals, revitalizing, renewing, finding a new and better way to express yourself.

CAR AND TRAILER:
May imply you are carrying a heavy load of responsibility along with you everywhere you go. Dream may imply a need to unload some of this or solve those problems, rather than drag them around with you.

DENTS:
Physical or emotional hurts, scars, hard feelings, battle scars of life, injuries that have not healed nor been eradicated from your mind.

DIRT AND DUST:
Riding through dirt and dust often depicts confusion, being unable to see your way clear.

FIRE:
Flames inside your vehicle can symbolize an inner cleansing and purification needed, impending, or presently being experienced. This is a good symbol, especially if you are calm about it in the dream or feel happy about it when you wake. A burning auto and a feeling of alarm can be an ESP warning of a car problem, or could represent an actual fever and illness about to overtake you. It could indicate a need to cleanse some burning anger/desire, or may denote you are "all burned up" about something.

LOSING YOUR CAR:
This can imply losing your self-esteem, your pride, your self-image, your job, your freedom, your present lifestyle or pet project. May denote feeling lost and out of touch with yourself or with life.

MOTOR TROUBLE:
If your car is not running properly, this may be a warning to check your health or your auto. May refer to the lack of power, potential, drive,

energy, vitality, or enthusiasm in a particular situation.

OUT OF GAS:
Out of energy, no go-power, drive, enthusiasm; feeling run down, cut off from your source, in need of revitalization and renewal. Possibly you need a physical check-up, vacation, a new diet, or a good supply of vitamins. Warning.

PARKING PLACE:
Place to stop and rest; may imply you need to make some "stopping places" in your daily schedule, to find a time to stop and relax inbetween activities. Or, this may be your own individual spot, your special place or niche, your private parking place, especially if this is in a parking lot or your usual parking area. Losing your place could be significant in this context.

Parking Place or Lot Filled with Ice, Snow: This may imply trying to find your place in life, where you want to be, but being unable to do so because of the many frozen talents and emotions (especially fears and inhibitions) which hamper both your progress and your ability to find your true place in life. Too much of your creativity, talents, and abilities are frozen, inaccessible, coated with old beliefs, thoughtforms, and inhibiting ideas about what you can, can't, or should do. You may have fears about leaving the safety of a good job to take a chance on doing your own thing, moving on to something more appropriate. Ice can depict a lack of faith in yourself. See the *Index* for more on *ice* and *snow*.

Can't Find a Parking Place: Can't find the time or place to stop and rest. No time out for yourself, much too busy; dream is pointing to your need to take time out to rest and relax a bit. On the other hand, this may indicate your inability to "find your place" in life, find your own particular niche, work, talent, place from which to do your thing or express yourself to the fullest—the spot where you belong.

POKING ALONG:
Implies you aren't making much progress, or may indicate an inner dissatisfaction with yourself and your accomplishments. Could imply that you don't really like what you are doing and you need to switch to something that makes you come alive again—unless, of course, you are quite happy with your pokey pace.

PUSHING YOUR CAR:
This may say you are pushing yourself too hard, making things harder than they need to be, doing things the hard way, struggling with life.

REPAIRS:
Since the auto represents your body, this could indicate a need for a physical check-up. Possibly some minor repairs or adjustments are needed for your best health, or could be your vehicle is due for a check up. Your feelings on awakening should give you a clue as to which is which.

SCRATCHES:
May imply that you or somebody has only scratched the surface of things, or could denote minor irritations, frustrations, and sore spots.

SCRATCHING OFF:
Showing off, lack of discipline or control; little respect for the body or for others.

SELLING OR TRADING IN YOUR OLD CAR:
Giving up old habits, old ways of doing things for newer ideas, better ways, greater health, a finer lifestyle.

SLIPPING, SLIDING:
Implies losing control of yourself in a situation, possible need to move a little slower.

SPEEDING:
Going hard and fast in dreams can be a warning that you are pushing yourself too hard and need to slow down a bit. Getting a speeding ticket would be a direct warning from your Higher

Self of your need to slow down your driving, your lifestyle, or both.

Speed may also imply strong impulses that tend to get out of control. Check the color of the car for the type of impulse or feelings.

SPINNING WHEELS:
Good symbol for using tremendous amounts of energy without making any progress.

STEERING:
Indicates your control, guidance, ability to handle, manipulate, and direct.

STUCK:
This implies being unable to progress, move forward, or generally get wherever it is you want to go. You may be stuck in your job, in your lifestyle, in your thinking, or in your general belief system. Low self-esteem is a common cause, lack of clear goals is another. Look to see what is blocking your progress.

> **Ice or Snow:** This is frozen water, frozen emotions such as fears and inhibitions, beliefs which say you can't or shouldn't, "What happens if I fail?" and other mental boundaries. Often snow is a symbol for talents, abilities, and creativity covered or inaccessible because you have been "snowed under" by "Not good enough," "You can't do that," and other such statements accepted as truth. These barriers to your progress are meltable. Faith in yourself and your abilities does wonders. Forgiveness of yourself and others for any wrongdoing will also facilitate the thawing process. See the *Index* for more on *ice* and *snow*.

> **Mud:** Mud and muddy water imply emotions which keep us from seeing clearly or firmly standing our ground. Churning mud or emotions imply being too upset to decide fairly or to move forward in a controlled, safe manner. Look to see what has upset you, what emo-

tions are controlling you or preventing progress. See *Muddy water* under *Water*.

> **Rut:** Ruts are made by taking the same path, mentally or physically, over and over. To be stuck in a rut would indicate being halted by one's own reluctance to change old habits, old ways of thinking and doing, unwillingness to try anything new, different, bold, or innovative. Being stuck implies we can go no further in life **unless** we make some changes, set new goals, dare to go beyond our former limits, and most of all to move past the ghostly wall of our fear of the unknown, of "what will happen if?" In short, ruts mean "Time for a change." Take a good look at where and how your lifestyle is bogged down or stuck.

TUNE UP:
This could imply that you need some minor adjustments or refills, maybe some vitamins, a better diet, a trip to the doctor for a check-up; taking care of minor things before they become major problems. Maybe your car needs it, too! Dreams speak on many levels.

UPHILL:
Can be a challenge to you physically, mentally, or both.

WASHING YOUR CAR:
Need to clean up your act! May imply a need to cleanse out old bad feelings, hurts, inharmonies; might even say, "You need a bath!"

WAXING:
This implies taking good care of your car (body), giving it some extra attention, cleansing, smoothing, polishing, taking care of its needs, nurturing. May say you need to nurture yourself, your health, treat yourself to something nice for a change.

Types of Automobiles

AMBULANCE:
Implies trouble, rescue, need for help. If you are driving, maybe someone needs your help in a hurry.

ANTIQUE:
This can denote an old body—out of date, incapable of keeping up with today's pace. Or, it can be a valuable treasure, an ageless beauty, something that has stood the tests of time. May imply old memories, nostalgia, things out of your past, or the condition of your life or body.

ARMORED CAR:
Heavy protection, possibly an overly-defensive attitude which keeps others out of your life and affairs. Can be inability or unwillingness to share the beauty, wisdom, and wealth of yourself you keep locked inside.

AUTOMOBILE SAME AGE AS YOU:
This would definitely represent your physical body and its condition.

BIG CAR:
Symbol of feeling big, important, capable, confident, prosperous, well-satisfied with yourself and your abilities (provided that you like big cars), or can imply "putting on the dog," acting like a big-shot, showing off, being pompous, overcompensating for low self-esteem, an exaggerated sense of self-worth, pretending to be something you are not. See *Limousine*, also *Small Car*, this chapter.

CAMPER:
Vacation, fun, and relaxation oriented. May imply using your body for fun and games or that your lifestyle is fun-centered. Could hint that you need some fun in your life, depending on the dream and your feelings.

CARDBOARD CAR:
Implies make-believe, pretense, absurd lifestyle, superficial, impractical, unworkable, unreal.

CONVERTIBLE:
Denotes freedom, changeability, a light touch, an open-mindedness, versatility, fun-loving.

DUNE BUGGY:
Implies a joy ride, fun and games, recreation, or may imply not using the body wisely, indiscretion, possibly self-centeredness or carelessness. Loose lifestyle.

EMERGENCY VEHICLE:
May denote an actual emergency in your body or lifestyle, could be ESP, or perhaps you live every day at emergency levels, breakneck speed, high stress. May be a warning.

FAMILY CAR:
This would symbolize your family and family affairs, family lifestyle, and general condition, problems, and concerns of the family as a group.

FOREIGN:
Can be a lifestyle that is foreign or some new, pet project that is different, unusual, or unfamiliar.

JEEP:
Built for ruggedness, hardship, and tough going with little thought for beauty. May denote a need for some beauty in your life as balance; could imply you have an all-work-and-no-play attitude; may depict excellent, robust health and vigor. Could denote the sporty lifestyle.

JUNKER:
Symbol of poverty, poor self-worth, low self-esteem, or a show of how you feel about yourself in general. To buy a junker would say you are

"buying" that concept of who you are, what you are worth. It can be a statement on your lifestyle, an "I don't care attitude," or a chronic health problem.

LIMOUSINE:

This can denote a very special occasion or lifestyle, or may show prestige, showmanship, excess wealth and materialism, pomp and power, an exaggerated sense of self-worth, a need to show off, and an intense desire to impress others or make a false impression. This can imply a super-ego, an overcompensation for complete lack of self-worth, a cover-up for poor self-esteem.

> **Big, Black Limousine:** Implies all of the above plus a generous supply of ultra-conservatism and unwillingness to make changes.

MODEL CAR:

Ideal lifestyle you may be toying with; could be trying to build your own lifestyle, an ideal way of life, a new way of putting things together; it isn't life size yet. Could be trying to model your life after a person or ideal, or the model you are setting for others around you.

POLICE CAR:

A no-nonsense attitude, discipline, control, justice. Strong sense of right and wrong, crime and punishment, guilt, rescue, or capture. Could say you are being very judgmental and harsh with yourself or others.

RACE CAR:

Could be a pun on your race or your attitudes about other nationalities; may imply hard-driving attitudes, your feeling of competition, or a need to win.

SMALL CAR:

This may portray a feeling of smallness, of inferiority, of not being as big, powerful, important, or as good as others. Can depict a generally poor self-esteem, an impoverished lifestyle, or

the belittling way you see yourself and/or your life work.

SPORTS CAR:

This could represent a pet project, hobby, belief system, or alternative lifestyle, especially if it is a second car. It may indicate a desire to look good to others or to be a sport. It could imply being a spoil-sport or a put-on. On the other hand, it can indicate having a more carefree, fun-loving attitude about yourself and what you do, depending on your personal feelings about small cars.

STATION WAGON:

Often denotes family responsibilities, daily chores, and family affairs. If it is a work car, may imply a feeling of being used, abused, overworked, overloaded, hard pushed, unless you really enjoy the work.

STOLEN CAR:

Someone stealing your thunder, taking your ideas, using your energies, taking credit for what you have done, pulling a fast one on you, using you or your resources.

Taxi Cabs

This could represent using other people's ideas and energies to get where you want to go. May indicate how you use people, unless you pay for the ride. Could also denote an alternate lifestyle, a different way to go, a desire to let someone else take responsibility, or might be a luxury you allow yourself. If you have been pushing yourself lately, it can be a hint to let someone else take part of the responsibility, delegate your authority, or ease up on yourself.

> **Yellow Cab:** May imply using the minds and ideas of others.

> **Blue Cab:** May denote using others' spiritual powers and abilities instead of your own, or a hint to use yours.

Red Cab: Implies using another's physical power, abilities, influences.

VAN:
These have been nicknamed "motel on wheels," sex vehicles, and party wagons. They are also used as work wagons or glorified station wagons. This could indicate a partying lifestyle, a work-a-holic lifestyle, or whatever. The final meaning would depend on your own associations with vans in general and your dream van in particular.

Trucks

Trucks can represent your work or your play, depending on the dream content and type of truck. Often they depict power, ability to pull heavy loads, toughness, endurance, dirty work, hard driving, burden carrying, heavy loads you carry or which are being put upon you. May denote a general lack of loving kindness or luxuries. A tough row to hoe.

As an overall symbol for your body, trucks could represent how you work or how you use or abuse your body—look at the action with the truck for this.

Trucks can also portray an all work and no play attitude you may have or indicate that you are using your body like a work horse. Hard driving, no luxuries, no tender loving care. Tuff stuff, hard life. May point to a need to soften up.

EMPTY TRUCK:
Could imply a feeling that your life is empty, that you are not pulling your share of the load, that you need something to make your life seem more rewarding or worthwhile; possibly you need to shoulder more responsibility, or it may be you just unloaded a bundle and it feels good! May imply you are ready for action.

LOADED TRUCK:
Alludes to the heavy load you are pulling. Can denote a loaded-down feeling, overloaded with care, a need to unload, or may point out a need to solve a problem rather than dragging it around everywhere you go.

MOVING VAN:
This could represent a move you are making or are about to make, could be the "heavy load" you are hauling these days. If it is being loaded, it may imply that someone is "unloading on you."

TRACTOR-TRAILER:
Implies pulling your own weight, pulling an extra-large load, weighty responsibilities, a "loaded situation," feeling overloaded, over-stressed. Could be a big job to do or a warning of your need to unload.

Work Vehicles

BULLDOZER:
This implies heavy work, big projects, much work to be done, or major changes to be made. Can be major changes coming into your life. If you are driving, you may be making your own path, doing your own thing, blazing new trails, finding a new way to go.

DIGGING EQUIPMENT:
Implies a need to dig deep for the answers, getting to the bottom of things, digging after success or knowledge, making preparations for better things to come, readiness to dig in and get the job done.

DUMP TRUCK:
You may be dumping your problems on others, or they may be dumping on you. You may have a heavy load which needs to be turned loose.

FARM EQUIPMENT:
Getting into the act of planting and growing new ideas in a big way.

Cultivator: May be the act of cultivating better attitudes, right thinking, better habits, disciplining the mind, weeding out negativity, making yourself over.

Harvester: Denotes readiness to reap what has been sown, to enjoy or deplore what you have earned. Part of the process of understanding "As a man thinketh in his heart, so is he," or "You reap what you sow."

FIRE ENGINE:
Great do-gooder, roaring out to the rescue with sirens going, everyone knows you are coming. Might imply that you are going like a fire engine, jumping at the sound of every alarm, charging to the scene of action, getting into the middle of things. Could imply a need for more discretion on your part.

GARBAGE TRUCK:
May imply you are dealing in or collecting worthless information or show a need to clean out old mental garbage, depending on whether you are collecting the trash or putting it out.

ROAD CONSTRUCTION EQUIPMENT:
Hard work, major changes, new paths to be made, whole new way to go, new outlook.

ROAD SCRAPER:
Scraping and smoothing the way for a new road, path, way of living. Could be a pun on just barely scraping a living or on scrapping (fighting) with others.

TRACTOR:
This could represent seeing yourself as a work horse or using yourself as one, or may be preparation for the planting of a whole new crop of ideas or houses.

WAGON:
Represents many things. Can be the wagon we fall off of when we break our resolutions, the loads we carry, or our potential for burden carrying and responsibilities. It may denote a heavy load, an overload, a useless or needless load, or

something we need to unload. Its condition may show how we feel about life's burdens.

Child's Wagon: Can indicate childish or playful attitudes about your work, or pulling your own load. Could say you are not equipped or prepared to do the job at hand. May imply a small job or childish work, thereby suggesting you take a more light-hearted, playful attitude toward your work. Can denote irresponsibility. Consider your own feelings and associations with toy wagons first.

Glass Wagon: A fragile vehicle, unable to hold or pull a heavy load, must be handled with care and caution. May denote your own fragile health condition which cannot bear a heavy load at this time. Warning to take care.

Loaded Wagon: This probably refers to a burden you are carrying which goes way back in time, either in this life or a previous one. Check to see if this can now be unloaded, forgiven, forgotten, or otherwise disposed of in some healthy manner.

Old Wagon: Might denote an old-fashioned way of doing or believing, or could be your old-fashioned ideas about the work you feel you need to do.

Buses

Buses take groups of people along predesignated routes, representing race-consciousness thinking, going along with the crowd, following a beaten track; preconceived ideas, prejudices, or old, familiar attitudes, whether sensible or not. Non-original thinking, worldly thoughts and actions, taking little or no control over the direction your life is taking, routine, habit, mass reactions, mass hysteria, ruts in your thinking, not making an effort to think things through for yourself, lack of originality or freedom, not being true to your own ideas and feelings.

There can be exceptions, of course. If you ride a bus to work, then buses can indicate your feelings about your career and represent your general attitude and outlook about your work, those you work with, or a group project.

BUS DRIVER:
As the driver, he can represent the one in control, the leader of the group idea, plan, or project, or he can be one who just drives around in big circles.

CHARTERED BUS:
This can be a group vehicle for reaching a special goal, accomplishing a particular group project; group cooperation; or, may symbolize a group lifestyle.

MISSED BUSSES:
These can represent passing opportunities to get where you want to go; therefore, to miss your bus could be to miss an opportunity or imply that you are always "running late" or that life is passing you by while you stand and wait.

SCHOOL BUS:
Symbolizes group action, group learning which can also be group progress or prejudice; group cooperation or group thinking as opposed to original, individual ideas, beliefs, and concepts.

STREETCAR:
In most cases this would represent old-fashioned trends of thought and action, outmoded ideas, by-gone days, memories, possibly even past-life events; or, if you are waiting for a street car, you could be waiting for a nonexistent opportunity.

Trains, Trolleys

Trains refer to your train of thought which goes down a definite track of thinking, race-consciousness ideas and prejudices thoughtlessly adhered to, taking the path of least resistance, going along with the crowd in thought and deed. Mindless acceptance of the status quo. No independence or originality, going along for the ride. Might depict an old-fashioned way to go, a chain of events, or could be a pun on training yourself.

DERAILED:
Losing one's train of thought or purpose, getting side-tracked, upset, demoralized.

ENGINE:
The power that moves the train, chain of events.

ENGINEER:
The authority figure, keeps you on track or on time.

FREIGHT TRAIN:
Can be a long, heavy load, long way to go; could imply a project or course of events which takes a good while to get started but, once set in motion, picks up speed and travels straight to a predestined conclusion. Can be difficult to stop, like a freight train going downhill.

MONORAIL:
Can depict a one-track mind, singleness of purpose, ability to stick to a goal.

ROLLER COASTER:
Similar to trains in meaning, since these follow on a fixed track. This depicts the ups and downs of life, our emotional highs and lows, strong desire for excitement, cheap thrills. Could imply thrills of booze, drugs, sex, or whatever turns you on. To ride this with a particular person may show how you feel when with that person, how s/he affects you and your equilibrium.

STEAM ENGINE:
May depict the pressure you are working under.

TRAIN TRACKS:
Depicts being on track, a set way of thinking and doing, a straight course, a prescribed course, fixed thinking, automatic actions and reactions, no new ideas, no original thinking or acting, old habit patterns, no individual freedom of choice.

Crossing R. R. Tracks: This can be crossing out old habit patterns in favor of new ones, going against the grain or set ways of thinking, breaking out of limitations, taking a new, different path or course of action. A breakthrough.

TROLLEY:

Generally has the same meaning as a train, but can also represent a one-track mind, obsolete, old-fashioned ideas, quaint ways of traveling or doing things. Could imply a trip into your past, an old-fashioned lifestyle, or can symbolize San Francisco!

Planes

Airplanes often represent your high ideas and ideals or a way of rising above the situation, but they are also an Aquarian Age way of travel. As a symbol of a lifestyle, they would symbolize a freedom of thinking and doing, a wider acquaintance with and acceptance of new ideas, customs, concepts, and beliefs. A far-reaching range of interests, ideas, and activities, ability to get from one point to another quickly, a great open-mindedness, a live and let live attitude, a strong desire for freedom, worldwide travel, friendships. Global thinking, thinking **big**.

Small, private planes would have about the same meaning as the larger ones with perhaps a bit more personal connotation—especially if it is **your** small plane. May depict your mental attitude, your mental body or "mental plane," or can represent your hopes, ideals, prayers, affirmations, wishes, thoughts, blessings, or curses you send out into the world which return to you for better or for worse. See *Airport* under *Background Settings*.

LANDING:

The return of your thoughts, ideas, wishes, will, intentions, or communications as karma for good or ill.

Coming In Backwards: Returning in an unusual, unexpected, round-about, or back-handed manner.

PARKED PLANE:

Ideas and ideals that never got off the ground.

TAKING OFF:

Your ideas, thoughts, communications going out into the world to do their thing.

WRECKED PLANE:

Broken ideals, dreams, aspirations; hopes which crashed or plans that failed. Could imply a lack of preparation or planning of a project you are about to launch or be an ESP warning of some kind of failure.

Boats

These often denote your spiritual vehicle, your spiritual body, your soul, and/or your spiritual progress. A ship can depict the voyage of life, the state of your soul, your soul's journey, or the path you are taking.

These can also depict other things such as prosperity, fun, vacations, social life, and many other things. The feeling of fun and games, relaxation and pleasure would go along with the boat dreams which represent leisure, while a special quality of peace, contentment, and high spiritual upliftment would accompany the spiritual progress type dream.

In boat dreams, look at the size and kind of ship and who is in command. Notice if the ship is in good condition, tied or anchored in one place or free to go, and how you feel about this trip.

You may have a series of dreams which show you sailing on increasingly larger and more luxurious vehicles. Eventually, you should be the Captain of your ship.

Ships may also denote ideals, hopes, and dreams—"when my ship comes in."

BOAT MARINA:

Center where many spiritual aspects of yourself come together. Could be a central meeting place of spiritually-minded people, a spiritual center. If you have a boat or visit a marina often, this could be an ESP dream or symbolize fun, vacation, social life, and so on, depending on the feeling and action of the dream.

FIRE INSIDE SHIP:

May be a sign of spiritual cleansing and purification going on within you or a hint that this is needed.

Kinds of Boats

CANOE:

Can denote a simple, serene lifestyle—certainly you would be moving under your own power and control, going at your own individual pace. May depict emotional balance and single-minded purposefulness.

LEAKY BOAT:

Your spiritual life is endangered in some way.

LUXURY LINER:

Easy going, rest and relaxation, prosperity, sense of well-being, good spiritual progress.

OCEAN LINER:

Full steam ahead, plenty of power to move ahead, luxury cruising, good spiritual progress being made, or may be ESP of a trip you may make.

Ocean or Sea: Psychic currents.

Smokestacks: These can represent channels of energy, God sparks flowing through you, possibly chakras open and running well.

PADDLE BOAT:

Could denote paddling your own way, going on your own power, no help from the outside. If alone, can say you are on your own or show a need to paddle harder. With a partner this could be light-hearted fun, or can imply you are not taking your spiritual life seriously, but playing. Possibly you and your partner are helping each other along.

PASSING SHIPS IN THE NIGHT:

Could be your spiritual opportunities, good fortune, and so on are passing you by because of your ignorance of how truth principles work.

PLEASURE BOATS:

These may symbolize a fun-loving, pleasure-oriented journey which may be anything **but** spiritual, or can indicate the joys of being "in the flow," depending on your feelings in the dream.

RAFT:

Can depict drifting through life, possibly alone and with no purpose or direction. You may feel a victim of circumstances. Implies rough going, could be a pun on having a "raft of problems," or as your spiritual vehicle, it may imply you have not built a firm spiritual foundation—there is much work yet to be done.

ROWBOAT:

Plugging along the hard way.

SAILBOAT:

May represent smooth sailing, going along with the flow of things, being in tune, unless of course you are having trouble navigating.

SMALL BOAT:

Limited spiritual preparations, going it alone.

SUNKEN SHIP:

Can imply your spiritual progress has come to a halt or has been drowned by the weight of worldly goods and activities or other treasures.

YACHT:

Implies luxury sailing, good spiritual growth and progress, prosperity, unless tied up. May also represent a vacation or other events, depending on the feeling in the dream.

Miscellaneous Vehicles

BALLOON:

This could easily imply rising above a situation, seeing things from a different perspective, doing the unexpected or the unusual, unpredictable. Could be open-mindedness, floating on air, a trial balloon sent to test something, or a new, untried concept or idea.

BICYCLE:

Balance. This may indicate a need for more balance in your lifestyle or possibly in your diet or your affairs. May show you just how balanced or unbalanced your lifestyle is at this point.

Motorbike: Can imply going it alone, keeping in balance, freedom of movement, getting there at your own pace and in your own style, or could be a very noisy way to go.

Training Wheels: Support, help in balancing your life, preventing the possibility of upsets, making sure, playing it safe. May also symbolize dependence.

Tricycle: Kid stuff.

Unicycle: This implies the need of a very delicate touch, a fine balance in your life right now. Definitely alone.

BIG WHEEL:

May be a childish way to go, immature lifestyle, or could be a pun on wanting to be a big wheel or acting like one.

CHARIOT:

This could be an indication of a past lifestyle or may be an old, old way of living and thinking. Unique.

GOLDEN COACH:

Symbol of royalty, a Cinderella type of rags-to-riches prosperity, magic, fairy tales.

HORSE AND WAGON:

Depicts old-fashioned person or thinking; slow, plodding ways; out-dated behavior; living in the past.

RICKSHAW:

May indicate that you are open-minded and possibly vulnerable in a way that is foreign or unusual to you. Being pulled, led, or manipulated by another.

Drawn by an Animal: Being led, motivated, or drawn by means of your animal instincts or your lower nature.

Drawn by an Oriental: Being led or motivated by ideas, impulses, or emotions that are foreign to you.

SKATES:

May be a childish way to go, immature lifestyle, or could be pun on escaping.

SKATE BOARD:

Same as above, but add a desire or tendency to show off.

SLEDS:

Could be childish or fun-loving and open-minded lifestyle.

SPACE VEHICLES:

These imply ability to travel far and wide, to go beyond human boundaries, to explore new ideas and places.

UFO:

Can depict being "spaced out," adventure, mystique, astral travel, untried concepts, or the unknown. May signify fear, new adventures, or new worlds to conquer. Many people experience UFO vehicles of various kinds in their dreams. Often these seem to be teaching tools or experiences that expand the mind. Sometimes they seem to be a rescue operation. Be reminded here that we not only learn lessons during sleep time but also serve on other planes of existence. This could be a memory of such an experience, or the UFO may represent the unknown and untried, new dimensions of mind.

My Own Vehicle Symbols

CHAPTER 42

Water

Water is the source of all life and as such symbolizes all life-giving energies, life essences, spiritual flows of truth, knowledge, healing, and refreshment. Water may represent spiritual realms, spiritual depths, spiritual experiences, healing, or refreshment. Water can depict our feelings and emotions as well as our subconscious depths.

Calm, clear water usually represents your spiritual attunement, while murky or muddy water would indicate the invasion of ulterior motives, unclean thoughts, muddled emotions, and feelings.

FROZEN WATER:
Inaccessible, hard, stiff, unmoving. Can depict frozen, hardened feelings and emotions we don't want to see, deal with, or have exposed or accessible to others. It may indicate the state of your spiritual or emotional affairs. Could represent unforgiveness.

MELTING ICE:
A loosening, thawing out, relenting of hard feelings, repressed emotions, old hurts, unforgivenesses. The beginning of a greater spiritual flow.

STEAM:
This may symbolize the process of change or transformation from one thing or quality into another. Could depict the purification and transformation of our emotions.

Lake

When the lake is calm and serene and the water is clear, this can represent peace, quiet, stillness, tranquility, and spiritual refreshment taking place within you, provided that your feelings and the rest of the dream concur.

If you are feeling stressed and out of sorts, this may be a symbol of your need to meditate and restore your peace of mind. Possibly the dream is depicting your need for seeking out such a quiet spot, or it could symbolize the peace and tranquility now being bestowed upon you. Such healing does occur in dreams, especially if you are praying for this.

WIND ON THE WATER:
Indicates the power of your thoughts upon the situation, also the direction. This includes your thoughts, prayers, affirmations, your spoken words, and your will power.

Ocean

The ocean or sea implies a large body of water. Most often this represents our feelings, our emotions, and their condition. It may depict being "all at sea" or can symbolize peace and serenity, psychic currents, depths of feeling, the unknown or unfathomable, unmanifested things, and the source of all manifestation—the ethers from which all things take form. Maybe the Sea of Forgetfulness.

It can also depict spiritual refreshment and renewal or upset emotions, depending on the clearness and calmness of the water and the feeling and action of the dream itself. This may also symbolize cosmic consciousness for those who are on the spiritual path.

GLASSY SEA:
Biblical symbol of perfect peace on all levels, stilled emotions, tranquility, serenity, or the meditative state.

MUDDY:
This represents emotional upheavals stirring within you, being unable to see clearly because of your emotional turmoil, or could be a family or work situation which is building up steam. Could be a warning.

NORMAL WAVES:
Represent normal ups and downs, emotional ebbs and flows, things running a fairly normal course.

PEACEFUL AND CLEAR:
Portrays serenity, refreshment, and renewal, especially if you enjoy the sea. It might also depict a need for you to go to the ocean for awhile—physically or mentally—to refresh yourself.

ROUGH OR CHOPPY SEAS:
Warning your emotions are getting out of hand, storm coming, need to take some positive action to release stress and emotional build-up.

SEASHORE:
Area where emotions (sea) and material levels (land) meet. A good place to balance (ground) your mind and emotions, to unwind, to refresh and renew both body and mind. Dream may be a hint that you need some spiritual refreshment and possibly a vacation.

STORMY SEA:
Emotional storms brewing, upheavals stirring within you, a big upset—possibly more than you realize—may be building in your life. Strong need to face into the storm and confront the problem before it overwhelms you. Some exercise can relieve emotional stress; a confrontation, forgiveness, or a good cry may also release the pressure.

TIDAL WAVE:
Extreme emotional upset, urgent need to correct the problem, forgive, change, or release your emotions before great damage is done or before you are completely overcome.

WALKING ALONG THE SHORE:
Can depict peace and serenity, quietly thinking things over, getting your life and thoughts in order, relaxing, getting in tune with nature, spiritually refreshing yourself.

WHITECAPS:
These are usually precursors of a coming storm or upheaval in our lives.

River or Stream

Rivers, when they are clear and flowing peacefully, usually represent the condition of your emotions—your ability to flow with life's events and live in peace and harmony with yourself and the rest of the world. As such, they can reveal your spiritual path or flow and your spiritual condition as a whole. (Anytime you become unhappy, angry, or upset in any way you are not in true harmony with the world or with your God-self.)

Rivers portray the flow of spiritual truth and knowledge, the source of life-energies. They symbolize the unceasing outflow of God's love or bounty, the constant supply of all your needs.

At times, rivers can denote a separation from one plane or state of consciousness to another.

STREAMS:
These are very similar to rivers in meaning but on a smaller scale. Often these represent your

personal lifestream, source, energy flow, or emotions.

BOATS:
Boats of any kind—large or small—usually depict your spiritual journey, but not always. They can be used to cross the river, to fish, for work or pleasure, so pay particular attention to the feeling of the dream so as not to miss the point. Notice whether or not you own the boat, who is in command, and whether the boat is free to sail or anchored in one spot. See chapter on *Vehicles*.

CROSSING A BRIDGE:
Symbol of crossing a barrier or moving from one state of consciousness to another, making an important decision, seeing the other side of things, making a big change, exploring a whole new area, or can mean a literal crossing over to the so-called other side (death).

CLEAR WATER:
Purity of spiritual purpose and endeavor, clarity of thought and understanding.

CLOUDY WATER:
Unclear purpose, emotional involvement or upset disturbing the clarity of heart and mind.

DAMMED:
Spiritual flow cut down or stopped entirely due to a blockage of some kind, usually within your own thinking-feeling nature. Think about how you may have "damned" yourself, cut off your emotions or your flow of good.

DRIED STREAM/RIVER:
This would symbolize being cut off from your Source, your spiritual flow, your oneness with God. (You may need to get to prayer and/or meditation practices!) This may also portray being out of touch with yourself, or you just may be physically or emotionally drained!

FLOOD:
This is an uncontrolled overflow of feelings and emotions pouring out on everything and everybody in its path—a definite warning that your pent-up passions are about to turn loose and spill out in all directions. This can imply that you are getting "carried away" by your emotions and need to exert some control and/or release some of these sentiments in a peaceful manner before they overwhelm you.

FLOODED HOUSE:
Overwhelmed by emotional upheaval. Note which floor(s) is immersed.

FROZEN STREAM:
Stream, source, feeling, or emotions still there but cold, hardened, stopped, unmoving, blocked. This may reflect hurt feelings you have "hardened" (which need to thaw and be dealt with sooner or later). It can be a type of unforgiveness, a strong emotion you are afraid of, or may signify the state of your spiritual affairs.

> **Thaw:** May be a needed loosening of your tight grip on your emotions, beginnings of forgiveness for yourself and others, a returning of warmer emotions, getting back into the flow of things.

IRRIGATION DITCHES:
These may represent channels for good, healing, helpful thoughts and feelings if the water is clear, or can show the directions your emotions are taking if the water is murky or muddy.

MUDDY WATER:
Indicates that your emotions are upset and in turmoil and denotes a need to take some positive steps to clarify your position. It also warns you not to make any final decisions until you can "see your way clear." (Emotions are literally muddy or muddle your thinking.)

> **Immersed:** In muddy or even murky water indicates you are in over your head in a situation, overcome by emotions, out of your element, in danger of being drowned by your

overindulgence in emotions. Dire need for control.

Wading: In muddy water can say you are wallowing in your emotions or that your understanding is rooted in emotions, not clear intellect.

POLLUTED:
Your spiritual flow influenced or poisoned by other people's ideas and beliefs. Need to go back to the Source.

PUDDLES:
These may portray small left-overs of your feelings and emotional upheavals not yet cleaned up by you.

WADING:
Getting your feet wet, starting something new. If the water is clear, this may imply a new understanding (feet) of spiritual things or putting your feet on a spiritual path. Could designate a cleansing of your understanding or a possible healing. Can be a pun on waiting.

Wading Pool: Can be a pun on waiting place. Could say slow down and wait on God's good timing.

WALKING ON WATER:
Supreme control over your emotions, exercising your spiritual mastery. May depict walking in faith or imply that you should "stay on top" of your emotions.

WATERFALL:
Symbol of grace and beauty, God's unlimited resources at your disposal, God's unlimited caring.

Clear, Sparkling Water

SPRING OR WELL:
A spring or well of clear water symbolizes spirit in action, the source of life and understanding; the source or supply of your spiritual good, whether it be spiritual refreshment, truth, healing, knowledge, prosperity, or whatever. The spring represents going straight to the Source—God. If in doubt about something, this may imply your need to go straight to God for your answers and ignore other people's opinions.

If you receive something from the spring or well, it may denote a gift or message from your God-source.

BATHING IN CLEAR WATER:
This implies the cleansing of impurities both within and without, a spiritual cleansing through prayer, meditation, or forgiveness which is given or needed by the dreamer.

DRINKING:
Drinking clear, sparkling water in dreams implies receiving spiritual refreshment or your need for it. Can be the act of being filled with spiritual outpourings, depending on the feeling of the dream. See *Index* for more on *Drinking*.

ICE WATER:
Spiritual refreshment but with reservations on your part.

FISHING:
Usually implies the act of fishing for spiritual food for thought, searching for enlightenment, or a spiritual quest of some kind. If it is your favorite pastime it may mean vacation, peace, serenity, relaxation.

FLOWING WATER:
Source of spiritual refreshment, flow of life-giving forces, spiritual flows.

GAZING AT STILL WATER:
This implies peace of mind, being "beside the still waters," contentment, mental and spiritual renewal, meditation, contemplation.

IMMERSED:
May be symbolic of a spiritual baptism.

LACK OF WATER:
May indicate you are neglecting your spiritual nourishment, or could imply you need to go to a new source of fulfillment.

RAINING:
God's cleansing being given.

SWIMMING:
Represents spiritual activity such as prayer, meditation, forgiveness, service to others, or exercising your spiritual mastery. May indicate your efforts to learn, study, and apply spiritual lessons or your search for truth.

Tap Water

Bathroom water usually refers to the emotions in your house (state of consciousness) and the ways you deal with them.

BATHING:
Denotes a need to cleanse your emotions or attitudes, to forgive, forget, let go, possibly to cry things out.

Soap: Symbol of cleanliness, need to clean up.

Shower: Same as bathing, but a shower tends to clean your aura as well as your body. This could be a hint to try a shower more often.

Tub: Same as bathing, if you are actually bathing and not just sitting. Sitting in the tub may represent your sitting in the midst of your emotions, possibly relishing them or wallowing in them.

HOT WATER:
Can be a pun for being in trouble or out of sync with others.

LEAKING WATER:
This implies pent-up emotions which need a fuller release. To withhold emotions is not necessarily the best or bravest way to handle things—it is more like the ostrich hiding his head in the sand, a useless gesture that only prolongs the problem. The longer feelings are held inwardly, the more likely they are to explode at the worst place or time. You may take out your spite on the wrong person, or you may not be aware of being short or snippy with others. Dream is pointing to a real need to release and forgive.

LAUNDRY:
Doing laundry refers to the need to clean up your attitudes.

TUB OR BASIN OVERFLOWING:
This implies your emotional build-up is really great and is spilling over on everyone. This needs your immediate attention.

My Own Water Symbols

CHAPTER 43

Weather

The laws of the universe can never fail...your own...(thoughts) will come back to you with mathematical exactitude.

— *James Allen*

The weather conditions in your dreams can indicate your moods, feelings, emotions, thought patterns, and the things and events you have set in motion by your thoughts, words, prayers, and affirmations. Weather can also depict your general emotional atmosphere. (Actually, our thoughts have a distinct influence on the weather we experience.)

WEATHER:
Can be a pun on "whether or not" as well as being a key to your mental-emotional state.

Air

Clear skies and sunshine can represent God's grace and love being poured out for all. It may indicate clarity of mind, a sunny disposition, or being in a happy, carefree state of mind. Sunshine itself often symbolizes wisdom, grace, and spiritual enlightenment being given to you or poured on your situation or state of consciousness.

SUNRISE:
Dawn symbolizes a special time of God's outpoured energies and blessings, peace, a time to greet God in prayer. Depicts the beginning of a new day, a new opportunity, a new cycle, new start.

SUNSET:
Symbol of the end of a day or a cycle, a time of rest, completion, renewal, and God's blessings; or, can imply the peace after a storm, beauty and harmony restored. This can be a statement of fact, or may be showing you the possibility of peace is at hand.

WIND
In *As A Man Thinketh,* James Allen states, "The most powerful forces in the universe are the silent forces...Thought forces are most powerful of all."

The wind indicates the general flow of your thinking—whether it is calm and peaceful, angry, frustrated and blustery, or somewhere in-between. The wind portrays your mind forces at work and the power of your thoughts on a situation. Its bearing symbolizes the direction of your thinking and the course of events set in motion.

A strong, steady wind can indicate the steady pressure of our will power. A blustery, stormy wind denotes anger, fury, frustration, and possibly a will to destroy or get even, rather than a will to do good. The stronger the wind, the more powerful the mentality involved. There is a possibility someone else's strong mental powers may be blowing you off course or trying to, so the dream can be a warning.

Wind

Symbol of spirit moving in a matter or of thought forces and the direction they are taking. Mental forces at work in a situation. Will power.

WIND TUNNEL:
A controlled, channeled direction of thought. Could depict a boxed-in channel with only one way to go.

Clouds

In dreams, the clouds forming in the sky symbolize our high ideals and show how our thoughts, prayers, hopes, words, and affirmations are beginning to take shape as we hold these in mind over a period of time. These are highly symbolic of *thought-forms.*

CLOUDS CHANGING SHAPES:
This could suggest flexibility and mobility in your creativeness or indecision as to what you really want to manifest; or, it could possibly denote your flights of fancy.

CLOUDS MOVING ON AIR CURRENTS:
This shows the direction your thoughts are taking.

CLOUDS MOVING AWAY:
This may be a situation you want to have removed, possibly something you have prayed about. Or, it may show that you are not putting enough effort into your prayers or affirmations to receive what you have asked for, and it is

therefore moving away from you or fading out of sight. Your feelings would give you a clue as to which way it is.

CLOUDS MOVING TOWARD YOU:
Symbol of your words, prayers, or affirmations (good or bad) coming into your life and affairs.

DARK CLOUDS:
Would denote negative thinking as well as an indication of the gathering storm of pent-up emotions beginning to take shape in the sky of your mind. These can forewarn of an emotional storm or upheaval on your horizon.

> **Moving Toward You:** Emotional outburst, tears, or turmoil headed your way. Dream gives warning that there is still time to change the course of things.

FLUFFY WHITE CLOUDS:
These denote your ideas and the size, shape, and form your thoughts are taking. White clouds would imply purity of purpose, positive thinking, and planning. The shape of the clouds in your dreams may give clear hints as to just what you are creating mentally.

HEAVY CLOUDS:
May represent clouding the issue, blocking out the light, limiting our vision.

LARGE MASSES OF CLOUDS:
These may imply mass ideals, mass or group thinking, strong movement of group ideas or prayers, coming trends of thought.

Rain

A gentle rain or light shower usually denotes God's mercy, forgiveness, and cleansing being poured out upon you. It is a beautiful symbol of God's grace freely given.

FOG:
Depicts limited vision, emotion-filled mentality, a lack of clear perception, poor understanding, inability to see your way clear, general con-

fusion, and strong need to clear the air mentally and emotionally.

Foghorn: Danger signal, warning of something you cannot see.

FREEZE:
Halting of all emotional flow. Feelings shut off. May indicate a hardening of the heart or mind.

GOLDEN RAIN:
Particularly symbolic of God's blessings being poured out.

HAIL:
Hardened thought-forms, solidified emotions, "hard feelings!" Could be hate bouncing around. Need to thaw out your feelings and deal with problems before they solidify.

ICE:
Frozen emotions, hard feelings, showing a tendency to freeze up when hurt rather than talking things out to the satisfaction of all concerned. Poor defense mechanism. Being prone to protect your tender emotions from pain or exposure, or a tendency to put your feelings "on ice" to take care of them later—too much later. Dream is a warning to handle things as they come up and/or to melt down the barriers you have put up over the years.

MIST:
Lack of clear perception in the low spots, partial emotional blocks, limited vision; spotty, faulty understanding; a need to clear the air mentally and emotionally.

RAIN ON THE ROOF:
Denotes spiritual ideas, concepts, and blessings coming to mind.

RAIN ON THE WINDOWS:
Implies spiritual ideas and insights being brought to your awareness.

RAIN ON WINDOWS COMING INSIDE:
You got the message! Depicts your openness to spiritual teachings and concepts.

RAIN SEEPING THROUGH:
Emotions affecting your home, health, and state of consciousness; getting to you.

RAINBOW:
Peace after the storm, God's promises to us, protection, happiness, joy, good things to come.

SNOW:
Frozen assets, frozen feelings and emotions, need to thaw these out and release or resolve them.

SNOWFLAKES:
These can represent purity and perfection of design or can be God's blessings bestowed but you aren't ready to accept them yet.

SNOWSTORM:
A snowstorm can represent a snow job, someone snowing you under, or can depict frozen assets, unused potential, abilities and talents, or an icy reserve. Snow can also be blinding, hampering your ability to see your way clear.

Crusted Snow: Frozen state of your feelings; restrictions, limitations, barriers, protection you have placed over your tenderest feelings; love, compassion, lovingness you are or have been afraid to express. Qualities, emotions, and gentle feelings you have "kept on ice."

Storm

Dark thunderclouds building up in size and intensity often represent your own pent-up feelings and emotions which are gathering and building energy deep within your being and are needing release. Combination of mental and emotional forces out of balance (accumulation of negative and discordant thoughts). The greater the imbalance, the more severe the storm must be to restore balance.

Storms can be any emotion from self-pity or disappointment to absolute outrage and full-blown fury. The intensity of the storm gives you an idea of the power of the emotions behind it. Actually this can be a blessing in disguise, as it is a needed release. You need only to make sure you do not vent your storm of anger in the wrong place. You may try to release the problem in other ways, such as forgiving yourself or another, as the case may be.

Storms can clear the air and release the turmoil which has been building up within and, handled rightly, can be extremely cleansing for all concerned. Your dream warning can alert you to the possibilities ahead of time, giving you a chance to guide the energies into productive channels rather than destructive ones.

LIGHTNING:
These can be intuitive flashes and illumination which can help you to understand the problem and clear the air without having a storm. It can also be an alert or a quick flash of inspiration or insight. May be the power to change things quickly.

WIND AND RAIN:
Indicate both mental and emotional forces building up and working out into manifestation.

STORM COMING TOWARD YOU:
Forewarning of tensions, turmoil, and an emotional upset and needed cleansing coming your way. Possibly a storm of tears about to break loose. At this point you can forestall, circumvent, or clear up the problem.

STORM IN PROGRESS:
Upset is upon you, need to release your own way *now* or fortify yourself against what is already in process. If you are feeling great, it *could* be that someone else's upset is about to engulf you. Be warned and ready.

THUNDER:
Mental forces in action, warning of a coming storm, need for preparations.

TORNADO:
Destructive mental forces, temper tantrums, extreme emotional upsets.

UNDISTURBED IN THE MIDDLE OF THE STORM:
Peace is one of the first fruits to manifest in your life once you have set your mind on spiritual attainment; therefore, to see a storm raging all around you while you stand at peace, untouched by it all, is loving encouragement for you to keep on working on your inner peace. This would definitely indicate that this kind of tranquility is now possible for you to attain. Congratulations!

My Own Weather Symbols

CHAPTER 44

XYZ & Potpourri

While symbol names can be found in a standard dictionary and their meaning pretty accurately derived from that source, I have listed a few extra ideas you may need plus some miscellaneous symbols not applicable in the preceding categories.

A

ADVERTISEMENT FOR A JOB:
An appeal for help and talent or list of alternatives, choices, and opportunities to choose.

ACTING:
Implies an act, a pretense, something make-believe or not real. This often involves the personality level as opposed to the real, spiritual you. It can suggest insincerity, a facade, an intent to conceal the truth or to defraud or mislead in some way. Check to see if you are being true to your own self and your ideals or acting a part, pretending to be satisfied, being insincere in the way your treat yourself. Also check the possibility that someone you are dealing with is acting.

AGITATING:
Search to see who or what is agitating whom. It could be an aspect, habit, or attitude of yourself which is stirring things up or causing your problem.

AMEN:
It is finished, or so be it.

ANKH OR CRUX ANSATA:
Key of life. Ancient Egyptian symbol of immortality and eternal life. Venus or "mirror of Venus."

ANNOUNCEMENT:
Proclaiming or calling your attention, stating a fact, affirming, declaring, making intentions clear to all.

ANUBIS:
Jackal-headed Egyptian god who represents the evolution of consciousness, self-consciousness, intellect. Same god as Hermes or Mercury.

APPLE:
Can be a healthy food you need to eat, a symbol of temptation, or forbidden fruit.

Golden Apple: Spiritual reward.

AQUARIUS:
Sign of the man or the water-bearer. One who pours out new, innovative ideas, is interested in groups and community projects; concerned with the good of all people.

ARIES:

Astrological symbol for spring, new growth, people who are active, ardent, pioneers, leaders, and doers.

ARROW:

Represents aim, goal, direction, one-pointedness.

Broken Arrow: Broken vows; can mean peace, change of mind.

Golden Arrow: Spiritual ideals, aims, goals.

Two-Headed Arrow: Opposing ideas, two sides to consider, dual awareness.

ART SUPPLIES:

May represent your creative abilities and potentials, or may suggest that you be more creative.

ARTIFACT:

Buried treasure, creation from a past life, an old talent, gift, habit, fear, pattern, or memory. Could be a situation from your past resurfacing to be examined and perfected.

ASLEEP:

Unaware, not paying attention, dead to the world.

AUTOGRAPH:

Signature or mark, endorsement or approval, usually of someone famous. This can represent your desire to emulate the person whose autograph you seek or may suggest those talents are yours also. If someone seeks your autograph, this may denote fame is coming your way or that you are giving your consent or approval to someone.

BACKING:

Can suggest backing up, backing out of a situation, reversing an opinion, decision, agreement, an attempt to get out of an undesirable predicament; a backward person, or may depict a person who backs or supports you. Backing away may also imply going back and forth over a problem; indecisive, vacillating.

BAG, BAGGAGE:

Place for your favorite attitudes and ideas. May be a bag of tricks, "in the bag," arrangements made, agreement assured, package deal, or pun for "bag lady," trash bags, litter bag, lunch bag, wind bag, and so forth.

Packing Your Bags: Getting it all together.

BAIT:

That which lures, entices, invites, motivates; a desire to catch something or someone.

BALL:

May depict wholeness, earth, globe, oneness, or be a pun for keeping your eye on the ball or being on the ball.

BALLET:

Balance, poise, graceful motions, cooperation, and moving in a harmonious relationship with others.

BALLOON:

May be a pun on being full of air, puffed up, expanded, light-headed, easily blown about.

BANNER:

A standard, logo, statement, symbol of a group or of group-held beliefs. May depict your standards.

BATHING:

Implies the need for cleansing, purification (inner, outer, or both), releasing pent-up emotions such as anger, fear, tensions, or frustrations. You may need to cry, exercise, confront, or make peace in some way. Forgiveness of self and others is the main means of cleansing.

BAZAAR:

May be a pun on bizarre or represent a wide variety of ideas, crafts (craftiness), creativity, art, miscellaneous things, items, and choices.

BEARING:

Can be pun on "bare-ing" yourself to another or bearing a burden or gift; bearing as in putting up with a person or situation; your general bearing, demeanor, manner of behavior; may allude to your bearings in relation to your sense of direction. May denote bear as in unbearable, overbearing, ruthless as a bear, or even something you have to bear or have borne.

BEHIND:

Can be supporting, backing up, encouraging or prodding, urging, pushing, hiding, or menacing.

BENDING:

Ability to bend, flow, adapt. Flexibility may be needed, or possibility you may be too flexible.

Backward: Going out of your way to please.

Forward: Implies eagerness to do something.

BICYCLE:
Balance.

BINOCULARS:
Bringing things into sharper focus, taking a long look or closer look.

BIRTH CONTROL PILLS OR DEVICES:
May represent repressing, stifling, or blocking your creative urges.

BLINDERS:
Prevent distractions and interruptions, aid to one-pointedness. May imply keeping your eye on the goal.

BOARD:
May be pun on bored, boarding, or building.

BOOKKEEPING:
This could refer to keeping balance in your life as well as in your finances, a statement of your life's account, giving account for your actions, keeping records, being accountable, or may be a pun on keeping borrowed books! May indicate your need to keep records or a diary.

BORDER, BOUNDARY:
Line between two states of consciousness, two levels of activity, two areas of thought; edge, limit.

BOUNCING OBJECTS:
Symbols of your attitudes, thoughts, and ideas—showing the effect they have on your life and others.

BOWING:
Implies greeting, reverence, respect, honor, prayer, devotion, humility, acquiescence, submission, and bending of the will. Is the dream showing a need to bow? An unwillingness to submit? Too much submission or not enough?

BOX:
Container, framework, doctrine, restrictive structure, limit, block to progress, boxed-in or closed-in feeling.

BOXING:
This can be boxing things up, putting yourself or your ideas/goals in a box or bind, tendency or ability to put things away in neat boxes or categories. Much would depend on what you are boxing up. Boxes can also be blocks, protection, limitation, even hiding things. There is also

boxing as in fighting, warring, and struggling with yourself.

BRIEFCASE:
May depict profession, business, career, prestige, important work, group of important ideas. Could be a status symbol, a false impression, pun on making things brief, or depict a brief, temporary problem or situation.

BROCHURES:
May be an advertisement or information sheet or could be a pun on giving or receiving a "handout."

BROWN BAG:
Lunch! Home-made, personal; can be a symbol of humility, poverty, or independence. May be wrapping, protection, privacy, or can represent under-cover, hidden, esoteric, occult.

BROWN WRAPPER:
Usually used to conceal something from prying eyes. Wrapping, protection, cover-up, desire to hide, secret; can be a cover for "dirty" literature or anything one wishes to keep "under cover."

BULLFIGHT:
Area of man against beast, the struggle between animal nature and our higher, spiritual nature.

BUMPING:
Implies carelessness toward others, annoying and disturbing by thoughtless actions or remarks, lack of coordination, cooperation, consideration of people's feelings.

BURNING:
Fire and burning can symbolize anger, a fiery temper, or represent purification and transformation needed. May also indicate being all burned up about something.

BUYING:
Means to purchase an item, but also can say you bought or accepted an idea, situation, condition.

Might allude to how much you paid or the price you have to pay for this. Ask yourself what purchase you are considering, or what did you "buy" and is it worth the price?

C

CADUCEUS:
Staff of Mercury, messenger of the gods; symbol of healing, Aesculapius, wisdom, and ideas. Presently symbol of American Medical Association and of healers everywhere.

CAGE:
Symbol of imprisonment, restriction, confinement, or can be safe-keeping. Anything in the cage may represent an aspect of you which feels safe or trapped.

CAMERA:
Instrument to focus, capture, and record an essence or memory of an event, person, or place; or, could imply a need to get a clear picture, idea, goal in mind.

CAN:
May be a pun on what you think you can or can't do, use, store. May be pun on not being live.

CANCER, SIGN OF:
Astrological symbol for those born from June 21st to July 21st. Pincers depict holding power, tendency to keep everything. Cancer is known to be family-oriented, nurturing in nature, sensitive, emotional, and can be moody.

♋
CANCER

CANNING/PRESERVING:
Saving or putting aside an idea as food for thought, possible tendency to put ideas away for later rather than facing, consuming, or digesting new ideas right away. May imply that you can or can't do something or say, "Can it!" as in throwing it away.

CANNON:
Getting out the heavy artillery, something drastic needs to be done, possibility of a big blow-up.

CANOPY:
May be under cover, hidden, covert, or protection.

CAPRICORN:
Astrological sign of the mountain goat or the unicorn. Known for desires to climb the heights, caution, responsibility, capability. Can be workaholics. Capricorn as half man and half fish denotes blend of human and divine.

♑
CAPRICORN

CARNIVAL:
Farce, falsity, gaudy, ostentatious, based on sensationalism and fooling the senses. May be deceptive in nature, appealing to our lower self, or can be fun and games.

Carnival Rides: Going in circles, getting nowhere, cheap thrills, giddiness. Can symbolize sex play.

CARTOON:
Ideas in picture form done with wit and humor. May symbolize our need to laugh at small mistakes, add more humor to our lives.

CASH, MONEY:
This is a type of energy or exchange, depicting buying power, ability to come, go, and do.

CATALOG:
Wish book, wide variety of choices offered, choose!

Little or No Cash: May denote little or no spare energy, being low on vitality, needing to recharge one's batteries.

CELTIC CROSS:
Symbol of the Celts and Druid religion. (Scots, Welsh, Irish, and Bretons.)

CENSOR:
Pot for burning incense. If burning, this indicates prayers or devotion being offered up, spiritual cleansing, raising vibrations to a higher level. Can be a pun on censoring.

CEREMONY:
Outward symbol of an inner change or intent to change.

CHANNELS:
Tubes, pipes, straws, chimneys, wires. Anything which channels or carries water, smoke, energies, vibrations, or messages can indicate an ability to carry, direct, give, or receive information, messages, healing energies, and so on.

CHANTING:
Getting in harmony with God and the Universe or your need to do this.

CHARGE:
Can be an accusation, being in charge, taking over, buy now and pay later, or charging ahead in a situation.

CHASING:
Implies actively pursuing an object or goal.

Being Chased: Implies fear of whatever is doing the chasing, need to get away from a person, place or situation quickly, a feeling of helplessness or powerlessness, your "past" catching up with you.

CHECK:
Usually represents money, paying debts, or receiving payment for services rendered. Can be money coming to you or a pun on checking things out.

Blank Check: Can say, "Name your price," unlimited supply, unused potential, uncashed assets, unclaimed rewards.

CHRISTMAS:
Depicts spirit of Christ being born in you.

Christmas Gifts: Probably spiritual gifts being given or received or the spirit of Christ being shared.

Christmas Lights: When lit, Christ light shining in you.

CIRCLE:
Symbol of God, eternity, perfection, unending love, superconsciousness, perfected man, no beginning and no end; also circumvention, going in circles, joining or being enclosed in a circle.

Pointed Circle: Symbol of higher planes.

CIRCUS:
Temporary state of affairs, your animal instincts doing their thing, putting on a show, childish attitudes, pomp and circumstance, fun and games.

CIVIL WAR:
War with yourself.

CLAY:
Ability to be molded, shaped, formed.

CLIFFS:
Often represent challenge, fear of falling, failure, edge of danger, catastrophe.

CLIMBING:
This could refer to social climbing, ambition, desire to rise to greater heights in physical, mental, or spiritual areas, or may indicate your progress.

Climbing a Ladder: Can indicate ascending the ladder of success, especially when it is associated with your place of work, but may imply a need to climb or step up higher in the area indicated.

Climbing Steps: Can mean taking things one step at a time or a step up in life. All upward movement would imply a need or desire to reach higher levels in whatever area you are in, indicated by the building, room, or background of your dream.

CLOSING:
Closing doors usually indicates an ending, a shutting-off, a barrier, completion, or cessation. It may symbolize shutting out opportunities (often symbolized by doors), ideas, or people. What are you shutting out of your life? How do you feel about this?

Closing Windows: Windows usually represent our vision, perception, or view of the world. To shut these would be closing out perceptions of the outer world.

Closing Drapes or Blinds: Shutting out the light of truth, refusing to look at or face something.

CLUB:
Depicts virility, combativeness, preparedness, caveman tactics.

COLLIDING:
This usually symbolizes a literal collision with one of different culture, ideas, goals, or way of living which may shake you up, injure your ego, damage your pride, or upset you in some way.

COMMERCIAL PRODUCTS:
Worldly, material, race-consciousness things and ideas produced by our society. Includes rules, regulations, customs, beliefs, shoulds, ought-to's, no-no's, and other things of questionable value.

COMPASS AND SQUARE:
Masonic symbol for macrocosm and microcosm.

CONCH SHELL:
Ancient symbol of inner hearing, clairaudience.

COOLER:
Keeping cool in a hot situation, having emotions under control, or need to cool it.

COPY MACHINE:
One idea being copied, repeated many times; ideas multiplying, spreading; getting the word out; may depict tendency to copy others' ideas and beliefs without thinking things out for yourself.

COVERING:
This can be an act of protection or concealment by you or another.

CRAFTS:
May represent creativity, dexterity, and art, or may be a pun on craftiness.

CRAWLING:
Crawling in dreams usually means humbling or debasing yourself, possibly doing less than your best. Could be a childish approach, lowering your standards, or being unable or unwilling to stand up to a person or situation.

CROSS:
A cross can depict the difficulties we have to bear, the way of Christ, or may imply resurrection. The cross is a very ancient symbol dating back long before Christianity. It represents the incarnation of man on earth as well as death,

Celtic　　Tau　　Roman

Patriarchal　　Papal　　St. Andrew

Maltese　　Bottonee　　Egyptian

Easter, new life, and liberation. There are many variations and styles, most indicating a particular belief or organization.

CROSSING:
Usually indicates a change in our lives, a crossing over from one state of consciousness or area of thinking or living into another. May also be crossing the line.

> **Crossing a River:** This is usually concerned with making a spiritual decision or change-over.

CRYING:
May represent your disappointment or your soul's despair at your performance, a regret for something said, done, or decided. Could also be a cleansing, a releasing of emotions, or the need for release. To wake up crying is often showing the soul's sincere lament and a warning to change your ways.

CUBE:
Represents a square, being "square," earth, material possessions, the physical or mundane.

> **Rubik's Cube:** May indicate a puzzle, challenge, problem.

CYCLE:
Seasons, variations on a given theme of life.

D

DAM:
Part of you which restricts, withholds, restrains feelings and emotions, giving only a part of yourself or your power. Can be blockage or a pun on your power to bless or to damn.

DANCING:
Moving in harmony, in unison, in cooperation with yourself, your goals, with others, or being in harmony with the universe. It may imply your need to *get* in harmony. If you are stepping on other people's feet, there is a warning to watch your step and get yourself into harmony with those around you.

DATING:
This often refers to the attraction of opposites and the process of getting to know one another, with the idea of marriage or integration as its goal. This can be on a purely social level, or can refer to the integration and subsequent marriage with your High Self, which can lead to the mystical marriage.

DAWN:
Usually signifies the beginning of enlightenment, but can mean start of a new day, era, cycle.

DEADWOOD:
Ideas, habits, beliefs; programming no longer alive, relevant, useful. Need to remove or burn (purify) these.

DESPAIR:
Dream warning of wrong thinking, decision, action.

DIGGING:
Effort required to accomplish, find, uncover. May be a hint to dig further into a matter, to get to the bottom of things, to search, to bring a situation to light.

DINING:
Symbolic of taking in food for thought, ideas, teachings, training, disciplines. You may have this symbol anytime you read or hear a new idea or teaching. Take a look at what you do with the food. Do you eat it, leave it, reject it, or store it for later?

DIVING:
Taking the plunge. Could be moving in too quickly or getting in over your head, or there may be a need to dive in and do something quickly, depending on the overall action and feeling.

DOLL:
Denotes small aspects of ourselves, thinking small, belittling ourselves, being a plaything for others, lack of control. Type of doll is important.

DOZING:
This usually refers to being asleep at the wheel, unaware, inattentive, unknowing, non-alert; could be a warning to sit up and pay attention to what is going on. May also refer to an altered state of consciousness.

DRAIN:
May show a need for releasing or channeling emotional excesses, a pun for things going down the drain, loss, wasted effort, or can be something draining you.

DRAWBRIDGE:
Protection from invasion or intrusion, pun on where you draw the line, or possibly the need for this.

DRINKING:
First thing to consider is what are you drinking? What are you swallowing? Is it your pride? Is someone pouring something down your throat?

Drinking Pure, Clear Water: Symbolizes quenching your spiritual thirst, drinking in spiritual truth, or your need to do so. If you are reaching for the drink but can't get it, perhaps you need to seek a new spiritual home, church, teacher, group, or source of information.

Drinking Alcohol: Can refer to the amount of alcohol you consume and what it is doing to you from a spiritual point of view.

Drinking Poisonous Substance: Could be a literal warning telling you that your water source is contaminated, or may indicate that something you are drinking in or swallowing physically or mentally is poisoning you.

DROPPING:
Usually indicative of dropping or letting go of some plan, project, person, or idea. May imply carelessness, letting things slip through your fingers, inefficiency. If you are dismayed, the matter dropped may be much more important than you thought—you may need to reconsider. If you are relieved, you may need to drop something out of your life or schedule.

DROWNING:
To see yourself or another drowning often implies being "in over your head," being in "too deep," deeply involved, overwhelmed, inundated, or emotionally overcome, especially if the water is not clear. Drowning in muddy water symbolizes heavy emotional involvement, being overcome by the situation. However, there is always the *possibility* of an ESP warning of an actual drowning which could take place. Be aware on all levels.

DRY CLEANER:
May say you need to clean this without further emotion, or warn that someone is taking you to the cleaners.

E

EARTHQUAKE:
An earth-shaking experience, tremendous upheaval in your life, thoughts, or affairs. Drastic changes needed or coming. Things will never be the same. On ESP level, this could be an actual warning of a quake to come and/or area to avoid. Look at both possibilities.

EMERGENCY:
Can be an urgent situation or pun on emerge and see.

EXERCISING:
This can mean much moving around without getting anywhere, or can be a hint that you need to exercise your mind, body, or will power more than you do. Possibly you need to exercise more control over a situation.

EXPLOSION:
Sudden outburst of pent-up feelings and emotions, an explosive situation, or may warn you are near the bursting point, need to take care of this.

EYE OF HORUS OR SACRED EYE:
All-seeing eye, eye of God, or self-regenerative power source.

EYE IN A TRIANGLE:
Symbol of spiritual sight, understanding.

F

FABRIC:
Material from which we fashion our lives into creations of joy or ugliness. Result is what we make out of life.

FALLING:
Can symbolize a fall from grace, heading for a fall, falling in love, falling down on the job, falling short of a goal, disgrace, embarrassment. Could be ESP warning or be an astral-travel

remembrance of returning swiftly to your body. Feeling is important.

FASTING:
Abstaining from something. Can be food, habits, attitudes, or thoughts; a cleansing of the inner self from unwanted traits; a spiritual pruning.

FEEDING:
Symbol of nourishment, encouragement, fulfillment. You may need to nourish yourself more or support another, depending on who is feeding whom.

Feeding Baby: Need to nourish and nurture your pet project, new idea, or ideal.

Feeding Fish: Need to feed your spiritual ideals.

FENCES, BUILDING:
Building barriers, defensiveness. Setting yourself apart from others.

FILE, TOOL:
Hint to trim the rough edges of your personality, smooth out your relationships, speak and act more harmoniously, less abrasively.

FIRE:
Symbol of purification, spiritual fire, impulsiveness, zest, transformation, or temper, destruction, being all burned up.

FLAME:
Awareness, light, enlightenment, warmth, desire, or zeal.

Sparks: Can be God sparks, energies, effervescing, magical, enlightening, stimulating; or, can be destructive.

Golden Sparks: Spiritual enlightenment, encouragement; may possibly represent magical transformations.

FIREWORKS:
Lavish display of fire, enthusiasm, emotion, artistic talent, beauty, spectacle, celebration, os-

tentatiousness, general showing off, or can be temper tantrum, noise, and discord.

FLAG:
May depict patriotism, support of your country, group, or belief; may mark a spot, flag someone down, or signal a message.

FLOWING:
Being in a flow of ideas or events, ability to go along with the tide, being in touch with your guidance, your right path, or moving in the right direction, providing the flow feels right. If you are uneasy, it may mean you are going downhill, downstream, in an unwanted direction. May imply you are not in control of your life, letting it drift aimlessly. Can be warning to get things under control.

FLYING:
This can symbolize your ability or your need to rise above a situation or emotion, to avoid being involved to the point of reacting negatively. Ability to give good for evil. Flying could be an astral-travel remembrance, or can be a desire to move up to higher levels.

Flying Birds: Can be flight of ideas, joyousness, high ideals, or high hopes. Blue birds especially represent joy and happiness.

Flying Carpet: Would signify mystical, magical, creative properties of the mind that can take you places you want to go. Creative imagination, flight of the mind. Creative visualization.

Flying Feathers: Confusion, upset, fright, hasty retreat, loss of dignity.

Flying Objects: Usually represent high ideals or flight of ideas, reaching for the stars.

FOLDING:
Act of making something smaller or neater, putting things in stacks, preparation to put it out of sight and out of mind, possibly storing it away

for future need or reference. Could refer to turning things over in your mind or symbolize unfoldment, growth, learning. Note type and color of articles folding or unfolding.

FOREIGN:
Area foreign to your usual thinking, far out, a totally different idea, or a new way of seeing things.

FORGIVING:
Usually shows your need to forgive yourself.

FUSSING, FUMING:
Since all anger is really self-anger, this is an indication that you are upset, angry, frustrated over something. Look at the object of your anger and decide what aspect of yourself this represents. Fussing may be giving voice to your unhappiness, frustrations, and feelings and could imply a need to speak up for your needs and rights.

> **Fussing at Children:** Can be annoyance at some childish aspect of yourself, or children may represent the little things which are upsetting you. If you are trying to make them be quiet or go away, dream is saying you need to take care of these—they won't go away, they need your attention.

G

GEMINI:
Astrological sign of the twins, symbolizing quick-thinking, versatility, changeability, adaptability, and keen wit.

Ⅱ
GEMINI

GILT OR GILDED:
Could be a pun-on guilt, a cover-up, a put on, over-doing something, a pretense, or ostentaciousness.

GIVING:
Can symbolize your need to be more generous and giving, unless you feel you are giving in excess. Often this has to do with being able to receive as freely as you give. Look closely at what is given and how it is received.

GLUE:
Getting it together, sticking to a person, group, or thing; may be a pun on a sticky situation or warning not to get stuck with this.

GOING HOME:
Going back home to God.

GOLDEN CANDLESTICK:
Holder of spiritual light.

GOLDEN THREAD:
Brotherly love, continuous caring and affection, a loving connection.

GOOSEBUMPS:
Confirmation of what you have just said or heard, or may indicate fear.

GOUGE:
Forcing something out of its place, forcing action in a person or situation, prodding, pushing, making things happen possibly without regard to others' needs or feelings.

GRADUATION:
A symbol of achievement, additional skills, a readiness to move on to higher levels, to do better things; a time of celebration and joy. Could be a symbol of an initiation ceremony on inner planes.

GRASPING:
Symbols often have dual possibilities. You may need to grasp and hold on to some idea, dream, or ideal; on the other hand, this may say you are being overly grasping in your attitudes or habits.

GRAVEL:
Loose footing, tricky, dusty, difficult way to go.

GRUMBLE:
Symbol of your dissatisfaction and your need for a change.

H

HANDLE:
Can be a way to handle a situation, a way to grasp or hold something, or a need to get a firm grip.

> **Handle Broken, Bent:** Hard to handle, can't handle it, can't get the hang of it, difficult to grasp, hard to get.

HANGER:
Hang-up, trying to get the hang of something, could imply the possibility of entanglement.

HANGING CLOTHES:
Getting your attitudes and emotions out in the open, airing out the "family linen," exposing your feelings, being totally open, confronting issues, letting it all hang out, getting a fresh point of view.

HEADPHONES:
Getting a message no one else can hear, listening to a different drummer, tuning in to your own intuition.

HEART-SHAPED:
Symbolic of love, kindliness, sympathy; deep, loving feelings.

HEAVEN:
High state of consciousness, state of love and harmony, oneness.

HEMMING:
May refer to hemming and hawing, indecisiveness, or can be tying up loose ends, putting on the finishing touches, completing a project. Could refer to a stitch in time.

HIDING:
What are you hiding or hiding from? Your dream can point to your need to realize that you are hiding from or dodging an important issue, or you may be hiding the truth from yourself or another.

HOLDING:
We can hold things lovingly or grasp things we need to let loose. We can hold ourselves or others back from their needs or goals. Holding can indicate you are afraid to let go. Look at what are you holding and why.

HOLE:
Can be a pitfall, something we can fall into; trap, something to avoid, hole in our thinking, loophole in a document, or can be getting in over your head.

HOOK:
Type of hang-up, catch all, hold up, hook up, grasp. May warn of getting/being hooked on something.

HOPPING:
Jumping around from one thing or place to another, not staying in one spot long enough to accomplish anything.

HORN:
Can depict making beautiful music, expressing yourself through melody, a call for help, call for attention, act of blowing your own horn, bragging, assaulting (car horn), locking horns with another's ideas or hardening your mind to new concepts.

HORNS:
Represent hardened thought projections, thought-forms, the shape or tenure of long-held ideas. May refer to locking horns with another's ideas, or hardening your mind to new concepts.

HUGGING:

Holding something close to your heart; loving, caring, showing affection. Dream may show you a need to be more affectionate.

HURRYING:

Rushing, going off half-cocked, ill prepared, not centered, running scared; lack of planning and preparation, scattered.

I

ICE BAG:

Cold treatment!

I H V H:

Hebrew initials of Jehovah. Also represents the four elements: I, fire; H, water; V, air; H, Earth.

ILLEGAL:

Against the laws or rules, unorthodox, different, hidden, underground, undercover, not accepted by others.

INCENSE BURNING:

Prayer, meditation, invocation; loving, devotional thoughts sent to God.

Frankincense: Transmutation of physical into spiritual.

Myrrh: Eternity of Spirit, resurrecting power of love, surrender of mind to spirit.

INDIAN DRUMS:

Earthy rhythms, call to gather and worship, show of reverence for the earth and all its beings, often an intonement for nature spirits to come with aid or wisdom.

INSURANCE:

Can be protection, guarantee, support, backing, benefit, buffer, reward, or could be a rip-off.

IRON:

Instrument for smoothing out kinks, wrinkles, rough spots in attitudes and relationships.

Heavy Iron: Applying pressure, heavy going, difficult moves.

Hot Iron: May be applying heat, hot stuff; could be burned up or warning that you can get burned.

Steam Iron: Can imply strong emotional pressure.

ISLAND:

Can be isolation, separation; alone or on your own. Or, if populated, may imply that you, your aspects, ideas, and interests, are in a place by yourself—out of the main stream of life.

J

JUKE BOX:

May depict a kind of feeling (represented by the type of music), group beliefs or sentiments, morale, group consciousness, mood, atmosphere. May also be canned music as opposed to the real thing, cheap harmony, second best.

JUPITER:

Planet named after Jupiter, god of good luck, success, expansion, optimism, generosity, and extravagance.

JURY:

Implies judgment, possibly punishment, being put on trial, pleading your cause. Remember, jurors are aspects of yourself judging your actions. Can be warning not to judge yourself too harshly or that you need to forgive yourself. Could show how you feel in your present situation.

K

KEEL:
Built-in guide, balance, direction, control, will power.

KINK:
Can depict a kink in your thinking, in your hopes or plans; a problem with some connection or communication.

KISS:
Show of affection, enticement, or deception (Judas). May imply adage to kiss and make up or point to your need to show more affection.

KITE:
May be a high ideal you are holding onto, possibly showing you which way the wind is blowing or how you are struggling to succeed. Could be child's play.

KNOCKING, SOMEONE:
May be opportunity knocking at your door, a bid for your attention, or a pun on hard knocks in your life.

You Knocking: May be saying, "Don't knock it," or possibly you need to knock harder at the door of opportunity; maybe you are "knocking yourself out" over something.

Knocking Things Over: Can be "knocking" things with words or gestures, upsetting others, or being "ob-knock-ious!"

KNOTS:
"Nots" in your life—do not, have not, can not; the no-no's; also restrictions (yours or another's) placed on you. Some of these may need to be removed.

L

LABELS:
The labels you put on yourself, people, places, and situations. Your pronouncements of worth, good or bad, hard or easy. The judgments you make. "Whatever you name it, that shall it be unto you." (Genesis 2:19.) Dream may be pointing out how you are creating your good or bad by your judgments and pronouncements. May imply judging by label or appearance, rather than by fact or performance. Could be accepting other people's labels/judgments, rather than thinking things out for yourself.

LACE:
Delicate, fancy, possibly expensive, special, with a see-through quality. May be used to impress or persuade.

LAUGHING:
Unless you laugh often and easily, your dream is most likely suggesting that you be more carefree, relax, and have some fun; to laugh it off, don't take life too seriously, or may say that laughter is good for you.

LAUNDRY:
Implies condition of the attitudes and affairs of the owners of the laundry.

LAWN:
Combination of solid ground, earth and healing growth, balance. Condition of your lawn may indicate the seed (thoughts) you have sown and the results of your labors.

Walking the Lawn: May be a hint to walk the earth in a certain way symbolized by the dream, or imply your need to get closer to the earth, possibly to walk barefoot on the ground to heal and harmonize yourself.

LEACH:
Parasite which feeds on others, drains the life forces. Some people are similar in activity.

LEASE:
Can be signing a lease or agreement to do something, getting it in writing, making a commitment.

New Lease: Getting a new lease on life, new start, new goals, new ideals, new agreement or commitment for yourself, or turning over a new leaf.

Old Lease: May say time is running out, time to make a new commitment, new goals, new start.

LEMNISCATE:
Symbol for eternal life, harmonious interaction between the conscious and subconscious, serenity, harmony, dominion over the physical plane.

LEO:
Astrological symbol for Leo, the lion-hearted. Symbol of royalty, dominion, creativity, organizational ability, leadership, authority, affection, pride, and loyalty. Ruled by the sun, there is usually a sunny disposition and playfulness of spirit. Sign can mean any or all of these.

LIBRA:
Symbolized by the scales, Libra stands for balance, Justice, truth, fairness, diplomacy, peace, harmony, partnerships and cooperation. May indicate a need to develop these qualities. A scale with a feather on one side and a heart on the other—depicts the weighing of the soul (Egyptian).

LIFE JACKET:
Security, support, backup, reinforcement, safety.

LIFE-SUPPORT SYSTEM:
Can refer to people or things you rely on for support, a need for extra support, state of your reserve supply of energy, condition of your health, or your need to support someone else in their difficulty.

LIFTING:
May be lifting one up by prayer, praise, support, love, caringness; being swept off your feet; or, may be inspiring others to greater heights. Could be lifting your sights or goals, or possibly you need lifting.

LINE:
Can be guideline, clothes line, drawing the line, lining up, waiting line, or getting our actions in line with our words.

LINING UP:
Getting in a line can signify your need for alignment, being at ease, in touch, or in tune with yourself, your body, and its needs. Can also imply a long wait, patience, fortitude needed before completion.

LOCKING:
Making things safe, secure. Protection.

LUBRICANT:
The oil of love and caring which makes everything run more smoothly. Possible hint to add this oil to your lifestyle, especially with the person or situation symbolized as needing oil in your dream.

LYRE:
Musical instrument of harmony or a pun on liar.

M

MAGIC:
Something from nothing. A thing which appears, moves, or changes by non-physical means. Can be symbolic of the power of our minds to create or change our circumstances, or can depict unseen assistance from other planes.

MALPRACTICE:
Pun on your own lifestyle or habits, pointing to a need for change in the area indicated.

MAP:

Path, plan, outline, reference point, guideline, goal; alternative routes, way to go.

MARCHING:

Usually denotes a steady pace forward, moving in unison with others, group work, group progress, group force. A forced march would probably denote moving against your will or better judgment, something you are forced into doing.

MARKER:

Can mark your place, your progress, where you stopped, or pun for making your mark in the world.

MARS:

Symbol of Mars, god of war. Mars means energy, action, desires, aggression, courage, impulsiveness, independence, forcefulness, enthusiasm, and assertiveness. Can be defiant and destructive when challenged, otherwise a go-getter.

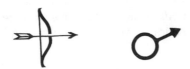

MARRIAGE:

Can mean partnership, cooperation, co-creativeness, togetherness, integration of an aspect or part of yourself. May be something you "have to live with" until you decide to divorce or separate yourself from it by taking some positive action, or could imply a mystical marriage, meditation, union with your High Self, listening to your intuition, being tuned in, in harmony with yourself, experiencing oneness.

MASSACRE:

Race consciousness ideas that lead to the death of all who follow blindly without questioning ideas or ideals of their leader. If this is in old-

fashioned clothing, look for possibility of a past life recall.

MECHANICAL DEVICE:

Automatic reaction, moving without thought, unwittingly acting, plodding, not really living or experiencing. Unaware.

MERCURY:

Symbol of the thinking mind, reason, alertness, dexterity, efficiency, changeability, analysis, versatility, awareness, calculations, communications.

MERRY-GO-ROUND:

Going around and around but not getting anywhere. Can symbolize worry or going in circles.

METER:

Measure of time or space. Can be a pun on how you measure up or what measures you are taking.

MISSING PARTS:

Implies not having what you need to solve your problem, understand the situation, reach your goal, or complete your task. Something may be missing in your life; you may have overlooked something important or missed the point.

MISSING TRAIN, BOAT, BUS:

These would indicate missing out on an opportunity to go somewhere or to gain something represented by the type of vehicle. It may indicate that you are waiting too long to decide or move or say, "Don't wait any longer" for a certain person or chance, lest you miss your opportunity. Could imply a feeling of being unworthy or unprepared, depict missing the point, the object, goal, or the good things in life. May be warning.

MIXING:
Can refer to mixing several ingredients together to create harmony or a new, better situation in some way; but, may refer to getting all mixed up, confusion, chaos, an incorrect combination of facts, or even a lack of all the facts which confuses.

MOVING:
Physical or mental action you are taking or need to take. Your progress or lack of it; how, where, or what you are moving into or out of. Might imply changing from one area of thinking, doing, or believing, to another; changing states of consciousness or reality.

Backward: Backing up, backing out, backtracking, going back over the same old ground, not facing up to what is ahead, avoiding the issue, or a fear of moving forward.

Forward: Advancing or need to go on with what you are doing. Taking the necessary steps to achieve your goal. If symbols are good this may be encouragement to keep moving, or may say this is the right way to go—everything will work out well.

Going in Circles: Can be a hint that you are not making the progress you think you are, that you are going in circles, beating around the bush, evading things, not gaining any ground, trying to circumvent a situation, or that you are not coming to any conclusions in the matter.

Sideways: Side-stepping an issue, taking a round-about route, not facing things squarely or being up-front about matters. Possibly showing insecurity or unsureness in a matter.

MUSIC:
Beautiful music symbolizes harmony, divine influences at work, peace, and serenity.

Loud, Rowdy, Obnoxious, or Upsetting Music: Can signify a lack of peace, harmony, attunement to higher things.

N

NEEDLE:
Suggests mending one's ways, a situation, or a relationship; creativity in arts and crafts; or, may imply needling someone.

NEPTUNE:
Symbol of the god of the sea, Poseidon (Greek) or Neptune (Roman). Represents inspiration, intuition, genius, clairvoyance, sensitivity, imagination, compassion, devotion, understanding, limitless expansion, and mysticism.

O

OIL:
The oil of love that makes all things run more smoothly, a remover of friction, healer of hurts. May be a hint to apply more love and caringness in your life, affairs, and relationships.

Baby Oil: Oil to soothe childish aspects, platitudes for childish thinking or behaviors, or oil to smooth out a new project, idea, responsibility.

OLD-FASHIONED:
Can mean being out of date, out of step, behind the times in your thinking, habits, or attitudes. May imply a preference for the old ways, wanting things as they used to be. Can show a basic

dissatisfaction with the way things are and/or be a subtle hint to change.

Articles: If only tools and articles are old-fashioned, this would imply your methods and habits are out-of-date.

Clothing: If only your clothing is old-fashioned while all else is modern, this would indicate out-of-date attitudes.

Entire Scene Ancient: When everything in the dream is old-fashioned, this may be a past life recall. See the chapter on *Historic Settings*.

OLIVE BRANCH:

Peace, love.

OPERATION:
May indicate your need to "cut it out" or to "get it out of your system." Calls for drastic removal of whatever is bothering you before it makes you physically ill. Could be an ESP symbol of a health problem. Look at the part of the body and the background area for further clues as to what has to "go." Could be a habit.

OPPOSITE:
Implies an awareness of what confronts you or opposes you, looking at the person or situation eye to eye, facing up to something, readiness to work out the problem as opposed to ignoring it. May be emphasizing a need to work out your differences.

ORDINATION:
Graduation ceremony giving you the earned right to do greater things, to serve others in the way you have chosen, a step up in the world, a new opportunity.

OUTER SPACE:
Can represent out of nowhere, out of nothing, apparent magic, mystical experiences. May also be a symbol of the creative productivity of your mind as you concentrate on your goals, plans,

and affirmations and they suddenly seem to appear out of the blue.

OVERSIZED:
Double emphasis on that particular habit, item, or quality, showing it is out of proportion, out of harmony, needs immediate adjustment. Examples: an extra-large coffee cup to indicate drinking too much coffee; a huge nose to imply nosiness or lying, as in Pinocchio!

P

PACK:
Can be a burden you carry which could be left behind or a compact way of getting it all together in a small package.

PACKAGE:
May refer to a package deal, more than meets the eye, a pig in a poke, meaning you don't know what you are buying or getting into, or a symbol for wrapping things up. May be a surprise package. Any wrapped package suggests the unknown.

PACKING:
Getting it all together in one parcel, package, place, unit.

Groceries: Food for thought.

PADDED WALLS:
Protection, possibly from yourself. Might depict safe limits or a need to soften the blows.

PARABLE:
Story, usually with a hidden meaning, teaching, or truth told in simple but symbolic terms.

PARADE:
Long line of people and things making themselves highly visible, stopping traffic, amusing and entertaining, or disrupting and distracting. Can show how we are side-tracked from our

purpose or how we stop ourselves from attaining our goals.

PARADING:
Suggests showing off, strutting your stuff, being up front, out in the public eye, in plain view, holding an audience, seeing and being seen, even making a public spectacle of yourself, depending on your feeling. Could be that you need to be more public and show what you can do.

PARASITE:
Irritating habit of taking from others, feeding on ideas, energies, things of others; dependent, non-productive, draining other people's resources, taking without giving. Can represent a habit or aspect of yours that drains your own vitality.

PARALYZED:
Feeling powerless, unable to move, to cope, or to do anything about a person or situation. Could be paralyzed by fear or indecision. Dream is emphasizing how you feel and your need to move.

PARKING:
Symbolizes lack of movement, standing still, not moving, not accomplishing, no constructive activity, not using what you know or have, not going anywhere in life. If you are parked where you don't want to be parked, you probably need to get moving; but if being parked feels good in the dream, it may be showing your need to get out of the fast lane, take a vacation or at least a brief rest period. It may be time to pull off and let someone else take the wheel (of responsibility) for awhile. Think about it.

PAYING:
May suggest the price you will pay for your action, decision, or indecision. May show who or how you will pay or how you will be paid/repaid.

PEBBLES:
Little rocks, little irritations, difficulties, challenges, rough spots, or uncertain footing.

> **Throwing Pebbles or Rocks:** Little things that hurt, gossip, criticism, nasty comments that can wound or kill.

PEDDLING:
This could be trying to sell, educate, promote, advertise, or extol an item or idea; or, could be a pun on pedaling along, even piddling around.

PEN:
Can be an tool of creativity or destruction, praise or criticism, expression of beauty and graciousness, or a damnation. Can represent one-pointedness or be a sex symbol.

PERMANENT:
Hair-curling experience, a change in your outlook or thinking, taking on a new look, becoming a different you, or possibly getting some kinks in your thinking!

PHALLIC SYMBOL:
Almost any pointed type of object which can penetrate or protrude is a possible sex symbol for someone, and as such it can represent sex and one's fears or feelings about this.

PICNIC BASKET:
Wide variety of food for thought together in one unit, easily handled, a chance to learn and share ideas and opinions with friends in a relaxed, easy-going manner. An outdoor scene here may suggest spiritual learning, a spiritual atmosphere, or both.

PIECE:
Can be a pun on peace or show that you only have a part of the whole.

PILLS:
This can be ideas that lead to healing, counteraction to negative ideas held in mind, hard lumps

or bitter pills we have to swallow in life, or preventive measures we may need to take.

Poisonous Pills: Poisonous ideas that can lead to illness or death of the believer, such as hate, resentment, greed; even self-pity can be harmful.

Truth Pills: Healing food for thought, affirmations, positive beliefs, statements, and prayers; healing principles.

PIN:
Can indicate a sticky situation, stick to it, stuck with it, or a haphazard way to put things together. Is someone trying to pin something on you?

PISCES:
Astrological symbol for great sensitivity, sympathy, caringness, service to others, readiness to suffer for a cause. These make great musicians and artists, but they sometimes wallow in self-pity.

♓
PISCES

PLAY:
May refer to the parts we play in life, the act we put on; or, could refer to all work and no play, our need to be more playful.

Rehearsal: Getting ready for the real thing, practicing our art and abilities, sharpening our talents, perfecting ourselves.

PLOTTING:
Making plans or need for some. Is anyone plotting against you? Do you need to make plans, goals?

PLUNGING:
May say you are plunging in over your head, diving headlong into things, possibly into the unknown, or maybe you need to plunge into things.

PLUTO:
Planet named for the god of the underworld, Pluto, symbolic of death, destruction, transformation, rebirth, consecration, transmutation, reformation, karma, instinct, intensity, struggle, light, or darkness.

♇

POLE:
Fixed connection, unmovable object, security, stability; an object one can use to lean on, hold on, tie up to, fasten to, grasp, or make secure.

PORTFOLIO:
Object to hold records, facts, important papers, business records, and transactions. May imply being neatly organized, getting it all together, or having facts readily accessible, available, usable, under control.

POWER COMPANY:
Source of power, source of strength, ability to move or accomplish. Can symbolize your God-power.

PRANA:
Invisible life forces we can breathe into ourselves.

PRAYING:
To see yourself praying, especially if you don't spend much time in prayer, would most likely be a reminder of your need to pray more in general or a need to pray about your greatest concern—possibly the matter you asked about before going to sleep. It may be telling you that prayer

can change this, or it could be saying you need to turn this matter over to God and let it go completely. Often prayers are not answered simply because we never **released** them—we just keep repeating them as though God were deaf. (Beggar's prayer.) Perhaps you need to learn to pray and relinquish all worry or thought as to **how**, **when**, or **if** it can be accomplished. (Prayer of Release.) You may need to work in your Garden of Prayer.

PRESCRIPTION:
Method, formula, program, therapy for solving a problem, healing a situation, fulfilling a request for aid.

PRESENTS:
Can be gifts you have, give, or receive or be a pun on presence. Take a good look at the kind of gifts and what you do with them.

PRICE TAG:
Notification of the price you have to pay for something you are considering.

PROGRAM:
Plan of events to come, planning what you want in life, setting goals, looking ahead, having a plan of action or a guide to go by.

PULLING:
This action implies struggle in getting things accomplished, pulling your share of the load, a long, hard pull, possibly pulling more than your share, or pulling others along as you go. Look at who or what you are pulling and reassess the situation. Dream may show how you are struggling to pull things, people, responsibilities, or situations which should have been unloaded long ago. You need to **flow**, not strain. Life should be joyous!

PUNISHMENT:
Can be giving yourself a hard time, refusing to forgive yourself, or making things harder than they need be. Dream may show where, how, or why you feel the need to punish yourself so you can change this.

PUPPET:
Can reveal the way you feel about yourself or imply you are allowing yourself to be controlled by another or swayed by others, not acting on your own, being manipulated.

PUSHING:
You may be pushing yourself to get ahead, pushing your luck, or pushing other people. Pushing and pulling both symbolize struggle, effort, and not **being** in the **flow**. Take a good look at who or what you are pushing.

Q

QUILT:
Type of cover-up, protection, security blanket. If it is a family heirloom, this would indicate family security or cover-up. May even be an "under cover" deal!

R

RAPE:
This could be an ESP warning or may symbolize a person or condition being forced upon you; taking advantage of a weakness, ignorance, or vulnerability; taking by force something which could be secured by gentleness; being compelled to accept or do something against one's wishes.

RACE CONSCIOUSNESS:
A composite of race-thinking—ideas which are generally accepted whether right or wrong, prejudices, group ignorance or pressure, going along with the crowd, everybody-does-it attitudes, and generally selfish, self-centered, non-original thinking.

RAMP:
Easy access in and out, on and off.

REACHING:
We reach to communicate, get in touch, give aid, comfort, support, or love to another; or, we reach to receive what we need from others.

Reach for a Male: Needing power, strength, stability, intellectual knowledge, and ability plus any known qualities that particular male may have.

Reach for a Female: Reach for intuitiveness, sensitivity, love, gentleness, nurturing plus any other qualities that particular female may have.

READING:
Can be a message to yourself if words are clear or a symbol of obtaining more knowledge, reading up on the matter, getting informed, need for further study. If possible, note the title of the subject matter. May possibly be a pun on "reading" for others (using your psychic abilities), or can say you need to go back to school to study, learn. Check background, feelings, and action of the dream.

RED LIGHT:
Danger, warning, need for caution. Could also symbolize prostitution of your physical body, talents, or abilities.

REHEARSAL:
Getting ready for the real thing, practicing your arts, gifts, and abilities, sharpening your talents, preparation for life.

REJECTING:
Are you refusing to accept the good things in life that are being offered to you? Look at what you are rejecting and the symbolism of it—who or what did you reject the day before? How do you really feel about this? The dream is pointing out this rejection for a reason. Reevaluate!

RIDING:
Can be going along at another person's pace with the ideas, beliefs, lifestyle of other people rather than doing your own thing, using your own original ideas, ideals; being "taken for a ride," unless you are in control of the ride. Look at the animal or vehicle ridden.

ROBBED:
Being shorn of valuables, money, dignity, job, or self-respect. Dream may point out your fear of these or may be picturing how you feel. Possible ESP warning.

ROCK:
Solid base, foundation, security, or truth concept. May also be cold, hard facts, a barrier, obstacle, difficulty, or challenge, depending on the dream feeling.

ROD:
May be a standard of measurement, a symbol of power or leadership, or an instrument of discipline and punishment.

Blossoming or Sprouting Rod: Symbol of God's favor, high spiritual attainment, spiritual gifts and powers.

ROPE:
A connecting link, a way to tie things together, hold things secure, line of escape or rescue, means to an end.

ROWING:
Can be a pun on a hard row to hoe, a tough or difficult way to go, doing things the hard way. Can also be a spiritual adventure or endeavor. You may need to row harder to make spiritual progress, or you may be running a good race, depending on details of dream.

RULER:
Measuring device, measuring up to standard, taking proper measures, giving good measure, accurate measurements or judgments, careful assessing of facts, rules, regulations, probabilities, and so on, before making a decision.

Ruler, Person: One who is in charge, takes responsibility, gives directions, has authority and dominion, makes decisions, sets things in motion, oversees results.

RUNNING:
Need to delineate running from jogging first. Is this a needed exercise or are you running into a situation or away from someone or something? A dream can show a strong desire to run from a situation or a need to run from temptation, depending on the feeling. If you were afraid, you may be running from your fears rather than facing them. Running may imply you are getting nowhere fast or you can't run from this! Note your feelings and the overall situation. Why are you running?

RUTS:
Implies old tracks your mind runs along in its thinking through force of habit. Old ways of thinking and reacting, old habits you have fallen into, things you do automatically. You may need to take a good look at your old habits.

S

SAFETY BARS:
Safety measures, protections, regulations, rules, something that bars you from danger but also limits your freedom of movement. Could be a warning to take some safety precautions in area covered by dream.

SAGITTARIUS:

$\nearrow$

SAGITTARIUS

Astrological symbol—half man, half horse, or the man with the bow and arrow. Signifies goals, aims, high ideals, philosophy, higher mind, lofty thoughts, optimism, intuition, perception, visions, directness, and bluntness.

SAILING:
Usually implies smooth sailing, flowing along with ease, being in the flow, unless of course you are having problems with wind, sea, or sail.

SATURN: ♄
Symbol of discipline, lessons, tests, delay, limits, constraint, caution, stability, conservation, time, death.

M,
SCORPIO

SCORPIO:
Astrological symbol for healing, transformation, regeneration, power, intensity of purpose, and ability to penetrate deeply into a matter.

SCREAMING:
Act of giving voice to your feelings, anger, fear, love, or whatever. Screams denote strong emotions, great need for expression.

Scream, No Sound: If you wanted to scream but didn't or couldn't, dream implies an urgent need to give voice to your feelings and confront the situation. Could mean that you are unable to name or give voice to your fear.

SCHEDULE:
Plan of action, set course, timing, goal. Losing a schedule may imply you do not really want to do this or don't really need it. May imply a need to either throw away the schedule or drop some-

thing off of it. Losing a class schedule can indicate you aren't sure what it is you want to learn or if you really want to learn it. Probable need to re-think your decision, possibly change or chuck the schedule or plans you have made.

SCREW:
Can be an important connecting link, the small detail which holds everything in place. May symbolize making connections, getting it together, or the little things—the small details which mustn't be overlooked. May be pun on screwing things up.

SCUFFLING:
Struggling, dragging your feet, reluctance.

SCURRY:
Fearful movements.

SEEING:
Perception, understanding, viewpoint, mental picture. See *Eye* under *Body and Its Parts*.

See Clearly: Indicates clear thinking, understanding, having a good grasp or perception of the situation.

Unclear, Fogged, Obscured Vision: Unable to see all the facts or factors involved, poor understanding, need for more information or understanding.

Seeing Through Knothole or Small Opening: Limited view, unable or unwilling to see more; or, can put extra emphasis on what you can see, increasing its importance, possibly over-emphasizing or exaggerating its import. Might indicate focus, concentration, and one-pointedness or an extremely narrow-minded point of view.

SEMINAR:
A learning experience or place of learning, expanding one's knowledge and understanding.

SEWING:
Mending, repairing, constructing, putting parts together. Creative, constructive endeavors. If you are working on clothing it may denote the repair of attitudes, mending your ways, constructing new attitudes, new ways of looking at things, even creating a new self-image! It could also be a constructive use of your creative energies.

Pattern: Guidelines, outline, shape of things to come, new habit patterns, parts of the whole.

SHAKING:
We usually equate this with fear, but it can mean the shaking up of old ways, old habit patterns, old thinking. May shake the old foundations loose in order to rearrange, reorient, or rebuild. Sometimes we have to tear out the old in order to build new and better.

SHOOTING:
Can be shooting off your mouth, shooting people down with words, volatile tempers erupting into violence, hurting others. Explosive situations erupting or about to erupt. Can imply the deadliness of words spoken without thought or the harm which repressed emotions can do when suddenly released.

SHOPPING:
Looking around for new ideas, knowledge, new attitudes, new food for thought.

SICKLE:
Symbol of labor, reaping; also Grim Reaper, Death.

SICKNESS:
Feeling sorry for yourself; excuse for not being responsible, keeping your promise, making decisions; way to avoid a person, situation, or decision.

SIGNING NAME:

Join, accept, charge; responsibility, seal an agreement, show support or approval; mark of identification, authority.

SINGING:

An act of joy, of being in harmony with yourself and with others, feeling good about yourself, spreading joy and uplifting others by your cheerful attitude. Dream may be encouraging you to do this.

SINKING:

Feeling of getting in too deep, over your head, being overwhelmed by an emotional situation, helplessness.

SIREN:

Alert, warning, attention-getter, alarm, call to be aware of a dangerous or emergency situation.

SITTING:

Inactive, not moving or doing anything. Reflective, idle, not applying what you know, doing nothing.

SKULL AND CROSS BONES:

Ancient symbol of warning, death, danger, poison, or deadly situations. It is also a pirate symbol with connotations of piracy, robbery, death, and deception.

SKULL CAP:

Holy attitudes, pious ideas, or symbol of prayer and devotion.

SKY – MORNING, NOON, CLOUDY, EVENING, NIGHT:

May be symbolic of Heaven or say the sky is the limit, look up, seek something higher, raise your sights. If there are clouds moving, these may show the direction of your thought and ideas.

SMOG:

Fear, confusion, upset emotions, poor visibility and understanding of a situation.

SMOKE:

Confusion, smoldering feelings, subterfuge, hidden forces, inability to see clearly.

SMOKING:

Implies emotional disturbance, confusion, upsets. Can depict being all burned up, smoldering about something, putting up a smoke screen, trying to obscure the facts; or, may indicate the person has taken up smoking!

SNAPS:

This can be a pun to indicate whatever you need to do will be a snap, not to worry.

SNEAKY:

Cautious, underhanded, covert, avoiding recognition. Could be a person or situation slipping up on you, a hint to be on guard or more aware. May show how you feel about a situation or your behavior.

SOLO:

Performing alone, on your own, no help or support, do or die; also "so low" as in low down, low profile (unseen), or low sound which can't be heard by others.

SORTING LAUNDRY:

Sorting through your attitudes and feelings, seeing what needs to be washed or worked on.

SOURCE BOOK:

Would represent your God source of knowledge, understanding, insight, intuition, inspiration, ideas, and help which come to you as you seek these.

SPILL:

To spill or upset a food could be showing you where your diet is unbalanced or an item which should be deleted from your menu. To spill things on others can be a pun on spilling the beans or can be a sign of carelessness and general inconsideration, upsetting others by your deeds.

SPIRAL:
Symbol of creative power, cyclic patterns, seasons, rhythms, reincarnation.

SPREAD:
May be a warning not to spread yourself too thin, or could imply a need to expand or enlarge your area of coverage in your work, expertise, interests, whatever.

SPYING:
Getting information not meant for you to have, watching others secretly, prying into another's affairs, secret investigations, nosiness, lack of respect for another's privacy. Who is spying on whom? Could be a warning.

SQUARE:
Basic, practical, worldly, fundamental, predictable, somewhat inflexible, stoic. May also be a box, represent a boxed-in feeling, limits, barriers, obstructions.

SQUIRT GUN:
May be a harmless spouting off of emotions, or could be a pun on sex play.

STAFF:
Symbol of office, rank, honor, profession, power.

> **Bishop's Staff:** Symbol of church authority, protection, power, faith.

> **Shepherd's Staff:** Symbol of the shepherd and his constant watchfulness over his flock (sheep or thoughts), also of compassion, protection, guidance, rescue, aid, caringness, and responsibility.

STAGGERING:
Implies lack of balance from overload, overdoing, or lack of something essential; possibly poor diet or health.

STAKES:
Can be support for the ideas growing in the garden of your mind, gambling for high stakes, staking your claim, or a pun on steaks.

STAND:
May be a flower stand, fruit stand, telephone stand, other furniture stand, or a pun on taking a stand, standing tall, standing up for your beliefs or rights, being proud of yourself.

> **Stand and Look:** Observing, contemplating, getting the feel of things, looking things over, summing up the situation, being cautious, or a hint to do these. On the other hand, it can be just watching, doing nothing, and a hint to get involved.

> **Stand on Bare Ground:** Can be standing your ground, having both feet on the ground, in touch with the earth, knowing where you stand, being well-grounded, feeling your way.

STANDARD:
Emblem of office, country, faith, or king served, loyalty, authority, power, rank, honor, or profession.

STANDING:
This can be asserting yourself, standing up for your rights, or your need to make a stand, to stand firm, take your place in a matter, confront, stand tall, be proud of yourself.

STAR:
Point of illumination, high hopes and ideals, or may be messages from other realms.

> **4 Points:** Higher powers, signal, message, warning, or foreboding. May also be a symbol for the star Sirius.

> **5 Points:** Pentacle, symbol of man, five physical senses, money, protection against evil spirits, star of the Magi, Order of the Eastern Star, and for all seekers of light and enlightenment.

Upside Down: Witches' foot, symbol of witchcraft, evil, devil worship, black magic; also logo for a few of the Orders of the Eastern Star (most use the pentacle).

Anti-Witchcraft or Hex Sign: Protection from witchcraft. Many variations of this symbol are seen on homes and barns in Pennsylvania Dutch areas to ward off evil.

6 Points: Star of David, Bethlehem, symbol of the Jewish nation or religion, love, peace, perfection, union of fire and water, balanced forces, union of low self with High Self, soul-infused personality.

7 Points: Said to be the *true* Solomon's seal. Represents the seven spiritual senses, spiritual perfection, or Son of God.

8 Points: Octogram, cosmic order, cosmic consciousness, radiant energy, attainment.

9 Points: Symbol of Holy Spirit (three triangles).

12 Points: Twelve Tribes of Israel.

STERILIZE:
To cleanse, to eliminate all feeling and emotion, withhold or repress all intuitive or creative urges; may imply that you think of yourself as unproductive or non-creative, or show a need to do something creative to fulfill yourself.

STICKY TAPE, GLUE, ETC.:
Can be warning about getting into a situation which will be difficult to escape, or that you may be stuck with something; a pun on a sticky or messy predicament, or may say stick with it.

STONE:
Changeless, solid, dependable, unbending foundation of truth, or can be an impenetrable barrier, challenge, or difficulty.

Stone, Uncut: Truth untouched or unchanged by man.

Stone, White: Pure foundation.

STUFF:
Miscellaneous creations, memories, attitudes, problems, fears, bits and pieces of our lives.

SUBSTITUTE:
Can be someone using you for something or someone else; may warn that you are not getting the real thing or what you think you are getting/buying; or, it may be pointing out your need to make some substitutions.

SUBWAY:
Underground travel or activities, subversiveness, covert action, subconscious levels, getting to the bottom of something, undercover, change, transfer.

SUITCASE:
Receptacle for getting it all together, especially your attitudes. May also say it's in the bag, or can symbolize vacation, travel, freedom, mobility, or changes.

Small Bag: Small or short trip.

Large Bag or Many: Long trip, many changes.

SULPHUR:
Associated with alchemy or with fire and brimstone.

SURFING:
May be riding the crest of emotional ups and downs, literally being on top of it, in control; or, can be danger of wiping out, being overwhelmed by emotional stresses.

SWAMP:
Emotional bog, uncertain ground, loose footing, insecurity, fear, suppressed feelings and emotions, being swamped or overcome with the weight of emotional stresses, can get in over your head, danger of drowning.

SWASTIKA:
Ancient Indian symbol for movement through life, spiritual forces at work, good luck, continuing life, hope. This is also a disguised cross used by early Christians.

> **Reversed Swastika:** Nazi emblem for evil or bad luck, now associated with Hitler, Nazis, great cruelty, and mass murders of World War II.

SWEARING:
Can imply your language or use of cuss words, but might also be to swear allegiance to a person or thing, commit yourself to a cause, to take an oath, make a promise. Could refer to swearing to do a thing and to whether or not you kept your promise to yourself or to another.

SWEEPING:
Can indicate the need to make a clean sweep of things, to get things out in the open, get rid of the guilt or negativity, clean up your act, make way for something better.

SWINGING:
Denotes going back and forth in a situation, trying to see both sides, vacillating, undecided, going from one extreme to another. This points to a need to make up your mind.

T

TALL:
If you stand taller than another, this may imply standing tall—standing up for your rights—or indicate you have outgrown or outranked that person and his ideas, teachings, and so on. May say you are head and shoulders above the crowd!

TARGET:
Can imply taking careful aim, having a goal to shoot for, or a need to have a goal. May be nitpicking, criticism, taking pot shots at another, or being a target for another's unkind remarks or missiles.

TAROT CARDS:
Symbols of life and ancient mystical teachings; may also be symbols of fate and fortune-telling or of self-evaluation, depending on how they are used.

TAU:
Tau cross, or symbol of manifestation in the physical plane.

> **Upside Down Tau:** Spirit descending into matter.

TAURUS:
Astrological symbol of the bull, of determination, stability, acquisitiveness, stubbornness, will power, gentleness, business acumen, and love of beauty.

TAURUS

TEACHING:
What are you teaching? We tend to teach that which we most need to learn and understand ourselves. Listen carefully both in dreams and in your daily life teachings.

TEARDROP OR RAINDROP:
Ancient Egyptian symbol for remembered wisdom.

THORNS:
Stickers, hang-ups, problems, catchy situations.

THOUGHT-FORMS:
The actual astral form your thoughts take as you think, especially as you concentrate or repeat the thought. Forms vary in shape and color according to the idea held and the emotions involved. These are not usually seen by the average person but can be viewed clairvoyantly or in the dream state. May also be felt or sensed by all.

THREAD:
Can be the thread of life, continuity, flow through, the interweaving of life's events, connecting links, or the proverbial stitch in time.

    Golden Thread: Cosmic love, brotherly love, a heavenly link, continuity of love, or the love connection.

TICKET:
Legal permission to enter, to have, to do something. Can be proof of payment, chance for a prize, a vote, a legal statement, or a summons such as a speeding or parking ticket.

TIE:
This can be emotional ties, karmic ties, financial bonds, love bonds, hate bonds, marital bonds, religious ties, obligations, manipulatory ties, memories, anything which can pull at your heartstrings or your neck. You can feel tied to a situation or person, in knots or nots, and have opposing ties.

TOOLS OF TRADE:
Talents, tendencies, abilities, knowledge, experience, preparation for your life's work, what you have to work with, your do-it-yourself kit, your potential which may be symbolized by the type of tools or by the talents of the person who owns them. These may represent your own unknown or unrecognized talents.

TOUCH:
Could indicate your need to get in touch with some person or thing; may say you are out of touch, too touchy, unreachable; may point out a need for touching, being touched or in touch, making a show of affection and approval to those around you.

TOYS:
Can represent playful attitudes, childish ideas, joys, freedoms, quirks, emotional securities, toying with an idea, ways you thought and felt as a child, or childhood itself.

TRACKS:
Set path of thinking and doing, ruts, automatic actions and reactions, no new input, no original thinking or doing.

TRAINING WHEELS:
Extra support to balance.

TRANSFER:
Moving or being taken from one place or level to another; can indicate changes or travel.

TRAP:
Means of getting caught, held, duped, fooled, deceived, misled, delayed, hurt.

TREATMENT:
Can be a therapeutic act or a pun on getting the full treatment, possibly implying how you treat others.

TRIANGLE: △
Symbol of security, immobility, solidarity, a geometric figure, love triangle, trinity, pyramid.

TRIDENT:
Symbol of Neptune, God of the Sea, or of creative energies, sensitivity, mysticism.

TUNING:
May imply getting in tune with others, attunement to higher forces or to your Higher Self.

TYPEWRITER:
Symbol of writing, communicating, neatness; can imply secretarial skills or creative ideas.

U

UMBRELLA:
Protection from outside influences or emotional storms. Can symbolize protection of prayer or of angelic forces.

UNABLE TO RUN OR CRY:
You can't run from it, can't cry for outside help—you must face it and deal with it.

UNFOLD:
Can refer to growing, unfolding, maturing, or can depict smoothing out things in your mind and affairs. Could be a pun on unfoldment.

UPSETTING THINGS OR PEOPLE:
Can be showing you how you affect others on a daily basis or the effects of yesterday's actions. This may point to a need to set things straight, to be more careful or considerate, or to be more aware of what you are doing and how your actions, words, and deeds can affect others.

URANUS:
Planet of the unusual, unexpected, intuition, new ideas and inventions, inner awakening, independence, genius, originality, freedom, individualism, rebellion, change, progress, reformation, and unconventionality.

V

VACATION:
Change of pace or place, recharging your energies, break, rest, doing something different, play, forgetting about work, exploring new areas. Dream may suggest you need a rest or a break from routine or rest. (When you are under heavy stress, frequent mini-vacations are not a luxury but are **necessary** for physical and mental balance.)

VACCINATE:
Could be "stuck with it," the proverbial ounce of prevention, the "hair of the dog that bit you," or a dose of your own medicine. Maybe you need to be immune to the situation or overcome your vulnerability.

VALENTINE:
A well-known symbol of the heart, being all heart, of love, tender feelings, showing affection, or possibly the need to express more love and affection.

VENUS:
Symbol of love, beauty, femininity, harmony, social affairs, fertility, desire, and personal love.

VIBRATING:
Active, moving, pulsating, filled to overflowing with invisible forces, spiritual energies, or possibly unknown influences.

VIRGO:
Astrological sign denoting purity, perfection, attention to detail and analysis, criticism, service to others. Always striving for greater perfection.

♍
VIRGO

VOTING:
Speaking your mind, letting your voice be heard, registering your affirmation, approval, desires; your OK or veto on an issue or on your subconscious.

W

WAITING LINE:
May indicate a period of waiting, the amount of time needed to accomplish or acquire. There is a waiting space between the time you pray, ask, affirm, or decree for a thing and the time your request (or curse) manifests into your life. Since we tend to give up too soon on our dreams, hopes, and prayers, the line may imply we have to wait awhile longer, or it may say your time is coming. Note the length of the line.

WAKE:
A gathering of friends and aspects of yourself to celebrate your death (change in consciousness), end of an old habit, or moving on to a higher level of life.

WAND:
Symbol of will, magic, power, transformation; the use of spiritual forces for good, ability to perform miracles. Beautiful symbol of your prayer power or love power.

WANDERING:
Moving about without any plan or direction. No goals, ideals, or aims. No strong motivation.

WATCHING MOVIES OR TV:
Daydreaming, pretending, wishful thinking, unrealistic attitudes, watching life pass you by, nonparticipation.

> **Cartoons:** Could say you are not taking your life seriously, life is a game to you; or, may say to get a little more fun or humor in your life and thinking.

WEATHER VANE:
Unpredictability, going around in circles, versatile, quick changes in direction, instability. Can be a pun on being vain, vanity, or doing something in vain.

WEDDING:
A ceremony bringing together two opposite parts, two differing opinions into union or agreement. Can be spiritual integration with your High Self, a long-term agreement, a pledge of love and devotion. May even denote a wedding!

WEENIE ROAST:
Can be a pun on sex play, toying with the idea of sex, playing around with it.

WEEPING:
This is a sign of your High Self (God-self) being distressed over your past actions or the decisions you are making. A warning that you need to re-evaluate what you have done or are about to do.

WEIGHING:

Taking stock of a situation, weighing a matter in your mind, trying to balance or need to balance, possibly saying you should look at both sides of the matter and consider carefully what you are about to do; or, a pun on waiting.

WEIGHT:

May be self-worth, self-esteem, importance, power, influence, ability to throw your weight around, or a pun for wait.

Overweight: Could say you overestimate your own worth or ability to influence, that you overdo something or over-weigh, over-rate, overdo a thing.

Underweight: Could say you think too little of yourself, have too little self-esteem and need to work on this, or that you are under-valuing something.

WHEELCHAIR:

Mobile support; implies inability to stand on your own two feet and a need to do so, unless you want to be "pushed around" all your life. Can be a temporary support system while the person gets his understanding healed and puts his feet on the ground.

WINGED GLOBE:

Ancient symbol of many religions representing the relationship existing between the body, soul, and spirit. It portrays the freedom of the soul, since the soul gives wings to the body, and symbolizes the earth and its soul. The winged globe is also the exact shape a prayer takes as it is sent out as a thought-form.

Winged Globe with Serpents:

Ancient symbol of the three persons of the Egyptian Trinity: Ammon, Ra, and Osiris.

WINGS:

Ancient symbol for soul, soul in its flight, freedom, joy, ability to visit the spiritual realms, freedom from the material level, freedom of mind or body, ability to rise above mundane problems. Can be wings of prayer or protection.

WIPE-OUT:

Losing it, loss of control; letting your emotions run you, upset your equilibrium.

WISHING:

Implies wanting something but not really expecting to get it. Wishing can be passive—waiting for someone to do it for you.

WORKING:

May point out a need to work something out, work through a situation, go to work on some project symbolized in the dream. Could imply a need to get a job done or to go find a job if you don't have one. May say it is time to look for a new career, depending on the action and feeling in the dream.

WRAPPING PAPER:

May signify wrapping things up, preparing your gifts for presentation; surprise, presents, or presence.

WRITING:

Putting thoughts into words, writing it down to get a better look at it, putting ideas in writing to make things clear to all concerned or so you won't forget. Bringing things up to your conscious level, impressing it on your mind, putting things on record. Possibly, the dream is pointing out a talent for creative writing which you need to encourage or practice. It may even be a pun on righting a wrong, setting things to right.

Writing a Check: Trying to make amends, to pay-up a debt, to bring things into balance or perspective, effort to pay as you go.

X

X-OUT:
To X-out is to cross out, cancel something off of a list or out of your life; to stop, end, quit, remove, take back, change your mind.

X-RAY:
To see through barriers and hindrances, possibly seeing through a person or situation.

Y

Y:
Fork in the road, your life, or career marking the time or place to make decisions or to choose which way you want to go.

YELLOW BRICK HOUSE:
A consciousness of your dominion over the material world and its affairs.

YOD:
Literally, "drops of light," an ancient Hebrew symbol of manna, favor, or the descent of life-force from God. May also represent power, skill, dexterity.

YOGA:
Symbol of self-discipline, control of mind and body.

Z

ZERO:
Absence of quality and quantity, absolute freedom, sign of eternity, infinity, super-consciousness, or cosmic consciousness.

ZOO:
A place of many varieties of animals, animal habits and qualities. An area of confinement, limited freedom for the animals or animal natures, instincts, qualities, abilities, and talents we may possess.

My Own Symbols

My Own Symbols continued...

My Own Symbols continued...

My Own Symbols continued...

Bibliography

Allen, James. 1968. *As A Man Thinketh*. Kansas City:Hallmark Editions.

Barasch, Marc. "Hitchiker's Guide to Dreamland." *New Age Journal,* volume and date unknown.

Besant, Annie. 1939. *The Ancient Wisdom*. Adyar: Theosophical Publishing House.

———. 1971. *Man and His Bodies*. London: Theosophical Publishing House.

Besant, Annie, and Leadbeater, C. W. 1901. *Thought-Forms*. London: Theosophical Publishing House.

———. 1913. *Man, Whence, How and Whither*. Adyar: Theosophical Publishing House.

Boone, J. Allen. 1954. *Kinship With All Life*. New York: Harper & Row.

Bro, Harmon H. 1968. *Edgar Cayce On Dreams*. New York: Harper & Row.

———. 1970. *Dreams in the Life of Prayer*. New York: Harper & Row.

Bulfinch, Thomas. 1970. *Bulfinch's Mythology*. New York: Harper & Row.

Campbell, Florence. 1931. *Your Days Are Numbered*. Ferndale: The Gateway.

Castaneda, Carlos. 1971. *A Separate Reality*. New York: Simon & Schuster.

Cayce, Edgar. 1960. *Gems and Stones*. Virginia Beach: A.R.E. Press.

Delaney, Gayle. 1979. *Living Your Dreams*. New York: Harper & Row.

Dement, Dr. Wm. 1976. *Some Must Watch While Some Must Sleep*. San Francisco: San Francisco Book Co.

Domhoff, G. W. 1985. *Mystique of Dreams*. Berkeley: University of California Press.

"Dream Interpretation." 1979. *A.R.E. Journal,* No. 6, p. 279.

D'Aulaires, Edgar and Ingri. 1962. *Book of Greek Myths*. New York: Doubleday & Company, Inc.

Ellison, Jerome. 1971. *The Life Beyond Death*. New York: Putnam.

Faraday, Ann. 1973. *Dream Power*. New York: Berkley Medallion Books.

———. 1976. *The Dream Game*. New York: Harper & Row.

Findhorn Community. 1975. *The Findhorn Garden*. New York: Harper & Row.

Ford, Arthur, and Bro, Marguerite Harmon. 1968. *Nothing Stranger*. New York: Paperback Library.

Fox, Oliver. 1962. *Astral Projection*. Secaucus:University Books.

Freud, Sigmund. 1938. *The Interpretation of Dreams*. New York: Modern Library Books.

Fromm, Erich. 1951. *The Forgotten Language*. New York: Holt, Rinehart & Winston.

Fuller, J. F. C. *The Secret Wisdom of the Qabalah*. London: Rider & Co. Date unknown.

Gawain, Shakti. 1986. *Living In The Light*. Mill Valley: Whatever Publishing.

Garfield, Patricia. 1976. *Creative Dreaming*. New York: Ballantine Books.

———. 1979. *Pathway to Ecstasy*. New York: Holt, Rinehart & Winston.

———. 1984. *Your Child's Dreams*. New York: Ballantine.

Gray, Mary. 1935. *The Gateway of Liberation*. La Canada: De Vorss.

Gurudas. 1983. *Flower Essences and Vibrational Healing*. Albuquerque: Brotherhood of Life, Inc.

Hall, Calvin. 1953. *The Meaning of Dreams*. New York: McGraw-Hill.

Hay, Louise L. 1984. *You Can Heal Your Life*. Farmingdale: Coleman Publishing.

Heline, Corinne. 1944. *Magic Gardens*. Los Angeles: New Age Press.

Hodges, Doris M. 1961. *Healing Stones*. Hiawatha: Pyramid Publishers.

Hodson, Geoffrey. 1927. *The Brotherhood of Angels and Men*. London: Theosophical Publishing House.

Horvath, Al, Jr. 1983. *Beyond Dreams*. Scottsdale: Harmonious Publications.

Ismael, Christina. 1973. *The Healing Environment*. Milbrae: Celestial Arts.

Jung, Carl. G. 1961. *Memories, Dreams and Reflections*. Edited by Aniela Jaffe. New York: Random House.

———. 1964. *Man and His Symbols*. London: Aldus Books, Limited.

———. 1974. *On The Nature of Dreams*. Princeton: Princeton University Press.

Gris, Henry, and Dick, William. 1978. *The New Soviet Psychic Discoveries*. Englewood Cliffs: Prentice-Hall.

Kelsey, Morton T. 1978. *Dreams: A Way To Listen To God*. New York: Paulist Press.

Kelzer, Kenneth. 1978. *The Sun and the Shadow*. Virginia Beach: A.R.E. Press.

Kilner, Walter J. 1965. *The Human Aura*. New York: University Books.

Krippner, Stanley, and Rubin, Daniel. 1975. *The Kirlian Aura*. New York: Doubleday/Anchor.

Kubler-Ross, Elisabeth. 1975. *Death, The Final Stage of Growth*. Englewood Cliffs: Prentice-Hall.

LaBerge, Stephen. 1985. *Lucid Dreaming.* New York: Ballantine Books.

Leadbeater, C. W. 1899. *Clairvoyance.* London: Theosophical Publishing House.

———. 1971. *Man, Visible and Invisible.* Wheaton: Theosophical Publishing House.

McGarey, William. "Be Thou the Guide." *The Searchlight Bulletin,* an A.R.E. publication, Vol. 16, No. 10.

Monroe, Robert A. 1971. *Journeys Out of the Body.* New York: Anchor Press/Doubleday.

Moody, Raymond A., Jr. 1975. *Life After Life.* Covington: Mockingbird Books.

Murphy, Joseph. 1963. *The Power of Your Subconscious Mind.* Englewood Cliffs: Prentice-Hall, Inc.

Noone, Robert, with Holman, D. 1972. *In Search of the Dream People.* New York: Wm Morrow.

Parrish-Harra, Carol W. 1982. *A New Age Handbook on Death and Dying.* Marina del Rey: DeVorss & Company.

Powell, A. E. 1925. *The Etheric Double.* Wheaton: Theosophical Publishing House.

———. 1927. *The Astral Body.* London: Theosophical Publishing House.

Ring, Kenneth, M.D. 1984. *Heading Toward Omega.* New York: Quill.

Ronan, Colin. 1976. *Lost Discoveries.* New York: Bonanza Books.

Rubin, Howard J. "Awake in Your Dreams." Publication and date unknown.

Sanford, Rev. John. 1968. *Dreams, God's Forgotten Language.* Philadelphia: Lippencott.

Sechrist, Elsie. 1968. *Dreams, Your Magic Mirror.* New York: Dell Publishing Co.

Sparrow, Gregory Scott. 1976. *Lucid Dreaming: Dawning of the Clear Light.* Virginia Beach: A.R.E. Press.

Steadman, Alice. 1966 *Who's The Matter With Me?* Marina del Rey: DeVorss & Co.

Stearn, Jess. 1967. *Edgar Cayce, The Sleeping Prophet.* New York: Doubleday & Company, Inc.

Stevenson, Robert L. 1892. *Across the Plains With Other Memories and Essays.* New York: Scribner.

Sugrue, Thomas. 1942. *There Is A River.* New York: Dell Publishing Co.

Tart, Charles. 1969. *Altered States of Consciousness.* New York: John Wiley & Sons.

Taylor, Ariel Yvon, and Hyer, H. Warren. 1956. *Numerology, Its Facts and Secrets.* North Hollywood: Wilshire Book Co.

Ullman, Montague, M.D. 1979. *Working with Dreams.* New York: Delacourte.

Welles, Gloria. 1986. "Wake Up to the Benefits of Dreams." *U.S.A. Weekend,* June 20-22.

Yogananda, Paramahansa. 1972. *Autobiography of a Yogi.* Los Angeles: Self-Realization Fellowship Publishers.

"Your Dreams." *Searchlight Bulletin,* Vol. 2, No. 21-22.

Index

A

Abortion, 289
Abuse of sex organs, 136
Acorn, 205
Accident, 230, 301
Acting, 323
Actors, 271
Advertisement, 323
Aerobics. *See* Games
Affirmations, 40
Afghan, 218
Agitating, 323
Air, 319
Airport, 107. *See also* Building
Alarm clock. *See* Clock
Alien, 272
Alley, 281
Alligator, 100
Altar, 147
Alter, 156
Amen, 323
Ancient
  places, 107
  scenes, 215
  themes, 215
Angels, 272
Animal
  oversized, 92
  restraints, 92
Animals, 91
  domesticated, 92
  running, 92
  running free, 93
  young, 92
Ankh, 233, 323
Ankle, 137
Announcement, 323
Ant eater, 100
Antique, valuable, 294
Anubis, 323
Apartment. *See* Building
Applauding, 131
Apple, 323
Apron, 168
Aquarius, 323
Arbor, 203

Arch, 137
Arches, 156
Archway, 156
Area, sun-lit, 113
Areas, 285
Arena, football, 148
Aries, 324
Armor, 168
Arms, 131
Arrow, 324
Art center. *See* Building
Art supplies, 324
Artifact, 324
Artillery, heavy, 117
Ashtray, 218
Asking directions, 281
Asleep, 324
Attendant, 272
Attic, 156. *See also* Room
Audience, 272
Auras, 173
Auto racing, 301
Autograph, 324

B

Babies, 269, 291
Back, 131
  backbone, 131
  curved, 131
  damaged, 131
  muscles, 131
  turn your back, 131
  wrenched, 131
Back burner, 189
Background settings, 107 - 114
Backing, 324
Backing up, 301
Backward, 339
Badger, 100
Bag, baggage, 324
Bait, 324
Bald, 128
Ball, 198, 324
Ballet, 324
Balloon, 311, 324
Bandages, 230

Bank. *See* Building
Banner, 324
Banquet, 189
Bar, 218. *See also* Building
Barefoot, 137, 166
Barking, 96
Barn, 93. *See also* Building
Barren ground, 203
Basement, 156. *See also*
  Building; Room
Basin, overflowing, 317
Basket, 239
Bat, 120
Bathing, 325
  an animal, 93
Bathing suit, 168. *See also* Bikini
Bathroom. *See* Room
Battlefield, 107
  familiar, 108
  new, 108
  old, 108
Battles, 115 - 118
  bedroom, 116
  dining room, 116
  kitchen, 117
Bazaar, 325
Beach, 108
Bear, 101
  teddy, 101
Bearing, 325
Beast, 101
Beasts
  wild, 105
Beauty parlor. *See* Building
Beaver, 101
Bed, 218
Bed wetting, 14
Bedroom battles, 116. *See also*
  Room
Bedspread, 219
Bee. *See* Bugs
Beer, 191
Behind, 325
Bells, 156, 219
Belt, 168
Bending, 325